THE TIMES
OF TIME

A New Perspective in Systemic
Therapy and Consultation

THE TIMES
OF TIME

A New Perspective in Systemic
Therapy and Consultation

Luigi Boscolo

Paolo Bertrando

Translated by Stephen Thorne

W. W. Norton & Company · New York · London

Printed in the United States of America.

First Edition

The text of this book was composed in Elante. Composition by Bytheway Typesetting Services, Inc. Manufacturing by Haddon Craftsmen.

Book design by Justine Burkat Trubey

Library of Congress Cataloging-in-Publication Data

Boscolo, Luigi.
    [I tempi del tempo. English]
    The times of time : a new perspective in systemic therapy and
consultation / Luigi Boscolo, Paolo Bertrando ; translated by
Stephen Thorne.
        p.   cm.
    "A Norton professional book."
    Includes bibliographical references and index.
    ISBN 0-393-70163-8
    1. Family psychotherapy.   2. Time—Psychological aspects.   3. Time
perspective.   I. Bertrando, Paolo, Ph. D.   II. Title.
    [DNLM: 1. Time.   2. Family Therapy—methods.   3. Referral and
Consultation.   WM 430.5.F2 B74t 1993a]
RC488.5.B648513   1993
616.89′156—dc20   93-20599 CIP
DNLM/DLC
for Library of Congress

W.W. Norton & Company, Inc., 500 Fifth Avenue, New York, N.Y. 10110

W.W. Norton & Company, Ltd., 10 Coptic Street, London WC1A 1PU

1 2 3 4 5 6 7 8 9 0

To Jacqueline
and Paola

CONTENTS

FOREWORD

THERE WAS A TIME WHEN THE United States was some sort of a Holy Grail for family and systems therapists worldwide: Everything new and inspiring seemed to come from there. But that time now seems past, as this book well shows. Like the seminal works of the well-known American pioneers it evinces a wealth of ideas, an experimenting spirit, and a pragmatic down-to-earth approach guided by the experiences and requirements of clinical practice. In addition, it gives evidence of an impressive humanistic scholarship and, together with that, of the authors' ability to explore and untangle philosophical and historical complexities. It is these qualities which continue to thrive particularly well on European—and especially on Milanese—soil. I know few books in the psychotherapeutic realm that reveal them as convincingly as does the volume at hand.

The authors invite us to look at psychotherapy and consultation through a new lens: the time lens. This lens, so they believe, complements other postmodern lenses, such as those of radical and social constructivism and of so-called narrativism (which views reality constructions as an expression and consequence of the construction and narration of stories). That is true and yet remains an understatement. It would be more appropriate to speak of an exploratory journey which leads us into ever new territory, reveals ever new connections, opens up ever new perspectives, while constantly eyeing their relevance for clinical practice.

At the same time, the book documents the developments and process of differentiation that the so-called Milan model has undergone up to the present day. We need to remind ourselves: The original team around Mara

Selvini Palazzoli, which gave us *Paradox and Counterparadox,* ceased to exist some time ago. Out of it has sprouted, so to speak, a number of successor models, one of which is presented here by Boscolo and Bertrando. It bears the imprint of newer developments, such as second-order cybernetics and radical constructivism, as well as of the two authors' unmistakable personal styles. The ease and seeming effortlessness of their presentation and simultaneous abstention from polemics testify to their mastery. They have succeeded in writing a book that is both a scholarly achievement and a guide to perplexed practitioners. It will, I am sure, find many admirers.

Helm Stierlin

INTRODUCTION

THIS BOOK WAS CONCEIVED IN 1988, when we began to recognize the importance of the relationship between time and change in clients' and therapists' expectations. As we looked more closely at the influence of time on both therapy and everyday life, we became increasingly curious.

Ordinary literature in the field of consultation and therapy proved to be of little help. We then turned to a number of books: first in the domain of philosophy, then of physics, finally of several other disciplines; gradually we were absorbed in a fascinating journey, looking for that mysterious object that is time, continually eluding our grasp. A meditation by St. Augustine—one of the authors we were reading with great interest—captures the sense of such a journey: "What, then, is time? I know well enough what it is, provided that nobody asks me; but if I am asked what it is and try to explain, I am baffled."

This challenged our *hubris*, triggering the desire to understand, to explain—first to ourselves, then to others—what time is. So we proceeded on our interesting journey, which was full of beautiful surprises but also of disappointments. Just as, when visiting Venice, one gets lost in the labyrinth of the narrow passages but always perceives that, from the darkness of the winding passages, s/he will eventually reach the grandiose Piazza San Marco—the final destination—so we wandered.

We think—*a posteriori*—that our journey was successful, because it enabled us to see human relationships, particularly therapy and consultation relationships, through a new lens: the time lens. The way in which we "see" our clients—and ourselves in the process of seeing and acting—has been so enriched that we now propose a new perspective in systemic therapy and consultation.

The time lens is coupled with other lenses which have recently appeared in the field of family therapy and consultation: the lens of premises, of language,[1] of narration, of post-modern thinking. Many of these models emerged as alternatives to the systemic paradigm, based on the cybernetic metaphor. However, we are still at ease within the systemic paradigm, based on first- and second-order cybernetics. The time lens is a complementary perspective, not an alternative, to the systemic one. In the second part of the book, which deals with clinical cases, the reader will notice how our way of doing therapy, which remains grounded within the Milan approach, has become richer and more complex with the addition of this perspective.

Back to our research: We followed at first a crooked pathway. We asked what philosophers, physicists, historians, anthropologists and sociologists meant by time. The answers we found were most diverse, indeed, a plurality of times: objective time and subjective time, family time, institutional time, cultural time. Confronted with such diversity, we recognized the importance of coordinating different times and wondered if a lack of coordination might result in problems, sufferings, pathologies.

Our clients, it seems, present problems that may be seen as problems of time coordination: the time that stops, does not evolve, in the depressed person; the scattered time of the schizophrenic; or the chaotic time of the troubled organization. The different temporal horizons and perspectives that can be seen in persons, cultures, organizations, and social entities increase the complexity of our analysis.

Therapies have their temporal perspectives, too. Some therapeutic models deal mainly with the present time, others with the past, others mainly or exclusively with the future. In our approach, we try to relate present to past and future; we are interested in the relationship among the three "dimensions" of time, taking into account the variable temporal horizon of the client and its possible evolutions. We take care to coordinate our time with our clients' times. Clients often see time in a linear-causal way: past determines the present, and the present leads inexorably into the future. The therapist's task is to introduce a reflexive relationship among the three dimensions of time, what we define as the reflexive loop of past, present and future, making time for hypothetical pasts and futures in the present.

---

[1]Which we have recently considered in a study, described in "Language and change: The use of key words in therapy" (Boscolo, Bertrando, Fiocco, Palvarini, & Pereira, 1991).

These are only a few of the aspects of time that are important to human relationships. Our exploration involved a journey of two clinicians in domains that are not their own, such as philosophy, physics, geology, and sociology, and we apologize in advance if our version sometimes sounds naive. We want to emphasize, however, that from our journey in a strange land, we took along some metaphors (especially from physics and philosophy) that are extremely useful in considering the process of consultation and therapy. Of course, such metaphors must not be taken at face value but considered for what they are.

The book is divided into ten chapters, which deal both with theory and with clinical practice. The first chapter is an introduction to our way of working with time in therapy, illustrated by two clinical cases (a whole therapy and a one-session consultation). The second chapter initially approaches the metaphors of time we find in philosophy, history, geology and physics, and then discusses the three main domains of time — i.e., individual, cultural and social time — and their interconnection. In the third chapter the research shifts to the different models of family interaction, considered through the time lens. The fourth chapter deals specifically with our systemic therapy model and its evolution as we developed our ideas about time, while the fifth chapter discusses modifications in therapy and consultation technique.

The fifth chapter introduces in a clinical dimension, with the transcription and analysis of a session. The sixth and seventh chapters deal respectively with the creation of a past and a future in therapy, by means of narrations and transcripts of clinical cases. The eighth chapter is about the temporal aspect of therapeutic rituals, illustrated with several brief clinical cases, while the ninth chapter focuses on three cases followed through their complete development. The tenth and last chapter analyzes one session, with commentary comprised of a dialogue between the two authors.

We know that some readers may find the first chapters of this book too theoretical, abstract, sometimes a little boring. We therefore suggest two possible pathways for the reader: a direct reading, from the beginning to the end (in our language, from the past to the present to the future); or a reading that shifts immediately from the first to the fifth chapter, both centered on clinical cases, through the final five chapters, focused on clinical practice, back to the three theoretical chapters and then, possibly, back again to the clinical ones. The reader may thus follow a circular path: going from present to future, then back to the past, and then to a new present.

Coming to the end of this introduction, we ask ourselves what colleagues might acquire from this book: we think that — as happened to us — the interest in the time dimension may open new perspectives, so to broaden their theoretical and clinical view, promoting greater versatility in their work. We are well aware that our time-based model is still in development. However, we hope that the book may stir in the readers the same curiosity as the concept of "the times of time" stirred in us, leading them to propose ideas to sharpen the time lens we have found.

ACKNOWLEDGMENTS

For this English language edition, we would like to thank first of all Max Cornwell, who painstakingly read the whole first draft of the manuscript, offering valuable suggestions for its improvement. Carlos Sluzki and Peter Steinglass helped us to perfect some of the basic ideas outlined in our paper, "The Reflexive Loop of Past, Present and Future in Systemic Theory and Consultation." Our gratitude to Susan Barrows Munro, our editor, whose hard work has contributed to the completion of this book.

Luigi Boscolo
Paolo Bertrando

THE TIMES
OF TIME

A New Perspective in Systemic
Therapy and Consultation

1

A JOURNEY IN TIME: THE BEGINNING

PRISONERS OF TIME

The Campi family came to our center in February 1991. The family consisted of the father Armando, aged 46, a freelance engineer, the mother Rosa, aged 42, a housewife with an accountancy diploma who worked part-time at home, and their two children, Mario, aged 14, in his second year at junior high school, and Gustavo, aged 6, in his first year at primary school.

The father had phoned us to say that the problem was his son, Mario, who (he said) had suffered from various disorders since birth: he had been a late talker and had also developed walking difficulties. His doctors had decided to put his legs in plaster casts for two months, and had then fitted him with prostheses. Mario had resisted the orthopedists and nurses and they had been obliged to force treatment on him. As if this were not enough, a congenital heart condition had also been diagnosed; this required lengthy clinical tests, some by well-known heart specialists. Fortunately, the condition had not proved serious and no clinical symptoms had resulted. Mario had also developed rather serious muscular coordination problems and had been seeing physiotherapists since the age of five. The treatment had not been very successful: Mario still had a certain amount of bodily stiffness, and his movements were slightly uncoordinated. Psychological tests had also revealed mild mental retardation. The combined effect of all this had been to make Mario a deeply insecure child with very low self-esteem. Socially he was rather awkward and shy, and avoided interactions with children of his own age, who often made fun of him because of his strange gait. He had no friends at all. He had changed

1

school several times since the age of six (in some he had had a special support teacher) and his school work had been poor in all of them.

Therapy—twelve sessions held at varying intervals—lasted almost two years from February 1991 to January 1993. The sessions were conducted by a female trainee in her third and fourth years at our center, with her group monitoring sessions from the observation room under the supervision of Luigi Boscolo.

At the beginning of the first session the father immediately launched into a detailed account of Mario's story: all the problems they had had, the *via crucis* they had had to walk, their uneasy relations with the orthopedists, heart specialists, neuropsychiatrists, speech pathologists and physiotherapists they had consulted, and the school teachers who had called them in to discuss Mario's problems. Mr. Campi, who suffered himself from a physical impairment (a slight lameness), repeatedly stressed that the specialists had given them little real help and had solved none of their problems. The only person he was not wholly negative about was a physiotherapist Mario had seen on numerous occasions, with fairly successful results. The parents were especially resentful of Mario's teachers (and, as we shall see, of Gustavo's teachers, too), and they had changed his school several times. Neither Mario nor his parents had undergone psychotherapy. When asked why they had decided to come for family therapy, the father said he had heard a radio broadcast about our center's work and had decided that it might prove beneficial to explore their family relationships.

The most important feature of the first session was the behavior of the two sons. Mario sat stiffly and spoke in a mechanical, monotonous voice, glancing often at his mother or father. His facial expressions were fixed and expressionless. In contrast, Gustavo seemed hyperactive. He spent the whole of the session moving restlessly around the room, frequently disturbing his parents and pinching his brother hard (which the parents did nothing to prevent). Mario accepted the pinching and teasing without complaint. One unusual—and highly significant—feature of Gustavo's behavior was that he would sit sprawled in his mother's lap. She accepted this and embraced him passively, often without looking at him and making no attempt to coordinate her body movements with his.

Although attention focused on the elder son, it became apparent during the session that the younger son also had problems, especially at school. The therapist told the parents, inevitably enough, that Gustavo seemed uncontrollable and that they did nothing to restrain him. They justified this by saying they had given Gustavo as much attention as they could to compensate for all the attention Mario had received because of his handicap: Gustavo was a clever, sensitive, psychologically vulnerable child and they had to be as tolerant as they could of his behavior to prevent him from feeling left out. It is worth noting here that, at a certain point, the mother, ignoring Mario's feelings, said: "If Gustavo had been our first child we probably would have decided to have four or five."

The first three sessions were held with the entire family. The impression was that the parents had a close, almost symbiotic relationship with their children, whom they treated as if they were much younger than they really were. Lavishing all their energy and attention on the children, the parents seemed to have no separate life of their own as a couple. The parents' explanation for this was that the children were not yet sufficiently independent, and so needed intensive care. They seemed completely unaware of the vicious circle that bound them to their children: that all this intensive care, their attempts to find a solution, had become the problem itself. Any attempt, however indirect, to draw attention to the problem produced a dismissive reaction in the parents: a barrage of "reasonable" arguments from the father, and silence from the mother.

Despite this, the family came willingly to the sessions and became very attached to the therapist. The atmosphere during sessions was relaxed and sometimes cheerful. One important change happened in Gustavo, who grew quieter and better behaved during sessions. The parents seemed to be coming to therapy to win recognition for the extraordinary abnegation and self-sacrifice the care of their children involved—to feel that their misfortune had been understood, to receive consolation for the wounds life had inflicted on them. The team felt that the possibility of endless therapy was developing, so at the close of the third session they decided to see only the parents in order to break the deadlock.

In subsequent sessions with the parents only, inquiries about their relations as a couple produced evasive answers. The parents continually led the therapist back to the usual subject of their relations with the children, and the strength of the bond with their children became increasingly apparent. The father said that they never left their children with others ("We aren't used to it, and they've got too many problems anyway") and that, on the contrary, they often looked after other people's children. The father said—and his wife agreed—that he couldn't understand how some of his friends could go out so often, leaving their children alone: "When our children aren't with us we feel like divers without aqualungs." The parents continually gave the impression of being contented slaves, of having chosen to live in the gilded cage of their family, of having accepted parenthood as their lifelong mission. The father had even resigned a short while ago from his job as a manager in an important company to work freelance from his home. Let us quote now from the report on the seventh session.

The group and the observers agree they are dealing with a powerfully homeostatic family system based on a kind of four-way symbiotic organization
that tends to engulf and then reject any expert it comes into contact with
who tries to alter the family situation. Perhaps the father, who has a physical
impairment, fears that his wife, an intelligent and very beautiful woman,
may leave him, so he pins her down in the role of mother. Conversely, the
mother may be devoting herself so intensely to her children to avoid couple
relations with her husband. Both may be competing to see who is the best
parent in the eyes of their families of origin and acquaintances. Naturally,
the children are adapting their behavior to meet the expectations of their
parents.

At the end of the session it was decided to call in the whole family in
an attempt to break this second deadlock.

At the start of the eighth session, Gustavo sat between his parents,
ensconced on his chair like a little boss, complete with a pair of dark
glasses. Mario sat near his mother. Gustavo behaved more calmly than on
previous occasions, with the parents intervening periodically to prevent
him from interfering with others or invading their space, as if to show that
they had accepted the therapist's suggestions. The atmosphere was calm
and relaxed. The therapist worked mainly with Mario in the first part of
the session, and it became apparent that he was trying to adapt his behavior to the idea his parents had of him. His goals, he said, were to travel,
ride a motorbike, dress like an adolescent, go to high school, and then
become a surgeon. Gustavo and the parents listened with interest to the
dialogue between Mario and the therapist.

At a certain point the team called the therapist out and asked her to
broach the theme of "girls" with Mario. The parents' response was immediate and significant: they appeared incredulous and rather irritated, dismiss-
ing the idea with wry smiles. The team recalled the therapist, who was
evidently in difficulty, to discuss what to do next. Since Mario had made
it quite clear that he felt happier at home than out of doors, they decided
to suggest that he might remain a "mommy's boy" for the rest of his
life. The therapist's stance usually remains unchanged in our work, but
sometimes, in situations of prolonged deadlock or real emergencies, the
supervisor joins the session. In this particular case, it was decided that the
trainer-supervisor should join the session, openly challenge the family's
premises, and possibly play the role of the "baddy" so the therapist could
continue to be the "goody."

When the trainer joined the group the family instantly went on full
alert. He took the initiative immediately and launched without further
ado into the theme of the relations between the parents and their children.

TRAINER: What Mario has experienced—being made fun of or not being understood by others—happens to all young people sooner or later. But luckily they usually find a boy or a girl to talk things over with when they feel they're being laughed at. I think Mario's had the misfortune to find no one, not even a friend, who understands him. Now he feels unhappy at school so he stays at home and . . .

FATHER: And he feels unhappy at home, too!

TRAINER: But at home there's the risk—and I'm saying this to Mario, I'd like him to know it so he can think about it—the risk that in the future, because of this, he'll feel so happy at home that he'll find it more difficult to become independent, which is very useful to be—everyone enjoys it—and he might grow into a mommy's boy.

MARIO: Mommy's boy?

TRAINER: If you become a mommy's boy, you might get so used to it that you won't be able to change later on. Do you see? Because home becomes the only place where you feel accepted.

FATHER: I don't think he's accepted by children of his age either inside or outside school, so when he's at home with his family we spend hours trying to make up for everything he doesn't get outside: at least he's among the last of the runners-up instead of being rejected. That's our task, that's the problem we've concentrated on. We hoped it wouldn't go on for too long, that we'd get some outside support—from psychotherapy obviously, and also from what we're trying to do now.

TRAINER: Let me speak to Mario now.

FATHER: Yes, of course, but it's a rotten life, really rotten.

TRAINER: I agree about Mario's problems. (*to Mario*) I heard you say you'd like to travel, be a surgeon, that you'd like to do all those things, and I thought, a bit like my colleague, that when you said those things you said them because you think they're what your family wants you to be like, that you'd really like to be a surgeon because you'd make your parents happy. Am I right?

As his comments make clear, father is ambivalent. On the one hand, he implies that Mario is ill, handicapped, and can only stay that way; on the other, he seems to be thinking about another son, the one Mario should have been, and urges him to enroll at the science high school, the school he himself attended. The incongruity is that although the father does not advise his son to try a less demanding type of school, he goes on reminding him that he'll only be one of the runners-up, that in the end he'll never make it. Mario is caught in an impossible bind and becomes increasingly confused. It's as if his father is constantly urging him forward, and at the same time telling him he'll never make it. Basically, the father doesn't seem able to accept his son's handicap. In other words, he seems to fluctuate between images of a son caught in an unchanging past and of a mythical son evolving towards a positive future. The mother doesn't seem to agree entirely with her husband, but doesn't interfere, perhaps to defend the myth of a united family that would be challenged by open conflict.

The trainer now introduces the idea that Mario still has untapped potential, despite the limitations his biological handicap entails. In this way he introduces the future, stressing the existence of unknown possibilities. This provides an element of freedom lacking in the father's deterministic logic: "If Mario is the way he is, it's hopeless: his future will be a future of failure." We might comment here that Mario is, in effect, being denied a future and conceded only a past. The future belongs only to the hypothetical, unhandicapped Mario who can live up to his parents' expectations.

> TRAINER: I said earlier that you might become a mommy's boy. In your view, do you think your brother is a mommy's boy? Has he got this really strong glue, like superglue—it's a bit like superglue, isn't it—that might also make it difficult for him to break away? Do you think he has more glue than you?
>
> MARIO: Yes.
>
> TRAINER: (*showing amazement*) Really? And has the glue stuck him to your mother or your father?
>
> MARIO: To mother.

Further questioning revealed strong rivalry between the brothers, with both avidly seeking their parents' attention. The trainer began to ask Mario if Gustavo sought the attention of friends outside the home, as well as that of his mother in the home.

> TRAINER: (*to Mario*) Has Gustavo got friends, does he like going out?
>
> MARIO: Yes . . .
>
> TRAINER: How is he doing at school?
> (*The whole family starts talking noisily all at once.*)
>
> FATHER: (*getting the upper hand*) Very badly! Very badly! I can tell you that now! Very badly!
>
> TRAINER: Do the teachers say he is doing very badly?
>
> FATHER: Certainly they do! We're always being summoned to the school. That's the problem. They scare us even when we try to re-

assure ourselves, or have tried to before, because we don't think it's as bad as all that . . .

TRAINER: Bad because of his behavior or because of his work?

FATHER: Both! You'd have thought he was a genius, never had a problem in his life, but he's doing exactly the things Mario did, and we've changed his school, too.

TRAINER: Is it you who talks to his teachers?

FATHER: Both of us, not just me.

TRAINER: I'd like to know what the teachers say about his behavior.

FATHER: Well . . . that he masturbates in class. We changed his school. That's it. (*The mother tries to intervene. Gustavo becomes noisy.*) The teachers went berserk when we did that. Then there was group therapy, psychotherapy . . .

TRAINER: Gustavo, are you following all this?

MOTHER: Listen, please.

TRAINER: Do you agree with what your father says?
(*Gustavo doesn't answer.*)

TRAINER: What about other people, how does he get on with them?

FATHER: He complains that they tease him, but it's he who teases them. In his previous class there was just one he picked on, but they see each other again now and they're great friends. Now there are three of them who say he's become one of the plagues of the class.

TRAINER: It was strange, I noticed today that Gustavo stood up only once today, and came twice to you, Mrs. Campi. The other times he went over to his brother whenever he liked, pinching him, pestering him.

FATHER: Yes, yes.

TRAINER: It seemed as if Gustavo had no rules to keep him in check.

MOTHER: Yes, he's changed over the past two years, you see. Before he never behaved badly, he was quiet, a nice boy. Now he's probably . . .

TRAINER: He's very intelligent. He certainly does it to show me that he doesn't want to listen to me, because he's clever. For example, he's being so clever today he's saying: "Today I'll obey the rules." The other times he didn't obey them, and did what he liked. Today he began by saying, "I won't let you speak," but now, a short while after . . .

MOTHER: He's calmed down.

TRAINER: Today, he's decided to stay calm and obey the rules. But sometimes he doesn't control himself, he does what he likes and expects other people to accept it. He asserts himself when he wants you to hug him; he asserts himself when he goes to his brother; he stands in the way when his brother is talking to you. In other words, he's decided not to obey any of the rules, so I'm not surprised he does the same thing at school. Sometimes, at school, he says: "I'm the one who makes the rules. I'll masturbate, I'll pull my willy out." And he enjoys seeing how he can impose his own rules at school, all the teachers who are powerless to stop him . . .

(*The father and mother talk excitedly at once.*)

MOTHER: He doesn't even seem to realize that there . . . but then, let me say something . . .

FATHER: There's something that explains . . .

MOTHER: Yes, there's an explanation, I know, I fell into that trap too. I don't have the courage to say: "Go away, why are you still here, can't you see I'm doing dictation with Mario."

TRAINER: Gustavo, are you listening? If your mother was a nice cake, who would get to eat most of her? Who has more of mother here in the family, who gets more than anyone else?

MOTHER: (*to Gustavo*) Well, do you understand?

GUSTAVO: Yes. Me.

TRAINER: And doesn't he (*pointing to Mario*) take a bit of cake, a bit of his mother. . . ? Oh, I see, you don't want him to!

MOTHER: I must say that in number of hours Mario certainly gets more time than Gustavo.

TRAINER: So when you see Mario with your mother, when she holds his hand, cuddles him, what do you do? Don't you like it?

GUSTAVO: I push him away and take his place.

TRAINER: Why do you do that? Why?

GUSTAVO: Because I want to be there.

TRAINER: Why don't you let him have some of your mother too? Why don't you arrange with him to take turns? Why is she all yours?

GUSTAVO: She's mine because she was in the hospital with me once when I was small.

Gustavo's reply — "She's mine because she was in the hospital with me once when I was small" — is another example of arrested time seen from the child's point of view. This is the kind of arrest of time that happens when a past event is seen as the cause of a present situation — for example, when a spouse attributes present unhappiness to an act of infidelity in the past, without taking into account the complexity of human relations. This may be a good way of describing what von Foerster (1981) calls the "trivial machine" which is a dominant feature of mechanical systems.

TRAINER: (*to the children*) Do you leave some of your mother for your father, or take her all for yourselves?

MARIO: Yes, we do leave some.

GUSTAVO: We leave some.

TRAINER: But you leave very little of her, don't you? Very little. Isn't your father hungry? Doesn't he need a bit of your mother too, a bit of cake to eat, instead of you two gobbling her all up?

MARIO: Father wants some too, because he always says he never manages to spend any time with mother.

TRAINER: He complains sometimes that he never manages to be with your mother?

MARIO: Yes, maybe he goes on a trip with her sometimes, but mother always thinks about us.

TRAINER: So you take all of her away with you. Listen, do you let your father have her at night, or not even at night? Do you sleep with your mother as well?

MARIO: Yes, a bit, at night Gustavo wants mother to read him stories, and mother goes away afterwards when he's fallen asleep.

TRAINER: Where does she go?

MARIO: She goes to her own bed.

TRAINER: And maybe your father has already fallen asleep waiting for mother. Maybe your father waits for your mother because he wants to . . . do you know what intimacy is between a man and a woman? Do you know what they do?

MARIO: (*He nods, laughing mischievously.*) I certainly do!

TRAINER: Do you think your parents do it, or that they don't have time? Do you think they have time?

MARIO: Well, on Sundays.

TRAINER: They make love?

MARIO: Yes, but sometimes not even on Sundays because Gustavo wakes up before eight and gets into bed with mother and father.

This exchange shows how the sons, within the pattern of strong attachment we have already seen, end up preventing the parents from relating to each as a couple. We might well hypothesize that before the birth of their children the couple's time—its horizon and temporal perspective—was different. With the birth and growth of their children, mutual coordination of the times of all the family members seems to have halted development in the family system. The parents seem to expect nothing new of the future. Their attention is focused on the past and present, and the past has a deterministic influence on the present. In other words, they don't expect to be doing anything different in the future from what they are doing now: their system is organized as a closed system in time. Even their work, which they once did outside the home, is now done at home; they rarely go out and never leave their children with a baby-sitter. Their future is one of lifetime parenthood that permanently freezes their "handicapped" son and "immature" son at somewhere between the ages of three and five. Their future is the future of people who live in a prison.

> TRAINER: So early on in the night Gustavo wants mother for himself. (*to the mother*) Why is that?
>
> MOTHER: Well, I can tell you what I think. Since so much time during the day is given over to Mario, that hour in the evening, perhaps not even hour, sometimes it's me who gives in . . . that hour is sacred and inviolable to him.
>
> TRAINER: (*to Mario*) Is your father still waiting, or has he already fallen asleep when the hour's up? Does he call her sometimes . . . what's your mother's name?
>
> MOTHER: Rosa.
>
> TRAINER: Do you hear him calling: "Rooosa, Rooosa . . . "?
> (*They all suddenly start speaking at once.*)
>
> TRAINER: Don't you sometimes hear him calling?
>
> MARIO: (*laughing*) Yes, he calls her "Bubu."
>
> TRAINER: Oh, he calls her "Bubu."

Note that Mario seems well informed, fully aware of what happens at home and shows much more understanding than his parents credit him with, especially his father. Note also that in this session Mario is much more natural and articulate than when therapy started, and seems appreciably more intelligent. This led the team to wonder whether the diagnosis of mild mental retardation had been made when he felt seriously inhibited and should now be questioned.

The trainer tries hard to make distinctions—sibling time, children-parent time, couple time—but his efforts are continually frustrated and neutralized. Paradoxically, it seems that Mario, the handicapped son, is more aware of role distinctions then the others; this may throw interesting light on the communicative "innocence" handicapped people usually show when confronted with the complexity and ambiguity of the language demanded by social conventions.

MOTHER: But it isn't true! More often than not your father's still at his computer . . .

TRAINER: Do you think your father's happy with this situation? If you were him would you do what he does, or would you end up saying "Now I'll have her"? Would you do that?

MARIO: No, I'd be patient, like father.

TRAINER: Why would you be patient?

MARIO: Because father's a good person.

TRAINER: Who is he good to?

MARIO: Everyone.

TRAINER: Everyone?

MARIO: He puts up with them.

TRAINER: You mean he resigns himself, is that it? He's someone who resigns himself.

MARIO: When we went to France, Gustavo slept on his own, he always slept on his own, you know?

TRAINER: Your mother's a good person too, a person who devotes herself to everyone.

MARIO: Yes, she is.

The statement that Gustavo always slept alone when the family went to France is important. It shows he is quite capable of doing without his evening rituals and managing on his own (a psychoanalytical reading here would relate this to activation of oedipal desires in the home environment). However, what strikes us most in this part of the session is the description of the mother and father's altruism (Mario experiences it positively), which the parents are so visibly pleased to acknowledge. Both seem to want this recognition, and there is even the impression that they are subtly competing with each other to see who is the "best" parent. When their altruism is questioned by teachers or specialists, they immediately react in an irritated, hostile way until the relationship eventually breaks down. We could say there is a potent family myth here—the myth of the parents' goodness—which like all myths stops time and lays down appropriate behaviors and meanings for all members of the family.

TRAINER: She has no time for herself. I imagine that having three males . . .

MARIO: No, two males! The third male is her husband.

TRAINER: You are three males and your mother is completely devoted to you. I imagine she spends all her time on you and doesn't have much for herself. Am I right?

MARIO: Yes.

TRAINER: So both your parents have little time to be with each other, and she has little time for herself. Am I right?

MARIO: Yes.

TRAINER: And do you think that's a proper state of affairs?

MARIO: No.

Here the trainer is clearly trying to introduce distinctions between private time, couple time and sibling time by appealing to the children. He would have failed if he had tried to do it through the parents.

TRAINER: Don't you think it would be useful if you and your brother began helping them to have some time for each other as well?

MARIO: But he's still small, and I'm not very good at doing my homework.

TRAINER: But do you agree with what I said?

MARIO: Yes, but I can't manage on my own.

TRAINER: You can't manage on your own?

MARIO: And he's still small.

TRAINER: Would you help your parents? Couldn't we work out some way of helping you and Gustavo to let your mother and father have some time for themselves, and be with each other, too?

MARIO: Yes, mother can't even go to the hairdresser's . . .

TRAINER: Otherwise, what sort of a marriage have they got? They've had two children and all their time is devoted to them, twenty-four hours a day, and they have no time for themselves.

MARIO: Mother always helps me with my homework so she doesn't have to pay for private lessons.

TRAINER: Would you like to do without her lessons sometimes so she can have an hour to herself? Or would you find that too difficult? You could try a little, couldn't you? . . . Do you see what I'm saying?

MARIO: Yes.

The trainer is working here on the theme of public and private time (in the mother and couple, but also, implicitly, in the children). He does it by talking almost exclusively to Mario, treating him like an intelligent person who well understands what she is saying: The more Mario is treated like an intelligent person, the more he shows he is capable of responding intelligently.

> TRAINER: You're already 15, you're making plans that seem very positive to me, you're an intelligent boy. Of course, you'll still have problems because of your physical difficulties. Of course, I understand your attachment to your parents, but it's possible that your attachment to your mother will grow so strong that it'll be very difficult to break it. Mario, I'd like to ask you—then we'll think about Gustavo (*who is creating a noisy disturbance.*)—would you like . . . sorry, Gustavo, I'll ask you afterwards. Mario, would you like your mother and father to help you become less of a mommy's boy?
>
> MARIO: Yes.
>
> TRAINER: So what advice would you give your mother and father to help you become less of a mommy's boy?

These last two exchanges are a dual reversal of punctuation: in the first phase the parents are placed in the active role of helping their son; in the second, Mario is placed in the active role of advising his parents how to do it. Hoffman (1981) has described this kind of punctuation as a reversal which often works because it counteracts a commonplace, accepted view: it's usually the parents who help their children. One interesting implication of the second exchange might be that if the children help their parents to help them break away from them, they might also help their parents to break away from the therapists. In this way, an evolving temporal perspective connecting all members of the therapy system (which obviously includes the therapists themselves) may take the place of a static perspective.

> MARIO: Well, I could tell her just to help me with my homework, and not cling onto her at other times.

Significantly, Mario says "not cling onto her" instead of "not cling onto me": the slip reveals the strength of his will and attachment.

> TRAINER: I see, you could advise her to leave you alone sometimes. You could say: "Listen, mommy, could you leave me alone for half an hour?" Could you do that? Because that way your mother will

help you to stop being a mommy's boy. Do you see? Mrs. Campi, do you understand what I mean?

MOTHER: Of course.

TRAINER: Do you agree? If he says . . .

MOTHER: Of course. Only yesterday, so it's a recent example, he worked on his own almost the whole afternoon. But Mario's in a difficult situation, you know.

TRAINER: Of course he is, we agree on that, your devotion is admirable. But did you understand what I mean? I'm trying to talk to Mario about helping you to help him, and vice versa, so he must express his needs in the way he feels. Mario can start saying: "Look, mommy, I'm going to do my homework now for half an hour, or an hour; do something of your own for a while."

MOTHER: Then he'll try to study and perhaps get nowhere.

FATHER: (*speaking over her*) It's the difference between the situation he's in and what he should do: that's the point! He spends an afternoon doing only a third of what he should, so then he fails his exams and I have to sort him out. Look, I don't know if you follow me. From his first year in infant school . . .

Here the mother subverts the attempt to reduce the attachment and the father steps up the pressure! They certainly seem to believe in carrot and stick as a way of teaching children.

TRAINER: So what if they failed him! If they fail him and he doesn't go to school, he'll do something else. He'll work. There are so many other possibilities.

Here the trainer falls into the trap. He should have insisted on the healthy/handicapped ambiguity by saying: "He'll do what he can, the teachers at school are aware of his difficulties too . . . "

FATHER: (*becoming even more excited*) Yes, but we're talking about junior high school! Junior high school! He can't even manage junior high school!

TRAINER: In the future he'll do the things he can, he'll use the potential he has, he'll do what he's able to do.

FATHER: I agree, but . . .

TRAINER: Sorry. We were talking about how to help him develop his potential.

FATHER: Oh, I see.

At this point the trainer envisages that Mario will turn to his father for help in establishing relations with his peers because his father, too, was once his age and knows about the issues that arise in relations between young people. The father responds irritably, raising his voice and saying he's sure that no boy could ever establish a lasting bond with his son: "I'd find him a friend all right, one of his own age. But then he'd leave after five minutes because he's got lots of other interests, other abilities. I'd have to find him one who's at least five years behind. We're talking about him as if he's normal, but he isn't."

Visibly annoyed, the trainer now focuses on Mario's potential in order to shift attention away from the restraints his problems impose to the possibilities they offer. The father repeatedly responds by returning to the idea of "diagnosis," of a label, which is by definition timeless, while the trainer tries to stress the potential, which points to a developing future. The mother unexpectedly intervenes to agree with the trainer.

In this part of the session the team hypothesized that the father was projecting his anxiety about his son's handicap onto Mario. This hypothesis was also supported by the father's tragic past: he had lost his own father during adolescence and, as a father-brother, had had to look after a younger brother. It seemed as if history was repeating itself. The father and mother are now looking after a "handicapped" son and an "immature" son, and seem to see the outside world as threatening and deceptive.

The session came to an end. Before the therapist and trainer left the room, the trainer abandoned his previous role as a challenger of the family's premises in order to establish a joining, understanding role with the parents. This took place in a dialogue conducted with his colleague in front of the parents.

TRAINER: (*to the therapist*) I still get the impression that these two parents, Mr. and Mrs. Campi, have purely objective problems, so I understand why they're so touchy. It's understandable: they're faced with specialists like us, or other . . .

FATHER: But . . .

MOTHER: My husband's been telling me that for years.

TRAINER: They devote all their energy, all their effort . . . (*as if making fun of experts*) then along come these experts who're so relaxed about everything, who've read a few books and seem to know everything. They can make you really angry sometimes! I'm trying to put myself in their position, and I think I understand them. Of course they've become sensitive to criticism, so sensitive that perhaps they see criticism where none is intended. I also understand that given their situation, where things go on happening but nothing changes, they end up getting used to things, they try one expert after another but they see the years rolling by just the same . . . but it's as if the years don't really pass, as if time has stopped.

MOTHER: There's nothing more we can do.

TRAINER: But because hope dies hard, and there's always the hope that the experts can help you, it's easy to imagine how bitter they feel when they discover the experts have failed again . . . it's as if time has stopped for everyone, they're caught in a vicious circle and they give up hope. When you enter this state of mind you really can't see the possibilities that might be there. Because there are possibilities. Not miracles — no one can work miracles — but possibilities. It's important to give up the idea of miracles, and better to take a fresh look at small things, small events, and start building again from there so that new possibilities gradually emerge that were hidden before. That's the point. We're trying to help them discover the potential both their children have, because if you don't think in this way there really isn't anything you can do.

In this conversation with the therapist the trainer focuses on the relationship between static time and evolving time, between a predominantly synchronic vision and a prevalently diachronic vision. The message is that if the clients and the experts don't share the same ideas about the potential of the children, it's like saying that nothing new can happen, that time has stopped.

In the next session, conducted by the therapist alone, it was decided to concentrate more on the children, who were already showing some signs of change and seemed less impervious than their parents to the possibility of evolution. In other words, the children seemed to be living in evolving time, their parents in static time. The therapist told the boys that her colleagues behind the mirror had noticed they had grown and now looked like two young men. She then asked them if they thought their mother was happy about spending so much time with them. Shaking his head, Gustavo immediately replied he didn't because his mother never had time to do what she wanted. Mario suggested to his brother that they should help their mother at home, and Gustavo agreed, suggesting in turn that they could help her with the shopping.

The two children were then asked how much time they needed from their mother every day. Mario said he needed two hours a day, three when his school work wasn't going very well; Gustavo said he needed only an hour. The question was important because it implied that the mother's time wasn't wholly at the disposal of her children, but could (hopefully) be divided into private time, time for her children, and time for her husband. By answering as he did, Mario showed he understood the opposite punctuation, that the children's time needn't necessarily be the mother's sole concern.

Probably as a result of the therapist's positive response to the children's increasing maturity, as well as their answers to her questions which clearly showed a new awareness of what independence means, the wall the parents had erected against the therapist from the very first session began to crumble. The mother admitted that the housewife's role wasn't what she had really wanted: she would have preferred to continue with her previous work as a consultant. The father said he had been dissatisfied with his previous job as a manager and was also dissatisfied with his present badly paid job at home which he had only decided to do because of Mario's needs. He revealed that his dissatisfaction was also the result of his bitterness at not having had the career his family of origin had expected of him (significantly, he consistently avoided speaking of the accident that left him with a limp at the age of 18).[1] Now he couldn't even look after his family on his own, and this weighed heavily on him. "Now," he said, as if challenging the therapist, "make the associations you think are best."[2]

Immediately afterwards, however, he went on to criticize his wife for not being firm enough with the children. "There's no pleasing you!" was the comment she let slip. It seemed that the questioning of the children, which had revealed the immobility of the parents, had placed them in a critical position. The fact that the children had began to glimpse how they might develop in future—and so also their future independence—was forcing the parents to take a hard look at their own relationship.

---

[1] One member of the group who had had psychoanalytical training advanced the hypothesis that the father's leg injury was an oedipal punishment. Mr. Campi had lost his father some years before the accident and had brought up the younger brother with his mother. By taking the place of his father, he symbolically associated the oedipal punishment of castration with his leg injury, which he sought to repress, understandably enough. This may also explain his "fixation" with his handicapped son, onto whom he projects his own conflict.

[2] In a rapid exchange of views on the other side of the mirror, a point of view very different from the one Mr. Campi held emerged: the view that the rest of the family, and Mario especially, concealed the intolerable failure of Mr. Campi's life contrasted his view, that he was the victim of his family's misfortunes. His existential bitterness and his profound need to have it acknowledged seem his only consolation for the existential defeat he has suffered under depressing and tragic circumstances. Given this situation, it is quite understandable—and only to be expected—that his children's growing independence and success shakes the fragile edifice of his beliefs to its foundations.

The tenth session was held after the summer holidays, which the family had spent with the maternal grandparents, both because the grandmother had been unwell and because of the family's chronic money problems. The two brothers, who seemed calm and relaxed, said they had spent a lot of time together and had got on very well with each other. Mario especially spoke in a more self-assured way, reporting that he had been able to concentrate and study better without his mother around him all the time. Gustavo had also managed to do his homework on his own and felt pleased about it. When the therapist asked, "What would your mother and father do if they didn't have all the worries you cause them?" Mario replied emphatically, "They'd have nothing to say to each other." The parents didn't agree, although at the end of the session the father admitted that the children had improved, immediately adding, however, that there were still a lot of problems.

Mrs. Campi did not attend the eleventh session because she had to visit her mother, who was ill. The session went smoothly, with the evolution we looked at earlier apparently taking its natural course. At the end the father was told that the team agreed the situation was developing positively and that the mother should be told about it too. The team decided that the family should be told at the end of the next session that an irreversible process of positive evolution had begun, so that therapy should be terminated. The family was informed that only the parents should come to the next session, in order to stress, among other things, that the children were now able to handle their own futures.

The twelfth and last session was held at the end of January 1993. The parents seemed unusually relaxed and at first talked in an almost friendly way. This led the team to suspect that they were very involved with the therapist and were preparing themselves for endless therapy in which the team would either assume the role of wise grandparents who could help them to guide their children through future stages in their life-cycle, or fill the void in their relations as a couple, or keep them in touch with the outside world through their meetings at the Center.

Consequently, the team decided to terminate therapy at the end of the session, both to avoid the risk that the parents would become chronically dependent on us (and so create the conditions for endless therapy) and to restore the couple to full parenthood. The therapist made the following communication to the family.

THERAPIST: Today we want to tell you that we've decided to terminate therapy. To sum up the situation, you yourselves have noticed that your children have started to be more independent: Mario is slowly growing into adolescence and Gustavo will soon enter puberty, and these are both periods in which parents can start devoting more time to their private lives and their relations as a couple. Our impression is that you are very responsible, and above all, altruistic parents, in the sense that you devote most of your time and effort to your children, and that the passing of time has no effect on your attachment to them. We respect your choice, and our work stops here. We'd be very interested to meet you again in six months' time to see how things have developed.

CLASHING TIMES

During a seminar conducted by Luigi Boscolo in the United States, Dr. Stewart, a psychiatrist who worked in a psychiatric hospital located in a midwest town, told the group she was quite concerned about the life of Nancy, a self-injuring, highly suicidal, 22-year-old woman. It was decided to do a live consultation, conducted by Boscolo, with the whole family. Dr. Stewart called the parents, but they categorically refused to come, because "we have had enough with her, we don't want to have anything to do with her." Then she called the hospital and talked to Nancy, who accepted the consultation for the following day.

Nancy was the second of five siblings. Her elder sister Mary was married and lived with her husband, while John, 18 years old, Ted, 14, and Elizabeth, 11, were living with the parents. Her father, a teacher, was described as a very rigid, moralistic, at times violent man. Nancy reported that she was scared of him: he would frequently check her clothes, and if she was "not properly dressed" he would punish her and call her "a slut." In particular, he would get quite upset if her dress did not cover enough of her legs. Her mother was described as a "victim," a submissive woman, on the defensive anytime he raised his voice. A few times he physically harmed her. Nancy sided with her mother; for as long as she could remember she had always tried to alleviate her mother's burden by being a mother to the younger siblings and trying to console mother whenever she was upset. Mary, father's preferred daughter, was described as being very outgoing, lighthearted, a "joker," very different from Nancy.

Nancy described an interesting episode that occurred when she was 15—interesting because it raises the question of whether the content of her narration reflected what happened then or represented an elaboration of the event due to reading of psychology books or talking to experts. She remembered that at that time she had been very upset because of the frequent fights between her parents and started eating very little. As an effect of her fasting, one day she overheard them saying they were worried about her weight loss. She decided then to "become anorectic" to attract their attention, so they would fight less.

Three years later Nancy's mother initiated psychotherapy with a young male psychologist; as a result she became less depressed, less obsessed with the family, and more interested in herself and her appearance. The effect on her husband, according to Nancy, was striking: he became softer and at times seemed to court mother, as though he were afraid to lose her. Nancy remembered that in this period she missed her mother's closeness and started feeling lonely. At the age of 19, still a virgin, she was raped by a boyfriend, which had the effect, later on, of making her anorgasmic ("I did sex just for them—men").

A few months later, her anorexia turned into a severe form of bulimia, with repeated vomiting causing electrolyte imbalance, which led to her hospitalization at the age of 20. The symptoms of bulimia, in particular the repeated vomiting, made her parents turn their back on her, to the point that they refused to visit her in the hospital. At that time she developed the delusion of having inside a girl aged 15, named Mildred, who enslaved and bossed her around. She attempted suicide; she repeatedly self-inflicted wounds with razor blades or burned her arms with cigarette butts. Over the previous two years, she had been hospitalized seven times on Medicare.

The consultation took place in a room connected by a closed TV circuit to another room where Dr. Stewart and the other seminar participants were observing. Nancy was sitting next to the accompanying nurse, who later on confessed to Dr. Stewart that she had been scared of her possible acting-out during the car trip to and from the consultation. Asked whether she wanted to have the nurse in the room, Nancy agreed, as though she were in need of protection. She impressed the group as being an attractive, intelligent, tormented young woman. Most of the session she sat rather rigidly, rubbing her hands, with her forearms in front of her so that her scars were visible. Her legs most of the time were crossed, with the upper leg moving rhythmically.

During the first half-hour, the consultant inquired about her present life in the hospital, her relationship with Dr. Stewart, and her past life in the family. Most of the above information came from such inquiry. At the beginning, the atmosphere was fairly relaxed; Nancy even smiled at times and seemed to develop a positive relationship with the interviewer. When the consultant felt confident that Nancy perceived him as reliable, he decided it was the appropriate time to go into the hot issues of her delusions.

CONSULTANT: I was told by Dr. Stewart that you have a girl named Mildred inside you. What does this girl tell you?

NANCY: She tells me she's going to make me do things that will kill me.

CONSULTANT: Why does she want you dead?

NANCY: Because she thinks I am bad, I am a slut, I am fat . . .

CONSULTANT: You hate her or sometimes you like her?

NANCY: She's more a friend to me, I like her.

CONSULTANT: It may be because she's now the only person close to you. As a matter of fact, your family doesn't want to see you, people you know in the hospital are just acquaintances, and Dr. Stewart is just a therapist. So, the only person you have now is Mildred . . .

NANCY: Yeah.

CONSULTANT: So you love and hate her.

NANCY: I love her, she knows me well.

CONSULTANT: Would you like to be like her?

NANCY: (*smiling*) Of course, she's 15 and she's like a skeleton.

CONSULTANT: Do you think she has sex?

NANCY: Oh, no, no!

CONSULTANT: She's a virgin, she's perfect.

NANCY: Yeah.

Nancy appears dissociated and talks about Mildred as though she were part of herself and not related to a delusion. The consultant's hypothesis is that—as in case of multiple personality—Nancy and Mildred represent two opposite parts of the client's personality. Mildred would be the ideal, young, thin, virgin, who persecutes Nancy, the older, fat slut, to the point that she wants her dead.[3] The dissociated consciousness state could have occurred as a result of the unbearable anxiety triggered by her mother turning her back on her and maybe by the traumatic episode of the rape which occurred before the onset of her psychosis. The devastating consequences of such anxiety could be related to physical, sexual, or psychological abuse in early childhood, which interfered heavily in her evolution from childhood to adulthood. Mildred would represent the girl who does not accept becoming a woman and punishes the elder Nancy anytime she gives herself pleasure, keeping her in a state of terror.

---

[3]A psychoanalyst could see Mildred as a representation of Nancy's ego ideal or/and her persecutory superego.

This tragic situation must be linked to her family life. Her father was described as a stern, punishing, puritanical, at times physically violent man, who psychologically abused both her and her mother, while he preferred the eldest daughter. Her mother, as Nancy underlined, preferred the boys. Nancy's role of "helper" in the family could be motivated by her wish to be accepted by her mother. As has been told, when her mother broke her ties with her, she became "crazy." The real world started to make no sense. Her inner world became violent and pitiless, mirroring the perceived external world.

Her individual subjective time, then, lost its unity, giving way to the individual, synchronic, still time of Mildred, and the individual, diachronic, flowing time of Nancy. Time horizon and perspective narrowed considerably. Her attention became mostly a prisoner of the present time, caught in the web of her constant fears of punishment. Her future perspective was bleak.

> CONSULTANT: It's hard for Nancy to be Mildred, because she should go back in time, go backward; besides, she cannot become a skeleton because she would die before that.
>
> NANCY: Yeah . . .
>
> CONSULTANT: You cannot become a virgin, you cannot become a skeleton, maybe almost a skeleton, like a few anorectics. You can become *almost* like Mildred, but never her. You cannot go back in time.

Obviously, Nancy's attempts to go back into the past, to become younger, to become Mildred, pertain to the logic of psychosis. This is one of the consultant's attempts to match this logic of psychosis with the logic of common sense, thus making possible the appearance of a new story.

> CONSULTANT: How do you explain that Mildred came inside you and did not go inside Mary or other members of your family? Why did she come to torture you. . . ?
>
> NANCY: Actually she's trying to help me, she's trying to make me perfect.
>
> CONSULTANT: But she tortures you . . .
>
> NANCY: Sometimes it is a torture, sometimes I can't stand it, I'd throw . . . ashtrays around because I don't like what she's saying. She gets me angry and I lose control; usually I don't lose control.

In this segment, as elsewhere, the consultant introduces an epistemology of "either . . . or" by attributing to Mildred the characteristics of aggressor and to Nancy the characteristics of victim, thus creating a polarization between "bad" and "good." At the end of the session, he will introduce an epistemology of "both . . . and," by positively connoting both girls, aiming at a dialectic synthesis.

CONSULTANT: You said you are the one in your family who had been all good, all straight; you supported your mother, you tried to be your siblings' mother. You even became anorectic trying to attract your parents' attention towards you, so they could stop fighting . . . so, you are the helper . . .

NANCY: Yes, I can't stop helping, sometimes at night I clean the hospital's floors for hours.

CONSULTANT: But after having done all these things for everybody, you are the one who suffered the most. You are in the hospital, you have to pay, you are in a kind of jail, Mildred is your jailer . . . how can you make sense out of all of this? As a result of your goodness, you're punished. How can you explain that? You are in a jail, and cannot escape.

NANCY: That's right! That's why I want to die.

CONSULTANT: You are tortured. You are in two jails: an inner jail with a tough girl torturing you, and a second jail—as to say—the psychiatric hospital.

NANCY: (*laughs bitterly*) Yeah.

CONSULTANT: Your young jailer is so tough on you that she doesn't even want you to live, you cannot even escape, you may die or become crazy. A price you might have to pay is to become crazy. (*pause*) Do you understand?

NANCY: Yeah, yeah.

CONSULTANT: Are you afraid to become crazy?

NANCY: Yeah. Since I am in the hospital, Mildred gets worse and worse. She tries to make me a young girl.

CONSULTANT: It seems she either wants you to become crazy or to die. To become crazy is like dying; craziness is called "psychological death," you know?

NANCY: Yeah.

CONSULTANT: Now I have a big problem. I have to understand why a generous 22-year-old lady has to go through these terrible things and why a 15-year-old girl wants to kill her . . . I don't understand . . .

NANCY: (*with a bitter laughter*) Hmm-hmm.

CONSULTANT: (*pause*) I feel bad now. I feel bad because I cannot make sense.

NANCY: I wish I would help you, I wish I could do something to get out of this situation.

CONSULTANT: I feel disturbed now. Why does this girl want to drive you out of your mind and prevent you from going forward in time? Do you think I have my finger on something important?

NANCY: Yeah.

CONSULTANT: OK. Since I have to make sense, can we stop now? I would like to talk with the colleagues in the other room, especially to the women; I hope they are going to help me.

NANCY: (*laughs*)

CONSULTANT: Let's meet in half an hour.

In this segment three main points can be highlighted:

1. Her story of having been generous and altruistic is matched by the consultant with the story of her punishment and ordeal, to emphasize the absurdity of her present life.

2. As an example of depathologizing in language, a diagnosis of "craziness" made in the past is framed as a possibility in the future.

3. The consultant takes upon himself the confusion, the "illness" of the client, and asks her to help him get rid of the symptoms of confusion and malaise. This reversal of the position between client and therapist, whereby the helper becomes the client, offers the client the possibility of becoming the observer of her own drama enacted in front of her. The client, therefore, becomes a spectator of a drama lived by the therapist on an imaginary stage. Of course, the empathy and genuine feelings of the consultant must be real and evident here.

CONSULTANT: I went to talk to my colleagues to understand why, being so good, you ended up in such tragic situation. They are puzzled too. They asked me to ask you this question: How long do you think Mildred will make you suffer before you will become free again . . . how many months, years. . . ?

NANCY: I'll end up dead in a year. She wants me dead.

CONSULTANT: But if Nancy dies, what will Mildred do? Is Mildred going to visit some other girls?

NANCY: I think she will die too.

CONSULTANT: Why?

NANCY: Because she's part of me; she will die within me.

CONSULTANT: I wonder whether she will die within you. It might happen that she goes inside somebody else, maybe inside Mary, your older sister, or the younger.

NANCY: (*forcefully*) I hope not the younger one.

CONSULTANT: Why?

NANCY: Because I like her very much. I don't want her to be tortured that way.

CONSULTANT: How about if she goes to visit your mother?

NANCY: (*laughs*) Even better.

This segment shows three relevant issues:

1. The consultant enlarges the context from three people (Nancy, Mildred, and himself) to four, by asking the client questions regarding the relationship between Mildred and Nancy. With this linguistic operation he implicitly talks to the client as *one* person, and addresses the relation between two other conflicting characters (Mildred and Nancy). Later on he will unexpectedly try to solve the conflict and thus unify the dual personality.

2. A hypothetical future question about how long Nancy will have to suffer before being free again brings forth a bleak, deadly future.

3. As Nancy predicts her imminent death, the consultant challenges her with a riddle: where would Mildred go after Nancy's death? Her expected answer, that Mildred will also die, is confronted with the possibility that Mildred will go to visit another family member. This is an example of the consultant using uncommon logic, instead of common sense logic, appearing more "crazy" than the client.

CONSULTANT: Another question my colleagues ask me to ask you: When, for example, you will be 32, will Mildred be 25 or will she be the same age as today?

NANCY: The same age!

CONSULTANT: So it's possible, if you don't kill yourself before, that when you reach the age of 60, you will have a 15-year-old girl who will tell you what to do or not to do.

NANCY: (*laughing bitterly*) I won't live that long.

CONSULTANT: How come Mildred wants you dead?

NANCY: Because I'm not perfect like her. (*with passion*) She's a skeleton, I love skeletons. I would like to have them hanging over my bed
...

CONSULTANT: I'm confused; Nancy seems to be a victim of Mildred. It is incredible that Nancy likes Mildred; she likes to be punished by her.

NANCY: (*raising and showing her scarred forearms*) I like pain; sometimes I burn my arms with matches to see how much pain I can take. Sometimes I cut my wrist and I like to see the blood flowing down on my hand and see how much blood I could get out before dying.

CONSULTANT: Wouldn't you rather like to love life instead of death?

NANCY: (*showing despair*) I think that would be nice, but I never loved life. . . . I wish I were an abortion.
(**Long pause. Both consultant and client seem caught in an emotional grip.**)

In this segment Nancy reaches the depths of her hopelessness. Time and time again she tries to convince the consultant that there is no hope for her, that she is living in a timeless inferno, that she has been left only one wish: to die. The consultant, on his part, time and time again emphasizes the primacy of hope and life. Above all, he introduces the flow of time. Soon he will start to track her with a series of questions that will introduce new meanings and emotions.

CONSULTANT: Suppose I ask Mildred to give Nancy a little break once in a while. Would she listen to me?

NANCY: I doubt she would leave me alone.

CONSULTANT: Would Nancy like me to talk to Mildred?

NANCY: (*pause*) Hmm-hmm.

CONSULTANT: What would Nancy like me to tell Mildred?

NANCY: (*with a slow, deep voice; she looks down and starts to move her head and trunk rhythmically back and forth, as though she were in a hypnoid state*) Just let me alone, stop screaming at me . . .

CONSULTANT: Do you think Mildred will listen to me?

NANCY: No, she's going to kill me. Now she's telling me you're a jerk.

CONSULTANT: I'm not surprised. (*appearing emotionally involved, and speaking in a warm, empathic tone*) I'd like to tell Mildred that she has a terrible life, even more terrible than Nancy. I feel compassion for her. It's terrible for such a young girl to love death, not life. . . . Mildred is so unhappy, maybe she's more unhappy than Nancy.

(*pause*) What did Mildred do to deserve such a terrible life, maybe more terrible than Nancy's?

NANCY: I don't know why.

CONSULTANT: But do you understand me?

NANCY: Yes, yes.

CONSULTANT: I don't understand, it doesn't make sense to me. Can you help me to find a sense? (*pause*)

NANCY: No, I don't understand you now. Mildred wants to say what she wants to say. . . . (*shaking her head*) I don't know, you're getting blocked down in some place now.

CONSULTANT: Maybe Mildred is telling you now not to listen to me. Is she telling you? . . .

NANCY: I think so, yeah.

CONSULTANT: Does she want you to talk to me?

NANCY: Not really. (*long pause, tense atmosphere*) Because she thinks you know too much, you understand too much.

CONSULTANT: (*embarrassed*) I might help Mildred. Wouldn't Nancy like me to help Mildred?
(*silence, long pause*)

CONSULTANT: How do you feel now?

NANCY: (*with a low, almost inaudible voice and the head down*) Confused. (*long pause*)

CONSULTANT: Would you like me to continue or to stop here?

NANCY: (*slowly raising her head*) To stop.

The consultant's change of punctuation related to the possibility that the aggressor (Mildred) might suffer and be more unlucky than the supposed victim (Nancy) provokes a very significant effect: Nancy appears upset; she first tells the consultant he is "getting blocked down in some place," then that Mildred doesn't want the consultant to talk to Nancy because "she thinks you know too much, you understand too much." The consultant is perceived as getting too close to "the truth." If he accepts Nancy's invitation to close the session, he leaves his work unfinished: relying on her trust on him and on his experience, he passes the Rubicon and decides to go ahead.

CONSULTANT: Why do you want to stop?

NANCY: Because Mildred is getting angry, I'm afraid that when I go back to the hospital she's going to do something to me. . . . (*pause*) Do you think she will harm me when I go back to the hospital?

CONSULTANT: I don't think so. Mildred knows that you're going to obey her anyway. She thinks Nancy will be with her and I think that Nancy will forget what I've said and will go back to obeying Mildred. (*pause*)

The consultant tries to reassure Nancy that she will go back to Mildred and that the alliance between Nancy and him is too threatening and revolutionary. Now he tries to connect the two "women" positively.

CONSULTANT: Why doesn't Nancy try to get another kind of relationship with Mildred? Why don't they start accepting each other? Why don't they try to find out what they have in common and stop being like two enemies? I would like to help *you* to have both Nancy and Mildred try to find some way to enjoy each other rather than control each other. They could find another way to be together. I think they could become good friends or like two sisters, even better, like *twin sisters*. I think this would be good not only for Nancy, but for Mildred who, I think, suffers even more than Nancy. Do you understand what I mean?

NANCY: Yeah.

CONSULTANT: Probably, if Mildred listens now to what I'm saying she will start to have some doubts about what she's doing to Nancy.

NANCY: Yes, she's just suffering.

CONSULTANT: Because she did not learn another way of living. Maybe if she listens to me, instead of getting angry at Nancy, she might find out what a sad life she had . . . and she might start to make connections and start to enjoy life. They could enjoy each other, like you were enjoying your mother when she was close to you. When she disconnected from you, you suffered.

NANCY: Yeah, yeah.

CONSULTANT: What I see is that both Mildred and Nancy are in the same boat. They are desperate, and they are compelled to be the jailer of each other instead of being friends. If this would happen, the whole thing will start to make sense to me. . . . Does what I'm saying make sense? You might ask Mildred what she thinks about what I'm saying.

NANCY: I hope she listens . . . usually she yells at me when I talk to her, and tells me to do what she says.

CONSULTANT: It seems as though there is a way out for both of them: to become friends or sisters and start to have good moments. That's the last words I like to tell you. . . . I would like to stop here. It's possible that Mildred will start to listen now, because she understands that both of you are suffering. . . . If both of you connect, you will start to love life more than death. OK, let's stop here. . . . Thank you very much.

In the final part of the session, the consultant opens up new scenarios in Nancy's inner world, by introducing positive emotions, such as empathy, compassion, and love of life, and subsequently connecting Nancy and Mildred in a reciprocal accepting relationship. These new scenarios are very different from the ones perceived in her past. By underlining positively the relationship between the two girls, as like twin sisters, the consultant aims at bridging the rift between the two, so that the two different subjective times that characterize her life could become one flowing time, which could then coordinate with the times of others and with the times of living systems.

As an immediate follow-up, the nurse reported that during their trip back to the hospital Nancy, all of a sudden, asked her to stop at a nearby shop, to buy some chocolate. As she started to eat with pleasure a big piece of chocolate, she said smiling: "Mildred will let me eat, now." In the hospital she rapidly improved, was discharged, and went to live with another patient in a sheltered home. A year later, Dr. Stewart met the consultant and told him that Nancy had just gotten married and seemed to be doing fairly well. Mildred had left her not long after she left the hospital!

2

REASONING ABOUT TIME

SOME PARADOXES

The problem of time has exercised the minds of many writers over the centuries. The abundant literature is full of paradoxes; we shall look only at some of the more important ones here. Let us start with Zeno of Elea's famous paradoxes of time and movement, which date from the sixth century BC. In Zeno's fable, Achilles can never catch up with the tortoise because just as he reaches the place where the tortoise stood at the start of the race, the tortoise has already moved on a little, and by the time Achilles has made up the ground in between, the tortoise has already moved forward again, and so on *ad infinitum*. In another example, Zeno says that an arrow can never reach its target because it first has to cover half the distance to the target, but before that it has to cover half of that first half, and so on, again, *ad infinitum*.

A thousand years later, Augustine of Hippo addressed the question of time in his *Confessions*:

What, then, is time? I know well enough what it is, provided that nobody asks me; but if I am asked what it is and try to explain, I am baffled. All the same I can confidently say that I know that if nothing passed, there would be no past time; if nothing were going to happen, there would be no future time; and if nothing *were*, there would be no present time.

Of these three divisions of time, then, how can two, the past and the future, *be*, when the past no longer is and the future is not yet? As for the present, if it were always present and never moved on to become the past, it would not be time but eternity. If, therefore, the present is time only by reason of the fact that it moves on to become the past, how can we say that even the present *is*, when the reason why it *is* is that it is *not to be*? In other words, we cannot rightly say that time *is*, except by reason of its impending state of *not being*. (*Confessions*, Book XI, section 14)

Writing in our century, McTaggart (1927) proposed that there are two quite distinct series of time. In Series A, events are at first located in the future, then move through the present to come to rest in the past, while in Series B, events are located one after another in a fixed sequence. Obviously, the significance of events is very different in the two series. In Series A, they are in constant movement. Before Caesar was born, for example, the event of his birth was located in the future; at the moment of his birth, it then shifted from the present to arrive at its definitive location in the past, which is where we now perceive it to be. In Series B, Caesar's birth always has the same fixed "siting" in time — before the birth of Newton, for example. Given these discrepancies, McTaggart decided that neither series worked and concluded that time, as we normally think of it, does not exist.

In his essay "New Refutation of Time," Jorge Luis Borges carries the arguments of British idealism to their logical conclusion. If, as Berkeley says, reality exists only when perceived by the senses, and if, as Hume says, a subject can only be a simple sum of perceptions, Borges concludes that the notion of time as a sequence of different moments can easily be refuted. In the absence of an objective external point of reference — astronomical time, for example — it is not possible to distinguish the two identical moments: they may overlap, fuse into a single moment. And so, Borges concludes, time as we normally think of it does not exist.

In their various ways, our Greek philosopher, African bishop, Scottish logician, and Argentinian writer all end up refuting the popular notion of time. We have drawn attention to their paradoxes here because they illustrate very well what happens to popular concepts of time once we examine them closely: how they immediately become slippery and elusive and show a disconcerting refusal to obey the laws of common sense. There are many reasons why time is an intrinsically difficult subject; what concerns us most here is that *there is more than one kind of time*. The time we never have enough of in our daily lives is not the time we can measure with atomic clocks. Equally, the unceasing momentum of our personal lives has nothing to do with the office time that measures our working lives. Augustine's concept of time is different from Newton's.

To say there is more than one kind of time does not mean, however, that we share a single reality which contains many different kinds of time. Any group of people constructs its own reality using shared cognitive schemas to extract information from the outside world and organize it coherently. In other words, each group constructs its own reality, each with its own concept of time. Talking about these realities takes us into the realm of description, so concepts of time multiply still further. The time of external reality (objective time) is different from the time — or rather, the times — of the multiplicity of internal realities.

The paradoxes of time are created and transmitted by language. Zeno's paradox is produced by failing to distinguish between duration, in which one moment is inseparable from another, and the arbitrary fragmentation of time into separate moments. Augustine's emerges in the shift from how we experience time (which is fully comprehensible although untransmittable) to how we describe it (which is always difficult because we cannot step outside time to describe what time is). McTaggart's arises when his series become two versions of reality we have to choose between, rather than alternative, mutually compatible ways of describing time. As Bateson (1972) says, it is words, not things, that end up in a muddle. Time is misunderstood when it enters language; equally, things that have been said can be misunderstood.

We shall now look at some major stages in the development of the concept of time in Western thought, but only briefly, because they serve merely to introduce the main subject of our study. However, this brief survey will enable us to understand, at least in part, why the terminology of time has become so complex.

If we are to avoid falling into some of the traps we described earlier, it will be as well to remember that what follows has no *direct* relationship to therapy. All the ideas we examine are useful to therapists only as *metaphors* of time. They may serve to orient our thinking, but they cannot be transferred directly to therapy without appropriate modification. This in no way diminishes their importance, however. As Borges once wrote, "perhaps universal history is the history of a number of metaphors" (1964b).

METAPHORS OF TIME

Naturally enough, our survey starts with the Greeks because it was they who laid the foundations of Western thought. In addition to the many basic concepts they have handed down to us, they also developed an unusually extensive vocabulary of time in which the basic concept of time we find so confusing now can be expressed in three different ways, as *aion*, *chronos*, or *kairos*.

For the Greeks, *aion* meant "the always," limitless duration without past or future (Curi, 1987a). *Chronos*, on the other hand, meant measurable, countable time in constant movement from the future to the past. That this already suggests the familiar Western dichotomy between being and becoming in no way detracts from the insight of the original distinction. Finally, *chronos* means time that is susceptible to measurement, while *kairos* suggests time with *meaning*, time as a series of episodes with a beginning and an end, the time which provides the frame for human action (Kermode, 1967). So this second dichotomy distinguishes objective, measurable time from subjective time, time as we actually experience it.[1]

Aion, chronos, and *kairos* imply the existence of three quite distinct realms of time. *Aion,* although much less influential in the West than it once was, has been especially important over the centuries in religious thought, and the *distinction* between *chronos* and *kairos* still remains basic to our ways of thinking. *Chronos* is objectified, identifiable, divisible time that can be managed and regulated, the time of the science and technology that has made possible the use of the clock and the collective synchronization of human effort, the time of Aristotle, Newton, Kant, Whitehead and Popper. *Kairos* is the time of unique, interior, irreducible human experience, the time of existential philosophy, the time of Augustine, Kierkegaard, Bergson, Husserl, Heidegger and Sartre. This subjective-objective duality lies at the heart of our thinking about time. We use it as a matter of course in our daily lives, quite unaware of the philosophical debate that raged around it two and a half thousand years ago.

It was Augustine, one of the Church Fathers, who produced the first truly *introspective* theory of time. Indeed, he places his discussion of the interior experience of time even before the time of objects and movement.

Quispel (1957) warns against seeing Augustine as a modern philosopher before his time, an inventor of concepts that would be fully accepted only centuries after his death. Certainly, Augustine's interest in the nature of time should be understood in the context of the purely theological debate about the nature of creation and history in which he was involved; even so, there can be little doubt that some of his insights were fundamental to later philosophical attempts to define the nature of time. Indeed, his solution to the celebrated paradox we looked at earlier amounts to a psychological theory of time.[2]

---

[1] The classic notion of "the time we actually experience" (*temps vécu*) was first elaborated by Minkowski (1933), although Marsh's distinction (1952) between "chronological time" and "realistic time" expresses more or less the same idea.

[2] On Augustine's modernity, see Jaques (1982, chapter 1). Toraldo di Francia (1990, p. 98) also concedes that any attempt to penetrate the real nature of time is a hopeless undertaking, and that very little progress has been made since Augustine's time.

What is by now evident and clear is that neither future nor past exists, and it is inexact language to speak of three times—past, present, and future. Perhaps it would be exact to say: there are three times, a present of things past, a present of things present, a present of things to come. In the soul there are these three aspects of time, and I do not see them anywhere else. The present considering the past is the memory, the present considering the future is expectation. If we are allowed to use such language, I see three times, and I admit they are three. (St. Augustine, *Confessions*, Book XI, section 20)

But how does this future, which does not yet exist, diminish or become consumed? Or how does the past, which now has no being, grow, unless there are three processes in the mind which in this is the active agent? For the mind expects and attends and remembers, so that what it expects passes through what has its attention to what it remembers. (St. Augustine, *Confessions*, Book XI, section 28)

By locating time unequivocally in the mind (the psyche), Augustine came closer than any other Christian philosopher to reproducing the earlier Greek concept of *kairos*.

In spite of Augustine's fundamental insights, it was *chronos* that eventually triumphed in Western thought, and this new doctrine was given the final seal of approval by Newton himself, whose concept of time would remain unchallenged by science for the next two centuries, and live on in everyday thought for even longer than that:

Absolute, true and mathematical time, of itself, and from its own nature, flows equably without regard to anything external. (Newton, 1966, 1:6)

Thus, Newton saw time as a uniform, universal continuum independent of the movement and even the existence of objects.

Kant (1781) accepted the absolute autonomy of Newtonian time, but removed it, together with space, from the universe of *Ding an sich* (the thing in itself) and made it fundamental, instead, to the development of knowledge. For Kant, time and space are the two basic preconditions for experience: they are not the outcome of experience, but experience is needed to bring them into operation.

Modern philosophy raises as many questions as it answers, and this is also true of time. The certainties of Newtonian—and also Kantian—time have been challenged and finally overturned as much by physics as by philosophy and psychology. We shall look briefly later on at Einstein's theory of relativity, which raises insuperable doubts about the possibility of any unified concept of time in physics.

Of all the modern intellectual disciplines, phenomenology, sociology, and anthropology have been most concerned with defining the nature of time. Existential philosophy has given pride of place to the nature of human existence *in time* because its main interest has always been humankind's concrete, real existence and destiny in life. Husserl (1966) dwelt at length on the phenomenology of time or our awareness of inner time and the meaning we give to it once we remove it from our "scientific" consciousness and allow ourselves to indulge in introspective analysis. Time may well only exist in the present, says Husserl, but it is equally true that the past and the future are essential to our awareness of time, even if we are conscious of them only in the present.

Heidegger distinguishes four temporal dimensions—past, present, future, and a fourth dimension we use when passing from one of the previous three dimensions to another. Since, by definition, it is mobile and inconstant, his extra fourth dimension is in a way the most important, the "first," so to speak, because it is the dimension in which we actually *experience* time. However, in his key work, *Being and Time* (1927), Heidegger goes beyond straightforward analysis of how we experience time to discuss the meaning we subsequently give this experience.

We either experience being in time (*Dasein*) as a continuous referral from one thing to the next—an essentially anonymous, impersonal process—or find that we are able to step outside our existence in the present. By doing this or, as Heidegger says, by accepting the encounter with nothingness, we can muster and organize our possibilities in life; in other words, we can project ourselves into the future. Thus, time has *ethical* value for Heidegger—it is neither a revelation of the objective world nor a psychological function, but an aspect of what it means to be a human being.

By contrast, sociology has adopted an interactive approach to time, seeing it as an abstraction that shapes social institutions. Kant had already questioned the universality of time in his formulations of *a priori* concepts, although Norbert Elias (1989) prefers to see them as *a posteriori* concepts deriving from the social and cultural experience of the subject. Kant saw time as an innate mental function that "precedes" experience, while Elias sees it as the outcome of a learning process—we learn to live in time in the same way that we learn to live in space. In Elias' view, time is the outcome of individual learning occurring within the set of collective constraints determined by a society's history. Time comes to seem nonhuman—a fact of nature—only when it has been interiorized by learning processes of this type, and its enormous symbolic power can be brought to bear on subsequent experience (this also happens once the three dimensions of physical space have been interiorized). Elias attempts to solve the riddle of time by constructing a five-dimensional model of human experience whose fourth dimension is, obviously, time, and the fifth, human culture.

The constructivist approaches of von Foerster (1981), von Glasersfeld (1987), Watzlawick (1984) and Ceruti (1985) are based on similar assumptions. If reality is "invented" by an observer (or rather, a community of observers) and is not an objective, incontrovertible fact of experience, time itself must also be regarded as a shared construct of man.

Von Foerster (1981) was responsible for the central constructivist assumption that our experience of time is the construction rather than acquisition of an external reality. In constructing his or her representations, each observer has to reconcile simultaneously the permanence (or invariance) and the change of things in the world. Objects—or rather, their representations—are perceived as durable and unchanging, while events (or their representations) are perceived as mutable, as subject to change. On this basis, the observer constructs a computational "grid" with a "simultaneity axis" containing all contemporaneous events and a "duration axis" containing all identical individual events occurring at different moments in time. Time is thus a function of the way we construct reality, and so may be regarded as a representation of relationships rather than an external entity we can perceive and grasp. "The environment does not contain information. The environment is what *is*" (von Foerster, 1981, p. 167).

Other disciplines, too, have produced evidence to support the view that logical categories like time are the result of interaction with the environment. Piaget's genetic epistemology (1937, 1946) offered a more complex theory of how children acquire the concept of time, in which priority is given to the exploratory activity that enables children to relate to their environment. However, Piaget looks only at objective, measurable time, ignoring the rather nebulous concept of subjective time, which he regarded as illusory and so not worth the effort of explanation. Paul Fraisse (1976), another developmental psychologist who has studied time closely, to an extent takes issue with Piaget by insisting that the abstract notion of time does not develop before the age of 15. In effect, Fraisse shifts attention from objective time to subjective time (which Piaget regarded as mistaken). Indeed, Fraisse sees subjective time as basic to our understanding of objective, measurable time.

Finally, anthropology has concentrated on the cultural dimension of time. Observation of the interactive temporal schemas and concepts of "primitive" peoples has shown that the usual European and American ways of thinking about time are far from universal. Historical studies have also shown how different the awareness of time in past civilizations has been from ours in this century. However, even a brief survey of time in contemporary thought would be far too long for an introduction of this sort. As far as the psychology of time, we shall look at some aspects of it later on.[3]

We shall now look at a different way of considering time, the way of physics. Physics has been the premier science of the Western world since the time of Aristotle, which perhaps explains why it has always provided metaphors essential to our ways of thinking about the world. The metaphors of time it has given us have certainly been no exception, especially those which have helped to illuminate our relationship with the future.

Our commonsense view of time oscillates between the idea of a predictable future that can be programmed and an absolutely uncertain, unknowable future. During its long history, physics has also touched on both extremes, veering from the fully predictable future of classical mechanics to the unpredictable future of modern quantum theory. Modern physics has given us two further dichotomies to play with: the distinction between Newtonian absolute time and Einsteinian relative time on the one hand, and on the other, the distinction between reversible time (as in Laplace's mechanics) and irreversible time (as in thermodynamics from Boltzmann to Prigogine).

Our vision of time would be incomplete without the concepts physics has given us, but two points should be borne in mind here. First, these concepts are certainly useful as *analogies* — in this sense, they may even be more useful than some of the other ideas we have looked at so far — but to transfer concepts that are meaningful in physics directly to psychology, and from there to psychotherapy, would only complicate still further the very issues we want to clarify. Second, and more personally, our knowledge of physics is perforce limited, so our account of the scientific ideas that interest us will be found less than satisfactory by those who know more about mathematics and physics than we do. We would ask them to bear with us in what follows.[4]

Time has been inextricably linked to space since the earliest days of physics — "before and after" have always seemed to make sense in relation to a "here and somewhere else." In *Principia Mathematica* (1687), Newton rejected the concept of absolute space by saying that the position of an event in space *does* depend on the observer. We might take the example

---

[3]Much has been written about the nature of time, nonetheless. For general interdisciplinary surveys, see Fraser (1981); Fraser and Lawrence (1975); Whitrow (1980). For the psychology of time, see Vicario (1973); Giovannelli and Mucciarelli (1979); Reale (1982); Fraser (1989). For time in psychoanalysis, see Sabbadini (1979).

[4]We are much indebted in the discussion that follows to Hawking (1988) and Prigogine and Stengers (1984), who should be consulted for a more detailed treatment of the arguments presented here.

of a person who, seated in a railway compartment, seems immobile to another person on the same train, while s/he is obviously moving at 50 mph to an observer on the ground. However, Newton *did* believe that time was absolute: whatever the position of the observer, the interval between two events can be accurately measured by any observer in possession of a clock. As a result, the clock has come to symbolize absolute scientific time, and the metaphor of the perfectly regulated clock is generally used to represent the Newtonian concept of the universe.

The publication of Einstein's *Relativity: The Special and General Theory* in 1905 cast fundamental doubt on the absoluteness of clock time. The universal constant in the special theory of relativity is the speed of light, so observers watching a ray of light travel from one point to another see things rather differently from Newton's earlier observers. In a Newtonian universe, an observer would reason that, since space is not absolute but time is, the light had traveled different distances in the same period of time, and so conclude that the speed of light is not constant. But if the speed of light is constant, as in relativity theory, it must be time itself that varies. If light travels different distances at constant speed in different times, then different observers will see that their clocks have recorded different times *for the same event*. As Prigogine and Stengers point out (1979), Einstein's time is in effect a local time associated with a specific observer or observers. It is as if Newton's perfectly regulated cosmic clock had been broken down into countless smaller clocks, each with its own time that applies within its own immediate vicinity.

Unlike the special theory of relativity which had dealt only with bodies traveling at constant speed in straight lines, the general theory of relativity (cf. Einstein, 1916) examines how gravity causes bodies to accelerate along curved paths. Its most important discovery was that space is curved. Because light rays bend when they pass near large masses like the sun, but are less affected by smaller masses like the earth, the curvature of the space in the immediate vicinity of a mass is proportional to the size of that mass.

The general theory also states that time is "curved," in the sense that it passes more slowly in the presence of large masses. The "paradox of the twins" has been used to describe this extraordinary phenomenon. If one of a pair of twins journeys through space in a vessel travelling close to the speed of light while the other remains on earth, the first twin will be older than the other when he returns.[5] In a sense, then, relativity theory is a

---

[5]Note that the same thing happens if one of the twins goes to live on a mountain top. The only difference is that the discrepancy in aging would be so slight as to be unnoticeable.

prime example of the spatialization of time carried to its logical limit. Time has become the fourth dimension of space.

One logical consequence of this—that the universe must be spatially and temporally finite, i.e., must have a beginning and an end—is now fundamental to twentieth-century theories of the origins of the universe. Newton's static, nonhistorical universe, where motion was constant and perpetual, was like a perfectly regulated clock set to run by the Divine Clockmaker for the rest of time. By contrast, the post-Einsteinian universe began with an explosion—a "singularity" as Hawking (1988) calls it, or in common parlance, a "big bang"—and is still expanding, although it will presumably contract or implode in a "big crunch."

Absolute time, entirely composed of repeated rules or events, was central to Newton's thinking, but physicists like Einstein came to regard time as just another dimension that only seems irreversible because imperfect human beings fail to perceive it correctly. In his own words:

> For committed physicists like ourselves, the distinction between past, present and future is only an illusion, although a rather tenacious one. (cited in Prigogine & Stengers, 1979, p. 273)

Another important step in the development of concepts of time in physics was the shift from statics and dynamics to thermodynamics. In dynamics, any event in the physical world is reversible, but in thermodynamics they are irreversible. The second principle of thermodynamics implies an irreversible process: the world's energy is constant, but in time it decays to heat, tending towards absolute zero. In this irreversible process, measured by an increase in entropy, i.e., increase of disorder and chaos, irreversible time (time's arrow) enters the world of physics.

Classic thermodynamics has made extensive studies of systems approaching equilibrium, but has tended to ignore those far from equilibrium. In isolated systems approaching equilibrium, spontaneous or artificially created variations gradually decrease until they cease completely, with the result that the system returns to its original state. Ilya Prigogine has adopted a highly creative approach to dissipative systems far from equilibrium in which, as in open systems, outside energy is transformed with a consequent increase in organization (negentropy). Linear time—time's arrow—is crucial in these systems: even a slight variation can be amplified to the point where it exceeds the parameters of the system and creates a totally new configuration as unpredictable as the initial variation itself. In such cases, we can say that order is born of chaos.

Prigogine offers a new interpretation of the second law of thermodynamics by showing that increased entropy does not lead only to the nondifferentiation and eventual death of the universe—a pessimistic view of the future. In certain situations (i.e., in dissipative systems), entropy itself becomes a source of organization and order. This produces one of the paradoxes of time: as the universe moves irreversibly towards decay and death, a part of it simultaneously moves towards higher levels of complexity and self-organization.

With this version of thermodynamics, physics acquires a historical dimension, although not in the sense of a deterministic concatenation of events in which the state of any given instant defines the state of the instant that comes immediately after it. The future can be conceived of only as probability in which chance plays a decisive role. The future is thus freed from any kind of deterministic prediction.

In Prigogine's own description of the heavens, time and irreversibility romantically enter the cosmos:

> ... where classical science used to emphasize permanence, we now find change and evolution; we no longer see in the skies the trajectories that filled Kant's heart with the same admiration as the moral law residing in him. We now see strange objects: quasars, pulsars, galaxies exploding and being torn apart, stars that, we are told, collapse into "black holes" irreversibly devouring everything they manage to ensnare. ... Time has penetrated not only biology, geology and the social sciences, but also the two levels from which it has been traditionally excluded, the microscopic and the cosmic. (Prigogine & Stengers, 1984, pp. 214–215)

Just as relativity theory was beginning to question the absoluteness of time, another mechanistic certainty—predictability—was also starting to crumble. The world of classical mechanics was totally deterministic: if every event has an ascertainable cause, anyone with total knowledge of the universe at any given moment would be able to predict the future with absolute certainty.[6]

Heisenberg showed, however, that it is impossible to determine the exact position and speed of subatomic particles because to do so you first have to illuminate them by bombarding them with photons, and this

---

[6]Omniscience of this sort was, in fact, postulated by Laplace at the beginning of the nineteenth century in his celebrated description of an all-knowing "Demon":

> If an Intelligence were able, at any given moment, to know all the forces that animate nature and the individual situations of all those beings who live in it, and if it were powerful enough to analyse all this data, it would be able to yoke the movements of the largest bodies in the universe and the smallest of atoms in the same formula. Such an Intelligence would never know uncertainty, and the future, like the past, would be present before its eyes. (Laplace, 1967, p. 243, cited by Capra, 1991)

changes their energy state, speed, and trajectory.[7] Thus, measurement can be only approximate at this level. The laws of probability enable us to establish statistical trends in a particle's probable movements, but we can never have an exact description of them.

Heisenberg's uncertainty principle in effect replaces determinism with *probability*, because at subatomic levels it is impossible accurately to predict the outcome of certain measurements. The best we can achieve is a distribution of probabilities; we can never know for certain which path a particle will follow (Jauch, 1973). While Einstein introduced relativity in the present, Heisenberg introduced uncertainty into the future. The essence of the uncertainty principle is that, on a microcosmic scale, beyond a certain level of reality, it is not possible to obtain exact measurements, and thus know how subatomic particles behave, because *the act of measurement alters the thing you are trying to measure.* This does not mean, of course, that the laws of the macroscopic world are rendered invalid. They remain (more or less) valid because there would be no point in applying quantum equations appropriate to a microscopic world on this larger scale. Another fundamental discovery of quantum theory was that elementary particles can behave like particles *or* waves. Since it is impossible to know if a particle will behave like a particle or a wave, physicists prefer to speak simply of "matter waves" or "probability waves."

The different concepts of time in physics are similar in some ways to the kinds of time we experience in our everyday lives. Classical, deterministic time thus corresponds to our commonsense notion of time: events are ordered causally in a single temporal flow in which we all participate. The past determines the present and the present determines the future, and our lives are governed by necessity. Relativity time corresponds to subjective time: I have *my* time which is real to me; everyone has his/her own time which may well not be the same as mine. Quantum time is random and uncertain: the "real" exists in a nondeterministic relationship to the "virtual." Finally, the thermodynamics time of dissipative systems is oriented irreversibly towards the future.

But we should remember, once again, that although physics provides useful metaphors for therapists, these are still only metaphors. Poincaré (1913) distinguished very clearly between relativity in subjective time and

---

[7]Heisenberg was one of the first men of science to stress how the observer and his instruments inevitably change what is being observed. More generally, this is related to von Foerster's second-order cybernetics in which descriptions of the world are filtered through the biases, theories, and experiences ("instruments") of the observer who makes them.

relativity in physics—the same word is used, but conceptually they are quite different—and this is equally true of "uncertainty" as it is used in Heisenberg's Uncertainty Principle and Prigogine's dissipative structures. Certainly, it is exciting to find that physics uses concepts like irreversibility or the centrality of the observer, which are now also a part of systemic theory, but we should never delude ourselves that the uncertainty of a therapist talking to a patient is the *same* as that of a physicist trying to establish the position and speed of a particle.

What is most useful to us in our day-to-day work is the ability to adopt different or even, in some cases, contradictory points of view. It is interesting that general relativity, which deals with large masses, and quantum mechanics, which deals with subatomic particles, offer completely contradictory descriptions of the world. But, as Toraldo di Francia (1990) says: "Physicists are justifiably unwilling to give up either [view] and use both quite happily according to situation." Similarly, Elkana (1984) says that we should be realists within the confines of any single theory, but relativists when we compare different theories.

We believe that some knowledge of the various metaphors of time we have looked at so far is essential to therapists. Not only will the scope of our work be broadened, but we shall also develop the ability to move more easily between different universes of discourse. This is entirely consistent with what has been called "the epistemology of complexity" (see Bocchi & Ceruti, 1985), which regards knowledge as a set of relationships which establish connections between distinct universes of discourse. The logic of any one universe is quite incompatible with that of another universe, and no universe ever proves more important or more fundamental than another. "Perfect knowledge" is impossible (Morin, 1985). Knowledge of time is multiple. Each universe of discourse has its own time.

This passage from the end of Robert Ornstein's study of how we experience time shows how complex the fascinating subject of time really is:

> Returning to the beginning question, "What is time?", we have gone through all this to find that we cannot answer it. Time is too diverse a concept to be amenable to one answer. Time is many things, many processes, many types of experience. . . . The different times of experience will require different types of explanation. . . . (Ornstein, 1969, p. 109)

TIME AND RELATIONSHIPS

Our attempts to observe relationships through the lens of time often lead us into a mire of contradictions, inconsistencies, and sometimes, even paradoxes. One reason for this is the problem of self-reflexivity (when speaking of time we still remain *in* time), but another probable reason is that there are also many *kinds* of time, each associated with different ways of seeing reality. If, in the past, it has seemed impossible to reconcile subjective time with objective time, measurement with duration, and so on, for our purposes the problem *can* be solved if we bear in mind Elias' warning (1989) that time is not an object, but an abstraction deriving both from our experience of succession and change and from the realization that objects undergoing change remain constant nonetheless.

Time may be perceived differently by different people, different groups, or even the same person at different moments in time, so it would be wrong to say that one time is "more real" than another. Phenomenologists believe that subjective time is real because it is the one we experience, and physicists that clock time is real because it can be measured objectively, but the gulf between them can easily be bridged if we remember that different observers produce different descriptions of time, each real enough in its own — but only in its own — descriptive domain. When a description of reality wins the assent of a significant part of a community, it assumes the status of "reality"; equally, different descriptions of time will be regarded as "real" if they win widespread assent. In the West, physics time has won most assent, and inner, individual time the least. The rigors of relativity theory were needed to correct Newton's conceptions, yet it remains very difficult to "correct" a depressed person's perception of time because for him it never seems to pass at all.

Let us now look at three time domains more closely related to our work as therapists. We shall start with the individual, although the choice is, of course, arbitrary in the sense that any other situation would do just as well.

The time an individual perceives when he decides to observe himself is called individual or *phenomenological time*, because phenomenologists have been most interested in defining time in this way. At the opposite extreme we have *anthropological time*, based on the general assent of the individuals and human groups that make up a culture, so called because anthropologists have been responsible for defining time in this way. Midway between the two, we have the time of interactive systems (state departments, companies, schools, etc.), where individuals interact with one another, the social or *sociological time* that is the main concern of sociologists.

It should be remembered, however, that these three time domains can be conceived within their own contexts and that each one constitutes the context for the others. Their relationships will be more closely explored later on.

Individual Time

We begin not with individuals in the abstract but with real people living in the Western culture we all know. Our starting point will be the perception of time—one of the individual's most real yet also most perplexing experiences.

Our experience of time depends above all else on how we experience the immediate present. Many writers have attempted to define how long the present moment actually lasts,[8] but as Bergson (1889) points out, it can never properly be isolated because, when isolated, it has already moved from the present into the past. In many ways, our experience of the present moment is of something that can never adequately be grasped or described. Indeed, Jaques (1982) has gone so far as to say that we experience the present moment only in the unconscious mind.

Perception of present time is closely linked to perception of duration, or what is usually called "time sense." Chronobiologists (Fraisse, 1974; Luce, 1971) have proved the existence, in living beings, of a plurality of inner rhythms of varying duration,[9] which influence time sense by enabling us to experience time in a number of different ways.

In his list of some of the factors that influence time sense, Dossey (1982) includes personality, social competence, motivation, drugs, psychic disorders, and even changes in light and temperature. It is well-known, for example, that hallucinogenic drugs can radically alter our time sense. Many subjects under the influence of mescaline have the sensation of living through centuries or even millennia without losing awareness of themselves as integral human beings. There is no feeling of time passing more quickly, as in a speeded-up film. The time they experience seems quite natural, with the difference that once the effect of the drug has worn off, they realize that the clock has moved barely three minutes forward (Sonnemann, 1987).

However, time sense can be modified without resorting to artifice of this kind. We become highly alert when alarmed or exposed to danger, noticing more detail and performing more actions in any given unit of objective clock time. There are also corresponding changes in the physio-

---

[8]There have been many attempts to establish *what* the immediate present is. Reale (1982) gives a long list of interesting, though inconclusive attempts to establish its duration. Fraisse (1976) puts it at four seconds, Michon (1979) at from 50 milliseconds to a few seconds, and Stroud (1956) at from 60 to 200 milliseconds, while Miller (1956) states that a simultaneous perception can contain 7 + 2 "elements," such as a random sequence of numbers or letters.

[9]Chronobiologists have made extensive studies of circadian rhythms. See Cohen (1967), Orme (1969), Reinberg (1979), and Halberg (1979).

logical and neurochemical state of the body itself, which instantly adapts to the threat of danger. Adrenalin is secreted by the adrenal gland, blood pressure increases, the heart speeds up, blood rushes to the brain, and the entire nervous system is put on the alert. As a result, time seems to pass more slowly. Anyone who has experienced the terror of earthquakes lasting only a few seconds knows that those few seconds can seem an eternity. On the other hand, practitioners of Eastern meditation techniques can meditate for hours by totally draining their minds, yet report later that, during meditation, only a few seconds seemed to have passed, or even that time had stopped altogether.

Age also influences time sense. Small babies under a year old have no time sense at all. The word "today" first appears at the age of two, followed six months later by "tomorrow." "Yesterday" appears at three, and "days" at five. According to Dossey (1982), the adult concept of time is fully developed by the age of 16. As they age, most people have the impression that time passes more and more quickly. This is in part because we experience time cycles as percentages of the life we have already lived — a month is a long time for a girl of 15, but negligible to a 70-year-old adult.[10]

From his studies of the development of objective time sense in children, Jean Piaget concluded that time sense is linked to perception of speed: "Time is a coordination of speeds, or rather, of movements each with its own speed" (Piaget, 1946/1970). Until about the age of six, children have what Piaget calls an "intuition of speed," but cannot understand succession. At this stage in their development (Stage 1), they cannot associate "behind" with "in front," which Piaget regards as the conceptual precursors of "before" and "after." Thus, they can draw the various stages of a process as it happens, but cannot sequence their drawings correctly later on.

Between the ages of six and eight (Stage 2), children learn that objects can travel different distances in the same interval of time, and so acquire concepts of "before and after," simultaneity, succession and duration. Stage 3, critical to the understanding and measurement of time, is reached around the age of eight. By associating duration with succession, the child develops the conceptual ability to understand time retrospectively, as when, for example, two children of different ages are able to understand which was born first: they have learned about reversibility.

Experimental psychologist Robert Ornstein (1969) has made an outstanding contribution to our understanding of the experience of time and especially of duration. According to Ornstein, the term "time sense," as

---

[10]There may be more a existential reason for this: the nearer we are to the end of our lives, to death, the shorter the duration of what remains seems to us.

commonly used, implies the existence of an object called "time" in external reality, as well as a human "sense organ" able to perceive it with varying degrees of accuracy. He prefers to say that our experience of time depends not on "time sense" as such but on the amount of information we can store in a given interval. When we try to increase the amount of information stored in any given interval,[11] we experience more and remember more, and so perceive time differently (Ornstein, 1969, p. 103).

Ornstein's experiments demonstrate that the experience of duration ("magnitude" of time) is related not only to increased stimulation but also to *complexity* of stimulation and to how we code and organize the stimuli we receive. If sets of stimuli can be encoded in large units (for example, when we encode a succession of apparently unrelated movements into a single dance step), perceived duration will be shorter. Perceived duration can also be shortened retrospectively if the subject learns to organize stimuli *after* having perceived their succession. Thus, duration shortens in memory.

> The important variable, then, is the input which is registered and stored, not merely that in the stimulus array. An increase in the input registered and stored increases the storage size of that interval and lengthens the experience of the duration of that interval. (Ornstein, 1969, p. 82)

Ornstein's theory explains quite well how time seems to pass slowly and duration seems interminable when we are bored: duration seems longer because we are forced to attend to a sequence of events we find unimportant. His experiments also explain why pleasant events seem short when they happen, but are remembered as long: we have more memories of pleasant things because we remember them in greater detail, so when we look back on them their duration seems longer.

By contrast, during states of emergency we process more information, certainly, but in longer intervals, so less information is stored (coded) in the same interval and time seems to pass more slowly. Thus, when duration *lengthens*, time seems to *slow down*, and when it is shorter, time seems to speed up. This is an extremely important point, and we shall return to it later.

One other point should be made. We have already seen that variations in individual subjective time depend on a wide range of factors, such as

---

[11]As Ornstein himself warns, "registration" and "storage" are, again, metaphors and are not intended as descriptions of mental or cerebral realities. This is also our view.

genetic makeup, upbringing, cultural and social experience, etc. We think that Orme's concept of "inner time units"—an individual's ways of coding time data—accounts for these variations very well (Orme, 1969, p. 166). Each individual encodes time differently, depending, as we have seen, on a number of external factors. As therapists, we must be constantly aware of how the inner time units can vary in duration during interaction. If two people acknowledge each other's differing awarenesses of time, i.e., different time units, dialogue is possible. If they don't, and prefer to believe that there is only one way (the *right* way) of experiencing time, then dialogue is impossible. The possible clinical consequences of this will be examined in the concluding chapters of this book.

In physics (including relativity), succession is easy to study and measure, but in phenomenology it is more complex and eludes precise definition. Yet none of us could live without the concepts of present, past and future, which determine how we perceive succession, despite Augustine's fundamental insight that the past and future have no existence except in the present. This paradox intrigued countless scholars and intellectuals over the centuries, but none more so than the phenomenologists of recent times.

Merleau-Ponty (1945) developed Husserl's idea that human consciousness experiences time as duration within a clearly perceived though constantly changing temporal "horizon" that enables us to relate any given "now" to corresponding moments in the future or past. Moment follows moment in the flow of experience, but each moment can be separated and brought into focus. That we are able to experience time at all depends precisely on this ability to experience the present simultaneously both as flow and as a discrete moment, in contrast to the past and future.

We have already seen that we have a dual awareness of past and present because the present we attempt to describe at any given moment has already become the past. This matches very well the interchangeability of figure and ground in the Gestalt theory of perception. Both figure and ground are co-present but they cannot be seen *simultaneously*, only successively, just as an observer trying to concentrate on present time (figure) is drawn inevitably to the past (ground), and back again. Thus, we *experience* time simultaneously as flow and succession, but we can only *analyze* time alternately as either flow or succession.

Jaques (1982) speaks of an "intention axis" that complements and completes the "succession axis" of clock time. At any given moment, he says, an observer is aware of a past (memory) and a future (intentionality) that orient his actions in the present. Heidegger (in Steiner, 1978) expressed in a more profound way a similar concept: "Temporalization is the bringing

of time to maturity." Through higher awareness we may be able to tran-
scend and reevaluate the "banal triad" of past, present and future, the
time frame in which we live.

Without seeking to authenticate the experience of time or to commit
ourselves to the kind of secular mysticism Heidegger seems rather fond of,
we believe that his "banal triad" is, in reality, anything but banal, that
the succession of past, present and future can be seen as a cybernetic
self-reflexive loop. We shall explain what we mean by this in more detail
later on.

For now, it can hardly be disputed that the situation we are in at any
given moment determines whether we are more preoccupied with the past
(remembering) or the future (planning). The past and the future endow the
present moment with specificity by giving it the coordinates we need to
render it "active." As Jaques (1982) says, the active present defines the
temporal horizon of an individual's activity, and this present may vary
from actions of only a few minutes' duration to longer-term strategies
requiring days, months, or years for completion. Since it is mobile and
variable (depending on the kind of "focusing" we give it), the present may
hold actions of only immediate relevance, such as lighting a match, or the
more far-sighted actions needed to bring a long-term project to fruition.

We now move from the straightforward *perception* of time to the more
complex *notion* of time that each individual holds. An individual develops
only a part of his total potential as a human being. In physical terms, for
example, one develops a personal repertory of movements that forms a
basic constraint on how one interacts with the environment. Equally, we
develop our own cognitive and expressive styles: preference for a visual,
auditory, or kinesthetic style varies from individual to individual (Bandler
& Grinder, 1975). Each individual has a personal notion of time determined by the degree to which his relationship with the environment enables him to realize his biological potential; similarly, his biological potential shapes his relationship with the environment. These notions of time
influence the behavioral and linguistic style of each individual.

Fraisse's term "temporal horizon" (1976) suggests very well the unique
cognitive and emotive features of an individual's perception and experience of time. As we shall see, his term suggests more than just the static
features of individual consciousness. Temporal horizons are dynamic because notions of time change according to context. We shall give examples
of this later, when we discuss the temporal horizons of clients, therapists,
and therapy teams. Temporal horizons can vary enormously. Age is important (children tend to be oriented towards the future, the elderly towards
the past), as are cultural factors.

In therapy we are especially interested in marked attachments to the past, present or future in individuals or families. Clients are often oriented towards either the future ("Do something!") or the past ("It's all hopeless"). It is also important to remember that individual temporal horizons are shaped by the same factors (age, culture, social status, contingent factors) that influence temporal variables as a whole. These factors can even lead to clinical symptoms like depression, in which temporal horizons are limited to the past; manic syndromes, in which they are limited to the present; and schizophrenia, in which temporal horizons are fragmented.

An individual's subjective time can be described by analyzing the "inner time units" revealed in the rhythms and modulations of his/her discourse (especially analogical, or nonverbal, discourse). A therapist can also gauge breadth of temporal horizon from the extent to which an individual ranges from future to past while speaking (once again, we are obliged to use metaphors of space to talk about time). Preference for past, present, or future can be assessed from the form as well as the content of discourse: a recurrent use of past or future tenses, the use of the indicative rather than conditional mood, and so on. Naturally, observation of subjective time is influenced both by context and the relationship between the observer and the person observed. Objective knowledge of rhythms and temporal horizons is impossible because they are shaped by interaction between observer and observed and so also by the observer's time. To see how this interplay of subjective times works in practice, let us now look at how time functions in the interaction between two individuals.

When two people meet, their individual times interpenetrate to produce an area of "shared time." For simplicity's sake we shall ignore social and cultural context for the moment.

When two individuals, A and B, meet they can interact in two major ways.[12] They may be indifferent to each other, as in casual day-to-day contact outside the home: for example, we stereotype the person who sells us an article of clothing as a "shop assistant," and for our immediate purposes need only have knowledge of that stereotype; so far as we are concerned, we know "everything" about that person. Similarly, the driver of the car on my right in town is fully contained by the phrase "driver of the car on my right" and I need know nothing more about him. Such stereotyping is very common in complex urban societies, and of course, the kind of interaction it implies barely affects our awareness of time because no shared time is created.

What might be called "face-to-face" encounters are a rather different

---

[12]We are indebted here to Berger and Luckmann (1966) and Reiss (1981), although we have adapted their ideas to fit our model.

matter, however. Reiss (1981) describes this kind of interaction as "those encounters between two or more individuals in which there is relative freedom in each person's experience of the other: freedom from convention, freedom from stereotypes, freedom from highly simplified conceptions. In a face-to-face encounter, each individual has an immediate, emotionally charged sense of the uniqueness of the other" (Reiss, 1981, p. 161).

In this type of interaction, A and B may choose to agree or disagree over their individual times. If they agree, the temporal assumptions of both are mutually reinforced; if they disagree, each feels that his assumptions are being challenged. At this point, they will try to negotiate agreement. Face-to-face encounters also generate emotions which are difficult to avoid; indeed, the only way to avoid them is to withdraw from interaction altogether. In face-to-face encounters, then, the following situations may be found:

1. A and B try to impose their respective individual times on each other. A's assertion of the rightness of his own time reinforces B's conviction that *his* time is right, so B then asserts the rightness of *his* time, and so on.

2. A and B agree to establish a new time by mediating (more or less consciously) their respective individual times.

3. A and B oscillate symmetrically between non-acceptance and acceptance of each other's times.

More detailed analysis of face-to-face encounters reveals, above all else, a discordance of *rhythm*. For example, if A is quicker than B, if his time units are shorter and his rhythms are faster, this can easily be observed in how A and B communicate (especially non-verbally). In extreme cases, discordance may threaten maintenance of contact and lead to immediate distancing.

With an A who is healthy and a B who is profoundly depressed or maniacal, B's extremely slow or fast time may make A *uneasy* and threaten the continuance of the relationship, or even make it impossible to establish one in the first place. If B has the discontinuous fragmented time of the schizophrenic, the breakdown will be even more serious.

So far we have considered dual relationships that are artificially removed from their cultural and social contexts, and this has naturally had a marked effect on the kinds of individual time we have been able to describe.

Each individual can live in a wide range of quite distinct temporal contexts—in our daily lives we are constantly obliged to adapt ourselves to situations and relationships which call for different kinds of time—and yet, in any individual, we can almost always observe a particular time that seems to underlie all the others.

Cultural Time

The study of cultural time involves the identification of commonly held assumptions about time, where "assumption" means, to paraphrase Bateson, a recognizable expectation regarding, or a definite implication deriving from, certain aspects of cultural behavior[13] (1958, p. 219). To study these assumptions, we have to understand how different cultures perceive time because the notion of time varies enormously from culture to culture. For example, Whorf, in his study of the language of the Hopi Indians (1956), notes that their language has no concept of temporal flow as we understand it. Hopi verbs have no tenses and so do not distinguish between past, present and future, and yet the Hopis live perfectly well in their own cultural context.

> It is a common impression of those who visit foreign countries that the natives are either faster or slower, brighter or duller in their reactions than the members of the observer's own community. This impression is no doubt due to some form of cultural standardization of the personalities concerned, and should be investigated. (Bateson, 1958, p. 255)

Individuals are born with a range of potential characteristics. Some are subsequently selected by their culture, while others tend to be excluded or even actively suppressed. Thus, everyone is capable of experiencing time as both irreversible and cyclical, but a European or American will tend to experience it as linear, while a (traditional) Indian will see it as circular. This is in line with Gregory Bateson's view (1958) that cultures standardize their ways of perceiving time, and that this standardization varies from culture to culture.[14] This has an important impact on the daily lives of individuals in whichever culture we choose to examine.

The assumptions and expectations of individuals within a culture are

---

[13]By "culture" and "cultural" we refer to the entire cognitive, affective, and social organization of a given population.

[14]The more so since Whorf's original hypothesis (1956) has still not been verified experimentally. For example, the theory that color perception varies with culture has still not been demonstrated. Experiments (see Gardner, 1985) have shown that color perception is independent of culture; it is the *social use* of color that varies enormously.

the result of a learning process instigated by that culture, but the opposite—that a culture is the sum of the assumptions and expectations of all
its members—is equally true. The relationship between a culture and the
assumptions and expectations of individuals within it is, of its very nature,
self-reflexive.

Moreover, the standardization of time within cultures can only be approximate. In his study of the perception of time in primitive societies,
Lévi-Strauss (1974) concluded that any culture contains four distinct kinds
of time:

> a) progressive, irreversible time made up of ordered sequences, like
> our linear time;
>
> b) static, reversible time in which identical terms are repeated over
> generations; this repetition neutralizes time, making it "empty";
>
> c) fluctuating, cyclical, reversible time in which two terms (e.g., day
> and night) alternate continuously;
>
> d) closed, circular, loop time containing a succession of more than
> two terms (e.g., the seasons).

Residual concepts that have lain dormant since time immemorial in the
stratified historical assumptions of our culture can suddenly come to life.
Thus, if someone reared in a peasant culture moves to a town or city, he
will easily find ways of preserving "islands" of the cyclical time he understands and prefers best, no matter how "modernized" his environment
may be. In his discussion of cyclical time, perhaps the most fascinating of
all his studies, Eliade (1949) also agrees that someone living in a rural
environment will never be entirely well disposed towards irreversible, historical, linear time.

Many examples could be cited of this. What really matters is that an
individual's cultural assumptions and expectations about time can thus be
both cyclical *and* linear. The resurgence of "primitive" concepts about
time in culture can easily lead to muddle and misunderstanding. Indeed,
this is only inevitable when changes that formerly required precise and
specific sanctioning (as in rites of passage) are now open to free negotia-
tion. Who now would be able to say at what age a child becomes an
adult?[15] These "islands" of culturally deviant assumptions may emerge in

---

[15]There are examples in our own society of social rituals authenticating the
passage from childhood to adulthood: in practicing Jewish families at least, the bar
mitzvah is one such case (Davis, 1988).

individual or group interaction, producing inconsistencies in the perception and experience of time.[16]

Social Time

The idea of social time, or "sociological" time, implies seeing time as a means of social coordination, i.e., as having *instrumental* value. We live in a complex society structured in regular, hierarchical ways; Zerubavel (1981) has shown that the temporal ordering we give to the world is equally regular. If our social time were not regular and sufficiently predictable, our social life would rapidly crumble.[17]

Developing Merleau-Ponty's idea that man sees objects only as figures against a ground, Garfinkel (1967) says that our social expectations and routines are, in fact, grounds of this type. Time and *regularity* of time create an important ground against which our day-to-day social lives are enacted. However, coordination, regularity, and flexibility in social times vary enormously between countries, even between Western ones that share the same production system. For example, punctuality, organization, and coordination are much more valued in Switzerland and the Scandinavian countries than in Italy or Spain. In Germany, you can set your watch by the time a train arrives, while Italians would be amazed if a train arrived on time. In some countries, perfect coordination of times is a feature of specific sectors like the army (think, for example, of the USA's impressive time management in the Gulf War) or companies (especially private ones) which have to organize their internal and external times in an exact though flexible way to cope with strong competition. In some countries, such as Japan, management of social times seems to have been a key factor in spectacular economic growth, although it has to be said that many feel this has not always led to a corresponding improvement in the quality of life.

We can distinguish various social times in any culture. Since all jobs have their characteristic rhythms, one of the most important of these is work time. For example, a peasant's time has a much slower rhythm than an industrial worker's, and this can create serious problems when people move from the country into cities.

---

[16]I.e., the interpretation of time is only one of many cultural variables affected by this process.

[17]Regularity depends on repetition. There is a certain irony in the fact that the "empty" cyclical time of ancient ritual lives on in our most ordinary routines, such as coffee breaks or the end of the working day.

Zerubavel gives us the four "parameters" of regularity in time:

> One fundamental parameter of situations and events is their *sequential structure*, which tells us in what order they take place. A second major parameter, their *duration*, tells us how long they last. A third parameter, their *temporal location*, tells us when they take place, whereas a fourth parameter, their *rate of occurrence*, tells us how often they do. (1981, p. 1)

For such regularity to be possible—for events to have fixed duration, rigid succession, and regular collocation and frequency—social time has to be not only linear and irreversible, but also *measurable* and *divisible* into fixed units. Also, for human activities to be *synchronized* and coordinated, the time we devote to them has to be *compartmentalized*.

In the social life of the modern Western world, leisure time is an unfortunately rare commodity. One of our commonest experiences is the sensation that we won't have enough time in which to do things. In *Modern Times*, Charlie Chaplin epitomizes the relationship between man and time in a Taylorian world. The character he plays clearly feels the anxiety of a man obliged to adapt to rigid, alienating rhythms. Lack of time is a result of the multiplicity of times that exists in modern society.[18]

The situation of primitive peoples is quite the opposite: they live by slower natural rhythms in clearly differentiated sacred and secular times that have been prescribed and handed down by tradition.[19] But modern people have no traditions, no ancestors, no rituals, and in a way, no masters. They live in a world that has its natural roots severed, caught up in a network of increasingly complex and demanding social relationships, a world whose rhythms and times are also becoming increasingly complex and more tightly organized. There is a time for work, which is public, but also a time for social contact, which is also public. There is—or should be—a time for the family, a time for solitude, and time for oneself, for leisure and reflection.

We often read that modern life is a source of anxiety, stress and neuroses because of the hectic rhythms it imposes. In her book *Tempi di vita. Studi e proposte per cambiarli (The Times of Life: Studies and Proposals for Changing Them)* (1991), Laura Balbo seems to come down in favor of our

---

[18]See also Thompson (1967) on work schedules, Jaques (1982) on "discretionary periods" in bureaucracies, and Merton (1984) on social expectations of duration.

[19]The rituals that mark off the Jewish Sabbath from the rest of the week are particularly good examples of the separation of times. See Zerubavel (1981, Chapter 4).

modern way of organizing times, arguing that it allows citizens to manage their own time (to a certain extent, at least) and so gives them a greater degree of independence, self-organization, and choice:

> Things were not like this at the height of the industrial revolution when the predominant temporal mode—the production time of the "industrial model"—was first created and then increasingly imposed. . . . Nor would it be right to idealize pre-industrial society almost as a golden age of natural rhythms and collective rites that were rich in shared values rather than coercive of the individual. The vast majority of the people lived in circum- stances that offered no possibility of independence, freedom, or planning. (p. 13)

This seems to contradict what we said previously. It smacks of the familiar contrast between "the world was a much better place before" and "the world is a much better place now." We believe, in fact, that we could enjoy a much better quality of life if social times—individual, family and institutional—were coordinated better.

Let us cite just one example of uncoordinated social times from Balbo's (1991) book: It has been calculated that around 800,000 vehicles, 600,000 from districts lying outside Milan, pass through the city every day. On average, people living in the city who move from one place to another spend from a half to three-quarters of an hour in their cars, but an hour if they have to come in from outside. Every ten years, they spend five months of their lives traveling—five months multiplied by almost a million people. Many more examples could be cited. Balbo concludes: "I would like to draw attention to these dead times in our lives, unpredictable times, times we have no control over, governed by chance and, often, by the indifference and even arrogance of others." City life now brings "stress, tiredness, frustration, boredom . . . loss of time, never having time; or else, for some, the opposite: empty time, time that never passes" (1991, pp. 28–29).

This is the negative side of modern life; however, from the point of view of time there is also much to be said in its favor. In industrial society, social times were rigidly institutionalized and led to passivity among the citizens, because their lives were organized around a single working time. In the postwar period, with the gradual emergence of a post-industrial society and incredible growth of service industries, individual and collec- tive times have become more complicated but also more flexible, enabling individuals to choose and manage their times for themselves.

Also, important changes are now taking place in male and female times. In the past, the times of most of the population were rigidly differentiated and programmed by gender (men existed to work, women to produce children and look after the home, adolescents to learn). Now we are seeing a revolution in these times. Flexibility is replacing rigidity, and everyone, irrespective of sex and age, can now devote some time to work, some to learning, some to caring for others, some for rest, and so on. In this redistribution of social times, the result of new production and distribution methods, the development of new technologies, and the contribution of feminist movements have played an important role in freeing women from the tyranny of procreation and satisfying the basic needs of others, thus allowing them to find some time for themselves. Many would not agree with this view, though: the tyranny of family time and working time often make it difficult for women to have free time.

In Italy, the importance of coordinating social times has recently been recognized by legislators, who have passed a bill that attempts to reform the organization of times in cities: In some towns, offices dealing with working hours and times have already been set up. Their job is to study individual, corporate, and institutional times, analyze their complex interdependence, and assess the accompanying economic and social costs. When this has been done, strategies to increase the flexibility and coordination of working hours and times will be proposed. The overall quality of life may benefit from what we might call this "social therapy."

Time is especially important in companies that have to achieve a high degree of coordination among their various organizational levels if they are to remain competitive. In his book *L'Enterprise Polycellulaire (The Multicellular Firm)*, Hubert Lander says:

> Each level of organization in the system has its own rhythm. The coordination of the organizational levels fits the hierarchy of their different rhythms (e.g., short term, medium-short term, medium-long term, long term). The harmony of the whole, as a system developing in time, depends on these rhythms. Harmonizing one rhythm with another (e.g., short term with medium term) is the task of managers, who operate at the interface between two or more work groups. Thus, managers have to work simultaneously in two time scales, and their job may be seen as connecting coherent different levels of the organization both functionally and temporally. (1987, p. 208)

So far, our argument has ranged from individual times to social times and corporate times. We would now like to go back and look at individual time more closely. An individual is a social being whose interior "reality" is the outcome of relationships established in time with the outside world, the world of "the Other." The harmonization, "coherencing" (as Lander might say), and diachronically speaking, co-evolution of internal times and external times is necessary for a realization of individual potential that is compatible with the needs of "normal" life.[20] As therapists, we see clients every day who suffer tragically when this process goes awry (see Chapter 5).

Within his/her cultural and social context, an individual continually has to coordinate internal time with the times of other individuals as well as a whole range of institutional times. The person has to adapt to inevitable discrepancies in the times of transport systems, work, school, the family and so on. Obviously, problems in these areas can lead to problems not only for that individual, but also for the individuals with whom he or she interacts. An excellent clinical example of this is the relationship between an obsessive-compulsive patient and the people around him. The rigid individual time of the obsessive makes it difficult for others to harmonize with him, and vice versa.

We should like to stress here the importance of the dialectical relationship between "individual time" and "individual times." Individual time is the range of individual times a person uses to harmonize with external times. The more times a person has available, the more adaptable he or she becomes.[21]

Likewise, the more internal times members of a family or institution have available to them, the more likely they are to succeed in coordinating themselves with each other and with people and things external to the group. Thus, a wide range of possible temporal connections is crucial to the kind of interaction that occurs between individuals and their environments. For example, a person may find it (impossibly) difficult to adapt to rigid external times like those found in armies, or to their opposite, the vague, flexible times of a university that leaves students free to manage their own time: both situations may give rise to intolerable frustration and anxiety.

Jaques (1982) provides an interesting analysis of internal individual times. He defines an intentional human act as a "goal-directed episode" positioned in both objective and subjective (or intentional) time. Each episode has its own time span and perspective (the time assumed neces-

---

[20]We realize that this use of the word "normal" will jolt many of our readers out of their chairs. We should like to say here that we have tried many other words ("functional," "satisfying," "gratifying," "acceptable," "livable," etc.), but in the end opted for "normal," conscious that rivers of scholarly ink have run dry in the attempt to define exactly what it means.

[21]See the concept of restraint in Gregory Bateson's article "Cybernetic explanation" (1972a).

sary to complete the episode), with a beginning, middle, and end. But a person is evidently a multi-episodic creature, because in any given moment an individual may shift to different parallel episodes.

It is also important to note that *each episode has its own separate time.* Work time, for example, may seem slower than free time to any given individual. Moreover, each episode may be composed of a string of discrete moments which, although remote from each other in time, add up to a single episode with a discrete time span and its own "internal" time. So an individual tends to experience the moments of any given episode as continuous and interconnected. Naturally, this happens only when the individual is actually living (temporarily) in the time set aside for that episode.

In psychotherapy, for example, therapy sessions are usually experienced as being less separated in time than in fact they are. Sometimes the previous session is experienced as having taken place only "yesterday" (people will often actually say this), when in fact it happened the previous month.

If each episode has a separate time, therapy time is not one moment in a single time *continuum*, but a time *distinct and separate* from all other times. For example, a patient will say: "When I'm here, I believe in therapy, but there are moments outside when I don't believe in it." In such cases, we have a time in which the patient believes in therapy, and another (totally separate) time in which he refuses to accept it. Similarly, during working hours, he or she may not have time for therapy, for the rejection of therapy, or even for symptoms. As we have seen, this calls into question our whole organization of social time.

Minsky (1985) advances the interesting idea that the mind is a "society of the mind" whose different sectors are concerned with the performance of different operations. Similarly, we might say that individual time is a "society of times," with a different time for each sphere of activity.

However, the extreme complexity of our interaction with time probably justifies the view that, at any given moment, the individual exists within a whole range of different temporal horizons, even if he or she can give conscious attention to only one of them at a time. Following Jaques' (1982) theory, we live in different time episodes, each with its own subjective duration and perception of continuity. Because time episodes are usually independent, an individual will tend to unite segments of duration relating to a certain activity or state of mind into a single continuum. Thus, work times form one continuum, family times another different continuum, and so on. We might say that we have a time continuum for each and every context in which we live as individuals. Similarly, the same person can show different character traits depending on the context. To give just one example, Schafer (1983) observes that, in private, many psychoanalysts reveal a personality that seems quite at odds with the nature and quality of their work. In his view, this indicates that analysts have a "service" or "duty" self that they put to one side when they are off duty.

CO-EVOLUTION AND TIME

We hope we have now made our general approach clear. Distinctions between "individual," "social," and "cultural" time are the outcome of methodical observation on the part of countless observers working in different areas of the overall system (individual, institutional, cultural). There is no "cultural" time determining the form individual time takes; equally, individual time does not determine the nature of cultural time. There is only a continuous *co-evolution of times in time*. Elias (1989) describes this process in his discussion of interaction in time. The need for basic coordination in the simplest societies has evolved, in more complex societies, into increasingly complex and coercive rules, which in turn have created the need for calendars, timetables and clocks. This has meant, on the one hand, that abstract "time" has become increasingly generalized (as in philosophy or physics, for example), and on the other, that the intrusive constraints of organizational time (social time) have become increasingly apparent as their range of applications has widened. All this contrasts with inner "experiential" time, which is quite different from clock time.

In our account of time, we began with individual ways of experiencing time. Then we saw how broad individual similarities and correspondences within a culture unite to produce anthropological time, and how social systems also produce their own ways of organizing time. Since the converse (individual time is standardized by culture and social identity) also seems true, what we have is, in effect, a closed loop:

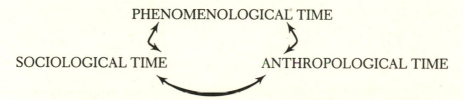

PHENOMENOLOGICAL TIME

SOCIOLOGICAL TIME   ANTHROPOLOGICAL TIME

In this loop, any separate term exists only in the context of the other two, and in turn provides part of the context for any other of the terms. Such self-referential aspect is not confined to the sphere of time alone. Pearce (1989) has found it in language, and Bateson (1958) in cultural *ethos*, and we might well conclude that it is present in all forms of human interaction. We also identified another closed loop linking past, present, and future. This means there may be two distinct loops in time, one diachronic (past-present-future), the other synchronic (individual-social-cultural).

All the different concepts of time we have examined are the outcome of a process of co-evolution, a collective co-creation that has modified time, as it were, right across the board. With his usual elegance and originality, Bateson (1972) compares the collective co-creation of time to the evolution of the horse. It would be quite arbitrary, he says, to see the evolution of the horse as the adaptation of the genus *eohippus* to the nature of the fields in which it browses. In reality, it is the ecosystem of horses and fields that has evolved—influenced, naturally, by all the other elements that make up the global ecosystem.

3

MODELS OF INTERACTIVE TIME: FAMILY TIME

F ERDINAND DE SAUSSURE IS ONE of the most interesting authors we have come across during the course of our research. Although familiar to linguists and linguisticians, he is virtually unknown to psychotherapists, and yet it is to him that we owe several key ideas about time and language. In his *Course in General Linguistics*, he writes:

> Certainly, it would be beneficial for all sciences to pay more careful attention to the axis on which all the things they are concerned with are located. This would mean distinguishing . . . : the *axis of simultaneity*, regarding relations between existing things, from which any intervention of time is excluded; 2. *the axis of succession*, on which only one thing at a time can be considered, but where all the things on the first axis, and their changes, are located. . . . To highlight better this opposition and intersection of two orders of phenomena regarding the same object, we prefer to speak of *synchronic* linguistics and *diachronic* linguistics. Anything referring to the static aspect of our science is synchronic, anything concerning evolution is diachronic. (de Saussure 1922/1966, pp. 99–100).

Nowadays we would probably prefer to say that the dichotomy is not so much between different phenomena related to the same object as between different descriptions produced by different observers. This means that every possible description has its own synchronic and diachronic axis.

As we shall soon see, anyone who has used cybernetic or systemic

61

models in therapy has had to come to terms with the problem of time. For example, our group, during the early seventies, used an essentially synchronic model, which took present relations in the clients' system into account: the "black box" theory (see Watzlawick, Beavin Bavelas, & Jackson, 1967) required only interactive observable behavior in the present to be considered. Later, when we discarded the "black box," emotions, meanings, and a wider temporal horizon became prominent. This shift can be seen in the new time-related terminology in the published literature: the use of *feed-forward* as well as *feedback*, *spiral causality* as well as *circular causality*, and a preference for *story* rather than *pattern*.

Let us now look at how we study the family—the system we most often deal with in our clinical work. Observing a family synchronically means describing the system of elements and relationships that enable us to say a certain group of people actually *is* a family. Synchronic observation confirms that the group belongs to the class of "family" and enables us to describe a family at the moment when it is observed.

If we observe the same family from a diachronic point of view, we describe it in terms of two quite distinct time frames: either as an instance of *stability* (time's cycle) based on recurring generational and transgenerational events, or as an instance of *change* (time's arrow), the irreversible events that make a family, at any given moment, completely different from what it was a short while before. These two points of view—one static, the other dynamic—can be reconciled because stability and change— time's cycle and time's arrow—are complementary aspects of family time as a whole.

Whenever we move from individuals to systems of more than one individual, we have to use the logic that applies to more complex entities comprising several individuals and their interactions. In this sense, the system is more than the sum of its parts, so descriptions of family time cannot be limited to the interpenetration of individual times: they must also take account of the time the family possesses *as a system*. The same is true of the relationship between family time and cultural time.

Thus, families vary according to how we choose to look at them. Every individual shows a set of fixed traits; at the same time he or she appears different with different people and in different contexts. The family is probably the social system in which the individual trait we are most concerned with here—awareness of time—can be observed in its subtlest and most complex form. To use Elias' (1989) terminology, the coordination of events in families is finely calibrated. Families often function as totally harmonious single units, so it really does matter whether we opt for holistic or analytical description.

In *Actual Minds, Possible Worlds*, Jerome Bruner describes two ways of thinking which he terms "paradigmatic thinking" and "narrative thinking." In paradigmatic thinking, we use category and concept to achieve the highest possible degree of logical consistency. The prime example is scientific discourse. Narrative thinking, on the other hand, is concerned less with consistency than with "the vicissitudes of human intentions" (Bruner, 1986). Meaning is kept open, giving not a blueprint for a reality that can be reproduced if rigorously defined parameters are observed but a story that unfolds in time, a diachronic image of a reality it may be possible to bring into existence.

Although the paradigmatic mode has long been considered the only proper medium for "scientific" discourse, most humanistic disciplines (history, for example) have invariably adopted the narrative mode, at least in part. Moreover, all men of science—including the most irreprehensible of them all, theoretical physicists—readily admit that the narrative mode is indispensable initially in formulating theories (as distinct from mathematical elaboration once they have been formulated). Paradigmatic and narrative thinking, individual and collective times, and synchronic and diachronic perspectives are the parameters we shall use in our survey of some theories of the family we have met with during the course of our work.

DESCRIBING FAMILIES

It may seem an easy task to describe the time of a family, or a family in time. Let us return to our two individuals, A and B, and assume that A and B are of the opposite sex and have decided to live together as a stable couple. The basis for the coordination of their individual times has already been laid, but it is likely—or even inevitable—that some rather important incompatibilities still remain.

For example, A may be a woman who looks well ahead into the future, while B is a man used to living from day to day who thinks only a few months ahead. Or A may be a woman with fast rhythms, and B a man with slow rhythms. As we saw in Chapter 2, differences of this magnitude can certainly create problems, although not always immediately. Problems may arise even when two individuals have closely coordinated identical times, as can clearly be seen in symbiotic couples, when one reacts dramatically to inevitable fluctuations in a partner's time to which he or she has not yet learned to adapt.

For individual times to develop in tandem, it is important that the couple has a wide range of possible times available to it. The importance of range is also true of bodily movements: the narrower the range of available movements, the greater the loss in adaptability. A young man has a wider repertoire of movements than an old man, is physically more adaptable. We could extend this idea to the members of a family, an institution, or any other social organization.

Diachronically, A and B will begin to influence each other's times by developing a set of shared assumptions and constructs, an ethos, and of course, a shared time. Just as A and B have their own times, so the "A-B" family will have its own rhythms, temporal horizon, and perspectives. In the incompatibility crises of new families, partners quickly realize that they have to harmonize the rhythms they have learned in their respective families of origin, and to try to establish a shared perspective and horizon.

Further crises are caused by critical events in family life such as birth, adolescence, separation, and death. When a child is born, the family is faced with a complex series of changes. The new arrival is not a *tabula rasa*, but a real person with a personal (if still not fully developed) time sense. The new baby—whom we shall call C for convenience—causes adjustments, or what Bateson (1979) calls "recalibration," to be made in the rest of the family. Rhythms are at first upset by the needs of the new arrival, but the family eventually "absorbs" his or her newness and individuality as he or she gradually assimilates their time coordinates[1]. Over time, a new temporal framework is established in the family.

Developmental psychologists are fiercely divided over the extent to which biological, genetic, and environmental factors influence behavior in the early stages of a child's life. Some theories stress the influence of environment, others the importance of biology. Newborn babies subjected to tactile or electrical stimulation immediately after the umbilical cord has been cut react differently in accordance to a Gauss curve. Their heart beat, arterial pressure, skin electrical resistance, and psychomotor response vary widely, from hypoactivity to hyperactivity. Clearly, this variety of response is established well before environmental factors come into play in the newborn, which would suggest that a child actively influences relations with its parents right from birth.[2] All parents being equal, there is a world of difference between dealing with a child who has been underactive and docile since birth and one who has been overactive. For example, a child who cries all night can cause considerable strain in families and produce emotional reactions in parents different from those produced by the child's brother or sister, with possible appearance of symptoms in the

---

[1]This is what Maturana and Varela (1980) call "structural coupling." Individuals are stimulated by their environment (in which other important individuals play a leading role). Equally, they stimulate the environment in order to produce change in it.

[2]To be more precise, we should take into account the environmental factors of the intrauterine life.

distant future. In other words, a baby can influence people, including members of the extended family with whom it has no direct contact.

TIME AND FAMILY MODELS

Let us now try to locate some of the more important family models on the three axes we identified earlier, namely the synchronic/diachronic, the individual/family, and the paradigmatic/narrative axes. We shall limit ourselves to placing some family models on the synchronic/diachronic axis. Any lasting relationship—therapeutic and non—has to be analyzed both in the here and now and in its wider temporal implications. Some models favor a synchronic view, and so emphasize distinction and discreteness, while others favor a diachronic view, and so stress continuity and flux.

For example, Minuchin's structural model (1974) lies towards the synchronic end of the synchronic/diachronic axis: the observer looks for structure, that is, the reciprocal position of the various components and how they interrelate at any given moment in the observed system. Although Minuchin takes in due consideration family change and development (as his penetrating studies of how "problemless" families originate and develop clearly show), he tends to describe families using spatial metaphors (boundaries, subsystems, etc.). Individuals negotiate with one another in this metaphorical space—form alliances, exert pressure on one another, cross boundaries, triangulate other members—so that the concept comes to resemble a microsociological theory. In other words, a structural family therapist looks for how the observed system is structured, how boundaries between subsystems and hierarchies are formed or breached.

In its original form, the Mental Research Institute's strategic model was also largely synchronic. One of its assumptions was that, for the observer, it was sufficient to know the present patterns to get an understanding of the observed system. Moreover, symptoms had the function in the here and now to maintain the "family homeostasis" (Jackson, 1957). The therapist aimed at changing the family's relational patterns, the idea being that other, more functional patterns would emerge. Other therapists, such as Haley (1963/1990), also adopted a synchronic perspective. A narrative aspect of the original strategic model can be seen in Ferreira (1963), with the introduction of the concept of "family myth," related to family homeostasis.

Moving on now to diachronic models, we might note Murray Bowen's multigenerational model (1978; Kerr & Bowen, 1988) which focuses on the complexity of generational and individual relationships and how they develop in time, and David Reiss' family paradigm theory (1981). Finally, recent narrative theories based on stories and meaning systems are currently arousing a great deal of interest (Anderson & Goolishian, 1988; White & Epston, 1990).

TIME AND CYBERNETICS

Most systemic family therapy models—ours is no exception—are rooted in cybernetics. The early therapists used the concept of first cybernetics based on *self-regulation*. Norbert Wiener, the founder of cybernetics, defined it as "the theory of control and communication in machines and animals alike" (Wiener, 1948/1961, p. 35). Attention centered on the processes by which self-regulating systems minimize the effects of environmental disturbance. The classic example was the thermostat, which seeks to restore environmental temperature to the desired level by means of *negative feedback*. This concept was central to what in future years would be called *first-order cybernetics*.

Cybernetics theory developed during the Second World War mainly in response to military need: the self-regulatory machines produced during that period developed from anti-aircraft aiming systems, which had to reduce aiming error to an absolute minimum by means of negative feedback. The early cyberneticists were anxious to find ways of predicting the future as accurately as possible: in order to be effective, anti-aircraft aiming systems had to predict with reasonable accuracy where a target would be in the sky. Moreover, this target had two important characteristics: it moved very fast and was guided by an intelligent being capable of taking evasive action (Wiener, 1961). Theorists in other fields automatically directed their attention towards ways of minimizing difference. For example, Cannon's concept of homeostasis (1932) was immediately used to describe the complex procedures that organisms follow to minimize internal variations by keeping major variables like pH, temperature and so on within acceptable limits.

Time is essentially cyclical in negative feedback. The thermostat works by minimizing the effects of time: whenever it restores a preset temperature, the result is that nothing has changed, nothing is new. Thus, first-order cybernetics saw time as a closed cycle in which any change can be reversed and stasis restored once more. And yet, the cyberneticists knew about thermodynamics and the idea that time is irreversible; they knew that perfect cycles are an illusion (Wiener, 1961). This led to a rather special concept of real, irreversible time in which great care was taken to predict how a system would *oppose* change, and what the probabilities of its being able to annihilate change were. Thus, first cybernetics time is stochastic, probabilistic, essentially predictable.

In this context, the family was seen as a system which, when disturbed, uses complex negative feedback to restore as nearly as possible the conditions that applied before change occurred. New conditions were seen as signals of potential changes to which the family would react by trying to minimize them. The emergence of a symptom in one member of a family was thought to be the family's way of avoiding more sweeping change in the system as a whole.

The earlier models offered by cybernetics and communication theory (used by the Mental Research Institute of Palo Alto and by the Milan group in its early period) considered the family as a self-regulatory system which controls itself through rules formed over a period of time through a process of trial and error. The observer needed only a view of the present state of the family relationship, a synchronic view, to "understand" the observed system. Such, at least, was the theory presented in *Pragmatics of Human Communication* (Watzlawick, Beavin Bavelas, & Jackson, 1967), which remained an important systemic theory and therapy text for years after it was published.

The early therapists could hardly have been unaware of the importance of time, yet cybernetics made it difficult to see change as a continuum, a process of becoming: it was more like a cinema reel, a sequence of discrete frames, a succession of static patterns rather than a flow. The two main reasons for this were the central importance of negative feedback in cybernetics and the example of Wiener's calculating machines, whose circuits are always able to return to zero or, in other words, to annihilate the time that had passed and so become a *tabula rasa* once again.

> Incidentally, note that one important difference between how we use machines and how we use our brains is that the machines work in successive cycles—which are devoid of mutual relations or have only limited, minimal relations—and can start from the beginning again with each cycle, while the brain, of its nature, can never, not even approximately, cancel out what it has stored previously. (Wiener, 1961, p. 165)

Obviously, a human system like a family can never behave exactly like a machine that can return to zero and start functioning from there: families have to preserve memories of themselves and maintain their ability to learn. It was this distinction between mechanical and living systems that finally exerted its influence.

In her article, "Deviation-Amplifying Processes in Normal Groups" (1971), Lynn Hoffman brought Magoroh Maruyama's second cybernetics—and so a diachronic perspective—into systemic family therapy. Magoroh Maruyama (1968) stressed that the difference in cybernetics between living and nonliving systems is that living systems are mainly morphogenic (positive feedback prevails in relation to negative feedback) while nonliving systems are mainly morphostatic (negative feedback prevails). He went on to describe two cybernetics processes, those (governed by negative feedback) which reduce difference, and those (governed by positive feedback) which amplify deviation. The latter can only be described in diachronic, developmental terms. Where before the observer was mainly interested in recording negative feedback, he or she now tried to record the *interaction* between negative and positive feedback and the tendency of the system to achieve either morphostasis or morphogenesis. The same event in the same system will have very different consequences depending on whether negative feedback (maximum stability) or positive feedback (maximum instability) is greater.

Using different terminology, Prigogine (Prigogine & Stengers, 1984), that tireless champion of the irreversibility of time in biological systems, concentrated on the relationship between change and systems far from equilibrium. Therapists usually are very sensitive to the conditions of stability/instability in the client system. As the system starts to destabilize, that is, goes far from equilibrium, change is more probable. Similarly, we can say that when individuals or families are in crisis they may rapidly exhibit major changes.

In the processes described by Maruyama, the effects of a negligible event can be either reduced (even eliminated) or amplified by dominant positive feedback that leads to increasing divergence from the system's original state. A tiny, unimportant difference between two members of a family—two children, for example—can amplify a time difference that may eventually produce two completely different stories and destinies. In our clinical work, we often see the effects of this process in the co-creation of psychiatric symptoms in a family member. "Scapegoat" theory and various sociological norm-deviation relationships may also be interpreted in this way.

Heinz von Foerster's ideas entered family therapy in the early eighties, most importantly with the role the observer plays in the process of acquiring knowledge. Von Foerster developed a "second-order cybernetics" ("a cybernetics of cybernetics"), that is, a cybernetics of the observing system, whereby every description made by an observer includes the biases, theories, and characteristics of the observer him/herself. This is very different from "first-order cybernetics," in which the observer is separate from what is observed.

Emphasis on the observer generated a constructivist approach in which the knowledge acquisition process assumes a central role in relation to the known object. Three authors in this field who have had—and continue to have—an important influence on systemic theory and practice are Ernst von Glasersfeld, Humberto Maturana, and Francisco Varela. The concepts of "co-creation of reality" and "co-evolution" are central to their thinking, since they are based on time's flow and generate a historical perspective. It is only a short step from their ideas to the narrative theories of more recent times.

Time and Paradox

We would now like to look back at a period in the history of the Milan group which illustrates the struggle we have had with the problem of time. In the early seventies, paradox was central to the theory and practice of the Milan group, and indeed inspired the title of a book, *Paradox and Counterparadox*, published in Italian in 1975 and in English in 1978. At that time our interest in paradox derived from readings of *Pragmatics of Human Communication* and, above all, Bateson, Jackson, Haley and Weakland's classic article "Toward a Theory of Schizophrenia," in which the double-bind concept was elaborated. Double bind was defined as a pragmatic paradox in which a prohibition is given and denied on two different logical levels with no possibility of resolving the contradiction or changing the terms of reference. When repeated in important emotional relationships, this form of double bind was seen as a source of pathology.[3]

In later years, the whole idea of double bind and paradox was questioned, especially by Dell (1981) and Cronen, Johnson, and Lannamann (1982). Their criticisms were mainly leveled at Russell's concept of logical levels on which Bateson had based his theory of paradox. As Cronen and his colleagues pointed out, double bind was based on the notion that language is a mirroring of external reality, and so excludes, by definition, the possibility of self-reference. This philosophy was carried to its logical limit in Whitehead and Russell's theory of logical types (1910–13), which states that a class cannot be a member of itself. Spencer Brown (1972) made the key criticism of Bertrand Russell and the theory of logical types when he said that the theory was suitable to the kind of logical system found in *Principia Mathematica*—an ordered, timeless world from which paradox has to be excluded to maintain logical consistency—but not to natural language, which is not so orderly and consistent and inevitably *includes* the paradoxes that help to give language its richness and creativity.

---

[3]Although Bateson states: "There is no single episode in the whole of my life that I regret more than that 'recipe' at the start of my early work on double bind" (1978a, p. 221).

Russell accepted Spencer Brown's critique in the end, and Bateson, in turn, agreed in his later works that the role of logical level theory in human interactive systems had to be reviewed. He described his change of heart in *Mind and Nature*:

> I suggest it is the attempt to deal with life in logical terms and the compulsive nature of that attempt which produce in us the propensity for terror when it is even hinted that such a logical approach might break down. (1979, p. 25)

We might say that paradox exists in logic, which is timeless, but not in real life, which develops in time. In logic, contradictions between levels produce paradoxes; in life, where there is sequence and succession, paradoxes appear when time sequences are cancelled out in language[4] (although we should remember that the resolution of paradoxes using time had already been described by Norbert Wiener in 1948[5]).

Watzlawick, Beavin Bavelas, and Jackson (1967), among others, cite Epimenides' famous paradox: "I, Epimenides of Crete, say that all Cretans are liars." In logic, this statement is paradoxical: the truth of Epimenides' statement cannot be determined. Bateson himself, who had cited this paradox as an example of an unsolvable situation, explains how it can be solved by introducing time:

> The truth of the matter is that logic cannot simulate all the steps of the causal systems operating in time.
> Logic breaks down when confronted with the paradoxes of abstraction— the Cretan liar or Russell's more sophisticated version of this, the question whether the class of classes which are not members of themselves is a member of itself. Logicians have been boggling at these paradoxes for 5000 years, but if such a paradox is proposed to a computer, it will answer: "Yes, no, yes, no, yes, no . . . " till it breaks or runs out of ink.

---

[4]Bateson, who studied logic in the early decades of the centuries, was also unaware that more recent logic had assimilated the dimension of time, which it had traditionally ignored. From 1950 on, temporal logic became an important branch of so-called "special logic" (Dalla Chiara Scabia, 1979).

[5]"Bertrand Russell's solution of his own paradoxes was to affix to every statement a quantity, the so-called type, which serves to distinguish between what seems to be formally the same statement, according to the character of the objects with which it concerns itself—whether these are "things," in the simplest sense, classes of "things," classes of classes of "things," etc. The method by which we resolve the paradoxes is also to attach a parameter to each statement, this parameter being the time at which it is asserted. In both cases, we introduce what we may call a parameter of uniformization, to resolve an ambiguity which is simply due to its neglect" (Wiener, 1961, p. 126).

The computer operates by cause and effect; it follows that when events inside the computer are used to simulate the "if ... then ... " of logic, the "then" becomes temporal. "If I close this switch, then (almost immediately) the light will light."

But the "If ... then ... " of logic contains no time. "If three sides of this triangle are equal to three sides of that triangle, THEN the triangles are equal." There is no time in that "then."

So, when simulated in the world of causality, the Russellian paradoxes come to work like this:

"If at time₁ the Cretan's statement is true; then at time₂, it is untrue; if it is untrue at time₂; then it is true at time₃; and so on ... " There is no contradiction, and the old "If ... then ... " of logic is obsolete. (Bateson, 1978a, p. 55)

So paradoxes arise when time is eliminated by making two or more events or behaviors occurring in temporal sequence happen simultaneously. If verbal or nonverbal meanings in the human world create situations where contradictory behaviors are simultaneously present, those situations are paradoxical. In other words, paradox is generated and lives in language. It is through language (verbal and nonverbal) that we deceive ourselves that our lives are governed by timeless logic; and in language, to quote Bateson (1972) once again, we often find that "things end up in a muddle."[6]

Naturally, these authors' attempts to revise the concept of paradox have been crucial to us in understanding the complex relationships between time and language. As we have seen, our interest in paradox waned toward the late seventies as the concept itself evolved, and we shifted our attention to time and language.

The assumptions that paradox does not exist in real life because time eliminates it, and that it exists only in logic and mathematics, which are timeless, were fundamental. As we have said, paradox can appear in real

---

[6]Cronen and colleagues (1982) reject even the terms "double bind" and "paradox" and use "self-reflexive loop" instead:

> We can say, as does Hofstadter (1979), that when two or more levels in a system are unclear as to which is of a higher level, a reflexive loop is formed. (p. 93)

> A temporal dimension is also present when a fully reflexive loop is formed: in a fully reflexive system a person first examines one aspect of the loop and draws an interpretation—"if this is helpful advising, that message must be a joke." The other side of the loop is then examined—"but if this message is an insult, then we are in an episode of domination." Thus, a fully reflexive loop involves an experience defined in part by time—a person experiences each side of the loop as a context for the other *during a constricted period of time,* while attempting to interpret *a particular unit of social meaning.* Logicians Brown (1972) and Varela (1975) both claim that reflexive relationships must be understood as movements through time. (p. 97)

life when time sequences are cancelled, as, for instance, when a parent simultaneously communicates to a child a confusing message like "Grow up/don't grow up" or "Leave/don't leave." At the time of *Paradox and Counterparadox*, we believed that symptoms were related to double binds, i.e., to paradoxes, and that these could be solved with *ad hoc* interventions (counterparadoxes). The therapeutic relationship itself acquired a paradoxical flavor since the therapist, as an agent of change, by connoting positively and prescribing all the clients' behavior, introduced the therapeutic bind "Good if you change/good if you don't change."

Similarly to Bateson's analysis of Epimenides' paradox, the introduction of time sequences cancels out paradoxes. A positive connotation of present behavior *now* may be followed by change *then*. The "now and then" which are in the mind of the therapist are transmitted—in the here and now of the therapeutic context—ambiguously, so that clients are put in a therapeutic bind: "It is all right with us if you don't change/it is all right with us if you change."

Elsewhere in this book we shall describe cases in which circular questions and rituals may create time sequences where their elimination had produced suffering, confusion, and madness. It should be remembered, however, that the elimination of time is also (one might even say paradoxically) a source of human creativity, art and poetry.

TIME AND PARADIGM

John Mince (1991, personal communication) has made an interesting and original attempt to connect cognitive and linguistic processes, from Spencer Brown's first law of form (1972) to Kuhn's concept of paradigm (1962), through a series of Linguistic Transforms operated by an observer. Here are the first seven of his ten Transforms:

Primal operation:	The *First Law of Form*:
	"Let there be a *distinction*."
1st transform:	The unity evoked is given a *name* (word).
	(At exactly this point bio-linguistics begins.)
2nd transform:	The unity is given *animation* through active/passive predication.
3rd transform:	A *description* is generated.
4th transform:	A description of the description, i.e., an *explanation* is generated.
	(We comment upon the description using causal or appositional linkage and modifiers.)
5th transform:	The explanation is accepted by the speaker and a listener, i.e., a *belief* is generated.

| 6th transform: | A series of beliefs coalesces through interaction with others into a *myth* over time. |
| 7th transform: | A series of myths coalesces in interaction with others over time into a *paradigm*. |

We insert Mince's seven propositions here because of the connections between terms like descriptions, explanation, belief, myth, and paradigm, concepts that will be dealt with shortly.

Of the many authors who have attempted to relate family interaction to time, we would like now to mention David Reiss (1981), a leading researcher in the field of family therapy. His work is an interesting example of how a static model can be developed into a dynamic view of how families actually work. In his early writings, Reiss had been concerned with defining what he called the "shared constructs" of families. These were necessarily static—almost snapshots of what a family is like at any given moment. However, as he developed his theory, he began to link these "shared constructs" in time to arrive at the concept of "family paradigm," which derives originally from Kuhn (1962). Thus, his work shifted from a synchronic to a diachronic point of view: the family paradigm operates at a higher level (meta-level) than the assumptions (shared constructs) a family elaborates to deal with specific events.

What Reiss calls a "paradigm" is the totality of these rules and assumptions. The process starts off as a way of dealing with contingent events, but gradually becomes increasingly abstract, losing all direct links with specific events to become a set of assumptions that are general enough to enable the family to orient itself in a vast range of different situations. It is interesting that the family paradigm is preserved not in the family's memory but in its unique way of organizing itself.

> We will argue that memory, as conventionally understood by individual psychology, is *not* the medium or repository for the conservation of the family paradigm. On the contrary, it is the structure of family interaction behavior which is itself the primary repository and conservation factor. (Reiss, 1981, p. 203)

A family's system of meaning or, if you like, its "thinking and premises" change constantly over time. The paradigm exists in and through the family's web of internal and external relationships. Mary Catherine Bateson relates this to:

> ... the kind of thematic consistency my father called ethos, the pervasiveness and congruity of style within a system that make any culture more than a list of traits and institutions. (1984, p. 81)

Time and Family Rituals

How does the paradigm manage to remain relatively stable over time? The answer is through rituals — distinct formal events — as well as the tiny, routine events that structure our daily lives.

David Reiss (1981) defines "ceremonials" as a special kind of ritual, highly charged emotional events with powerful symbolic connotations. They are episodic, in the sense that they occur on only a small number of important occasions, and require the presence of all the members of the family. Our definition of ritual is broader. It includes the ordinary events (Reiss calls them regulators) that determine the progress of our everyday lives.

Rituals are the family's most important way of maintaining continuity in time. We would like to mention one of Reiss' examples, a family organized around the aggressiveness and independence of its male members. The ritual perpetuating this value system was enacted whenever the father returned home from one of his long business trips. The father engaged in a brief physical tussle — arm-wrestling — with each of his sons while the mother stood approvingly to one side. Even such a simple ritual contains a surprisingly complex web of meaning. First, the family paradigm — carefully directed and controlled aggression — is used in a highly charged, emotional way; second, the potency of the father-children relationship is confirmed and strengthened. Above all, during the childhood and adolescence of his sons the father would restrain himself so as not to hurt them physically, while later on the children themselves would hold back so as not to hurt their 70-year-old father.

In the continuity it establishes, this ritual charts the family's irreversible biological evolution by allowing its past (the tradition of masculine toughness and independence) to enter and shape the present lives of all its members.

> Through each repetition the family reexperiences a crucial aspect of its past as if that past were present: the family's hardiness and success through competition of the remote past, and the family's more recent past, when the adult sons were children. Indeed, the fusion of the past and present crystallizes around the experience of fathers: the sons, one now a father, experience themselves as fathers of their father through a ritual whose special meaning comes from memories of themselves as small sons of their father. The experience of fusion in time, felt during the few and fleeting instances of this ritual, may be thought to live in the present, to shape and inform it. (Reiss, 1981, p. 238)

These "celebratory" rituals safeguard the continuity of the family, but there are other rituals which conceal or cancel out the past. Goffman

(1961) defines them as "rituals of degradation." A typical example is the choosing of a scapegoat, an act which many families cyclically repeat and reinforce until it assumes the regularity and inexorability of a ritual. However, its effect on family life is opposite to that of a ceremonial ritual because, instead of blending the past with the present, it blocks time in the present, *freezes* it solid. Positive values (attributed to others) and negative values (attributed to the scapegoat) polarize in the present, creating a new situation that conflicts with a previous one that was totally different but has now been forgotten. Where before each member of the family had his or her share of goodness and badness, now one person is black and the others are white, and collective forgetfulness totally isolates this reality from the past.[7] It is as if the family members were unaware of the past in the present. The family freezes into a repetitive pattern that prevents it from moving along time's spiral.

Unimportant, "regulatory" events act in and on time in a more continuous and subtle way. Since these are repeated actions that lend regularity to the daily life of the family, they *orient* the family in time by allowing each of its members to construct a personal temporal horizon and then synchronize it with those of other members. The degree to which these individual times have been synchronized is reflected in varying degrees of rigidity or flexibility, harmony or discord, conflict or peace in the family. We all know that there are "slow" and "fast" families, families that are well synchronized and families in which individuals stick resolutely to their own habits and personal timetables. Lack of synchronization can be a regulator like any other feature of family life because — as in any other human system in time — it is a family's way of establishing and maintaining coherence. Unsynchronized families of this type were studied by Minuchin and his colleagues in *Families of the Slums*. A synchronization scale for families ranging from "synchronous" to "nonsynchronous" could almost be produced; among other things, it would match Minuchin's well-known typology of "engaged" and "disengaged" families rather well.

In any event, synchronization is fundamental to many aspects of family development. If adequate linguistic, behavioral, affective, and cognitive synchronization (intimacy) is not achieved, the risk of dysfunction in the future becomes greater.

An especially elegant example of how family routines are established is given by Mary Catherine Bateson in *With a Daughter's Eye*. She tells how

---

[7]In one of his picturesque metaphors, Carl Whitaker describes family therapy as an event in which the therapist enters a family where the designated patient is the "black knight" and the other members are "white knights." His task is to make them all grey.

her mother, Margaret Mead, caught in a cross-fire of conflicting needs—
motherhood and career, desire to experiment and love of tradition—tried
to create around her daughter an environment that would give her both
a feeling of continuity and the possibility of becoming an adaptable, flexible person. To achieve this, she gave her a stable home and a solicitous
nanny—"No one who has had an English nanny can grow up without a
sense of continuity" (Bateson 1984, p. 29)—but also took her, together
with her nanny, to live in a home she shared with a large family of friends
and many children of different ages. As a result, Catherine grew up in a
stable environment but could also choose to be on her own when she
wished.

Emotional continuity, basic trust (Bowlby, 1982) and the certainty that
others will be there when needed are the first requirements for the building of a family. Emotional continuity provides the security we need to be
able to withdraw from others into ourselves. According to Eliot Chapple
(1970), we have an internal rhythm that dictates whether we can interact
with others and ourselves, conditioning our ability to live in "public time"
and "private time." Since the family is the primary social institution, it
provides the learning context for our ability to modulate our interaction,
to move from detachment to intimacy and vice versa. The need for intimacy is universal and is central to family life,[8] where we experience and
develop many kinds of intimacy: with parents, with brothers and sisters,
with a spouse, with children, and finally, with ourselves. Lynn Hoffman
(1981) believes that these intimacies are one of the reasons for the (continuing) existence of the family as an institution, beyond any cultural changes
that may occur. Consolidated, harmonious experience of intimacy in the
family fosters self-identity, makes individuation possible, and allows members to live both in collective family time and in private individual time.

In her book, Mary Catherine Bateson gives a vivid example of the
transmission of mother-daughter intimacy from one generation to another.
She describes how her mother, Margaret Mead, tried to balance the
rhythms of her work with the rhythms of her daughter so as to create a
new mother-baby system with its own unique coherence.

> When Margaret planned for my care and feeding, she set out to combine
> the generosity of most primitive mothers, who nurse their infants when

---

[8]It should be remembered, however, that the emotional closeness and intimacy
of the evolved Western family are not found in all types of family. In past centuries
(and even now in non-Western societies such as traditional Indian society), families
infrequently generated intimacy between partners or between parents and children.

they cry and remain with them constantly, with the resources of civilization, the clock, and this too meant recording. She would record the hours at which I demanded feeding and then, by analyzing these times, construct a schedule from the order immanent in my own body's rhythms which would make the process predictable enough so she could schedule her classes and meetings and know when she should be home to feed me. I have the notebook that records these feeding times and other observations, as I also have the notebook in which my grandmother recorded her observations of the infant Margaret and the one in which I recorded my observations of my daughter, Vanni, while I went off between feedings to teach a seminar and analyze films of the interactions of other mothers with their children. (1984, pp. 22–23)

This example shows how a mother-daughter relationship can be transmitted across generations. One of the authors of this book had lunch with Mary Bateson and her daughter Vanni in Tel Aviv some time ago. Mary explained that she was in Israel to show her 16-year-old daughter the Middle East, just as her mother Margaret Mead had done with her when she was 16. The very least one can say is that there was never any lack of continuity and intimacy in her family!

TIME AND NARRATION

The use of narrative as a metaphor to describe the structuring of family relationships and, most importantly, how they evolve in time is a relatively recent development, although Ferreira's writings on the "family myth" (1963) contain early examples of it.

The assumption that the narratives we tell construct our reality for us, and so become reality in their own right, is crucial in narrative theories of the family, in which the family is seen as a story narrated by its own members. Anyone who becomes important to the family as time passes — real people, imaginary people (an unborn child, for example), past people, present people — contributes to the story. As in ancient oral traditions, each person tells his or her own version of the story, which is thus both repeated and created anew. How all these stories interrelate constitutes an important part of the life of the family; agreement or disagreement between stories generates agreement or disagreement between the members of the family.

Carlos Sluzki says:

Our social world is constituted in and through a network of multiple stories or narratives (the "story" that our social world is constructed in or through multiple stories or narratives being one of them). This ecology of stories, with different degrees of dominance at different moments and in different contexts, establishes the frame within which we become aware of self and others. . . .

What we call "reality" resides and is expressed in one's description of events, people, ideas, feelings, and experiences. These descriptions, in turn, evolve through social interactions that are themselves shaped by those descriptions. . . . (1992, pp. 218–219)

The popularity of the narrative model can be explained in various ways. Perhaps the most plausible is that family paradigms as such are limited, and sooner or later reveal undeniable shortcomings.[9] Bruner (1986) points out that, when their theories fail, economists often resort to anecdotes about Japanese managers or other contingent aspects of the economic world to find some explanation for events:

These narratives, once acted out, "make" events and "make" history. They contribute to the reality of the participants. For an economist (or an economic historian) to ignore them, even on grounds that "general economic forces" shape the world of economics, would be to don blinders. (p. 42)

As we have seen, one of the earliest narrative metaphors of family interaction was Ferreira's concept of "family myth." "Myth" here means a set of beliefs shared by all the members of a given family from which they derive their personal identities; so it is also a "story" describing how they live and adapt inside and outside the family. Myth proper is a static, super-individual construct lying outside the flow of time. The family myth was seen as a story that shapes the interactions of the family: in keeping with the homeostatic paradigm current at the time, it came to be regarded as the family's way of stabilizing its interaction.

Like classical Greek myths, family myths have their own internal development in time, but seem timeless when seen from the outside. Thus, a family living a myth sees its own life as a process of becoming, while to an external observer it seems to revolve around itself and does not develop in any real sense: from the outside, a family appears static in relation to the cultural time in which it is embedded. If the discrepancy between internal and external reality becomes too great, disorders may occur. The Casanti family described in *Paradox and Counterparadox* was immobilized by a time frame unsuited to the culture it lived in, thus producing a conflict expressed by the onset of severe anorexia nervosa in one of the family members. We shall look at myth in more detail in Chapter 8.

---

[9]It is striking that Paul Ricoeur (1988) finds philosophical theories of time as limiting as family therapists do. In the end, "skepticism of temporality" can only be dispelled through the use of story-telling and narrative ways of thinking.

The eighties saw a revival of interest in the use of narrative metaphor. Of the many authors who wrote on the subject during the period, White and Epston (1990) are perhaps the most interesting. Personal story is central to their conspicuously diachronic model: when a person has only one story to tell, his future options are drastically reduced. Michael White (1984) developed his theory while working with encopretic children. In the families of such children, the only stories ever told were of shame, dirt and squalor, a continual harping on the physical shortcomings of the child and the disappointment of parents unable to persuade the child to control himself. Isolating those rare moments in these stories when children failed to live up to their parents' gloomy expectations of them became a way of formulating new stories that made it possible to shake off the symptom. Illness determined how these children saw themselves and their parents, so life became just a long series of failures. To break this pattern, it was necessary to find some point of discontinuit in their stories, a "unique achievement" that could provide the starting point for a new success story. Milton Erickson had adopted a similar approach years earlier when he urged therapists always to try to see the positive aspects of the stories their patients told them (this has also been a longstanding idea over several decades of social work theory).

White and Epston (1990) give an example of how injecting the past into one story rather than another can change awareness of present and future time and have wide-ranging practical consequences. Until the forties, the history of the North American Indians had been seen by anthropologists and the Indians themselves as the story of a glorious past doomed to oblivion in the vast melting pot of American culture. As a result, the daily life of the Indians was seen as an example of disorganization and dysfunction. In the fifties, a new interpretation emerged, in which the recent past became a period of exploitation and the future a period of rebirth. So although the daily lives of the Indians had not actually changed very much, the way the Indians and others saw their lives most certainly had: their poverty-stricken alienation was no longer interpreted as racial degeneration and inferiority, but as the dignity of an exploited people whose only option was passive resistance.

In more general terms, narrative theory, which owes much to the work of Michel Foucault, implies that a family is a set of interwoven stories drawing on events in the remote past. These stories not only shape the past and present but also impose real constraints on how all members of the family construct or envisage their futures.

The more flexible families are—the more able they are to listen to a wide range of stories even when they contradict one another—the greater their intellectual and emotional enrichment will be. Their members will be able to develop independent lives and individuate in the course of time. If a family can accept only a few stories or is huddled around a dominant myth, it will soon experience strain when faced with stories incompatible with its own. Certain periods in family life, especially adolescence, call for high degrees of flexibility and tolerance if new stories are to emerge. If this does not happen, anxiety, suffering, and frustration may lead to clinical symptoms. The Casanti family we mentioned earlier falls into this category.

Naturally, individuals and their families are immersed in a culture, one which—in the West at least—is currently undergoing rapid change. Our culture offers a repertory of narrative themes or models that can challenge myths or stories passed down in families over generations. In this sense, a "normal" family—with all the reservations that the use of the word entails—is one which is flexible enough to handle the conflicts that inevitably arise both inside it and between itself and its surrounding culture. Interweaving stories from past generations with those of contemporary culture can be either creative and life-enhancing or a source of symptoms and anxiety. In the professional literature, families of the first type are often defined as flexible, and those of the second type as rigid.

Sometimes people seek therapy, which may relieve their anguish and suffering, and reconcile personal and cultural stories.

> Within this frame, an encounter can be defined as therapeutic when, in its course, a transformation has taken place in the family's set of dominant stories so as to include new experiences, meanings and (inter)actions, with the effect of a loosening of the thematic grip of the set of stories on symptomatic-problematic behaviors. . . .
> In the course of the therapeutic conversation, the therapist scans the organization and delivery of the collective stories about the family's predicament and, through questions and comments, favors certain kinds of transformation in the *nature*, in the *telling* of the stories, and/or in the *relationship* between stories. (Sluzki, 1992, pp. 219–220)

In therapy, highly dissimilar and divergent stories dating from the distant past are sometimes told by family members living in close contact with one another in the present. One example of this was an 18-year-old anorexic girl, the second of three daughters, who came to us for treatment. In the third session, she told us that her mother had ignored her since childhood, and that she had felt so lonely and isolated that she had attached herself to the mother of one of her friends. Totally astonished to hear this, her mother told us that her daughter had always seemed the strongest and most self-sufficient of all her children, so that the mother had always given her all the freedom she wanted. She had never understood, however, why her daughter had repaid her with ill-concealed hostility. For years, mother and daughter had been telling themselves totally different stories about their relationship, which had forced them further and further apart. Each interpreted the other's behavior in terms of her own story, which only confirmed the apparent "truth" of their respective stories. Another example is Jim, a young adult whose life story totally differed from his mother's version ("He's telling the story of a boy I never knew"). We shall look at Jim in more detail in Chapter 5.

Families with psychotic members tell the most divergent stories: the strange, incomprehensible stories that psychotics tell tend to create incompatibilities and impede communication with other members of the family. One of the therapist's tasks is to establish contact with the psychotic, accepting the delusions, the private communicational code and logic, thus making possible the development of a dialogue during which he/she may build a bridge between his/her stories and those of others.

At this point, it is worth looking in more detail at the differences between myth and story. One major difference is their use of time. Myths are detached from the smooth flow of ordinary time; they are "finished" stories with a beginning and an end. Stories set in the present always have a future, while myths have no future: mythical time is frozen, imprisoned, while story time flows like a river in ordinary, day-to-day time: stories are open-ended.

One further point we would mention here is the distinction between system and narrative. By definition, "system" refers to a group of interrelated elements within a given boundary: it requires, of necessity, a spatial dimension. We have said elsewhere in this book that we used the Palo Alto cybernetic-systemic approach in the early seventies, based mainly on a synchronic view of relationships, but then adopted a diachronic view by bringing time into therapy. Since narrative is more properly concerned with time than with space—human affairs are presented as stories that develop in time—we obviously had no difficulty in accepting narrative paradigms. We now use both synchronic and diachronic approaches in a "binocular perspective" that enables us to orient ourselves in space and time.[10] As Bateson says, two points of view are better than one.

---

[10]The distinction between system and narrative is similar in some ways to the distinction made between structure and system in the seventies.

4

THE OBSERVER
AND TIME

WE HAVE CHOSEN TIME AS A KEY, as a special way of looking at human relations. Why time and not space? After all, time and space seem inextricably intertwined, as Kant in philosophy, Piaget in psychology and Einstein in physics have all said: each term of this dyad recalls the other. We rarely discuss space explicitly in this book, although it is present everywhere in our theorizing. Terms like "interior world," "external world," "horizon," "perspective," "time dimension," "system," "structure," "closeness," and "distance" in relationships, etc., presuppose a *representation*, a spatial frame that is necessary for consciousness to operate.[1]

Other authors have regarded time as an important aspect of psychotherapy, but we have chosen it as the *focus* of our inquiry, as the favored lens through which to observe interaction. In Batesonian terms, we could say that this lens now represents our epistemological premise, an observer bias.

For us, time is not only a means, a way of structuring and timing sessions, but also an end in itself, one of the aims of our interventions. How can a temporal horizon be changed? How can the sluggish time of

---

[1]Bateson defines information as a difference that makes a difference, a relationship. Visual, auditory, tactile, and proprioceptive perceptions representing spatial and/or temporal differences reach the central nervous system through binary impulses which are processed, integrated, and associated into sensations, images and thoughts. These are then contextualized in spatial and temporal frames.

82

a depressive be made to move more quickly? How can the diachronic connections lost in the fragmented story of a schizophrenic be re-established? How can the potential for development be restored to those who seem to have lost all sense of the future? Finally, how can the lens of time be used to observe and understand synchronies and dissynchronies between individuals, families and social systems, and how can we promote harmony between different individual and social times?

As systemic therapists, it is our job to look at how relationships work. Seeing relationships through the lens of time can illuminate aspects of therapy that are often overlooked. Let us look now at some aspects of the systemic approach to consultation and psychotherapy.

SYSTEMIC CONSULTATION
AND THERAPY

First, we should like to give a brief history of the systemic approach to therapy and show how the ideas of the Milan group (Mara Selvini Palazzoli, Luigi Boscolo, Gianfranco Cecchin, Giuliana Prata) have developed over the past 20 years. We know that this involves giving a description, and that the description we make of our present will become a past event for our readers, to which they will then attribute the meaning of their present. Telling this story will be both a reenactment of past actions and the construction of a bridge into the future. As we tell our story, we shall enter the self-reflexive loop of past, present, and future.[2]

After a psychoanalytical period (1967–71), the Milan group switched in the early seventies to the so-called Palo Alto method, a systemic approach strongly influenced by the ideas of Gregory Bateson, Jay Haley, Don Jackson, and Milton Erickson (Haley, 1963/1990; Watzlawick et al., 1967). In this initial period, until around 1975, therapy was always offered to the whole family in which a problem had arisen in one of its members (the "designated patient").

The therapy room and the observation room were linked by a one-way mirror. The therapeutic team would usually meet before each session to formulate a working hypothesis based on the information already available, after which the therapist, or more often a pair of therapists would begin the session while the rest of the team observed from the other side of the

---

[2]For a more detailed account of Milan systemic therapy, see Hoffman (1981), Tomm (1984, 1985), Campbell and Draper (1985), and Boscolo, Cecchin, Hoffman, and Penn (1987).

mirror. The session could then be interrupted by either the therapists or the observation team behind the mirror; in either case the therapist(s) and team would hold a short meeting in the observation room to exchange ideas. In a closing discussion at the end of the session, the therapist and team would meet longer, sometimes for even up to an hour, to develop simple hypotheses and integrate these to form a systemic hypothesis that made sense of the behavior observed in association with the symptom. This systemic hypothesis then provided the basis for a "final intervention," which could be either a reformulation, a prescription with tasks the family had to perform at home, or a ritual. The therapist(s) would then present the family with the final intervention.

The Palo Alto method was based on systemic thinking and first-order cybernetics, i.e., the cybernetics of observed systems, which assumes that the observer is separate from the entity he observes. The team would attempt to produce a systemic hypothesis based on how the family organized itself around the symptom or symptoms that had arisen, so that the hypothesis more or less represented what was then called the "family game." To be of any use, the hypothesis had to be an *ad hoc* representation of the family game or, at least, to "fit" it in the way a key fits a lock.

In most cases, it proved easy for the whole team to agree on a hypothesis and produce useful interventions. Many families without psychotic members finished their therapy after a few sessions, and appreciable success was also achieved with various cases of acute psychosis. Cases of chronic psychosis proved more intractable, however: therapy would often come to a standstill, and it usually exceeded the maximum of ten sessions stipulated in the initial contract with the family.

Paradox and Counterparadox (Selvini Palazzoli et al., 1978), which describes the group's work with 15 families with clinically diagnosed schizophrenic members, reports that dealing with those families was like entering a labyrinth. It was difficult to arrive at a hypothesis that made sense to the whole team, and this produced feelings of confusion and frustration. Like Bowen (1978), the group saw symptoms as aspects of a three-generational game in which the designated patient occupied a special position entailing the highest degree of disconfirmation, with resulting uncertainties over the perception of self and others, as well as feelings of confusion and pointlessness. Double-bind theory (Bateson et al., 1956) which we discussed in Chapter 3, based on the paradoxes that arise through mixing different logical levels, was central to the group's understanding of psychotic symptoms.

The aim of therapy was to dissolve the rigid patterns of dysfunctional behavior in order to make room for more functional patterns. This was achieved by attributing positive connotation to all behavior, whether symptomatic or not (paradoxical reformulation), and by using family rituals.[3]

Following the publication of *Steps to an Ecology of Mind* (1972), a collection of Bateson's most relevant work, the group felt that important new horizons had been opened up, and by 1975 had radically altered its ways of working and thinking. An attempt was made to transfer Bateson's cybernetic epistemology to clinical practice, to think systemically in order to act systemically.

Compared with the Palo Alto approaches we were then using, the systemic view of Bateson's original writings seemed both purer and more complex. The distinction between map and territory, the logical categories of learning, the concept of mind as system and system as mind, the notion of cybernetic epistemology and the introduction of semantics—all became extremely important. The clinical application of these ideas led to new information collection and processing methods and new types of intervention in human systems. Three principles were drawn up for the conduct of sessions—hypothesizing, circularity, and neutrality—which later became the distinctive features of the Milan approach (Selvini Palazzoli, Boscolo, Cecchin, & Prata, 1980a).

Hypothesizing is a way of linking all data deriving from observation. A hypothesis is regarded as systemic if it takes account of all the components of the observed system and offers an explanation of how they relate to one another. This explanation is neither true nor false; it is simply a working tool. The therapist uses verbal and nonverbal feedback from clients to assess the validity of his or her hypotheses.

Circularity is the process by which therapists use feedback to assess hypotheses and formulate new ones. It is important to keep changing hypotheses in order to avoid the trap of the "true hypothesis" that freezes interaction rigid and brings discourse to a halt. Hypotheses emerge from repeated interactions between therapist and family. In this sense, being a "real Batesonian" means attributing hypotheses neither to the therapist nor to the clients, but to both. Bateson himself (1979) once asked where, or what, mind is when a man is cutting down a tree, and concluded that mind is the circuit that connects the man, the axe, and the tree. In other words, mind and system are synonymous.

Similarly, where or what is the hypothesis? In the therapist's mind or

---

[3]In this brief account of our "Palo Alto" period, we used terms like "paradoxical eformulation," "dysfunctional behaviors," "effective interventions," "*ad hoc* hypotheses," "double bind" and others that belong to that period alone. We have not been used them since.

somewhere else? In the seventies it was regarded as in the therapist's mind, but now we would locate it in the total interactive context. This shift of perspective occurred during the writing of this book, and it may be taken as an illustration of how telling stories has the effect of changing them. Incidentally, this is the basic concept of the narrative model in therapy.

Circular questions—not to be confused with the concept of circularity we have just mentioned—developed when therapists asked various members of the family to comment in turn on the behavior of two or more other members of the family. The questions were devised to obtain information rather than data (Bateson said at the time that a piece of information is "a difference that makes a difference," i.e., a difference that establishes a relationship; it is different from a datum, then).

Circular questions are important because they make each family member the observer of the thoughts, emotions, and behavior of other members, and this creates a community of observers during therapy. Such questions challenge self-centeredness. Instead of *speaking*, each member of the family is *spoken about*, learns about the opinion of the others about him/herself, and thus may come to know them better.

We might go further and say that information obtained from circular questions is self-reflexive, in the sense that the therapist and family's perception of the situation is constantly changing as a result of the information each receives from the other. Circular questions draw attention to differences, to new connections between ideas, meanings and behaviors that can change the epistemology (personal premises, unconscious assumptions [Bateson, 1972]) of the various members of the family. Thus, circular questions are, in themselves, a form of intervention, possibly the most important kind available to the systemic therapist.

Initially described in the article "Hypothesizing, Circularity, Neutrality," circular questions were then studied and classified more accurately by various authors, including Hoffman (1981), Penn (1982, 1985), Tomm (1984, 1985, 1987, 1987a, 1988), Deissler (1986), Fleuridas, Nelson, & Rosenthal (1986), and Borwick (1990). Let us look briefly at two of these classifications.

Karl Tomm, one of the first to study circular questions, categorizes questions by aims and type. Taking into consideration the intention of the interviewer in asking questions, Tomm makes a distinction between informative circular questions and reflexive circular questions. The former aims to gather information, the latter to produce change (the aims are not mutually exclusive; questions are often mixed). The distinction between informative and reflexive questions lies not so much in their formulation as in their timing: depending on when it is asked, the same question can be informative or reflexive (Tomm, 1985, 1988).[4]

Both kinds of question have a similar function: to investigate and highlight differences, i.e., relationships. Tomm's differences can be related to type or related to time:

> Temporal difference questions are somewhat more complex. They focus on a difference between category differences at two points in time, in other words, on a change. The comparison is between relationships of certain categories in one time frame and comparable arrangements in another. (Tomm, 1985, p. 41)

Klaus Deissler (1986) has also stressed the importance of time differences. His PST (person, space, and time) systemic model uses three types of questions: "explicative" questions about the past to self-confirm clients' premises, "maintenance" questions about the present both to confirm and to create things that are new, and "solution" questions centered on future perspectives. The latter questions are supposed to have the maximum novelty effect.

The concept of neutrality is difficult to understand outside a diachronic view. Just as, by definition, "it is impossible not to communicate," so it is impossible to be neutral when we act. For example, when the therapist asks a member of a family to describe the emotions and behaviors of other members of the family, that member's active stance gives him or her an advantage over others. As originally defined by the Milan group, neutrality is active in time: the therapist refuses to enter into alliances or coalitions with members of the family or to associate with the ideas they express. Naturally, this process should be seen diachronically. For example, during a session a therapist may veer in one direction rather than another in order not to lose spontaneity and to prevent discourse grinding to a halt, but later on—possibly with the aid of colleagues behind the mirror or, if working alone, by reconsidering the situation in the interval before the next session—he or she will reestablish the former neutrality. The neutrality of the therapist is promoted by a circular view of reality and encourages the therapist curiosity (Cecchin, 1987) that allows new ideas and points of view to emerge.

---

[4]In his survey of the questions interviewers can use, Tomm also lists questions based, unlike circular questions, on linear epistemology, namely: *linear questions*, those which aim to collect data, and *strategic questions*, those which aim at producing change in a linear way.

With the development of systemic theories, we had to review the very notion of neutrality. As formulated in the seventies in first cybernetics terms, the concept assumed that observers and observed were separate. It was possible, then, for the therapist to place oneself "above" one's clients. Second-order cybernetics changed all this: separation was now impossible, the system had to include the observer and the observed, so the therapist could never be really "neutral" because one could never be neutral about oneself, one's biases, one's own ideas. This was also true of the team behind the mirror with its more abstract (partly because it is multiple) view: it too could not help being influenced by its own premises and assumptions.

Many attempts were made to expand or correct the concept of neutrality, including "curiosity" (Cecchin, 1987) and "multipartiality" (Hoffman, 1988). We now prefer to think in terms of a *tendency towards neutrality*, a therapist and team ideal which, by definition, can never be fully attained.

The Milan group split up in 1979 when Selvini Palazzoli and Prata left the center and continued their research on family therapy in another place. The research, based on first-order cybernetics, attempted to "discover" possible specific family organizations ("family games") related to specific syndromes, such as anorexia and psychosis. Later, in 1983, Mara Selvini Palazzoli, Stefano Cirillo, Matteo Selvini, and Anna Maria Sorrentino joined forces in studying family typologies; the results of their research were eventually published in *Family Games* (1989).

In the meantime, Boscolo and Cecchin had been developing an approach that had taken a radically new direction. In 1977, they had started a systemic family therapy training course for groups of 10–15 trainees from a wide variety of contexts (mainly social and health care services). Families were now seen by one or two therapists, often trainees, while other trainees and two trainers watched from behind the mirror. Thus, there was a shift from research about therapy to research about training *and* therapy. Roles became more complex: for example, a trainer would find it necessary to act as therapist, trainer, or supervisor at any given moment.

In the early eighties, Boscolo and Cecchin began traveling the world, presenting their method at conferences and seminars. Other teams in Europe and America began experimenting with what was becoming known as the "Milan method." This traveling brought them into contact with new colleagues, as well as a wide range of different organizations, ranging from small mental health groups to clinics, hospitals, universities, and other institutions.

Their personal and often lengthy discussions with Humberto Maturana, Heinz von Foerster, and later with Ernst von Glasersfeld were especially important. Maturana's key ideas were the centrality of the observer—"every thing that is said is said by an observer"—and the autonomous organization of living systems. From this, he concluded that "instructive interaction"—interaction that produces a certain changes directly in living systems—is impossible: the system always responds according to its organization and its history. According to Maturana and Varela (1980), reality emerges from consensus produced by language, so there are as many realities as there are conversations. Von Foerster (1981), for his part, developed the concept of second-order cybernetics—the cybernetics of observing systems—in which the observer is included in the description of what is observed, with the result that observer and observed can never be separated. Finally, von Glasersfeld (1987) pioneered the concepts of radical constructivism.

As a result of these new ideas, Boscolo and Cecchin broadened the concept of the family to include a much wider range of interacting human systems. Also, attention shifted from the observed to the observing system: both were now seen as organized "minds," in the sense that clients observe therapists as much as therapists observe clients. Thus, the emphasis in therapy shifted from the behavior of the observed system to the behavior, ideas, theories, and personal assumptions of the observing system, in keeping with constructivist approaches and the principles of second-order cybernetics. The family was no longer seen as a "homeostatic machine" that the therapist has first to know before he can put it right. More attention was paid to what actually happens in sessions, to exchanges of information, emotions, and meanings between therapists and clients. In short, the focus was now the therapy process itself, rather than the final intervention. Prior to this, the final intervention had been seen as the crux of the encounter between team and family, the only way of bringing about change. If change did not occur, it meant that the systemic hypothesis on which the intervention was based had not been truly *ad hoc*, i.e., it had failed to account for the total organization of the observed system.

Other changes in the working principles of the Milan group resulted from these new ideas (Boscolo, Cecchin, Hoffman, & Penn, 1987). Therapist and team no longer considered only the family system that came to sessions; instead, they began hypothesizing about the "significant system" attached to the problem. A significant system—the system of relationships that unite the people who have brought in a problem—includes, by definition, the designated patient, but may also extend to members of the nuclear family, the extended family (including its most important deceased relatives), the patient's friends and peers, the school, work, and most importantly, all the "helpers" and health and social services the patient may have had contact with over time. Of course, the significant system also includes the therapist, as an observer who brings with her or him all his or her theories and biases. Therapists now sought to understand how the patterns of ideas and meanings embedded in a complex significant system could produce, with the passing of time, the clinical picture they actually observed.[5]

The need to shift from families to wider social systems was the result of trainer-trainee interaction in the early training groups. Most of the trainees worked in public health departments, so hypotheses now had to include at the very least the patient, the family, the referring client, the clinical referrer and the health departments themselves, with their varying rules and wide range of personnel from different professions and practical situations.

The concepts of Maturana, Varela, von Foerster, and von Glasersfeld implied that the position of each observer within the meaning system had to be taken into account whenever a system was evaluated. The more points of observation there were in the system, the better the system could be known. If, instead of formulating hypotheses based on his or her own biases and unique point of view, the therapist tried to envisage and then correlate the hypotheses or points of view of other members of the meaning system to which they belong, it would be possible to formulate a more complex, multifaceted, and in a certain sense, collective hypothesis. Thus, the personal hypothesis, which always risks being one-dimensional, like a flat, monoscopic painting, is replaced by a complex, multidimensional hypothesis which, since it has real depth, offers a stereoscopic picture of the system.

Thus, the end result of trainer-trainee interaction was to introduce a macrosystemic dimension into therapy. This complicated the work of therapists quite considerably, since they now had to:

> 1. not only do psychotherapeutic work, but also deal with situations requiring social assistance, rehabilitation and interventions on organizational issues;
>
> 2. intervene not only verbally, as in psychotherapy, but also with actions, in contexts which require action.

It gradually became clear that what trainees learned at the center was not so much a technique as a new way of seeing and acting, based on Bateson's "cybernetic epistemology." Trainees had to learn how to act on

---

[5]In their article, "Problem-Determined Systems" (1986), Anderson, Goolishian, and Winderman describe a similar kind of therapy which is not based on cybernetics.

the basis of a systemic analysis of their own particular working context that would enable them to see what the most appropriate action might be. Thus, trainees about to embark on a course are now told that they will see done, and themselves do, consultations and therapy in which workers in a private clinic (in this case, the Milan Family Therapy Center) see the family as a system. The family thus becomes a workshop—a laboratory—in which it is possible to learn how to think and act in a systemic way.

TIME IN THE MILAN SYSTEMIC APPROACH

The Milan group's approach to time has itself developed in time, has had its own natural history, if you like. When, in the seventies, the group abandoned psychoanalysis in favor of the Palo Alto model (Watzlawick et al., 1967; Watzlawick, Weakland, & Fisch, 1973), the focus of its work shifted exclusively to the present, away from contemporary psychoanalytical approaches concerned mainly with the past. One famous example cited by Watzlawick et al. (1967) likens the present situation to a position in a game of chess. Looking at a given position in a given game, an experienced player can plausibly reconstruct the sequence of moves that brought the game to its present position. In practical terms, then, all one needs to know about is the present.

In the early years of the Milan group (1971 to 1975), the application of these ideas made the present the only focus of attention. The past was considered only from the moment when the symptom first appeared: inquiry centered on relationships created around the symptom in the present moment. The conduct of sessions became more complex when circular questions and hypothesizing were introduced (after 1975). Hypothesizing means asking exactly how a system is organized; how, out of all the possibilities open to it, it acquired the organization actually observed in sessions; how symptoms had come to be the way they were; how present relationships had developed. This also means tracking the logical sequencing of past interactions (including across generations), so this shifts attention away from either the past or the present to the *continuity* between past and present.[6]

Too much emphasis on the past can lead to linear, causal explanations of symptoms. Starting from the past rather than the present can funnel

---

[6]Without, however, constructing a genealogy or entering into transgenerational history in any detail. In this respect, it differs from Murray Bowen's (1978) transgenerational model.

everything into a narrow channel of causal necessity—only *this* reality exists, therefore it is the only possible reality, therefore a sequence of necessary events was needed to produce the situation we see now. Strict causality of this type means that a systemic vision (the present creates its own past) is replaced by a deterministic one (the past determines the present).

Our group began to realize that it sometimes never got beyond the "family game" hypothesis formulated in the first session: the initial situation had been frozen, as in a snapshot, so that subsequent changes were seen as something *added* to an initial situation, and the initial synchronic perspective invariably prevailed over a diachronic one. Subsequently, we recognized that such synchronic perspective had the effect of preventing the co-evolutionary process between the observing and the observed system.[7] The family system started to be seen as a new one at each session or, to use another expression, to be seen with new, fresh eyes. This is the process we refer to when we say: "Never marry hypotheses, flirt with them!"

Thus, the tendency to see therapy as a coherent, sequential "story"—a series of obligatory steps—was abandoned. Any given session has its own life, and there is no reason to link sessions one to another: *each session is "the first."* Memory of previous sessions acts only as a loose frame providing a background and some meaning to a conversation now in progress. The stories told in sessions have no linear plot; they are not traditional narratives. Each session may produce a different novel story.[8] In the unfolding of the stories, there is an high degree of unpredictability, particularly with regard to the content of the stories.[9] Whether there will or will not be a major change in the clients' system is fairly unpredictable.

The therapist's situation is strangely similar to the Trobriand Indian culture Ornstein mentions (1975), which is entirely centered on the present:

> When we ordinarily view the process of the maturation of a plant (e.g., a yam), we see a sequence. We experience the *same* yam turning from ripeness to overripeness in sequential time. The Zen monk does not share our view, nor does the Trobriander. The ripe yam (which in the language of the

---

[7]We might say that "synchrony" and "diachrony" are reminiscent here of Parmenides' *being* and Heraclitus' *flow*.

[8]This is why trainees are sometimes bewildered when they observe sessions conducted by Milan therapists: unless the method is fully understood its logic will be incomprehensible.

[9]When we adopt an *a posteriori* stance and describe or write about a clinical case, we give it a narrative coherence that resembles a deterministic concatenation of events.

Trobriander is called "taytu") *remains* a ripe yam. When an overripe yam appears, it is a different entity, not causally or sequentially connected with the ripe yam. It is another entity entirely and is even given another name, "yowana." (p. 107)

Thus, the client (an individual, couple or family) is always seen anew by therapists in each succeeding session. The therapist facilitates the loosening of the clients' deterministic causal relationships, which constrain their view of reality, keeping it within the realm of unresolved conflict and suffering. The client is seen by the therapist as a living system, ready to evolve and build a new future.

Although in therapy change is unpredictable, there is indeed a relationship between the therapist's *theory* of change and change itself. Different meanings are given by different therapy schools to the process of change. We shall concentrate here on the relationship between time and change in the theory of the therapist. Let us begin with an experience by one of the authors (Luigi Boscolo) during his psychoanalytic training.

In my training course, I had to analyze three clinical cases under the supervision of a training analyst. This was my second case, a 30-year-old man who had started analytic treatment, three times a week, in late June, and as it happened my supervisor was away on two months' holiday, so three months of analysis had already been done before I had the chance to report how things had been going. After those three months, my patient no longer had his original symptoms. On the contrary, he said he was feeling much better, and was already hinting that he was "cured" and could terminate analysis.

When I described the case, my supervisor showed none of the enthusiasm I had experienced. Abruptly, he asked me how I would explain what was going on with my patient, and I dared say—with hesitation—that I agreed with the patient. I did not expect his chilling verdict that the patient's improvement simply indicated that he had "seduced" me, that it was all a classic case of "flight into health," an obvious "resistance." Of course, I was quite disappointed, but I had to change my conviction that analysis was at an end. Moreover, being a trainee, I had to do what I was told.

I read the same disappointment on the face of my patient when I explained, in nontechnical terms, that his improvement was a "resistance," a "flight into health." I was curious to see whether he would accept the idea from me in the way I had accepted it from my supervisor. Well, he did, and the analysis turned out to be a long one. One could say that the client obeyed me, and I obeyed my supervisor, but whom did my supervisor obey? One could say, his experience, his teachers, and the textbooks of psychoanalysis, which prescribe an appropriate time to complete an analytic treatment!

This case has special significance for us, since it has triggered a particular interest in the issue of time and fostered insight into the relationship between time and change in the therapists' theories. The duration a therapist predicts for a therapy is obviously related to the time specified by the theory adhered to. For example, the time expected for a Freudian analysis to be completed, in the sixties, was anything from three to five years, at the rate of three or four sessions a week; a Kleinian analysis could take even longer. As our example shows, the theory of the therapist prescribes the time span usually necessary for major changes to occur, leading to the end of the treatment.

The Milan group, as we said before, used a psychoanalytic method when it started treating families and couples in 1967. Sessions were held once or twice a week over long periods, sometimes of years. Naturally, frequency of sessions and duration of therapy were those prescribed by psychoanalytical theory. In constructivist terms, we might say that, from the start of therapy, the therapists co-constructed with their clients a reality in which significant change could only be expected after one or two years of treatment.

When, in 1971, the group adopted the strategic brief therapy model, it was thought that therapy should last no more than ten sessions, at the rate of one session a week. The ten-session therapy introduced the idea of a beginning and an end. Most families showed significant changes within the prescribed period; more importantly, sudden and highly significant changes would often appear in the eighth or ninth sessions. In other words, the expectation of change within ten sessions possibly had the pragmatic effect of facilitating change.

The group debated at length the relative merits of change obtained by the psychoanalytic and the Palo Alto model, but in the end decided that it was a sterile discussion: the important thing was that change did occur. We became more interested in the relationship between the time needed for change and the time predicted by the therapist's theory. One crucial issue dealt with rigidity versus flexibility of the time frame of the therapist's theory. It goes without saying that therapists' flexibility about the time for change to occur allows them to coordinate their times with clients' times. An analyst who does not expect to see "normal behavior" until the third year of analysis and a brief therapist who expects it within a maximum of ten sessions are both imposing their own time frames on their clients. One can compare them to parents who have rigid expectations about their children's developmental steps: they may expect that, at a certain, specific age, their children should almost overnight exhibit adult behavior. The latter may react with frustration because behavior that was good up to then is suddenly not accepted; this can be the beginning of an escalating conflict.

One additional issue about the duration of therapy emerged. For reasons of geographical distance, it had been necessary to space out the sessions of a small number of families who had to come a long way (for example from Sicily) to the center in Milan. Instead of coming once a week, they were asked to come once a month. "Strangely," these families showed better results than the others, even if they had really serious problems to contend with. It was decided to make all the families come once a month, and the results were more than satisfactory. From then on, the monthly interval became a permanent feature of the Milan therapy, which changed its name from "brief therapy" to "long-brief therapy"—brief because of the small number of sessions, but long because of the overall duration of therapy.

In most cases, therapy was successfully completed by the tenth session, but some cases, especially families with chronic psychotic patients, needed more therapy and were offered a further course of ten sessions. Some of these families did not do well, and some dropped out before the end of the second cycle. Further experiences forced us to concede that families with a chronic psychotic member frequently need more time for treatment and other interventions, such as individual therapy, rehabilitation, and group experiences.

These cases contrasted strangely with the unexpected brilliant successes we had with some families that had interrupted therapy themselves, often in the first few sessions, without even informing us. Follow-up of these cases of spontaneous drop-out showed, surprisingly, remarkable positive changes that had taken place *after* drop-out. This was curious, and in some ways disconcerting, since at the time we did the follow-up we expected these families to be therapeutic failures.

A plausible explanation for such "strange" results could be that these families fled because therapy had triggered such change as to threaten their internal cohesion, with serious risk of disintegration. By abandoning therapy, these families were, in effect, slowing down the evolution that had suddenly begun to happen.

The group was elated by these unexpected results, and embarked on a sort of ego trip. For a while we thought that, if families were unchanged after the fourth session, it was our fault. In the language of those days, we would say that the therapists were not succeeding in identifying, or having any significant effect on, the "nodal points" of the system. We defined then the "nodal points" as the points where most of the system's functions converge, and where action would produce most change with the least effort (Selvini Palazzoli et al., 1978). It was the families themselves, especially those with psychotic members, who eventually brought us down to earth and cured us of our therapeutic omnipotence.

These experiences did produce the valuable insight that change may be (perhaps most importantly) discontinuous as well as continuous. These

ideas were validated theoretically by Prigogine's later accounts of dissipative systems (Prigogine & Stengers, 1984), and Thom's (1989) catastrophe
theory.

   We might also add here that all living systems already contain the potential for change and self-organization within themselves: all that is needed
for its spontaneous release is the creation of an appropriate context. A
blocked-up river provides a simple metaphor: as soon as the blockage is
removed, the river is perfectly capable of reaching the sea on its own
without waiting for its course to be remade.

CONTINUOUS AND
DISCONTINUOUS CHANGE

Different theories of psychotherapy imply different relationships between
time and change. All symptom-modification theories imply discontinuous
change. For example, in doing behavior therapy to treat phobia cases,
therapists need a certain period of time to diminish — and finally abolish —
the phobic response; once this is done, therapy ends. This also applies to
behavior therapies based on operational conditioning, aiming at producing
more appropriate behavior. Similarly, the aim of strategic therapies (Haley,
1990; Watzlawick et al., 1974) is to make symptoms disappear.

   In psychoanalysis, symptoms are regarded as epiphenomena of unconscious conflicts. The mere disappearance of symptoms is no indication of
"cure" because they may well be replaced by others as long as the basic
conflict remains unresolved. In spite of the many theoretical and practical
changes it has undergone over the years, as well as recent developments
that have brought it closer to hermeneutics and deconstuctionism (Jervis,
1989), psychoanalysis is centered on the growing process of the client
within the relationship with the analyst. For this reason, psychoanalytic
time may be considered continuous: by interacting with each other two,
three or four times a week, patient and analyst end up modulating each
other's times and rhythms, co-evolving in a continuous process. The analy-
sand's time is often measured by the rhythm of the sessions themselves.
Change is gradual and progressive. When, at times, sweeping, discontinuous changes occur, they are analyzed, interpreted, and incorporated into
the client's conscious processes, which may take a number of sessions.

   In systemic therapy, the main idea is that symptoms emerge when the
relationship of a person with her/himself (self-reflexivity) or with others
(family members have a particular importance) lose their meaning or take
on obscure, ambiguous meanings. In this sense, symptoms point to dilemmas in relationships: "What is my position in my family? What does my

family want from me? Does my mother prefer me or my brother? What is my position in the world?" Of course, these dilemmas also appear in other contexts such as school and work, or with peers and friends. Symptoms may appear when a person feels cut off by secrets and denied alliances (coalitions) within the group of significant people to whom he or she is connected. Persistence of the symptom—the expression of a dilemma in the group's relationships—keeps the members oscillating between alternatives. Especially for the symptomatic person, it is as if time had stopped: one's ability to evolve is markedly reduced.

In such cases, therapy may solve the dilemmas and ambiguities of relationships, so that the system is no longer torn between the alternatives open to it and can look for its own solutions. Therapy, according to this view of pathology, works through discontinuity.

In *Paradox and Counterparadox*, the Milan group had already advanced a theory of discontinuous change—change by leaps and bounds, in contrast to the concept of gradual change it had used earlier. Our current view is that, from the very first session, our way of doing therapy creates conditions for discontinuous change that follow no preset program or sequencing of stages ("each session is the first"). Naturally, there is the risk that such "leaps" might produce changes the therapist does not foresee or want. This is a good medicine for the "omnipotent" therapist, who learns how to be humble with the complex, often unpredictable events of life.

This does not mean that we do not have our own ideology—it would be impossible not to have one—but we constantly try to be aware of it and to avoid, as much as we can, influencing our clients. We see the therapist as a facilitator, a catalyst able to trigger change. Our aim is to create a context, with our clients, in which they can find their own solutions. We shall see later how this process can also be seen as the co-creation of possible worlds.

These ideas throw new light on Selvini Palazzoli's article "Why a Long Interval between Sessions?" (1980), which tried to explain why monthly sessions produce better results than weekly ones. The basic idea was that, following the therapist-induced perturbations in a session, the family needed a period of time to find a new equilibrium. If the next session were held before this equilibrium had been achieved, the therapist might have slowed or stopped the change triggered in the previous session, and s/he might well become enmeshed in the family. Someone once called this "hit and run" therapy, corresponding to a sequence of disequilibrium and equilibrium in the family system.

The same thinking applied to the issue of termination of therapy. The therapist would end therapy abruptly when significant, important change, likely to continue spontaneously in future without the aid of the therapist, had appeared. Families mobilized in this way are left with the task (and also the freedom) of managing their own change, their own future.

This concurs very well with the principle we outlined above, that the system—whether an individual or a family—already contains the information it needs to change of its own accord. Of course, it would be absurd to take this axiom too literally, for it would lead to the conclusion that any problem can be solved in a single session if only the right key could be found. This way of thinking may be applied to machines (trivial machines, Von Foerster would say), but not to human beings. Experience has shown us that repeated client-therapist contact is needed for new perspectives and solutions to emerge. Sometimes, as in cases of chronic psychosis, therapy alone is not enough and other interventions are needed.

The monthly interval—necessary, as we have said, for the system to achieve a new equilibrium—is obviously arbitrary. We did try to find explanations—some rather odd, like the menstrual cycle, phases of the moon, calendar months, etc.—to justify it. One thing was certain, however: most families liked the monthly interval, and we liked it too, because it made the organization of our work much easier. Naturally, the risk of rigidity is always present, whatever time interval is adopted. Sometimes, the first two meetings are held in consecutive weeks, and then meetings are scheduled at intervals of a month or more. Another factor affecting the spacing of sessions is the working context itself—working alone or with a team, in a public service sector or privately.

Two points should be emphasized here: it may be true that change in the therapeutic system is discontinuous, but it is also true that change *happens within a continuous relationship*. Also, the monthly interval, although useful for family therapy, appears to be too long for individual therapy, where a week or a fortnight works better. Individual therapy seems to require shorter intervals because more frequent contacts are needed to promote continuity in the dyadic therapist-client relationship. Families already have their own network of relationships, which reduces the need for frequent contacts with the therapist.

THE CO-CREATION OF TIME

A system can be defined in a number of ways. According to Maturana and Varela (1980), it is an entity an observer defines by distinguishing it from its context. It can also be defined as a set of elements that interact within given boundaries or, according to Gregory Bateson's definition (based on cybernetics), any unity structured on feedback.

As therapists and consultants, we deal with social systems—individuals, couples, families, institutions—that must deal with the issue of time. Any system has to be coordinated in time. If we consider an individual's physical (molecular) and biological (cellular, intercellular, hormonal) systems, we see that all the various elements are coordinated within narrow, clearly-defined limits. In such systems, time is deterministic. However, in social systems coordination is less closely controlled and less urgently needed; it is certainly not deterministic. Thus, our brain cells are strictly controlled and coordinated: their physical and biological times are bound by necessity. Human times are not.[10]

In social systems, time emerges through the consensus of a community of observers: human time is co-created through interaction. Every person has his/her own individual time, which fluctuates and varies according to internal and external circumstances. Individual time is related to self-reflexive loops in which each of us is an observer of oneself. In this sense, individual time, at a certain level, implies zero social consensus, and so may vary enormously from one individual to another.

As Varela has said, though, there is no such thing as a "self" isolated from context, from environment. The self is, in fact, a precipitate of past experience and interaction (especially with people who were important to us), so individual time becomes meaningful only if we think of it as encircled by ever-widening loops of other people with whom different interactive times were co-created.

In our daily life, we live in our own individual times, from which we establish links with the individual times of other people, with the times of groups, institutions, and finally, our culture. To understand other people's times is to understand how our own times interconnect with theirs.

In our work as therapists, we are fascinated—and often amazed—by the complex, unpredictable ways in which people relate to time: we see people immersed in the past, people who return continually to the past (as in post-traumatic stress disorders), people suffering from massive repression or amnesic disorders like hysteria and pseudologia phantastica, people like obsessive patients who reify time, and so on.

Like everyone else, people suffering from mental disorders try to make contact and establish coordination with other systems. What Wynne and Wynne (1986) call intimacy is closely linked to an optimum coordination of times. But in cases of mental disorder, such coordination is rather more difficult to achieve. For example, schizophrenics, even when they live

---

[10]In his theory of neuroses, Freud made "repetition compulsion" central to the production and maintenance of symptoms. As a result, the subject "loses his freedom."

together for years, as they did during the period of large psychiatric hospitals, have great difficulty in coordinating their reciprocal times.

Therapists, then, should try to facilitate time coordination and flexibility. This also means they should be aware of their own time assumptions and idiosyncrasies, and of the constraints that determine temporal relations with clients. For example, we are now used to doing "brief" therapy, so it would be difficult—if not impossible—for us to go back to therapy based on two-three weekly sessions extending over several years.

THE SELF-REFLEXIVE LOOP OF PAST, PRESENT, AND FUTURE

Let us now look more closely at the relationship between the observer and the three dimensions of past, present, and future in the time system. Every human system has a history, a past that defines the meaning of its present events. However, the past is also defined by events and relationships in the present, so this creates a self-reflexive loop in which past and present define each other. The loop becomes still more complex if we add the future, which derives its meaning from the past and present but alters them in turn: projects, strategies, and expectations can give meaning to actions in the present, and these in turn influence the structuring of memory (the past).

For example, a family myth rooted in the past influences perceptions and actions in the present and places constraints on future events which in turn modify the myth so that it may disappear. Another example, on a much larger scale, is the "American dream," rooted in the pioneer days of the United States. This myth has influenced American life for more than two centuries, reaching its apotheosis in the Second World War and its decline during the Vietnam War. In the collective American (but also non-American) consciousness, this decline has produced a sense of doubt and loss, leading to a reevaluation of the assumptions of the myth itself.

Past, present, and future are united in a single self-reflexive loop, but it should be stressed that the present holds a special position in this loop. As St. Augustine would say, *all problems are problems of the present*: past and future problems exist in the present, together with present problems, but no problem can exist outside the present. If it does, it is no longer a problem: it is only the memory or possibility of a problem.

It may happen that a particular event—a betrayal, an error, a war, a loss—can acquire total dominance. Despite the passing of time, it colors present events and rigidly determines future possibilities. It is as if the self-reflexive loop has split to become a linear, deterministic chain: the event "which has passed" has a huge influence on the present and future without itself being altered by them. Examples of this are incomplete mourning, post-traumatic disorders in war survivors obsessed by memories or prey to anxiety dreams, or marital betrayal in which powerful emotions infect the whole life of the couple.

In his article, "From Versailles to Cybernetics," Bateson gives a telling historical example of this process. Towards the end of the First World War, the allies offered the Germans favorable surrender terms in President Wilson's widely publicized Fourteen Points, which said there would be no annexation, reparations, or punishment. Because the allies broke these promises in the Treaty of Versailles, a climate of resentment, mistrust and hatred was created that eventually triggered the Second World War. However, the people who started the new war believed they were acting from contingent, "present" motives, whereas in fact these had been strongly influenced by events in the past. One has to be cautious, however, in emphasizing the role of the past, because one runs the risk of legitimating wrong actions in the present (for example, the Holocaust).

The common denominator in all these examples is that ideas associated with an event come to dominate individual and collective consciousness, to the detriment of other ideas about the same event, or ideas, memories, and expectations about other events. In other words, the system becomes rigid. The more open an ecosystem's feedback circuits are, the more flexible, adaptable, "normal" it is, and this allows information to circulate more freely. By using hypotheses and circular questions especially, systemic therapy creates a context that dissolves "rigidity" and allows new circuits to be opened up, with the emergence of new ideas, meanings, and perspectives.

This happens in the therapeutic dialogue, in the here and now, when past or future problems are brought into the present. In psychoanalysis, this happens by evaluating the transference and countertransference through which the past is relived. In other types of therapy—behavioral and, to a certain extent, strategic and structural—it is achieved through the use of behavioral prescriptions or restructuring in the present. In more recent psychoanalytical and systemic therapies (Anderson & Goolishian, 1988) with a hermeneutic basis, emphasis is placed on conversation in the present and the meanings that emerge from it.

One interesting type of "future" therapy was devised by Milton Erickson and subsequently developed by de Shazer (1988). In "Pseudo-Orientation in Time as a Hypnotic Procedure" (1954), Erickson presents hypnosis as a way not only to go back into the past, but also to influence the future. The therapist suggests to the hypnotized client that he has *already achieved* the goals that represent his deepest desires. De Shazer achieves similar goals without resorting to hypnosis:

> It seems that in the therapy situation, simply describing in detail a future in which the problem is already solved helps to build the expectation that the problem will be solved and then this expectation, once formed, can help the client think and behave in ways that will lead to fulfilling this expectation. (1988, p. 5)

The "presentification" of the past and the future in the therapeutic relationship aims at introducing circularity and flexibility into the system, so that fluctuations, oscillations, repetitions, and blockings may disappear and time can flow freely again. Telfener (1987) gives an excellent description of how this can be made to happen:

> The renewed attention toward time allows clients to disconnect present from past and future; a different reading of the present allows them to choose a new past and imagine various possible futures. Change is the transformation rule that allows clients to disconnect the future from the past and to break a sequence often taken for granted by persons in therapy. (pp. 34–35)

POSSIBLE WORLDS

"Pathological" systems are often equated in the professional literature with "rigid" systems, i.e., systems with little or no flexibility. They are based on deterministic assumptions of necessity, which make them reproduce the same patterns, behavior, and explanations. Our clients usually have a linear, "historical" conception of time in which the past determines the present and places constraints on the future. One way of producing change, as we have seen, is to create a context that works on clients' deterministic premises, thus promoting creativity.

One useful and interesting conceptual frame in "explaining" how this may happen refers to logic, with the consensual creation of "possible worlds." In formal logic, "possible world" refers to a situation that may happen. First used by Leibniz in his *Discourse on Metaphysics*, its application produced perhaps his best-known aphorism: "Ours is the best of all possible worlds" (Allwood, Anderson, & Dahl, 1977).

> The real world is simple—too simple, I would say. It is schematic, lacking in substance.... Once things become human, everything changes because a fantastic range of possible worlds is added to our single schematic world. I think this is the real meaning of Leibniz' idea about what happened when man appeared in the universe. In a certain sense, a myriad of new universes was born. (Toraldo di Francia, 1990, p. 26)

Ordinary language tends to use predicative and propositional logic (All-wood et al., 1977), which sees only one possible world at a time and often takes its truths to be absolute, as if our statements about the world were the same as incontrovertible truths deriving from logical premises. Therapy's function is to introduce *modal* logic, which admits the existence of other possible worlds. Nelson Goodman (1978) says that, for the purposes of ordinary life, it is important for a person to think that the world is flat; otherwise there would be problems. Similarly, an astronaut has to think that the world is round; otherwise he or she would be in considerable danger. Both statements—"the world is flat," "the world is round"—are equally valid in two different possible worlds, i.e., two different descriptive domains.[11]

Giuliano Toraldo di Francia (1990) says much the same thing when he points out the discrepancies between the general theory of relativity, which refers to the macroscopic world, and quantum mechanics, which refer to the subatomic world. These contradictions do not make the theories any less useful to physicists; it is just that they apply to different descriptive domains.

Knowledge of the external world is not simply a kind of mirroring, but the dynamic construction of an observer who compares the "real" world with possible worlds by introducing time.

> A possible world is not a synchronic structure but a diachronic development of a structure: it is a history. The synchronic universe may perhaps seem too simple. But as soon as we introduce a historical dimension, everything is enriched and becomes marvelously complicated. (Toraldo di Francia, 1990, p. 29)

As Jerome Bruner observes (1986), possible worlds can be described using modal logic:

> In the new, more powerful, modal logic, we ask of a proposition not whether it is true or false, but in what kind of possible world it would be true. It is the case, moreover, that if it can be demonstrated to be true in *all* conceivable possible worlds, then it is almost certainly a truth that derives from the nature of language rather than from the world—in the sense that the statement "a bachelor is an unmarried male" may be true in all possible worlds. (p. 45)

---

[11]According to Goodman, "worlds" are produced by mental activity, which can thus create an infinity of "possible worlds," each with its own coherence. Each world is as real as any other, although Goodman, by no means a total relativist, devotes most of his time to defining the criteria that make one world "more real" than another.

Within certain limits, any discourse can be interpreted using different kinds of logic: each interpretation is valid within the assumptions we make about the world that is created as a result (using "world" in Nelson Goodman's [1978] sense of the term). The way we interpret speech and actions has an important effect on our lives, so changing the bases of these interpretations (and assumptions) is in itself one of the conditions for change.

Let us take an example. The statement "my son is not self-sufficient" will hold true in all logically possible worlds. In logic, this is expressed by the "modal operator" N, which implies "this statement is necessary, i.e., true in all possible worlds." By contrast, the statement "my son may become self-sufficient" is expressed by the modal operator M, which implies "this statement is possible, i.e., true, in some possible world." Therapy tries to eliminate necessary statements in order to introduce possible ones. We often use the word "idea" to represent a possible world: "When did you get the idea that your son isn't self-sufficient? Where did the idea come from? What would have to happen for another to take its place? Of the people you respect most, who could persuade you to change this idea about your son's self-sufficiency? Let's imagine that the idea that he isn't self-sufficient changed in a year's time. What would change in your family?" And so on.

Modal logic can be used in a diachronic perspective, i.e., in a temporal context that enables a statement to be related to other corresponding statements made at other "points" in the time continuum (Allwood et al., 1977). We work in a similar way. Possible worlds created from systemic hypotheses formulated and tested during consultation or therapy can influence the "real" world of our clients and also help them to think in terms of possible worlds. We could say, then, that consultation and therapy create not merely a learning context but a deutero-learning context, a context in which clients learn how to learn.

5

TIMES IN CONSULTATION AND THERAPY

VERY DIALOGUE HAS A TIME and rhythm co-created by the interaction of those who participate in it. In this chapter we shall see why analyzing how times interact in therapy or consultation is so important. We shall look first at various aspects of client time, therapist time, consultant time, and team time, and then outline how we investigate and use time in our work.

CONSULTATION VERSUS THERAPY

First of all, we should like to clarify the concepts of therapy and consultation and trace their development. "Therapy" has long been the main, or even the only, term used to describe clinical interventions in families. The term "consultant" has been used sparingly in the literature; however, the eighties saw increasing interest in consultation and its relationship to therapy. Some authors have even abandoned the use of the word "therapy" altogether (see Hoffman, 1988), even though they work with individuals, couples, or families in clinical contexts.

A book edited some years ago by Wynne, McDaniel, and Weber— *Systems Consultation: A New Perspective for Family Therapy* (1986)—discussed the reasons for the shift from therapy to consultation in the clinical field. These include, first and foremost, the inadequacy and imprecision of our ways of describing family problems: some would even say that no system of classification is conceptually adequate to the task of describing them. The idea that a family is "ill," "pathological," or "pathogenic", and so in need of therapy, is increasingly less widely held. For example, self-help champions totally reject the concept of family pathology.

Another reason is that clients often come in search of expert advice about a problem—a state of uneasiness or suffering—rather than to be cured of an "illness." If the expert suggests therapy too soon, discussion will be limited to "pathological" problems in the present and ways of solving them in the future, thus limiting the possibility of highlighting clients' resources. Families or individuals are not always prepared to undergo exhaustive questioning, to embark on a therapeutic journey that may well solve their problems, but at too high a cost (the appearance of uncontrollable conflicts, for example). This is a major reason for early drop-outs from therapy. A consultation context may avoid such risks and be useful because it stresses resources rather than problems, health rather than illness. It encourages a collaborative relationship in which clients are totally responsible for the choices that are made.

As we said in Chapter 4, the couples and families sent to the Milan Family Therapy Center in the early seventies first underwent a preliminary consultation session. At the end, clients were offered ten sessions of therapy if indications seemed to justify it. In that period we believed that the families with an "ill" member were "pathological" and that a therapeutic intervention was needed to "cure" them.

Later on, our sessions gradually shifted from therapy to consultation. In dialogue with clients we increasingly avoided words associated with illness, like "symptom," "session," and "diagnosis," thus avoiding the use of the language of pathology, to be consistent with the most recent theoretical developments (second-order cybernetics, constructivism, constructionism, post-modern views). We have abandoned the practice of offering ten sessions, which implied the presence of problems to be solved, and now prefer to fix appointments for the next meeting as we go along. Moreover, while our original aim was to eliminate symptoms by means of a "final intervention," we subsequently preferred to explore ideas, meanings, and emotions in dialogue with our clients in a context that made possible the change of the clients' premises and the co-creation of new realities.

In the past, both clients and therapists knew pretty well they were involved in a relationship defined as "therapy." Now things are less clear: although clients usually come or are sent to us for therapy, the meetings with them resemble consultation more closely than therapy. At times, the meeting is explicitly defined as a consultation: when a colleague asks us for an opinion on a clinical case, or when we are asked to work in nonclinical contexts, for example on problems that arise in private or public psychiatric teams. We are sometimes also called in for consultation by public services or private firms, to deal with organizational issues.

It is worth looking here at Schein's (1987) interesting classification of nonclinical consultations. Schein, a professor of management at MIT, distinguishes three types: "information-experience acquisition," "doctor-patient," and "process consultation." In the first, the client (a company manager or a group of managers) already knows what the problem is, what help they need, and who to go to for it, so they engage a consultant to find a solution. In the second, the client authorizes the consultant to "find out what's wrong, make a diagnosis, and prescribe what should be done." The client thus becomes dependent on the consultant without being encouraged to learn ways of solving problems independently.

"Process consultation" (rather like our way of working) differs from the other models not so much in content as in how the consultant structures the consultancy relationship. "The central assumption is that the problem belongs to the client and continues to belong to him throughout the consultation process" (Schein, 1987, p. 29). In the last analysis, only the client really knows the context he works in—its peculiarities, its resources, what does and doesn't work. In process consultation, not only are problems solved, but "more importantly, the client learns how to solve problems so that he can go on solving them after the consultant has finished his work" (1987, p. 30). In Batesonian terms, we might say—as indeed we do say in our therapy and consultation—that a second-order learning context (deutero-learning) is created in which clients learn *and* learn how to learn.

CLIENTS' TIME

A central point in our thinking is that coordination is essential to human interaction. All systems—living or nonliving—need a certain degree of coordination between their component parts if they are to go on existing. In mechanical systems this coordination can be very tight, with very little or no room for variation. Even in the simplest living systems—in multicellular organisms, for example—coordination is governed by necessity: we need only think here of cancer, where a few cell clones evade the laws governing the growth and coordination of the larger organism with disastrous results to the organism itself.

Things are very different in more complex systems, comprising several organisms, such as a human group in interaction. Even here, coordination, though extremely variable, cannot exceed certain parameters. There is a *range* of possible coordinations, beyond which there is the appearance of dysfunction and possibly the disintegration of the system.

So, coordination of times, rhythms, and temporal horizons has to be kept within a range, otherwise blockage and rigidity, on the one hand, or chaos and an unacceptable degree of unpredictability and distress, on the other, may result. As we have seen in the social times of cities (Chapter 2), poor temporal coordination of times can lead to these features. Similarly, in families lack of coordination may lead to the experience of painful conflicts, suffering, and symptoms. A good example of rigid, overstressing coordination of time relationships between man and machine can be found in Frederick Taylor's approach, known as "scientific management." In his book, *Images of Organizations* (1986), Morgan offers a good description of it:

> In applying his five principles, Taylor advocated the use of time- and motion-study as a means of analyzing and standardizing work activities. . . . All the "thinking" is done by the managers and designers, leaving all the "doing" to the employees. . . . The increases of productivity have often been achieved at great human cost, reducing many workers to automatons. . . . For example, when Henry Ford established his first assembly line to produce the Model T, employee turnover rose to approximately 380 percent per annum. . . . When General Motors decided to tighten up on efficiency in its Lords-town plant in the late 1960s, the speed of the assembly line was raised to increase output from 60 to 100 cars per hour. At this new pace, each worker had 36 seconds to perform at least eight different operations. (pp. 30–31)

A humorous though devastating criticism of rigid, "nonhuman" rhythms in industrial production in the age of Taylorism is made by Charlie Chaplin in his already mentioned movie, "Modern Times," where the assembly-line worker loses coordination with the machines and other workers and develops a series of tics (this demonstrates well how symptoms may be seen as metaphors of relationships).

Coordination of times in human relationships depends on biological, cultural, and social factors. When a group of people enters into a relationship it develops temporal coherence by coordinating its actions and meanings. The coordination of individual times is fundamental to this coherence. In clinical cases, we try to "see" this in the context of the group's meaning system (family, school, workplace, etc.), which is in turn part of a larger social and cultural system. Observing this complex system through the lens of time allows us to identify temporal harmonies and disharmonies in individuals, between individuals and their families, between individuals and social systems (school, work), and between families and the dominant culture. For example, frequent, serious time coordination problems in human groups are experienced among immigrants adapting to a new country and in multiracial societies.

Persons who have problems with time may describe them in many ways. They may feel unable to coordinate various internal times. They may feel blocked, unable to develop, or unable to live in the present, taking refuge in the past or in the future. They may feel time as a tyrant that oppresses, controls their life, or eludes them. Moreover, they may feel unable to coordinate their internal subjective times with external times (working time, socializing time, etc.).

We shall now report on some problems with time we deal with in our practice. We intend to give neither a systematic treatment nor a classification, but simply a survey of some problems we frequently encounter.

Disharmony Between Objective and Subjective Times in Couples

Let us begin with a literary example. Mr. Kawai Joji, a 30-year-old man of quite ordinary appearance and aspirations, marries a 14-year-old called Naomi, a sweet, good-natured girl of a quiet and modest disposition. After a couple of years, he discovers a complicated series of betrayals and realizes that his wife, who now seems an unrecognizable and even unknown woman to him, has her own needs:

> Then, from the depths of memory, the image of Naomi as I'd first met her in the Diamond Cafe came back to me dimly. She'd been much more appealing in those days than she was now. Ingenuous and naive, shy and melancholy, she bore no resemblance to this rough, insolent woman. I'd fallen in love with her then, and the momentum had carried me to this day; but now I saw what an obnoxious person she'd become in the meantime. (Tanizaki, 1985, p. 102)

Mr. Joji is, of course, a figment of Junichiro Tanizaki's imagination, but similar problems arise in our lives more often than we think. Such cases occur whenever one partner of a couple clings to an image of the other partner as he or she was years before. A growing disappointment sets in: the other person isn't the way he or she should be—or rather, was in the past. The different perceptions become the starting point of a deviation-amplifying process. Differences between the partners are amplified, and both gradually adopt rigid positions. What starts as minor tension soon develops into the mutual incomprehension that can lead to open conflict.

The difference between a present representation and a past one is similar to the difference discussed in Chapter 4, involving the therapeutic team and clients. In the early seventies, the Milan group clung to the systemic hypothesis formulated in the first session (synchronic vision), but later came to prefer a co-evolutionary approach (diachronic vision). Thinking and emotions can often become polarized in human (and therapy) relationships, as if a few frames had been chosen from the film of our lives rather than countless other frames we could have chosen.

The case of the Valeri couple illustrates quite well this process. Their life had lately been dominated by continuous flashbacks that returned them repeatedly to a single frame from the film of their past. Mrs. Valeri had been unfaithful to her husband about ten years previously and had been submissive with him ever since to avoid his repeated accusations. But the meeker she became, the more he accused her: "You can never cancel out what you've done!" Thus, Mrs. Valeri's guilt lived on in the family, perpetuating itself with no hope of reprieve.

Divergent perceptions of time can produce many other kinds of discomfort. The Rossis had made an excellent start as a couple, but had taken to arguing and seemed to be becoming increasingly intolerant of each other. The root of the problem was clear right from the start: Mrs. Rossi was a quick, wide-awake woman who made sudden, unexpected movements, while her husband was placid, slow, and static. Only a few exchanges were needed for it to be evident that Mrs. Rossi was exasperated by her husband's slowness and lethargy, and reacted by becoming even more energetic and rapid. This irritated her husband, who slowed down even more. As with the "nagging" wife and "withdrawn" husband described by Watzlawick et al. (1967), Mr. Rossi would answer the question "Why are you so slow?" by saying "Because my wife drives me mad with her rushing about!" and she would say "I'm always rushing about because he drives me mad with his slowness!"

Giorgio and Beatrice came to our center because they were having problems as a couple. After five relatively peaceful years of marriage, Beatrice's life-style had suddenly changed shortly after the birth of their daughter. Virtually overnight, she had changed from a submissive woman — a perfect housewife — into a socially active woman; moreover, she had found herself a job. In brief, she had started to be independent of her husband. His reaction had been disastrous: first he had found another woman, but when his wife had answered him in kind by finding another man, he had gone to pieces and fallen into deep depression. This had been the start of a stormy relationship, kind of *via crucis* for the couple, with both husband and wife going for individual therapy. Two years later, Beatrice had given birth to a second daughter and had successfully completed her therapy. Giorgio, instead, went on with his therapy, eventually reaching his seventh year of analysis with no result to show for it. His analyst had eventually suggested couple therapy.

The heart of the problem — Beatrice's newfound freedom after years of submissiveness — was evident right from the start. The therapist redefined this as the "First War of Independence,"[1] which had alienated the couple, with Beatrice now projected towards the future and her husband tormented because he couldn't accept her as she was, insisting that she should be as she used to be. Both were imprisoned by their divergent views of time: the wife could not understand her husband's stubbornness, and he could not understand the now irreversible change that had taken place in his wife. Able neither to separate nor remain together "as before," the couple no longer shared the same temporal horizon: he lived in the past; she lived in the future. As a result, they had been deaf to each other's views for years. Giorgio seems to be very similar to Tanizaki's Mr. Joji.

The problem with the Amendolas, a childless upper-middle class couple, was the husband's growing disinterest in his wife. During the first interview, the therapist discovered that Mr. Amendola attributed his boredom to his wife's age. "My ideal of beauty is the 20-year-old girl I once knew. I can't desire my wife anymore because she isn't the woman she once was."[2]

This is similar to our previous case, where the husband had clung to an image of his wife as a perfect housewife (a mother substitute, many psychotherapists would say). Here, the husband blamed his wife for changing physically. Both husbands were unable to associate their real wives with the ideal wives they desired (remembered) so much. A husband and wife usually live, change, and age together; they live together in the same time. When questioned, they are likely to say that neither sees the same signs of aging in the other that both see in other people. They are like trains traveling side by side at the same speed: two passengers looking at each other from opposite carriage windows, each seeing the other immobile. But if their "speeds" are different and differences gradually increase over the years, they may lose interest in each other, conflict is likely to break out, and uncontrollable hostility may develop.[3] All this happens because the couple fails to develop in tandem. When seen in this way, Mr.

---

[1] Italy reached the status of a nation in the nineteenth century, through three wars of independence. We often see cases like these in which couples find it difficult to adapt to new cultural models of the couple. Many men still seem unable to accept changes in sex roles, i.e., women's emancipation.

[2] Emotions like those of Mr. Amendola can trigger a potentially dangerous process in which the couple becomes estranged and pressure is exerted on the children.

[3] A couple in crisis eventually ends up talking either to a lawyer to arrange a separation, or to a therapist in an attempt to resume traveling together "in the same compartment."

Amendola's statement is only superficially incongruous: "I'm just turned 40, and now I find myself married to a woman who's already 40!"[4]

Disharmony Between Objective and Subjective Times in Families

Mauro Viale, a 15-year-old boy, had been having behavioral and adaptation problems for more than a year. His uncontrollable rebelliousness was directed mainly at his father. A series of questions clarified matters. Probably without realizing it, his father had decided that his son should start behaving like an adult as soon as he was 14. Mauro suddenly found, in the space of a day, that his behavior was being interpreted in a new and quite inexplicable way: what had always been all right in the past had now suddenly become "infantile." He had reacted by becoming even more "infantile," and also vindictive. He was punished for it, and a situation of mutual intolerance developed.

The case of the Pesentis, a well-off business family with four children, living in Northern Italy, was presented in a supervision group by a hospital psychiatrist. When the children had come of age, the parents had decided to divide half the family fortune among them. However, the parents felt that Mario, 20, had not yet given sufficient proof of seriousness and self-control, so they decided to put his share aside until he showed sufficient maturity and judgment. In the family meeting when this decision was announced to the children, Mario had become angry, refusing to accept his parents' "diagnosis" and stating that he was as able to manage his share of the fortune as the other children were. His rage was regarded by the parents, as well as by the other siblings, as proof that he really *was* immature and irresponsible, and they insisted that he was not trustworthy enough to inherit his share yet. Mario had become increasingly violent, the police had been called, and he had been taken to the hospital.

The examining psychiatrist diagnosed a dissociative disorder and had Mario involuntarily admitted to the hospital. Mario soon became a model patient and was sent home after a brief period of hospitalization. However, the symmetrical escalation that had put him in the hospital in the first place soon reappeared, the police were called again, and he was taken back to the hospital. Mario returned to hospital many times over the next five years. Eventually, he began to lose interest in battling with his family

---

[4]We have reported two cases in which the husband cannot accept changes in the wife; naturally, our case records contain just as many examples of wives who refuse to accept their husbands as they are and continually compare them with the husbands they ought to be.

and began to adapt to his status as a chronic psychiatric patient, i.e., he ended up accepting the label of madness.

Looking at how this case developed, we see that the initial "kick" came when his parents and siblings told Mario he was immature and was not developing according to their expectations. Understandably, Mario's disagreement widened the rift between him and the other children, who had come to seem even more mature and responsible thanks to Mario's behavior. This escalation had made outside intervention necessary. Both the police and the psychiatrist had openly sided with the family by saying Mario was mad rather than immature. For his part, Mario had soon calmed down once outside the family home, and had quickly been discharged from the hospital.

One wonders what would have happened if the psychiatrist's stance had been different, if he had viewed matters more positively than the family itself, and most importantly, if he had been more cautious in his diagnosis, bearing in mind that the first episode could have been a straightforward (though violent) family conflict that might have resolved itself differently if he had bided his time and remained neutral. In terms of the recent research on "expressed emotion" (Leff & Vaughn, 1985), we could say that the psychiatrist failed to reduce expressed emotion and thereby to resolve the conflict in the family; indeed, he ended up heightening emotion and increasing conflict.

THERAPIST'S TIME

The Context of the Session

A consultation or therapy session can be held with or without the aid of colleagues behind a one-way mirror. Many different schools of therapy use the former method, including our center in Milan.

Our sessions are generally held in a room where the therapist/consultant[5] or therapists/consultants are present with the family. The therapy room is separated from the observation room, where the rest of the team operates, by a one-way mirror. Everything that goes on in the therapy room is recorded on video. The therapy team meets at the start of the

---

[5]Beginning with this chapter, we should consistently connect the word "consultation" to the word "therapy," but for brevity we will use the word "therapy" more frequently. Moreover, we shall use the word "therapist" or "consultant" when referring to the person actually in the therapy/consultation room, although strictly speaking all members of the team are therapists/consultants, not just the one who interacts directly with the clients.

session (pre-session) to discuss the synopsis of previous sessions, or if it is a first meeting, to discuss the preliminary information about the clients logged in the phone register. During the session proper, conversation between the therapist and family can be stopped at any moment by the therapist or the team. When this happens, the therapist leaves the therapy room to consult with the team.[6]

There are usually one or two brief interruptions during a session. At the end, there is a rather long interval with the family waiting, while the team, in the observation room, exchanges comments, ideas, feelings, and information that cohere in increasingly complex hypotheses, to produce a "systemic hypothesis" about the meaning system that includes the team as well as the clients themselves. This hypothesis forms the basis of an intervention—the "final intervention"—communicated as the conclusion to the session when the therapist returns to the therapy room. The final intervention may simply be an appointment for the next session, or a statement, an expression of doubt, a reframing, or a story about what happened during the session. Prescriptions and rituals may be given, too.

Obviously, the session is held in the here and now, in the present, but the temporal horizon of the therapist's and team's conversation is much wider. The pre-session, especially, gives the therapists information about the past, which may be the past of the family alone (in a first session) or the past of the therapy system (previous sessions). When the therapist enters the therapy room, he/she and the clients will engage in what we earlier called "face-to-face interaction," during which actions, meanings, and times are coordinated.

We could say that the most important task for a therapist is to favor the engagement and the development of a positive trusting relationship with the clients. The coordination of emotion, meaning, and the individual times among the actors of the therapy system has been aptly compared to a dance—a "therapeutic dance," we could say—unique for each case. Sometimes events occur rapidly, sometimes more sluggishly. Each therapist in time develops his or her own "dancing" style, a range of possible movements and responses.

It is useful for the therapist to leave the "dance" now and again to view the client relationship with a certain detachment. One of the authors (Luigi Boscolo) has developed his own ritual to mark this shift from involvement to detachment. When he enters his own subjective time to analyze interaction between clients and himself, he withdraws from the external conversation and starts his own interior conversation. During

---

[6]See *Paradox and Counterparadox* (Selvini Palazzoli et al., 1978), pp. 21–22.

these brief periods, the clients usually are unaware that the therapist has withdrawn behind an imaginary one-way mirror, barely listening to what they say as he adopts the stance of an observer of both himself and the therapist-client system. Of course, his detachment can only be partial: he can never achieve the detachment of the colleagues behind the mirror. Nonetheless, he attempts to hypothesize not only about the observed system, but also about the observing system: for example, he questions the emotions and thoughts the clients are producing in him and vice versa.[7]

Timing

It is important that the therapist has the sensitivity to detect and eventually respond to certain themes at particular moments in the session if a climate of trust and mutual understanding is to develop. If the times of the therapy system are not coordinated, it may prove difficult to develop a fruitful relationship with the client. Unlike English, Italian has no corresponding verb for the noun "time," so even in Italian we use the English word "timing" to describe this kind of sensitivity. The therapist may too quickly broaden the temporal horizon to include past and future, or miss certain temporal sequences in the conversation, with the result that the clients dance differently or stop the dance altogether. Let us look at an example.

A family of three—mother, father, and only child, a son—came to our center for help with behavioral problems in the son. After a brief survey of the present situation of the small family nucleus, the focus suddenly shifted to its relationship with the extended family, especially the grandparents. However, the conversation soon came to a standstill, and the parents began repeating the same answers to the therapist's questions in an almost stereotyped way, with barely concealed irritation. The therapist also began to show visible signs of uneasiness, and subsequently decided to interrupt the session to seek the aid of his colleagues behind the mirror.

When questioned, the therapist said that he felt he had been treading water, his mind a blank, that there was resistance in the family he could neither understand nor explain. During the subsequent discussion, the team advanced the hypothesis that the therapist had moved the conversation too early into the minefield of the nuclear family's relationship with its extended families. It seemed likely that the parents, who had come to

---

[7]This is comparable to transference and countertransference analysis in psychoanalysis. However, an analyst has a more passive role, so his or her task is easier.

the center to solve a simple problem regarding their son, had reacted negatively to the therapist's attempt to involve the grandparents in the problem and were alarmed that the therapist might start looking for skeletons in the family closet. There are often conflicts and secrets in relations between nuclear families and extended families. It is better not to investigate these in the first session until the right atmosphere has been established.

In this particular case, the therapist had allowed himself to be carried away by his desire to know things the family was not yet prepared to reveal. The team agreed that the therapist had not waited until the possibility of discussing these themes had emerged naturally from the dialogue itself or until the family had established a relationship of trust with the therapist. In other words, the therapist had made a mistake in timing. It is our experience that clients will forgive such mistakes and other errors in the handling of the session if they already trust the therapist.

The team discussion broke the impasse by shifting attention away from the family's origins back to the present. As soon as the therapist returned to the session with this new attitude, the parents responded by taking up the conversation again.

Due regard for timing is useful not only in developing the therapy and consultation relationship, but also in choosing the right moment to make certain interventions and in deciding the frequency of sessions and when to terminate therapy. Let us look at some examples.

A 25-five-year-old man came to our center complaining of depression. At the end of the first exploratory meeting, the therapist, Luigi Boscolo, advised the client to have individual therapy at the rate of one session a week. The client agreed, but after a couple of months his symptoms began to worsen. At a certain point he exploded with frustration, "I feel worse and worse because one session a week isn't enough for me!" He laid on his complaint even thicker by mentioning a young aunt and a friend who were having therapy two or three times a week, although they seemed less depressed than he was. The therapist objected that the decision to have one session a week was based on his evaluation of the case and that this was the ideal choice in the circumstances—otherwise, he would have opted for more sessions. He also noted that his timing was out of step with his client's, so that they found themselves at an impasse. If the therapist had agreed to the client's demands, he would have gone against his own clinical judgment, as well as what he perceived his client's needs to be.

In order to break the impasse and satisfy both their needs, the therapist suggested that two other "sessions" be added to the weekly session with the therapist. The client should go into a room on his own at home, imagine he was talking to the therapist and, for exactly 50 minutes, write down in a notepad everything that came into his head, omitting and censoring nothing. He should then bring his notes to the next session. The following week he came along with a thick pile of notes, which he gave to the therapist. The therapist immediately gave them back and asked him to read aloud what he had written down. The client read for the whole 50 minutes with no interruption from the therapist. In the next session, as one could expect, the client brought only a few pages, "My mind was empty, only these things occurred to me!"

The client's mood improved and not long after he stopped the "phantom"—or better, the "self-help"—sessions, because "Nothing comes to my mind." He stopped talking about needing more than one session a week because he had started feeling better. The improvement possibly occurred because he felt that his need to have more sessions had been accepted. He had also stopped writing down and reading aloud his accounts of his "sessions" at home, possibly because he realized that this prevented him from having a dialogue with the therapist. Paradoxically, the more sessions he had, the fewer sessions he had.

One important aspect of timing, as we have seen, is knowing when to terminate therapy. Often, as we said in Chapter 4, therapy is terminated when the client system seems to have reached a turning point and is undergoing significant change that seems likely to continue until the problem referred for therapy has been solved. We think, in many such cases, that if therapy were continued the therapist would become part of the solution, i.e., would become an essential element in the system, with the risk that therapy would go on forever. This may be considered a mistake in timing.

THERAPIST TIME AND TEAM TIME

When therapists work in teams, as we do, the therapist's time and the client's time become linked to the observing team's time. The interaction of these times is rather complex.

We have already seen that the therapist alternates phases of involvement and brief periods of detachment during dialogue with clients. When therapy is done with a team, the functions of involvement and detachment are more clearly separated. From the observing team's point of view, there are moments for observation and moments for dialogue, i.e., interaction with the therapist. Most importantly, the team can observe the coordination of the relationship, the "dance," from the outside. The team observes not only the coordination of the times and temporal horizons of the therapist and client but also the rhythms of their interaction. Therapist and team come together when the therapist interrupts the conversation with the clients and enters the observation room to start a conversation with the team. Interrupting the session, metaphorically expressed as "stopping the tape," takes the therapist into the different time of the team, which was not in direct interaction with the client's time.

In this way, the therapist participates in two different conversational domains, each with its own physical location and its own special time. He/she is the go-between and thus may transfer emotions and meanings from the clients to the team and vice versa. He/she is an active, not a passive agent. It is the therapist who decides which meanings to filter and convey to the clients. Sometimes, as we shall see, he/she may choose to present team views to the clients that differ from her or his own; consequently, although only a part of the therapy circuit, the therapist is ultimately responsible for the choices that are made and so occupies a central position.

The team's job is to analyze the connections between the three subsystems. It may happen, for example, that the therapist (especially if a trainee) is not yet sufficiently expert or confident and so depends too much on the team and relates more closely to colleagues than to clients; or the opposite may happen, especially when the therapist is very experienced. The team may also help the therapist to discover his or her own time: to think about how sensitively he/she is harmonizing with other times, and perhaps how to use his/her own idiosyncrasies to relate to clients. Naturally, a therapist-team "dance" develops alongside the therapist-client "dance," so the relationship between therapist and team may also become disharmonious, with an overassertive team or an overreactive or passive therapist.

One variation on this working method is the use of a "reflecting team" (Andersen, 1987), in which the therapist remains with the clients and asks for a "reflection" from the team, rather than shuttling back and forth between clients and team. A two-way mirror is used so that the therapist-client system can observe the team discussion. This creates a mutual process of observation and reflection, and communication becomes totally circular without the barrier that separates the team from the clients.

Two clinical examples will illustrate the team's importance in redefining the temporal frame of sessions. The first was a family of three in which the father, in his fifties, had recently developed persecutory delusions accompanied by auditory hallucinations. During the session, the therapist could not get things moving because the discussion kept on returning to the paranoid fantasies of the father ("My neighbors talk about me behind my back; they all say I'm a fag!") and the attempts of his wife and daughter to convince him that he was being irrational. The therapist seemed enmeshed in the family's slow, boring rhythm, as if he had been sucked into a temporal perspective with no future. Suddenly, he left the therapy room and complained to the team that he felt he was at an impasse. He also advanced the hypothesis that the father was suffering from an "organic psychosis."

The team's ideas were very different, however. As the discussion gradually developed, the therapist slowly left the arrested time of the therapy room and entered the time of the observation room. New lines of inquiry opened up to him and when he returned to the therapy room a faster rhythm and a broader temporal horizon emerged. He then succeeded in unblocking the situation.

The second case was a family of four in which the 22-year-old daughter, Annamaria, the second child, had recently become anorexic. During the third session, the mother gave the team behind the mirror the impression that she had successfully drawn the attention of the therapist to a period in her life when there had been a serious break in her relationship with her mother-in-law and her husband had given her no support. The other members of the family transmitted subtle messages of disinterest, and then boredom, but the therapist did not notice them. On the few occasions when the therapist did make contact with the other family members, they no longer seemed to be as collaborative as they had been in previous sessions. Either the mother took over the narrative from the therapist or the therapist encouraged her to do it because he found her more collaborative. Called out by his colleagues, he was told what the situation looked like from behind the mirror. Two hypotheses had been formulated: that they were looking at something none of them understood, or that the therapist was fixed in the mother's temporal perspective and was excluding the other members of the family. The second hypothesis was eventually adopted. On returning to the therapy room, the therapist actively directed his attention to the other members of the family and began to interrupt the mother as often as was necessary to regain everyone's attention and participation.

These two examples show, then, that one of the functions of the team behind the mirror is to "correct" the therapist when he/she fails to coordinate with clients (which can lead to interruptions, slowing down, and blockages in the flow of time).

The Team as the Future: The Hayworth Family

The difference of perspective between the therapist and the observation team is like the difference between a footballer actually playing the game and a spectator watching from the stands. The attention of the player is focused on the moment the action is happening in, which perforce includes oneself, the ball and nearby players in a limited area of the field. As an observer, the spectator can see the whole field. He/she is at distance, and perhaps loses some of the detail and physical impact of the game, but can have a synchronic vision of the two teams as a whole, watch the movements of the players and the referee, and mentally imagine, i.e., anticipate, all possible strategies.

The spectator's role gives one a future perspective, while the player's role, because it implies active involvement, gives a present perspective. The spectator is in a better position to predict which area of the field will be free and which covered, which moves will be successful, and so on. This is why spectators often lose their tempers with players because they don't send the ball where they expect them to, forgetting that their point of view of the game is different and that their temporal horizons are much wider than those of the players.

This analogy illustrates very well what happens in therapy. We might say that the therapy team represents the future of the therapy system, the clients its past, and the therapist its present. Unlike the therapy room, the temporal horizon of the observation room is one of exploring possibilities and foreseeing different directions. The team may help the therapist by transmitting this openness of horizon. Let us look at a case study illustrating the pragmatic implications of this idea.

A mother came to therapy with her daughter to discuss the problem of the son, who knew nothing about their visit. The Hayworth family had had a rather unusual history. The mother, Angela, a woman who liked to see herself as a nonconformist, had run away to London from Milan at an early age and had met Charles Hayworth, a fascinating pilot from the Caribbean. She had married him against the wishes of her parents, who regarded the marriage as "rash." Two children were born, Vera and Sandy. The marriage had been an unhappy one: Charles, a reckless man, had had various affairs with other women, until his death in a plane crash several years ago. Angela had then come back to Milan.

Sandy, the designated patient, was now a 24-year-old who, according to his mother and sister, was incapable of finding an aim in life or making definite choices. The sister, an apparently solid, level-headed woman, had found work as a teacher and now lived on her own. Sandy still lived at home with his mother and had become something of a playboy, indulging in affairs with married 40-year-olds, cultivating a wide range of interests and only pretending — according to the mother — to look for work. For all these reasons, the mother and daughter said they were very worried about his future.

At the therapist's request, Sandy came to the next session. He seemed a charming, intelligent young man, well aware that he was the center of attention and his mother's favorite, rather than Vera, who remained on the fringes of her mother's life, regretful and seemingly irritated. Questioning revealed that Sandy, who was like his father, had also inherited his father's role in the family—being creative and reckless—and thoroughly enjoyed living up to expectations. Vera, on the other hand, seemed to have adopted the serious, pragmatic role represented in the family by her maternal aunt, who had raised her during much of her childhood. The team quickly developed an hypothesis: Vera and Sandy had literally inherited parts—as if they were in a Pirandello play—and, with the passing of time, were becoming increasingly committed to their roles. The mother, showing a great deal of worry, occupied the center of the stage, from where she kept a close eye on her son, a substitute for her dead husband. In the final intervention, we decided to emphasize the character differences of the two siblings, in the hope that a sort of osmotic exchange of personal characteristics might occur. Vera could give seriousness and pragmatism to Sandy, and Sandy could give creativity and frivolity to Vera. The two siblings reacted nonverbally with surprise and curiosity. They looked at each other and smiled, giving the impression that they liked the idea of an exchange. The mother, predictably enough, seemed far from pleased.

In the third session the siblings showed a different relationship from before. They were smiling, relaxed, and occasionally exchanged friendly glances. Vera no longer sat stiffly erect and had stopped hiding behind professional jargon, while Sandy had given up his affected speech and snobbish attitude. The mother still seemed anxious and tense, driven to externalize her worries. And in fact, it was her words and emotions that captured the attention of the therapist, who seemed unable to attach due importance to how much the two siblings had changed; indeed, she was seemingly unaware that Sandy was saying how he had started working in a photography studio and was thinking of devoting himself seriously to work.

As the session continued, the team became increasingly satisfied with the way *events* were going, but alarmed at the way the session was developing. In fact, there seemed a risk that the changes observed by the team were overlooked by the therapist. She seemed rooted in the ideas and emotions of the previous sessions. Instead of emphasizing and exploring the changes that had happened, she seemed passively concerned with Mrs. Hayworth's residual fears and barely took account of the evident changes in the siblings, who at first seemed puzzled, then somber, as if disappointed at the therapist's failure to acknowledge the changes that had taken place. Since the therapist seemed to have married the no-change hypothesis, she was called out.

The therapist, entering the observation room, appeared dejected and, before sitting down, stated, "I don't know what to do! There's no change, nothing! I think things are getting worse." She was convinced that the family not only was stuck but looked worse than before. Of all the elements that had emerged during the session, she appeared to have selected those that pointed to immobility. She seemed to have been more influenced by the mother's emotions and worries than by the almost cheerful expressions of the siblings who, as time went by, gradually changed their mood. In short, she got stuck with the image of the family that had been created in the previous session. Intense discussion was needed to overcome her skepticism and help her recognize that the changes observed at the beginning of the session were important and had to be emphasized. She accepted the opinion of the team and reentered the therapy room, giving the following conclusion to the family.

> THERAPIST: We've seen that there's been change in your situation, and we think it's now irreversible. In their own ways, Vera and Sandy are trying to build their own lives. Their mother will have to accept this natural development, which will lead not to loneliness, but to a more united family better able to support her, if she needs it. Since we no longer see psychological or psychiatric problems in your situation, we think it's best to terminate therapy now.

Predictably enough, the two children seemed relieved, but it was Mrs. Hayworth who came out with the most surprising statement. With a thoughtful expression, she declared: "Yes, I expected we would finish today." All three seemed in tune with the therapist, with the idea of terminating therapy.

To sum up: it was the team behind the mirror that, from the beginning of the session, had seen a different family. The therapist had remained with her own initial vision of the family, anchored in the past, failing to consider the changes that had happened. The therapist's pessimistic map had gradually influenced the family, inducing doubts whether change had actually occurred. The team had offered the therapist a different view, a future she had been unable to see. One could say that the team had "cured" the therapist of a potentially serious perceptual blindness: the family could have ended up sharing her static, pessimistic vision of the situation.

DEALING WITH TIME
IN THE SESSION

Especially in first sessions, we think it best to adopt a "centrifugal" approach to time and space. As regards time, this means starting with the present, then extending discussion to the past, and finally moving towards the future so that the whole temporal horizon is covered.[8] Therefore, the therapist's initial questions concentrate on the here and now—the symptoms presented, the people involved with them in the present (family members, teachers, employers, and especially, the professionals who have diagnosed and sent the case to us). Then, gradually, interest shifts to the period when symptoms were first noticed and described, to the action taken to modify or eliminate them, and then to analysis of relationships, ideas and meanings developed over time, especially in the situations that have led to the adoption of present solutions rather than others.

As the session progresses, attention finally shifts to the future: from exploration of existing perspectives to extensive use of hypothetical questions about the future, which indirectly convey new perspectives and possible solutions. In this way, it is the clients who discover or invent new meanings and make their choices.

Of course, this is only a formula, which can certainly be ignored if the situation requires it. Therapy is an art as well as a science. It is important that the therapist or consultant is sensitive to the signals given by people, especially nonverbal messages like emotional tone (expressions of boredom, attention, interest, etc.) and subtle changes of mood. The therapist's own emotional signals and the extent of client involvement are also important in assessing and understanding the meanings, ideas, and patterns that emerge during therapy.

Let us now look at an example of how we use time in conducting a session. We have chosen this case because it illustrates very well the importance of temporal perspectives in sessions and stresses the centrality of time in the analysis of relationships.

In the summer of 1990, one of the authors (Luigi Boscolo) held a consultation in an Australian psychiatric hospital as part of a teaching seminar. Those attending were Jim, a 24-year-old student inpatient of the hospital, his 48-year-old mother, and Jim's psychiatrist, a member of the hospital's staff who had requested the consultation. A group of other staff members watched the session from another room on a closed-circuit TV link.

The consultant had been told before the session that Jim had been transferred there from a psychiatric hospital in another town a month before, with a diagnosis of "schizophreniform psychosis." He had been admitted urgently to the other hospital with florid psychotic symptoms,

---

[8]We do not intend to deal with centrifugality in space here. Suffice it to say that we usually begin with questions about the narrower system (designated patient and nuclear family), and then move on to the extended family and the various social agencies the family and its members interact with. We also do this with patients undergoing individual therapy.

visual and auditory hallucinations, delusions and inconsistent behavior. His psychotic episode had started while he was traveling on his own.

The crisis had been overcome by the time the consultation started. Jim seemed relatively calm, had no really noticeable symptoms, and cooperated with the doctors and hospital staff. However, he was still on neuroleptics and seemed unable to resume normal relationships.

The family's story was as follows. The father had died in a road accident when Jim was only four. The wife had been left with Jim and his brother John, two years younger. Two years later, his mother had married Peter (a farmhand, like her first husband) and had had a third child by him called Sam, seven years younger than Jim.

Let us look first at the major theme that emerged before describing the session in detail. It appeared that, a year before, Jim had begun to show signs of restlessness, disorientation and social isolation. Two years before he had taken LSD for a while, experiencing "good trips," but after that period he had not used any drugs. Two months before the session, he had traveled alone to the remotest areas of Australia, but the onset of symptoms had cut his journey short. The psychotic break seemed to have revolutionized his perceptions of himself and of his past and present time. It was as if he had had a "psychotic insight" which had replaced his memories with a new story that neutralized his fears of competition and growing up. His mother told a quite different story about his life.

The consultation began with an inquiry on the present situation (present time) and relationships between client's system and experts' system.

CONSULTANT: Dr. Brown, who is here now, has asked me to do a consultation, to assess the situation. A group of colleagues from this clinic are observing the session in another room. (to Jim) How is the situation now?

JIM: (smiling) Better than when therapy began.

CONSULTANT: What brought you into therapy?

JIM: I've got a schizophreniform psychosis! (turning to his psychiatrist) Right?

CONSULTANT: Who first told you . . .

JIM: (looking at his mother and smiling) It was the doctor in the other hospital, right?

MOTHER: Yes, it was her.

JIM: I don't think I was diagnosed correctly before. But now, yes. I'm a lot better, too, the hallucinations and voices have gone away.

CONSULTANT: You seemed very pleased when you said you had a schizophreniform psychosis. . . .

JIM: (*laughing*) Yes. Every time I see a doctor, I feel better.

CONSULTANT: So you came to talk to me willingly. . . .

JIM: Yes. I think this is a great chance for me to get qualified professional help.

As he made this final statement, Jim sank back into his chair with a serene smile. Obviously, the initial hypothesis attempted to connect Jim's strange, inconsistent happiness at the idea of having a serious psychiatric illness with the context, especially with his mother who had accompanied him.

CONSULTANT: So you like talking to doctors. . . .

JIM: Yes, yes. I'm now hoping to be discharged from hospital and start outpatient therapy.

CONSULTANT: You said you feel much better now. Do you feel normal?

JIM: Oh, no! I feel better because I'm on medication, but I don't feel normal.

CONSULTANT: What's the difference between feeling better and feeling normal?

JIM: (*puzzled, after a pause*) Not much. I don't feel self-confident yet. I see that others do feel self-confident.

Here, Jim seems to be clinging to the illness that plays a major role in his present life. The consultant introduces the possibility of "normality" as a first step towards challenging the label of illness and suggesting other possible explanations.

CONSULTANT: Who inspires most trust in your family?

JIM: Sam, John, Peter, and then my mother. . . . (*looking at his mother*) I'm more like my father; I've got his ways . . . but she doesn't agree with me.
(*The mother smiles.*)

CONSULTANT: But do you remember your father?

JIM: No. My grandparents and my father's sisters told me I'm like him.

CONSULTANT: Did you feel pleased when they told you?

JIM: Yes, a lot.

Here, Jim gives his mother a low trust rating and introduces his dead father, whom he is pleased to be like, into the discourse. It may be that he is still attached to his old family and has not yet finished mourning for his father. Attention now shifts to the distant past.

CONSULTANT: When did you start thinking you didn't feel well?

JIM: I guessed there was something not quite right in me when I was six . . .

CONSULTANT: What?

JIM: I felt alone, lost . . . I think I was mentally ill. . . .

CONSULTANT: (*to the mother*) Do you remember that time?

MOTHER: Yes, but he felt unwell because he was physically ill, first with rheumatic fever, and then with osteochondritis in his knees. He had several operations on his knees after he was 16. He had to give up skiing and other sports.

In terms of Bowen's "let the calendar speak" philosophy, we could say that Jim dates his disturbances from the time when his mother remarried and became pregnant shortly afterwards with Sam. It should also be noted that John was dyslexic and needed special care — all events that might have suddenly deprived Jim of his mother's support. This is merely a hypothesis, limited to a particular transaction, and obviously does not claim to account for the total situation. Other hypotheses will emerge and be explored as the consultation progresses. Jim's replies sometimes smack of the prolonged contact he has had with psychotherapists, as well as books he has read, rather than of his own ideas or feelings. And yet, he had never been treated by psychotherapists in the past, so he is very probably the author of his own story.

JIM: I think the knee problem was caused by the psychosis. . . .

CONSULTANT: What do you know about psychosis?

JIM: Huh!

CONSULTANT: Try to say . . .

JIM: (*questioningly*) A chemical imbalance in the brain? A brain disorder?

CONSULTANT: Where did you hear these things?

JIM: In the other hospital. The doctor told me.

(*The mother nods in agreement.*)

It is interesting that Jim attributes even physical knee illness (osteochondritis) to brain dysfunction. The psychiatric diagnosis seems to illuminate his whole life, both present and past: Jim might have been anxious about his future, but now, as someone who has been labeled as sick, everything is clear to him. If he hasn't thought about a career or tried to work for an independent future, this is not his fault: his illness is to blame. Obviously, this is a dangerous belief which, if shared by family and doctors, could quickly lead to chronic disorder, i.e., to the "career" of a patient suffering from serious mental illness.

CONSULTANT: You said that when you were six you felt mentally ill, but your mother has said you were physically ill. . . .

JIM: It's difficult for a child of six to explain to his mother that he's got a psychosis, especially if he doesn't really know what it is.

CONSULTANT: How did the psychosis reveal itself?

JIM: Oh, first there was the trauma of my father's death, and then my mother got married again.

CONSULTANT: (*to the mother*) How did the children adapt to the new marriage?

MOTHER: I thought they had adapted completely. Peter has accepted them very well. He treats all three the same, although I think that deep down he may prefer Sam, because he's his own child.

CONSULTANT: When Jim says he was psychotic at the age of six, did you have the impression he was ill, that he was different from the other children?

MOTHER: No. I wouldn't say so.

CONSULTANT: What did his teachers say?

MOTHER: That he was like all the others. He could have got better results, but there was nothing wrong with his brain.

CONSULTANT: (*to Jim*) It seems no one realized you weren't well.

JIM: No, because I managed to hide my problems. When I realized at school that I had problems with literary subjects, with logic, with abstraction, I took up pottery. I enrolled in a pottery course.

CONSULTANT: Did you feel different from your brothers?

JIM: Yes. John was very attached to mother because of his problems at school, but he got over them with a big effort. He's very self-confident and plays a lot of sports. Sam's very intelligent and he's Peter's favorite. He's doing really well at school.

Two different stories are clearly emerging. The mother's disagreement is total. The two pasts that emerge from the narrative are disharmonious, discordant, two competing stories that diverge still further as the consultant continues his investigation. It should be added that Jim seems to place Peter and Sam in one camp and John and his mother in another, like two couples. He remains isolated between the two. He probably felt important before his mother's remarriage, but then his brothers and stepfather threatened his position and made it difficult for him to integrate into the new family. This may have been the result of his paternal aunts and grandparents choosing him as his father's spiritual heir, which made it difficult for him to mourn properly for his lost father. If to this we add the serious knee illness that prevented him from skiing and playing other sports, and so engaging in healthy competition with his brothers and friends, it seems likely that Jim was plagued by doubts, uncertainties, and anxiety about his future, and that this led to the crisis from which he emerged with a new story to justify his arrested development.

JIM: After the death of my father, I felt I had a great responsibility on my shoulders.

CONSULTANT: Who put that responsibility on your shoulders?

JIM: (looking at his mother) First her, and then Peter.

CONSULTANT: Because you were the oldest child?

JIM: I think so, but I wasn't very aware then, I felt under pressure.

CONSULTANT: So you assumed the role of son, husband and father.

JIM: A bit.

CONSULTANT: Did you feel your mother needed comfort, support?

JIM: Oh yes, so much, so much support!

CONSULTANT: (to the mother) Do you recognize yourself from this description?

MOTHER: No. Jim's describing the life of a child I never knew.

CONSULTANT: (to Jim) Might it be that you saw your mother on her own and so began to feel like her husband?

JIM: Yes. It could be, maybe . . . psychiatrically.

CONSULTANT: What does that mean?

JIM: (smiling) It's very difficult to explain, it's . . .

At this point, the therapist begins to introduce other possible stories as alternatives to Jim's and, implicitly, the mother's, which seems to oppose everything Jim says. It is striking that she seems totally unaffected by Jim's messages about uncertainties and suffering in the past. They seem a symmetrical couple. The idea that Jim wants to get back at her, make her feel guilty, seems increasingly plausible. As time passes, his attitude towards her becomes increasingly accusatory, and she in turn increasingly disagrees with and detaches herself from him.

It is interesting that Jim, faced with the idea that he had to play the role of son and husband after the death of his father, replies "yes . . .

maybe . . . psychiatrically." He does not seem to acknowledge that he has broken a taboo.

CONSULTANT: From the way you speak, it seems you don't belong to this family. Have Sam and John felt this way?

JIM: No. They had more attention from Peter and her. I felt isolated.

CONSULTANT: If I asked your mother if she realized that you felt so alone in the past, what would she say?

JIM: I don't know, ask her. I think she'd say no.

CONSULTANT: Can you ask her?

JIM: (*to the mother*) How do you think I've felt all these years?

MOTHER: I don't think you've been all that unhappy.

JIM: Don't you think there's been a death in the family?

MOTHER: Yes.

JIM: (*excitedly, in a single breath*) And that it traumatized me? Don't you think a four-year-old child who's lost his father suffers a trauma? That the new man who enters the home isn't the best substitute for a father? And that being the eldest son, he had bigger responsibilities? . . .

MOTHER: Just because you're the eldest doesn't justify all this.

CONSULTANT: (*to the mother*) What do you think?

MOTHER: I don't agree. I never told him he was an outsider, and he never gave me any sign that he felt like one. He's describing a son I've never seen.

JIM: In addition to the situation I've just described, I had rheumatic fever, knee operations, and then schizophrenia. When will you realize I'm ill? You never seem to have caught on.

CONSULTANT: Have there been times when you've felt she understood you?

JIM: Sometimes. But she had a more maternal attitude towards my brothers. She treated me like a weak human being.

CONSULTANT: You seem very angry with her. Are you angry with Peter?

JIM: No.

CONSULTANT: With your brothers?

JIM: No.

(*The mother looks at him and smiles, as if almost amused.*)

At this point, hypothetical questions about the past are asked, which may allow alternative meanings to emerge. Moreover, the consultant openly challenges Jim's stories and beliefs. He does this now because he feels it is the right moment: Jim seems highly engaged. The consultant asks some exploratory questions. If his challenge is not accepted, he will switch, of course, to other ideas and feelings. If the challenge had come earlier in the session, before a trusting relationship had been established, it would probably have caused a breakdown in their relationship.

CONSULTANT: You said that if your father weren't dead you'd feel well, right?

JIM: Yes, yes.

CONSULTANT: I don't understand. How come so many children who've lost their fathers don't react like you. . . . Even John reacted differently. Also, you've got a mother, a stepfather and two brothers, and yet you feel alone. I'm confused.

JIM: I don't know.

CONSULTANT: At first you seemed happy, you smiled a lot, you seemed almost pleased to be ill, to be speaking to doctors. Are you looking for a father in your doctors?

JIM: Maybe.

CONSULTANT: I don't understand. I'm trying to make sense of this, but I can't. I think I'm almost going schizophrenic. . . .

JIM: (laughs loudly)

Jim has made sense of the situation. The therapist would like to also, and asks for his help. The noisy laugh—the only laughter in the whole session—seems to show that the consultant has touched on an important point. Jim, with his illness, has made sense, found a new meaning in his life, while the consultant remains confused, failing to make sense of Jim's story and even feeling that he's "going schizophrenic." The confusion-schizophrenia equation is used here as a semantic link to challenge the label of mental illness, to demedicalize the present situation and begin to attribute other possible meanings to Jim's beliefs. The diagnosis—which Jim sees as the cause of his precarious present situation and, as we shall see, the basis for a miserable future—is being questioned. The consultant takes on himself the dilemmas that emerge from the stories. Clearly, Jim sees his past in a deterministic way: his father's death was the primum movens, the trauma that led to his mother's remarriage, to changes in the organization of the family, to new alliances, new traumas. And now, because of all these traumas, he is ill.

The consultant tries to break the deterministic links that connect past, present, and future by taking the dilemmas on himself, by becoming confused and looking for new meanings. It is as if he is saying "I don't understand why you've constructed this story." It could even be said that the consultant is seeking to deconstruct his client's past so that new stories can emerge.

CONSULTANT: *(in a bewildered tone of voice)* I must make sense of this, find a meaning. . . . Can you help me?

JIM: *(laughs again)*

CONSULTANT: Maybe you're pleased because, as a schizophrenic, you can find a new father in your doctors. Who knows. . . .

JIM: *(becomes serious again)* I became ill before I was examined by doctors.

CONSULTANT: I'd like you to help me to solve my dilemma. I don't understand why you've never found what John has found.

JIM: He was younger.

CONSULTANT: So?

JIM: *(rather irritated)* You're the psychiatrist, you should be telling me . . .

CONSULTANT: Yes, I'm a psychiatrist. But I have to understand before I can help.

JIM: I don't know what to say. I've already told you why I've been traumatized since an early age!

CONSULTANT: I understand your explanation, but you must also understand my confusion. You said you felt isolated in your family, but didn't you make any friends outside your family?

JIM: Yes, but friendship isn't enough. I always felt a bit of an outsider, and that's enough to send you schizophrenic! Isn't this explanation good enough for you?

Although his certainties are now being challenged, Jim returns peremptorily to his past traumas and repeats the belief that he is schizophrenic. At this point, the consultant changes the subject both to avoid repeating himself and, most importantly, to avoid antagonizing Jim too much. He begins to ask questions about the original families, especially the mother's. Significantly, it is said that the maternal grandparents looked after the mother and the children in the brief period between the first and second marriage. Jim remembers this as a period of stability in which he got on well with the maternal grandfather. When his mother remarried, relations with the extended family virtually ceased.

CONSULTANT: So you liked being with your grandfather. He was fond of you?

JIM: Yes, I think he was fond of me.

CONSULTANT: So why didn't you decide to adopt him as a second father?

JIM: I was too confused.

CONSULTANT: If your mother hadn't remarried, could you have stayed with your grandparents?

JIM: Yes. If she hadn't remarried, I wouldn't be in the situation I'm in now.

CONSULTANT: You mean . . .

JIM: I'd be coping with life much better.

CONSULTANT: You seem to be complaining that you haven't got the right kind of mother. Would you like to change her?

JIM: (*smiling*) I'd like a refund.

MOTHER: (*bursts out laughing*)

CONSULTANT: Let's imagine you could have, and want to have a refund. How long do you think it would take?

JIM: (*avoids answering*) I feel much better now.

CONSULTANT: But if your mother was the way you wanted her now, would you change anything?

JIM: No.

CONSULTANT: Would you say you need a father now more than a mother?

JIM: Yes, certainly, a father.

This search for a father, this lasting link with a dead father, will be a central feature of post-session discussion and the final intervention. At this point, the emphasis shifts to the future.

CONSULTANT: How do you see your future?

JIM: (*shaking his head*) Not very well, I'll be a potter.

CONSULTANT: Have you got a girlfriend?

JIM: No.

CONSULTANT: Have you ever had one?

JIM: Yes, I've had a few, but never anything serious.

CONSULTANT: Have you ever had sex?

JIM: Yes, but it was nothing special.

CONSULTANT: Do you think you'll marry in the future?

JIM: Oh no, I'll never marry and have children.

CONSULTANT: Why not?

JIM: Because I'd be incapable of bringing them up.

CONSULTANT: Where do you get the idea you'd be incapable of it?

JIM: I told you, I'm going to be a potter. I'm going to live on one of the mountains near here, open a workshop on my own, make pottery.

CONSULTANT: So you've decided to live alone in a nonliving system surrounded by pottery. . . . Won't you at least have a pet? . . .

JIM: No, a girl!

CONSULTANT: So the girl will become your pet?

JIM: (*laughs*) That doesn't seem such a bad idea.

CONSULTANT: (*provocatively*) But wouldn't you prefer to be ill all your life so that they (*indicates the psychiatrist*) can look after you?

JIM: No.

CONSULTANT: You still seem to be saying that you haven't had a family, that you've been a kind of orphan, that you've become schizophrenic. But haven't you found a family in your psychiatrists and nurses, a family that can now look after you for the rest of your life?

JIM: No, no, no, I've already said what I'd like to do, I want to work with pots!

Jim envisages a grey, lonely future. The consultant goads him humorously and envisions—provocatively—the even simpler future of the totally dependent chronic sufferer. Provocation can often make possible futures seem less likely. It is important, however, that the consultant remain neutral over the choices available to the client.

At the end of the session, the theme of separation from the family emerges and produces an unexpected about-face in the tone of the conversation. The mother genuinely weeps, and this surprises Jim.

CONSULTANT: (*to the mother*) When Jim leaves the clinic, will he return home or . . .

MOTHER: (*very seriously*) Peter and I have talked about this. If Jim leaves the clinic, it'd be better if he didn't come home. He should be looked after by specialists.
(*Jim stirs a little, yawns ostentatiously and behaves as if the subject has nothing to do with him.*)

CONSULTANT: (*to the mother*) When did you start thinking it would be better to detach yourselves from Jim?

MOTHER: (*a long silence; she just manages to keep back her tears*) When he began feeling ill, we thought that . . . (*she begins weeping, then speaks without pausing*) . . . because he's very ill, he's seriously ill . . . since he's mentally ill he can't live at home now, he can't even live on his own . . . he has to be looked after . . . being a schizophrenic, mentally ill, it's better he stays in a clinic now. . . .
(*Jim watches his mother weeping; he is alert, immobile, silent; the continuous shaking of his knee which began at the start of the session has now ceased.*)

Jim seems affected, almost cheered, by his mother's genuine distress and weeping: he has succeeded at last in touching her emotions. It is probably Peter who wants to get rid of him, so that the mother finds herself in a dilemma. However, her tears are signs of a love that seemed nonexistent before. The powerful emotions now emerging may be a prelude to change.

CONSULTANT: (*to the mother, who is drying her tears*) But how was Jim before all this?
MOTHER: He was the most affectionate of them all, the one who showed most affection. . . . For me he was the easiest to bring up, until he became ill. (*She turns to Jim and smiles.*)
CONSULTANT: What does Peter think about Jim coming home?
MOTHER: Peter has had no experience with mental illness. He doesn't openly oppose it, but I think that deep down he's very doubtful.

After a brief discussion with the group in the observation room, the consultant returns and makes the following intervention.

CONSULTANT: What has struck me very much in your story is the event of Steve's death, your husband (*to the mother*) and your father (*to Jim*). I think you all forgot this man too soon, and as a result he hasn't really been mourned for properly. . . .
JIM: (*with an air of surprise and discovery*) It's true, it's true . . . I hadn't realized. Forgotten too soon . . . that's it, that's it.
(*The mother also seems affected by this, and looks self-absorbed.*)
CONSULTANT: Now I'd like to give you a very important task that has to be carried out by the old family, that is, you (*to the mother*), Jim and John. You must devote one day a week, possibly the same day of the week, to Steve. On that day, it would be best if you speak about him, tell stories about him when he was alive, get out your photos of

him. If possible, you should also visit his grave on that day. On all
the other days of the week you are forbidden to speak about Steve,
whether between yourselves or with other members of the family.
Regarding the other members of the family, before performing your
task, at dinner this evening perhaps, tell your husband and Sam that
I, as a consultant, have given you the task I've just described. I'm
sure they'll understand, and won't object. You should perform the
task at least four times, over a month that is, and then go to Paul
[the psychiatrist] and tell him what results you've obtained.
(*The mother and son seem impressed and satisfied, Jim especially.*)

The aims of this intervention—a reframing and a ritual—were as follows:

1. To bring the problem of the death of the father—according to
Jim the cause of all the subsequent suffering—into the present.

2. To reinforce this process by saying that the father has been forgotten too soon, thereby strengthening the memory of him in the present.

3. To enable the mother, Jim and John share the same drama, as
victims of the death of a husband and father who has been forgotten
quickly so that they might avoid suffering too much. It may be that
the mother had to avoid talking about her first husband in order not
to antagonize Peter. This may have hindered mourning.

4. To encourage collective emotional experience that creates cohesion and puts all the members of the family (the first family) on the
same level.

5. To enable Jim to reenter his old family and feel accepted. In our
experience, if a family member feels part of the family, accepted by
others, he can leave the family and build an independent life. If this
does not happen, the outcome may be disastrous.

Feeling accepted by the old family also encourages engagement with
the new one once mourning is over. Prescribing the ritual for the mother
and her children by her first marriage, while relegating Peter and Sam to
the role of observers, makes it possible to create a new family from the
ashes of the old one.

We had an opportunity to follow up this case. Dr. Boscolo returned to
Australia the following year, and in one of his workshops met Dr. Brown,
who reported that the consultation had had a big effect on the family,
especially on Jim. The latter had shown, after the consultation, a remark-

able change, which we would consider as a discontinuous change. The hostility towards his mother disappeared, as well as his feeling of being left out of the family. Hope for the future and new interest in people and activities became prominent. Dr. Brown emphasized that, according to his family, Jim appeared to be much better than before his crisis. The family had performed the ritual with intense emotions, which had had the effect of renewing and strengthening their affective ties. In describing to the psychiatrist their emotional experience during the ritual, Jim's mother, with tears in her eyes, had shown to Dr. Brown the wedding ring from her first marriage, which she always had worn on a chain around her neck since her first husband had died!

6

PAST INTO PRESENT

ONE CENTRAL FEATURE OF OUR approach to systemic therapy is the self-reflexive loop connecting past, present and future. Our idea of how the three dimensions of time relate to one another is usually different from that of our clients. They punctuate time in a linear causal way, so the deterministic causal connections built into their stories mean that events or relationships in the past have a powerful influence on relationships in the present and impose severe constraints on how they might develop in the future. The opposite idea, that the future has an influence on the present and past, seems as alien to their ways of thinking as it is remote from the laws of ordinary common sense.

If the relationship between past, present, and future is seen as a self-reflexive loop, one obvious result is that we can act on any one of the three dimensions of time in order to produce an effect in any of the other two. For clients, it is often essential to change the past in order to change the present, and so also the future. By acting—as he/she can only do—in the present, the therapist can work on memories of the past in order to show that new relationships might have been or still are possible. This means, in effect, that he/she can also work on the future.

As we have already seen, however, all problems are problems of the present. This means that one of the therapist's first steps must be to bring not only problems, but also all possible *solutions* to them, into the present. Doing this implies the basic assumption that the past and future can be brought into the present—that a past and a future can be *created*—and this means, naturally, a past and future different from the ones clients

137

bring to us. Clients bring their own possible world with them, whereas the therapist introduces a whole range of possible worlds.

It is important to remember here that the present illuminates the past. We pay the closest possible attention to what actually happens during sessions because this gives us a basis for investigating the history of what we see. However, we see this history not as an irreversible linear process, but as an element in the self-reflexive loop we described earlier. By working in the present, we and our clients are concerned with events, meanings, and relationships that fall within the temporal horizon of past and future. This enables differences, new meanings, and new interpretations to emerge that can break rigid, deterministic chains of association. The changes likely to result from this can lead, in time, to a reorganization of meanings and relationships, and so also to solutions to the problems presented.

A post-modern interpretation of this process would be that clients' stories are deconstructed through therapeutic conversation in the present, leading to the construction of new — or, as Michael White would say, *alternative* — stories. Obviously, such deconstruction occurs over the entire temporal horizon.

THE BALANCE OF MEMORY

In his short story, *Funes*, Jorge Luis Borges describes a man who, as a result of brain damage caused by a riding accident, is overwhelmed by a power of total recall: he can remember, for instance, everything that happened to him over any period of 24 hours, but it takes him exactly 24 hours to do it. The result is that he is literally no longer able to live; he is condemned (and not by his physical immobility alone) to a life of pure contemplation.

> We, in a glance, perceive three wine glasses on the table; Funes saw all the shoots, clusters, and grapes of the vine. He remembered the shapes of clouds in the south at dawn on the 30th of April of 1882, and he could compare them in his recollection with the marbled grain in the design of a leather-bound book which he had seen only once, and with the lines in the spray which an oar raised in the Rio Negro on the eve of the battle of the Quebracho. (1962, p. 112)

Funes' total memory is not entirely an invention of fiction, however. Under operating conditions, the Canadian neurosurgeon William Penfield (Penfield & Rasmussen, 1950) attached electrodes to various parts of the brains of individuals suffering from serious forms of epilepsy. His patients, having been given a local anesthetic, were fully conscious during the operation. He found that electrical stimulation of certain areas of the brain activated a sort of total memory, a one hundred percent recall of past experience which simulated the immediacy of consciousness in the present. Like consciousness in the present, this "consciousness in the past" could be neither halted nor reexperienced. It was as if the patients were seeing a film of a part of their lives, reliving the past as they had lived it in the moment when it was the present. As with Funes, time seemed to have been eliminated because, as it were, they were *inside* time, they had lost the distancing that makes it possible to distinguish differences between different dimensions of time.

During the same period when Borges was writing his short story, Russian neuropsychologist Alexander Luria was beginning his study of two remarkable clinical cases. One of them, Shereshevsky, was a real-life version of Borges' Isidor Funes (Luria, 1987a); the other, Zazetsky, was, in a sense, his complementary opposite, a man condemned to live without memory as the result of a war wound (Luria, 1987).

Luria's two clinical cases help us to understand the function of memory (the past) in our lives. Shereshevsky quite literally lived off his prodigious memory by performing almost unbelievable feats of memory in public. Although an uneducated Russian, he was able to recite a Dante canto word for word in Italian, and even remember it years later.[1] And yet, all this memory seems to have helped him little in organizing his own life. He lived in the continuous expectation of some ill-defined future, planning and imagining much but never succeeding in achieving anything concrete. He was like a man without a future, with no realistic plans, living from day to day.

By contrast, Zazetsky seems to have been condemned to little more than a vegetative existence, unable to remember even the smallest things and deprived also of most of his short-term memory. Even so, over a period of 20 years, and at incredible personal cost, he succeeded in writing down an "autobiography" of 3,000 pages, and then in revising and ordering his material correctly. Although he never regained all his faculties, he was thus able to recreate his own past. His memories surfaced only during the

---

[1]It is interesting that so "total" a memory should function spatially, exactly as with Funes. Shereshevsky's stratagems for remembering things were all visual: he located sets of objects or facts, including numbers, in space, as if an excess of memory must perforce be expressed in terms of space rather than time:

> When S. read through a long series of words, each word would elicit a graphic image. And since the series was fairly long, he had to find some way of distributing these images of his in a mental row or sequence. Most often (and this habit persisted throughout his life) he would "distribute" them along some roadway and street he visualized in his mind. (Luria, 1987a)

actual process of writing; once written down, they would vanish from his mind, remaining only in the pages he had written.

When carried to their logical conclusions, Shereshevsky and Zazetsky's parallel experiences make the essential point that both the absence of a past and *too much* past produce exactly the same result: they affect our ability to project ourselves into the future. Both Shereshevsky, who spent his entire life waiting for "something important" to happen (cataloging his memories in the meantime), and Zazetsky, who was denied even the most basic kind of learning, seem to have been imprisoned in an hermetically sealed present in which looking back was obligatory and looking forward an unattainable dream.

In our daily lives, we have to achieve some sort of *balance* of memory in which the past, indispensable as it is, guides our actions without smothering the present under its enormous weight. It is probably no accident that, of Luria's two patients, it was Zazetsky—the man with a shattered world, virtually without a past and much more seriously affected in his capacities than Shereshevsky—who was able in the end to create a more meaningful existence for himself through the unending search for his own past. Zazetsky's quest enabled him to find new adaptation to his environment.

NARRATION AND THE PAST

The narrative function—the ability to create narratives—is basic to human existence. Julian Jaynes (1976) has even gone so far as to say that consciousness operates almost exclusively by cohering our actions in narratives, putting them into continuous and coherent development ("narratization"). All peoples have had and have their stories and histories, whether the myths of the ancient Greeks and Levi-Strauss' "primitive" peoples, or the obsessive, monotonous chronologies of the Egyptians.

Our Western concept of history as a succession of unrepeatable events moving towards a definite conclusion is found not only in the sacred texts of Christianity and our modern concept of "progress," but also in the forms of the romance and the novel. History—narration—underlies our very existence. We create our individual or family histories (stories) using the narrative forms that have been handed down to us (according to H. White [1981] we transform our annals first into chronicles, and then into real narrative *histoires*). Our humanness is expressed through our capacity to narrate.

In 1984, George Orwell describes a world in which historical memory is constantly being rewritten to adapt it to the present needs of an all-powerful totalitarian state. The hero, Winston Smith, is employed as a rewriter of old newspapers, whose reports have to be made to reflect Big Brother's present political policies. As the novel progresses, Smith comes to realize how the society he lives in renders life timeless. His search for an identity is achieved through a search for his unique past, and so also for the past of the society he lives in.

> To be cut off from this knowledge is to be cut off from a vital source of meaning and reflexion, to be cut off from the material out of which the self is constructed. (Assmann, 1991, p. 10)

We often find Orwellian situations in some of the families we encounter in therapy: for example, in families with members who develop psychotic behaviors. In relational terms, these behaviors are a coherent response to an "insane" context, the result of a massive disconfirmation of personal emotions, thoughts, and meanings in the designated patient: the patient feels obliged to believe exclusively in the ideas of other people, but actually doing so then invariably leads to disconfirmation. Such situations go even beyond Orwell, with the psychotic member living in a perpetual state of relational uncertainty and ambivalence that eventually leads to withdrawal into an autistic world. (One important school of psychiatry, however, would question this exclusively relational interpretation of the origins of psychosis. Biological psychiatry assumes biological vulnerability in the nervous system to internal and external stressors [Ciompi, 1983] as the base for the development of psychosis. In this sense, the term "designated patient," an essential concept in relational psychopathology, would be redefined as "biologically designated patient.")

Michael White (White & Epston, 1990) sees all relationships between individuals as stories. In our Western world, a story is an onward moving flow in which the past produces the present and points the way to the future. Our systems of meaning in the present are based on the past (history and stories) so, in the widest sense, history supplies the cultural bearings by which we live. The histories of the groups we belong to increasingly narrow these bearings and coordinates; the family is merely one among many of these systems of meaning, or histories. Our personal stories determine the meanings we give to events as individuals: they influence how we interpret the past, but they also have a profound effect on how we live today and tomorrow. Obviously, how others interpret our stories also affects how we live, and other people are influenced in turn by how we define ourselves and narrate our stories.

Guy Ausloos (1986) has devised a therapy technique—the historiogram—for the treatment of immigrant families in Canada that have lost a precise memory of their own pasts. Therapists ask the children to say what they remember of their family's history and to write down the most important dates and events on a piece of paper. If there are obvious gaps in the narrative, they encourage the children to ask their parents or other relatives to fill them in. In this way, the entire family is persuaded to reconstruct a continuous and consistent history of its past.

It may happen that some alien, traumatic element suddenly enters the regular flow of our stories. This might be the revealing of an ancient secret, the emergence of a suppressed memory, a confession, a perverse interpretation of present events, or even a prediction, the anticipation of some future possibility. In short, the traumatic element may come from inside or outside the system, and may refer to past, present, or future events.[2] It has the effect of disarranging the story so much that—as in the case we shall look at soon—doubt is cast on the very identity of the individual and the entire system of his or her interactions with others. As Erik Erikson (1968) points out, identity derives from the faith that our ability to sustain interior sameness and continuity corresponds to the sameness and continuity of other people who are important to us. As an example, let us look at a part of a clinical study.

The man, a 45-year-old professional from a small mountain village in Northern Italy, had always led the life of an exemplary husband, father and citizen. He had three children, and his professional life was satisfactory in all respects. During an unusually stressful period, he was stunned by a sort of "revelation," the discovery of something absolutely unbelievable in his past.

He was overwhelmed one night by the memory of an act of sexual violence inflicted on him 40 years before by his father. With increasing clarity (and despair) he remembered a series of homosexual experiences totally at odds with his ordinary life, with the effect that the story he had always told himself and others was no longer consistent with his new memories. He now felt out of harmony not only with himself (he could not integrate the two sets of memories) but also with others. How could he know if he was talking to someone who knew only the blameless side of his existence or with someone who knew about the other story? How could he be a respectable father when he no longer respected himself?

Our patient's sudden revelation had disrupted not only his vision of himself and his family of origin, but also his interpretation of his own story (i.e., his life) up to that moment. His identity was now split down the middle: he began to see himself as a Dr. Jekyll and Mr. Hyde character.

---

[2]Destiny often depended on prediction in the Ancient World. Oedipus' destiny could well be regarded as one of Watzlawick's (1984) self-fulfilling prophecies.

He also began to doubt his father, the seemingly irreproachable man who had homosexually raped him 40 years earlier.[3] Thus, the patient's life had become difficult because of constant though unsuccessful efforts to repress this "terrible memory", to force it back into his unconscious mind from which it had surfaced. In the end, he had begun to think that someone might be beginning to unearth the homosexual experiences of his past, and this had quickly led to mild paranoia.

He had become a man without a definite, coherent story. He felt he was living in a confused present ("I don't know who I am anymore") with no future ("I don't care what happens anymore"). His life had become a constant remembering of the past because his present was, in effect, fully taken up with the attempt to *erase* that past, throw a mantle of forgetfulness over it. His future was now devoured by the anxious expectation that, sooner or later, everyone would come to know of his terrible secret. It was quite impossible for him to live this new, as yet unformulated story. As he himself said in the first session: "How can someone used to the limelight accept a backstage role?"

CREATING A PAST

Karl Popper (1982) has said that if we believed that time were reversible, we would be able to cancel out the horrors of Hiroshima. But the horrors of Hiroshima or Auschwitz *exist only in the memory if they exist at all.* This is why it is so important for every person and every culture to "have a past." History does not "exist" until it is recorded. For example, the Hittites had no existence in our civilization until they were "rediscovered." This is why it is necessary for the survivors of the death camps to *remember* the holocaust (see Levi, 1947): if it were forgotten, it would cease to exist for the conscience of the world. Remembering it in the present keeps alive the mourning for the victims and avoids the repetition of similar tragedies.

According to St. Augustine, the past and future do not exist as such for individuals; they exist only as "the past in the present" and "the future in the present." But if the past exists only insofar as it is constantly recreated in the present, this means that "retrodiction," the construction of the past from the present (Jaques, 1982), is just as uncertain as prediction, the construction of the future from the present. In other words, there is no

---

[3]The patient expressed this idea using a brilliant though unintentional metaphor: "Our house looked onto the main street of the village, but the rear courtyard led to one of the most notorious areas in the whole place."

certainty about the past, just as there is no certainty about the future. As Hampshire observes:

> If the objection is pressed further—"But something might happen at any moment in the future to make me change my mind," the same can be said about the past; something might happen at any moment (perhaps new testimony from others) to change my mind about the past. (1982, p. 127)

The less agreement there is about the past, the easier it is to change it. No one questions a definite, universally accepted fact like, for example, the date on which the First World War was declared, but dozens of books have been written about why the war started, each with its own different view. The margin of uncertainty surrounding events in the lives of individuals or families is very wide indeed and, as a result, reconstructions of them tend to be changeable and various. As human beings, we constantly interpret and elaborate not only our experience but also our *memories* of that experience. We remember by interpreting: we usually don't even remember "crude" experience until it has been organized and interpreted *after* it has happened. Freud (1916–1917) described the same process in psychoanalysis: by analyzing transference and countertransference, the analyst reconstructs the patient's past with him and reveals the effects it has had on the present situation, thus promoting insight into new emotions and meanings. It is well-known that pasts reconstructed under analysis reflect the analyst's theories, so a patient may acquire a Freudian past, a Jungian past, or a Kleinian past, just as systemic therapy patients will acquire a past that revolves around relationships.

However, we can go well beyond Freud's original theory of change if we assume that the past can never be "reconstructed" as it actually was but only constantly recreated in the present. Gardner (1985) describes an interesting experiment in which a group of Americans was asked to listen to a story and then describe its plot.[4] The story, a Hopi Indian myth, might well have seemed incoherent and inconclusive by Western standards, and yet most of the subjects (who remembered the details of the story quite well) were able to make sense of it by reworking the details into a logical, coherent Western narrative with a beginning, a middle, and an end. Their memory of the story was thus based on expectation rather than fact.

---

[4]The experiment was based on Rumelhart's theory (1975) of narrative grammar, which creates expectations: we expect a story will develop in a certain way, will have a certain plot, and so on. When people encounter a story that does not meet these expectations, they remember it differently so as to make it correspond more closely to their expectations.

However, this experiment can be interpreted in a different way. The human is a semantic animal, which has to find explanations for events. These explanations are constructed by finding a logical sequence that begins in the past, leads into the present, and opens out into the future. This is, of course, Jaynes' concept of narrative-making we mentioned earlier.

We evoke the past in the present using sets of relationships we establish with ourselves (our fantasies, our interior world) and others. This means that micro- or macrosocial interactions can change our view of the past on a number of different levels (individual, social and even cultural). "Historical memory" is really no more than an interpretation of the past which is shared by a culture — or by its generally recognized historians — i.e., the creation of a past through consensus on the largest possible social scale.

In his celebration of Renaissance Florence and Italy, the historian Flavio Biondo da Forlì (1492–1563) invented a concept that would influence the writing of history in Europe for centuries to come. What he did was to yoke together the thousand years from the fall of the Western Roman Empire to the emergence of the Medici dynasty in Florence in a single period, the "Medium Evum" or Middle Ages, to produce a narrative sequence that carried history from the glory of Ancient Rome through medieval decadence and barbarism to the splendors of the Renaissance and the Quattrocento. Later historians then imposed this inflexible sequence on the history of Asia, so that Chinese and Indian "Middle Ages" were also invented, as obscure and barbaric as their European counterparts. Centuries would pass before this bias against the "Dark Ages" was eliminated (Boorstin, 1983, pp. 580ff).

Therapy has quite specific ways of creating pasts. In the simplest way, we can construct them using Jerome Bruner's basic dichotomy (1986) between "paradigmatic thinking" (scientific knowledge, logic) and "narrative thinking" (story-telling), although any reality can be described equally well in either way. However, narrative discourse, in which intrinsic coherence and verifiability are rather less important, usually tries to keep meaning open so that it can be interpreted in as many different ways as possible. Thus, narrative discourse succeeds in:

> *subjunctivizing reality*. . . . I take my meaning of "subjunctive" from the second one offered by the *OED*: "Designating a mood (L. *modus subjunctivus*) the forms of which are employed to denote an action or state as conceived (and not as a fact) and therefore used to express a wish, command, exhortation, or a contingent, hypothetical or prospective event." To be in the subjunctive mode is, then, to be trafficking in human possibilities rather than in settled certainties. An "achieved" or "uptaken" narrative speech act, then, produces a subjunctive world. (p. 26)

However, the narrative each individual extrapolates from his or her story is usually (though not always) in the indicative rather than subjunctive mood: facts tend to be given one interpretation only, and to be seen from only one point of view. Such stories expressed in the indicative mode reproduce the paradigmatic mode of causal, linear thinking. Therapy may transform a client's past into a narrative which meets the three criteria proposed by Bruner (1986): the creation of meanings that are more implicit than explicit, personalization of the story, and multiple points of view.

Dialogue with the therapist can introduce a subjunctive reality because the therapist usually offers clients not only a new point of view, but *more than one* point of view, without necessarily indicating which one should be preferred. If the conversation is not with an individual but with families or couples, each person is given the chance to express his or her own point of view, so that the story acquires a number of facets and becomes much more than the simple sum of each individual story. In this way, a "subjunctive past" may emerge on which the vice-like grip of causality has been loosened. Metaphor is another linguistic device that helps us to create this "subjunctive past." Finally, the various points of view of the therapy team—mediated by the therapist or communicated directly by a reflecting team—can sometimes enhance the interplay of perspectives by implying that the past can be subjected to an infinite range of interpretations.

To continue our analogy with literary texts, the basic difference between the indicative stories that therapy takes as its starting point and the subjunctive past that subsequently emerges is that a subjunctive past enables its "reader" to rewrite the past in his own terms, shifting from the structure of the story as given to how it might actually unravel itself in time, from general situation to particular details. To return to one of Bruner's metaphors:

> So a reader goes from stones to arches to the significance of arches is some broader reality—goes back and forth between them in attempting finally to construct a sense of the story, its form, its meaning. (1986, p. 36)

For this reason, it may be inadvisable for the therapist to adopt a single or overly restrictive point of view.

There are other ways of creating pasts, apart from using metaphors, verbal modes and other rhetorical devices. The most important of all is, quite simply, the question mark—in other words, questions. Rhetorically speaking, the question transfers the responsibility for attribution of meaning to the recipient of the message.

One special type of question is the "hypothetical" question (Boscolo et al., 1987), which may be directed equally well to events and meanings in the past, present, or future. In the case of an anorectic patient, for example, we might ask the following about the past: "If you had decided to stop refusing food in the past, how might, let's say, your grandparents have reacted?" This question implies that its recipient can reformulate the result of a game going back over three generations. When sessions are conducted in this way, it is possible to create new pasts by bringing them into the present: the "new" past restores flexibility, the possibility of development, to the system by initiating self-reflexive feedback between past and present. A similar question could be asked about the present and the future: "Let's imagine that you now decide to stop refusing food, how would. . . ?" or "Let's imagine that you decide in future to stop refusing food, how would. . . ?

Recreating a Family

Therapy can sometimes construct a "new" past in unusual and even extraordinary ways, especially when conversation alone is unable to carry the therapy process forward. Let us look at two examples. The first, a case of individual therapy, concerns a 28-year-old woman suffering from fairly acute depression. After five months of individual therapy, at a rhythm of one to two sessions per week, the therapist had not observed any results. The patient continually communicated that she was a hopeless case, that her life had no meaning, that any effort was useless. In her opinion, the cause of this incurable depression lay in her childhood—to be precise, in the five-year period she had spent in a tiny apartment with an alcoholic father, numerous brothers, and above all, an uncaring mother "who didn't even bother to look at me." Her recollection was that she had not even had a mother; she had felt an unbearable sense of loss, had suffered from it, and the further forward she went in life, the more she felt burdened by the weight of her past.

The therapist's hypothesis was that the patient had fixed the cause of her problems in the past; consequently, her efforts to talk about the present and the future could have no effect because results could come only from a change in the past itself.[5] The therapist intervened, explaining to the patient that she could change only if he succeeded in changing her past. He continued: "The only possibility of changing you is for me to become the mother you never had. So from now on I will try to be the

---

[5]It could be said that the patient had placed herself in a double bind involving an "injunction on the past." We shall return to this idea later on.

mother you did not have in 1966, and I will try to behave in the way you would have wanted your mother to behave. You must signal to me from time to time, by raising a finger, if I am being that mother or not." With this approach, her depressive symptoms began to recede in a few sessions. In this case, the therapist, while accepting the irreversibility of the past, asked the patient to act as if the past were reversible. Obviously, it was not the past that changed; rather, the change that took place in the present had an effect on the patient's interpretation of her past. As the past (in the patient's memory) became new, the reflexive loop reopened, allowing the present to change.

A similar case encountered by the Milan group around 1975 is described in *Paradox and Counterparadox* (Selvini Palazzoli et al., 1978). The mother of a family with an acutely psychotic daughter was convinced that she had been the "cause" of her daughter's psychosis because she had made so many mistakes in her relationship with her own parents. Here, too, mythical blame had been located in an intolerable past. In order to produce change, the two co-therapists offered to become the mother's parents, so as to change her past and open up possibilities for a new present.

Whether or not a past can be deconstructed and reconstructed depends, obviously, on how we interpret the notion of "becoming." If we consider living systems from an *a priori* point of view, we arrive at a probabilistic vision implying a high degree of unpredictability, so that it becomes impossible to predict how systems will develop. But if we look at them from an *a posteriori* point of view, as systems that have *already* developed, we see them in terms of necessity, as if the events that have produced this particular present are arranged deterministically. As we have seen, humans are semantic animals, always searching for explanations. Causality does not lie in the external world: it is a principle, an instrument an observer can use to give meaning—*a* meaning—to what he or she observes. What he has observed is explained *a posteriori* in a deterministic way. But to try to explain future events in living systems deterministically is a mistake, because unpredictability is excluded. If, for example, we observe the development of a species *a posteriori*, we see that it had to evolve in just the way it did. But if we ask *a priori* how it will develop in the future, we shall never have an answer.

Clients who come for therapy often apply *a posteriori* points of view to *a priori* situations. In other words, their past rigidly contextualizes their future. The initial reaction of observers to events in Eastern Europe in 1989 was an epistemological error of just this kind: no one had future horizons flexible enough to foresee and then accommodate radical changes that had been unthinkable for the previous 40 years. An open viewpoint must be able to embrace moments of instability, when the process of change is at its most unpredictable, the moments which Prigogine and Stengers (1984) call "bifurcations." In narrative metaphor, this idea corresponds to the production of alternative stories. Using Bateson's terminology, we might say that the systemic action of the therapist changes the epistemology[6] of the client by making it approximate more closely to von Bertalanffy's concept (1969) of equifinality, in which different antecedents can produce similar results and similar antecedents can produce different results. A client-therapist relationship based on this kind of epistemology opens up new perspectives for change.

The Henry Street Settlement:
How to Create a Past

Temporal horizons vary according to culture and social class. As we saw in Chapter 2, the Western middle classes typically project themselves into the future from a known past (Coser & Coser, 1963), although this is by no means always the case. A dominance of the present in American culture is best seen in the nation's lower social classes, especially in alienated social groups.

One of the reasons why the temporal horizons of alienated classes are restricted to the present may be that they have to adapt themselves, in the here and now, to the environment in which they find themselves. Frequently they have to deal with social workers who are mainly concerned with immediate problems—social services needs, payments, assistance (a job, a home, financial aid, etc.)—rather than longer-term problems. Many of these people seem to have sprung from nowhere and retain only vague memories of the groups they belonged to in the past. They live exclusively in the present or in the immediate future and immediate past on either side of it.

Therapy, if successful, always changes the past, that is, our memory of the past. In some cases, certain hypothetical questions can be used to relate the past as remembered to another possible version of the past (a world in which another past would be or might have been possible). Let us take an example. Henry Street Settlement is a social agency located in the Lower East Side of Manhattan, one of the more economically deprived areas in New York. Its clients include a large number of recent immigrants from Central and South America, people who are often in the earliest

---

[6]In the sense of "system of premises."

stages of adapting to their new environment. In many cases, these persons act as if they have only the vaguest memories of their past. Perhaps because of their distrust of the therapist or suspicion about the safety of the therapy setting, perhaps because of a repression of traumatic memories or because of past deprivations, the therapist often has great difficulty in soliciting from these clients any details about their past lives, especially their childhood experiences. Social workers and these clients operate within a temporal horizon restricted exclusively to the present, and their interaction is based on routine dialogue and activity of a stimulus-response type. In Heinz von Foerster's terms,[7] they tended to interact like trivial machines.

Traditionally, interventions in such cases are concerned with rehabilitation and social support. But language difficulties often lead to dialogues with social workers in which clients tend to behave like trivial machines, giving only the most parsimonious and literal answers to questions being asked. Conversations resolve around present issues and generate monotonous, repetitive answers.

Some of the staff members of Henry Street Settlement underwent Milan approach training, but then went on to use the approach in a very original way, developing an unusual and very long (two hours or more) format for the initial session, which was then repeated in similar form after six months (L. Ahto & S. Sampieri, personal communication). In the interval, the patients received standard support and assistance. In the sessions, two staff members would be the interviewers, with other members behind one-way mirror. The interviewers would try to "create" a past for the clients by posing hypothetical questions. During the session, the consultants tried to create not only a past but also, and more specifically, a *family relationship* within that past: a family, a group to which their clients could feel they belonged.

This is reminiscent in a way of Pirandello's *Six Characters in Search of an Author,* which opens with six characters begging a theater director and his actors to give them a story. As in the play, the Henry Street therapists put themselves in the director's position and constructed a story for their characters, the difference being that in Henry Street it was the authors

---

[7]This *trivial machine* "can be defined analytically because we can analyze the machine . . . the machine is independent of history because, whatever input it is given, it will not remember it, and will behave the next time by following the laws that applied the previous time . . . finally, it is predictable: you always know what the machine will do when you give it a particular input" (von Foerster, 1985, p. 128).

who were begging the characters to enter into the new story that was being written for them.

For example, if the client had no father, or remembered nothing about him, the interviewers would ask questions like: What father would you have liked to have had? What occupation would you have liked your father to have had? If you had had a sister, what kind of father would you have wanted for her? What kind of relationship would you have desired to have with your father when you were a boy? When clients said they had been neglected by mothers who had led chaotic, promiscuous lives, the therapist would ask: "Let's imagine that your mother had an easier childhood, that she could have built a real life. How do you think your mother would have behaved towards you, your sister, your father. . . ?" And so on. These hypothetical questions were also directed towards schools and past relationships between clients and their teachers or friends of the same age.

The idea was to co-create a group to which the clients could belong and thereby establish a more complex and secure identity for themselves: hypotheses could become realities when clients had groups to care for them, people who thought it possible, or indeed likely, that they were normal people just like any others. This past, co-created in the here and now, established premises that eventually enabled clients to reject the emptiness of their alienated lives and enter into new stories.

Interventions like these have two important effects. First, they create a new history where previously either there was none or it was being actively suppressed. Moreover, the clients receive a totally new message. The questions asked imply that they can create a positive past for themselves, that have had a family that they associate with a positive "story." This makes it possible not only to have people tell genuinely new stories, but also to root them in a past with positive features. In this way, clients may acquire new self-esteem and a fresh attitude toward the future. They are thus released from their "deviant" status. From the point of view of present interaction and future perspective, the fact that the positive past is hypothetical has little relevance.

Working in the past is important for the therapist or consultant not only in cases like these, where there seems to be no past, but also in cases where the temporal horizon is weighted exclusively towards the past. It means, above all, introducing hypothetical ideas and encouraging the development of alternative stories that will later open out into the future. If, in the Henry Street cases, it is appropriate to speak of constructing a possible story from fragments and clues supplied by the client, in cases of the latter type the co-creation of new stories develops out of the simultaneous deconstruction of a past story.

The Therapist's Past

In narrative terms, the therapy process can be explained in at least three ways. In the first, the clients bring their story to the therapist and confer upon him or her the task of rewriting it (as happens in psychoeducational interventions[8]). In the second, the therapist creates a context in which the clients rewrite the story exactly as they wish (Anderson and Goolishian's preferred method). In the third, the story the clients bring is jointly deconstructed and reconstructed by the client and therapist, so that it becomes a story with two authors. In the first case, the author of the story is the therapist, in the second the client, and in the third both the client and the therapist. Let us now look at a case that can be described in the third way.

Silvio Castelli came to therapy with his mother, a housewife, and his father, a doctor. He was suffering from acute bulimia, a pathological craving for food. Twenty-five years old, a slim, elegant young man, he was prey to attacks of uncontrollable hunger which had required hospitalization twice in only one year for the treatment of electrolytic imbalance. In the first session, Silvio gave a detailed account of these attacks, which were already costing his father more than he was able to earn. When in the grip of an attack, he would oblige his mother to cook for him for days on end. When she collapsed with exhaustion, he would then reserve a private room in a small restaurant next to home and eat enormous quantities of food, as much as 50 pounds, sometimes for an entire afternoon. To manage this, he would repeatedly go to the washroom and poke a coarse table napkin down his throat to induce vomiting. This practice had led, among other things, to esophageal bleeding.

During the course of the interview, a memory emerged which seemed very significant to the therapist, namely that Silvio had had a younger brother who had died at the age of eight, when Silvio was 12. The team decided to incorporate this fact in the final intervention of the first session.

THERAPIST: What strikes us about your family is that you are the survivors of a death that has not been completely mourned yet. (*to Silvio*) A year ago, you decided deep down to break off your studies because you were afraid your parents wouldn't be able to cope with you

---

[8]This is individual and family therapy—usually for schizophrenia and bipolar affective disorders—in which therapists teach patients and families how to cope with their illnesses by suggesting solutions that are more appropriate and functional than the ones they would find for themselves.

leaving home after losing one child already. You then developed a behavior that obliges your mother to prepare food for you, and forces your father to work just to keep you alive. This is your way of reassuring them that for now you're not going to leave home. (*to the parents*) We also understand your behavior: you are two parents who have had a big loss and are now doing your utmost to keep your surviving son alive.

SILVIO: (*puzzled, to the therapist*) Is this why I eat—for my dead brother?

THERAPIST: Yes, possibly. Now we're going to try to find a way to help you all to mourn, so that when Mario is truly buried you will be free to return to your normal lives again.

At the start of the next session, the family announced, "A miracle has happened!" Silvio said that the therapist's words—especially the idea that he was a survivor and had not yet mourned for his dead brother—had stayed with him over the next 24 hours. The next day he had felt what he described as an "inner peace" and had realized to his amazement that he was no longer a slave to his hunger: his appetite had returned to normal. He had called friends he hadn't seen for a year and had spent the weekend with them. From then on, his bulimia had disappeared completely.

After the session, the team wondered how such an amazing change could have happened. During the first session, the observers behind the mirror had noticed that the therapist had seemed unusually emotional while delivering his final intervention, whereas the three members of the family had been in an immobile, almost trance-like state. The therapist remembered that the universal theme (death) that emerged in his interaction with the family derived from his own past experiences: Silvio's reminiscences had suddenly reminded him of his own younger brother who had died in infancy (this had been a major theme in his own personal analysis). The therapist's memories and emotions contrasted sharply with the family's seemingly unemotional account of the death of their own little boy.

This eventually produced the rather unusual hypothesis that the clients might change when they could see a therapist enacting their own unresolved emotional conflicts. A similar process might be induced in them (the process Mony Elkaim calls "resonance"): they would change, while the therapist—paradoxically—would remain burdened with his own conflicts, essential to solving their problems. Thus, therapy would be *cathartic*, as in Aristotle's concept of drama: in both cases, spectators see their own, universal dramas acted out before them.

A SHATTERED MYTH

In the case study we are about to discuss, the onset of a couple's difficulties coincided with a gradual divergence of the partners' interests. For a number of years, the couple had stuck to their myth of a static, immobile past. As usually happens, the myth eventually proved unable to accommodate outside input, which opened up conflict between the individual times of the two partners. Sudden change in the wife—greater independence as a result of individual therapy—now contrasted starkly with the static inactivity of her husband.

The couple consisted of Fabio, a 34-year-old employee in a commercial company, and his wife Anna, a 29-year-old high school teacher. Anna was a shapely woman, classically beautiful in the manner of early twentieth-century prints. Fabio, who was slender, seemed almost gaunt by comparison. However, the contrast between the two was not just physical. Anna appeared immediate, intense, and in touch with her emotions, while Fabio was cool, composed, and apparently humorless. He was noticeably fastidious and seemed to need to keep himself under tight control. The couple had a five-year-old son, Emanuele, an unusually self-confident, extroverted boy now attending nursery school. Relations between the parents had become increasingly strained over the past year and they had decided to try couple therapy because of the "lack of contact" between them. Therapy took place in six sessions over a period of ten months.

During the first session—the only one in which Emanuele was also present—the therapist carefully explored their disagreement and their explanation for it. The following story emerged. Before marrying, Anna had been a restless girl, intolerant of her parents, until Fabio had "liberated" her and given her freedom and a sense of her own life. For the first five years of their marriage, Anna had lived in Fabio's shadow, admiring him for his rectitude and devotion to his family, as well as for the unusual breadth of his culture. She had regarded him as her teacher.

The first signs of strain in their relationship coincided with the birth of their son. Both parents were strongly attached to Emanuele, but Fabio's attachment had become obsessive, and he looked after his son with exceptional care. He said that his attachment was strengthened by the fact that his own beloved father had died when he was only 14 years old: "I want to give my son the father I never had." Anna, in turn, had been affected by this situation: her child seemed distant from her and always sided with his father. "I'd like to be touched," she complained, "but Fabio and my son touch each other, never me!" Emanuele's analogical (nonverbal) behavior confirmed the strength of the bond with his father.

When Emanuele was two, Anna had begun individual therapy for a depressive anxiety syndrome. It had lasted two years and, she said, "helped a lot." However, as often happens, individual therapy had caused an imbalance in the couple. Anna had developed and was living in a temporal horizon increasingly open to the future, while Fabio had remained immured in his past. The team hypothesized that Anna had reacted by halting her development because of the risk that it might destabilize her marriage. The couple's conflict derived, then, from disparity between their internal times: one of the partners had developed much more rapidly than the other.

In the second session, both partners seemed very sad. Anna, especially, seemed depressed and said that immediately after the first session she had begun to suffer from a form of "exhaustion" involving depression, apathy and insomnia. Such symptoms were by no means new to her, however. According to Fabio, every Christmas (the second session was held in January), Anna entered a period of depression that would last until the summer, to be followed by a period of euphoria. At this point, the therapist hypothesized that Anna might be suffering from a form of cyclical mood disorder. Fabio, for his part, was exceptionally dissatisfied with the situation. As an intellectual, he had tried in vain for years to teach his wife how to "improve herself," but in less than two years her therapist seemed to have changed her more than he had in years of well-intentioned, affectionate teaching.

During the session, Fabio also showed a certain ambivalence towards his wife. "Anna excites me a lot when she's bubbly and euphoric, although I'm always afraid she might do something rash. She doesn't excite me at all—in fact, she makes me furious—when she lets herself go and puts on weight!" When read as injunctions, Fabio's statements seemed riddled with paradox and double bind.

The climax of the session came when the therapist reformulated Fabio's attitude towards Anna as that of a "teacher and policeman." Fabio accepted this impassively and again voiced his worry about the excessive strength of his father-son bond and the apparent lack of a bond between mother and son. The final intervention of this session is given below in full.

> THERAPIST: My colleagues agree about what we were saying earlier, especially the work that you, Anna, have done with Dr. Neri. You've begun to grow, you've worked very well, you've begun to feel well, to feel more secure and full of life. You've pleased your husband with this, but you've also alarmed him. Any couple can tolerate only so much change. Then perhaps it changes, and so can tolerate yet more change. But in any period it can only tolerate so much change and no more.

What my colleagues seem to have noticed is that you've somehow been *too* well, *too* secure . . . this is what happens when, either through therapy or some other experience, a married woman begins to feel like a woman, to feel sure of herself. This is what we call a *war of independence*, because in their original families women are often used to coming after their menfolk, to being slaves, to believing that they are inferior. Then, when they're married, many women rediscover themselves through a variety of experiences, including psychotherapy. They begin to rediscover their femininity and independence.

When you were saying how impressed you had been by Fabio in the beginning, how you had married him and had been very dependent on him for a long time, one of my colleagues noticed how much this is like the old model of the relationship between men and women, between masculine and feminine. Then, as a result of maturing, let's say, or because of other stimuli . . .

ANNA: . . . I broke free. . . .

THERAPIST: You broke free of this stereotype, and emerged as a woman who is sure of herself, who wants to develop, perhaps to do new things, new activities that suit her better as a person. When all this happened, Fabio liked it very much. He didn't like the idea of having the usual frivolous sort of woman as a wife. As I understand it, Fabio, you aren't a man of just ordinary tastes, you're original, so you like this woman as she is now, you feel exhilarated by her and admire her enormously.

But then you started to get frightened because there are limits to how much Fabio can tolerate. His fear is that you are taking on too much, that you're ignoring him, that you'll leave him for someone else. So he becomes like a small child. So what has happened since you started feeling better, until this latest period when all the depression started . . . I imagine you feel . . .

ANNA: . . . worthless.

THERAPIST: Worthless, exactly. So, you've come back to reassure him. You knew you had reached the limit.

ANNA: You mean, I'm going back on myself. . . ? I'm reassuring him.

THERAPIST: Exactly. You had reached the limit. Sometime now you'll begin another phase of growth, and at a certain point, as usually happens, he may begin to grow too. This is what we usually see.

The couple was then assigned a ritual that would introduce the possibility of establishing a different parents-son relationship.

THERAPIST: What we'd now like to ask is that you, Anna, take your husband to one side twice a week, on Tuesdays and Thursdays for example, in a place where you can be alone, and tell him what you think about the relationship he has with his son. The meeting should last at least half an hour.

The prescription was carried out to the letter. Two important changes were apparent in the next session: the child had distanced himself from his father (and vice versa) and had come closer to his mother, and Fabio had stopped worrying about the past and was much keener on thinking about the future, especially the future of the couple itself.

Anna noticed that the child had started coming to her again, and not only to his father, as before. At the beginning, Fabio felt that his son had become "like a stranger" to him, but after a week he began to respond when the child sought him out. The therapeutic dialogue was thus able to concentrate once more on the relationship between the parents. Fabio stated that his work was rewarding, but that at home he "no longer felt stimulated" and "got nothing from his wife."

During this session, as in all the others, the husband and wife were rather ambivalent about each other. When they spoke, both agreed that a rift had come between them and that they were increasingly indifferent towards each other (including in bed), yet they remained unusually close and spoke exclusively about themselves as a couple, virtually never about outsiders.

In the final intervention in this session, the therapist stated his view of their situation:

THERAPIST: You love each other too much, you're too close, almost in symbiosis with each other. This excessive closeness has made you worry about being too close, and also about separation. You have created a myth, that loving each other means standing still in time. This, Anna, is why your new independence caused problems in your relationship. We see that you are both trying very hard to construct a more real love for your future. Your coming for therapy has been an attempt to do this.

In the fourth session, the parents reported that Emanuele was much calmer and more independent, and that they had established their own independence from him as a couple. Fabio said he couldn't shake off the fear that Anna (who had put on a fair amount of weight in the meantime) would become fat. The image of Anna as an obese woman in the future disgusted him: "The thought that my wife will become unsightly, like my mother who was tremendously overweight when she died, frightens me. I wish I knew what it is inside me that makes my wife's weight irritate me so much. It even irritates me to see my wife undressed. I know these are stupid ideas, but they're the ideas I have." (This led to a series of hypotheses on how Fabio saw other men and women, which we shall not discuss here.)

For her part, Anna felt that she was being judged by weight, like some product for sale, and feared that she had put on weight simply because her husband was so obsessed with his desire to see her thin. Emanuele, meanwhile (according to their descriptions), seemed the most satisfied of them all, and appeared happy with both his father and mother. During the course of the session, attention shifted from the importance of Anna to the importance of mutual differences between the partners. Their relationship seemed complementary: Fabio was logical, his emotions completely stifled by logic and reasoning (he would curb Anna's emotions with logic), while Anna's emotions injected warmth into her husband's chilly logic. This reframing seemed to have a positive effect on the couple.

In the fifth session, Anna and Fabio at last seemed happy: their relationship had visibly improved, and they had made love for the first time in months. Anna said that Fabio was no longer irritated by her, and Fabio agreed that he felt much better. He added, though, that he was still worried that their happiness "might disappear in the future," probably because he wanted to prevent the team from saying that its work was done.[9] Anna then added with great satisfaction that she had gone on a diet because she wanted to look good in a new swimsuit she had bought. She added, however, that she wouldn't lose any more weight just for the sake of her husband because she felt this was a kind of blackmail: "I love you when you're thin; I don't love you when you're fat."

During team discussion, it was agreed that the couple had broken its impasse. It was decided to terminate therapy.

> THERAPIST: My colleagues behind the mirror have discussed the general situation with me and we agree that, at the moment, we see no psychological or psychiatric problems that need our attention. So

---

[9]It often happens in couple therapy that a significant improvement in the relationship (which leads the therapist to think therapy may be nearing its end) produces a resurgence old problems or the appearance of some new unexpected problem that postpones the termination of therapy. In such cases, the real problem seems to be the prospect of losing the therapist, so new problems are invented that require his attention. If the therapist is unaware of this, conditions requiring long-term or even permanent therapy may be created.

we're telling you that we're terminating therapy—we've seen the start of a change in your relationship as a couple, as a family and with your child, a positive change, so we don't think you need us anymore. Of course, we expect you'll have your ups and downs, like all couples. Life is a problem, conflicts and arguments are normal. So I agree with you that happiness, if we can call it happiness, isn't continuous. Life itself isn't continuous, it has its moments of indifference, of arguing. Living together means finding solutions, compromises, and so on. We now think you're able to find your own solutions.

ANNA: For the rest of our lives?

THERAPIST: What we see now, as therapists, is a couple, a family, that's evolving, looking for a new equilibrium. We think you now have your own resources to handle the conflicts and difficulties life will throw at you. We see that, between your ups and down, you are moving in this direction. When you ask "for the rest of our lives?" we can't really give you an answer. If you think you need help in future, you've got our address.

The feedback from the spouses was quite lively, as if they had been taken unawares by the termination of therapy. Fabio (who had given the therapist the impression that he considered him his adoptive father) said he felt "almost a feeling of loss." Anna, by contrast, said she at last felt able to cope with their relationship as a couple, but was also a little worried about succumbing to depression again and "starting everything all over again."

After this kind of final intervention, the couple or family usually continues the development that has been initiated. In rare cases, clients later ask for more sessions. As far as this case is concerned, three years later Anna called and asked if she and Fabio could come and talk about the problem of her weight again. The termination of their therapy had been followed by a very positive period: Anna had become pregnant, and a "beautiful child," now a year old, had been born. Emanuele was doing fine, and the couple had established a satisfactory *modus vivendi* until six months previously, when Anna had started putting on weight and Fabio had begun to complain, saying that her body disgusted him. Anna had answered his criticisms with phrases like "either you want me or you want my body," or "you love people by the kilo," and had aired the idea that she could find lots of men who liked her just as she was. Fabio answered that he couldn't help himself because his ideal woman was a thin, and so on. The couple came for a further two sessions, which proved sufficient to bring this repetitive game to an end.

EMENDING THE PAST

Orestes and Electra were both well-educated graduate professionals in their forties. Orestes had finished individual analysis some time ago, but still felt the need to consult his analyst now and again. He had recently been advised to come to our center for therapy with his wife, who had also started analysis some years before and was still seeing her analyst. Couple therapy was proposed at the end of the first meeting, on condition that their respective analysts give their consent. Since he had actually sent Orestes to us in the first place, the husband's analyst had already tacitly given his consent. However, the wife's analyst, a Kleinian, had not answered her question, as Electra had expected, because she usually intervened very little in their sessions. Electra read her silence as consent.

Electra had literally been dragged in for therapy by her husband, who was tortured by his sexual problems with her. He would ask her obsessively for sex, but when she consented, he would then say that nothing was "like it was before," referring to an earlier infidelity ("misdemeanor") of his wife's. Events had followed a course now common in the couples we see, a result of changes in sex roles in Italy since the war. After the birth of their first child, four years into their marriage, Electra had started analysis and had soon become more independent and self-confident. She had also become respected at work, and found her job rewarding. Then she had become infatuated with a married colleague at work. Their affair had lasted two months; then she had repented and confessed everything to her husband, hoping he would forgive her. Her revelation had come as a "bombshell," from which he had "never recovered." He had become pathologically jealous, tormenting his wife with questions, "What was it like with him? Exciting? Did he satisfy you better than me? Was he more expert than me?" and so on. He had begun an affair with another woman to "get even" with her, but had never managed to get over the blow to his male pride.

Their relationship as a couple had deteriorated to the point where Electra, totally exasperated, had begun talking about separation. At the same time — strangely to them but not to us — she had become pregnant, and plans to separate had been dropped. The pregnancy had been a fairly calm period, perhaps because Orestes had felt she couldn't betray him, but it had all started again once the child had been born. His jealous tantrums and obsessive questioning of the past had become increasingly frequent.

Faced with renewed threats from his wife to leave the "hell" they were living in, Orestes, with the aid of his analyst, had succeeded in bringing her to our center for couple therapy. In the second session, the wife openly admitted that she had only come along to "cure" her husband; she had her own analyst and was quite satisfied with her. For his part, the husband had given us an impossible task: to change the past.

It was as if he were saying to his wife: "Everything will go back to the way it was before if you'd never met him!" (obviously, the sequence of tenses here has been totally violated in an unsuccessful attempt to convey the temporal chaos such a statement implies).[10] Any injunction can only be directed at the future, but here the forbidden act had already taken place, so the injunction was, of its very nature, impossible to obey. The only way to have obeyed it would have been to invert time's arrow: in other words, Electra would have had to obey a prohibition regarding something she had already done, something located—most importantly—in a past they both shared. But, of course, attempts to obliterate a shared past can only fail; as they increase in scale, they quickly become as hectic and confused as they are ineffective, as psychotics and obsessives know to their cost.

Therapy soon proved difficult, with both partners sticking to their entrenched positions. The husband would describe a past that had been idyllic until his wife's betrayal had changed his life. While admitting that she had done something she shouldn't have, the wife maintained that her decision to break off her affair and freely confess everything merited his understanding at least, if not his forgiveness.

At the end of the second session, the team decided to prescribe a ritual to create a temporal sequence midway between past and present, a ritual that would contain the traumatic experience but bring it back to life only on the day of the week specified by the therapist. Every Thursday had to be spent remembering the events connected with, first, the wife's extramarital relationship, and then the husband's. They were to relive their intense emotions to the full, accusing each other of the wrongs they thought had been done to them, with the proviso that they should stop as soon as they felt they might lose control and become violent. They were forbidden to speak about these events on any other days, and any comment on or discussion about what had emerged on the day devoted to the past was strictly prohibited. Instead, they were to bring the results of their Thursday discussions to the next session.

---

[10]Another way of describing an "injunction on the past"—one that we ourselves would probably have used some years ago—would be to see it as a double bind which, superficially at least, does not conform to Bateson's classic double-bind "recipe." There is only one negative injunction in our double bind. Paradox results not so much from the negation as from the *reversal* of time. An injunction applied to the past forms a paradoxical recurring loop.

The aim of the ritual was to create a clear past/present sequence by marking off a time for discussing and hopefully solving past problems, leaving other days free for the present and the future. Rituals like these can often reduce tension in couples by putting negative experiences into "temporal brackets" totally separate from the rest of their time. Couples usually cannot do this on their own: there is always the suspicion — and the expectation — that the other partner is thinking about the traumatic events of the past.

When the couple returned, it was immediately obvious that the ritual had failed. In her first attempt to perform the task she had been given, Electra had attacked Orestes and he had responded in kind, thereby making it impossible to continue. Over the next three weeks they hadn't even tried to perform the ritual.

> THERAPIST: (*sometimes using technical language to match the couple's own language and knowledge of psychology*) We are very struck that the depth of your conflict has prevented you from performing the task we gave you. We're in a Pirandellian situation here. First, what's being asked is to change an event that happened in the past which, by definition, can't be changed precisely because it is in the past. Second, it's very Pirandellian — and you, Orestes, are showing it in everything you do, with words, with suffering and tears — that the person most important to you, your wife, the person you are most tied to, has had this experience in the past which you continue to mull over in the way a soldier returned from Vietnam mulls over his war experiences, which can never be changed because the war happened, and you can't change the past. This is also the person you continue to tell us you feel tied to, and yet you're doing all you can (and you'll probably succeed) to make her leave you. We are watching a drama here, and it will probably lead to breakdown in your relationship sooner or later.
>
> For you, Orestes, this past experience has become your reason for living. Since it's a past experience, logically it can never be changed. That's why we set you a task which tried to break this Pirandellian situation, or paradoxical situation, if you prefer. . . .
>
> ORESTES: What do you mean?
>
> THERAPIST: By definition, this past experience can never be obliterated because it's over. Third, as a corollary of this which makes your situation seem Pirandellian from the outside, there is your reaction, Orestes. Someone like you could have reacted in any number of ways when faced with a situation like this: accept the past, the idea that the past is over and done with, and start a new life; refuse to put

up with the past, leave your wife and find another partner; or, yet another reaction, leave your wife and have nothing more to do with women! There are thousands of possible reactions, and yet the one we see happening here is that you have remained in the past and go on thinking about your wife's affair with that man, and your wife can't stand it anymore. So I repeat again that you can't change the past. If you go on in this way, doing all you can to lose the person you're most tied to, you're creating the basis for irreversible evolution.

I, as a therapist, and my colleagues, we're witnessing a Pirandello play—or, I don't know, a Verdi opera like *Otello*—a drama whose internal force is not only stronger than the actors performing it but also stronger than the therapists. You told me the last time, "Give me a Palo Alto intervention," but beyond a certain point there can be no more interventions. The drama is bigger than you, and us. If you agree, I'll give you an appointment in six months' time and we'll see how things have developed. But right now, we're saying that this situation, this drama, will probably end in separation, given the circumstances. Either of you can take the step of separating, it doesn't matter. You might (*to the wife*) because you'll reach the stage where you can't take any more and you'll want to show that the past is the past. Or you might (*to the husband*) because at a certain point you'll get tired of it all: you've tried and tried and it hasn't worked, so you'll leave her.

This is probably the way things will develop. Alternatively, given the circumstances, and if you continue with this relationship, it's possible that your pain and powerful emotions will become like what we see in those complicated dramas where everything becomes expiation because time has stopped. That is, the future becomes expiation. You, Electra, have to make amends for and constantly witness your husband's grief, which comes out in a thousand ways. These dramas can last a lifetime, there's a whole nineteenth-century literature about them, whole novels have been written about them. . . .

ORESTES: This isn't an alternative!

THERAPIST: It's the alternative these circumstances produce: the continuation of situation in which even your therapists—I myself but also your individual analysts—are always, how could we say. . . ?

ORESTES: Spectators.

THERAPIST: Spectators in a drama that needs witnesses for expiation to occur. In which you'll have to spend the rest of your lives externalizing a grief that's timeless, that can never end.

ORESTES: But don't you see an alternative?

THERAPIST: I don't see any alternative in . . .

ORESTES: But there must be some way . . .

At this point, the husband (but also, nonverbally, the wife) rebels at the future outlined by the therapist. It is interesting to analyze in detail the role of time in this fragment of the session.

> 1. The therapist makes the husband's demand explicit, i.e., that what can never be changed should be changed.
>
> 2. The irreversibility of time, time's arrow, is stressed: the past, since it is over, cannot change, cannot be amended in any way.
>
> 3. At the same time, the temporal horizon opens towards the future. The therapist begins to construct hypotheses, first about what could have happened in the past, by presenting a series of possibilities: making up, immediate separation, searching for a new partner, isolation. Then he suggests hypotheses about what might happen in the future.
>
> 4. Having admitted that he is powerless, the therapist is described as a "spectator" by Orestes, and accepts the definition. The therapy team declares that it finds itself at an impasse. The husband and wife are thus handed back the responsibility for being actors in their own drama.

The rhetorical structure of the discourse presents all these elements not in sequence, i.e., in successive moments of time, but in a circular way. Every argument leads to another and then returns cyclically to the one before. The phrase "you can't change the past" is repeated again and again.

Modal logic replaces deterministic logic, but by declaring himself powerless the therapist offers only two possibilities (separation or continued suffering), which are both equally painful. It is interesting that the husband becomes openly rebellious when faced with such intransigence. The therapist has employed a logic midway between the husband's original logic and modal logic proper. There are only two alternatives, and they are rigidly determined. But this reversal of roles, in which the therapist now says real change is impossible, suddenly produces the opposite attitude in Orestes, who until then had indicated that he was in favor of things staying the way they were. The spouses now find they have to find a solution. No one, apart from themselves, can ever change the way they are.

ORESTES: But there must be a method. . . .

THERAPIST: The method is to change your relationship, because if you can't change the past, you can at least change your relationship.

ORESTES: Just a moment. If we start with the assumption that the person who set up this mechanism is me, and the person who's fixated on that moment is me. . . .

THERAPIST: Just a moment, please. I'm stopping you there because I don't agree. It's always because of the relationship that this happens. Being an actor in the drama, you could behave in many ways, but only after your wife, the other actor, has put you in a situation that enables you to do so. You are certainly not the only person responsible for this; it's the interaction that's responsible.

At this point, the therapist brings circularity back into the husband's discourse. The husband implicitly gives himself the role of leading actor by pointing to linear causality ("I'm responsible"), just as before he had made himself the victim by blaming his wife for his suffering.

THERAPIST: All your behaviors depend on the nature of your relationship, and our predictions based on your relationship point to two possibilities. A breakdown seems the most likely. . . .

ORESTES: You don't see a normal life as a possibility?

THERAPIST: No, not unless circumstances change.

ORESTES: Let's be clear about this. What you said earlier about the future seems obvious, I think no one would deny it's true, that the past determines the way things are now, and today determines the way tomorrow will be.

With this logical stance, Orestes perfectly expresses many people's deterministic assumptions about time, in which present conditions determine all future development, with no room for the unexpected. Orestes is now faced with the logical consequences of his own ideas. If he pursues his logic, he ends up with a future he doesn't want. The only way out is to think differently, but that's even harder for him to accept.

Furthermore, the therapist also says it wouldn't matter which of the two decided to leave the other. By doing this, he releases the couple from another kind of symmetry, in which one partner is always waiting for the other to make the first move, so as to feel victimized and be able to blame the other. The dialogue has both denied this possibility and broken the stalemate. This was done in an apparently casual way, with no special emphasis, so as to make both partners more receptive to the idea.

ELECTRA: (*to the therapist*) You speak of relationships, but what you say is also true of individuals, in the end.

THERAPIST: No, no, it's got nothing to do with individuals. It's about relationships.

ELECTRA: Yes, but when he gets fixated, or I . . .

THERAPIST: It may be that your relationship will change one day when he says something or you do something . . . perhaps when, for the first time, your husband thinks, for example, that he's as good as, or better than the man you had an affair with, and puts an end to all this, forgets his obsessive doubts. Is that clear? It may happen, you never know. It's a random possibility, it might happen. It could be anything—a gesture—I don't know, if I knew I'd tell you, and this might change the relationship. If the relationship changes, he might see you in a different way, and vice versa, and there might be some way out of this Pirandello play you're in. Is what I'm saying clear?

ELECTRA: Yes, yes, very clear.

In reply to the interesting statement from the wife, whose individual therapy seems to have been more successful than the husband's ("what you say is also true of individuals"), the therapist says that their relationship conditions their individual behaviors, which in turn condition their relationship. He introduces a link between their relationship (as the outcome of both their behaviors, which they are unaware of), and their individual behaviors (which they are only too aware of). This opens up a circular view of the situation, linking their actions and the meanings they attribute to them. This enables them to abandon their linear-causal—and moralistic—stance in which "the other is to blame."

At the same time, indeterminacy and unpredictability in human relationships are introduced by implicitly challenging their deterministic ways of thinking. The stalemate is broken by introducing unpredictability into their relationship. Both of them are waiting for the other to "want" to change or, in therapy terms, for "the doctor to do something to make him/ her want to change." However, the therapist merely admits he's powerless, introduces the idea of unpredictability, and outlines a range of different futures. Change is now no longer just the result of the will to change: it may also happen by chance. The therapist challenges the sterile, static order of the couple with variables that imply fertile disorder. Prigogine would describe this new situation as a system far from equilibrium in which reorganization is very likely to occur. The couple now has the chance to become flexible, to end their self-imposed imprisonment.

THERAPIST: To conclude this meeting, apart from the two possibilities we mentioned earlier, it may be that you, Electra, will begin to feel that he isn't the man you once knew, that the experiences he's had have changed him. And you, Orestes, something might happen to free you from your obsession with your wife's crime, and this might change your relationship. Now time must do its work. So the next meeting will be in six months' time.

REMEMBERING AND FORGETTING

Remembering and forgetting are indispensable to human existence. They form a complementary pair: too much of one or the other tips the balance towards either an excess of remembering, as with Shereshevsky, or an excess of forgetting, as with Zazetsky. If the balance between remembering and forgetting is disturbed, the ability to adapt to environment is also affected.

These extremes apart, excessive remembering can also acquire pathological significance. The major symptom of post-traumatic stress disorder is a continual return to a traumatic event that can never be erased from memory. Hysterical amnesia — in a sense the outcome of an inability to forget — may be regarded as the opposite of this. Whether mediated, somatic, or symbolic, the suppressed memory always finds a way of surfacing: amnesia may be effective, but at the huge cost of enormously reducing the scope of normal social life. The hysteric is always prey to a memory that will not allow itself to be suppressed.[11]

Remembering and forgetting also play a part in interaction. Let us look at a case study. The Tebaldis, a pair of 35-year-old school teachers, had two children aged 12 and 8. They had come to us about their children, who had developed an intense mutual rivalry over the past year, accompanied by frequent arguing and increasing rowdiness. From the very first session, it was clear that the parents argued frequently about how to deal with their children. The husband especially complained about a "loss of memory" in his wife that had coincided with the start of their problems with the children, and attributed great importance to it. His wife was unable to account for her sudden loss of memory and acknowledged that, if it hadn't been for her husband's totally reliable memory in domestic matters, the family situation would soon have taken a dramatic turn for the worse. When asked, the husband, too, was unable to explain her mysterious loss of memory.

The team's hypothesis was that her loss of memory — and also the problems with the children — had started when the husband had begun attending a course in psychotherapy. He had found the course rewarding in

---

[11]Perhaps only rituals can unite remembering and forgetting *in the same event.* For example, the social rite of the "Day of the Dead" revives memories of the dead, but also confines these memories within ritual time, thereby allowing the dead to be forgotten in everyday life.

itself, and it also relieved the tedium of a job that had become routine and repetitive. He was a "husband-on-the-run," but his wife's loss of memory, and the need to make up for her deficiencies, had had the effect of involving him in household affairs: he would do the shopping (which his wife would regularly forget about) and so on. As he himself said, he had had to develop a "super-memory."

One of the most useful interventions in the whole course of the therapy was the following, which concluded the third session.

> THERAPIST: We see that there is a very powerful bond between you, even if there has been some frustration lately. We believe that, over time, you have developed a relationship in which you, Mrs. Tebaldi, monopolize forgetfulness, and your husband monopolizes memory. This is very positive because it has been of great use to your family. But we also think it's very important to remember *and* forget in our lives. The problem we see in you as a couple is that all the forgetting is in one person, and all the remembering in the other.
>
> We think it's important that for two days a week, on Tuesdays and Saturdays, you do what we ask you. (*to the husband*) You will stop remembering things, while (*to the wife*) you will try to remember whatever you can. It's essential, Mr. Tebaldi, that on those two days you never try to remind your wife of anything.

The atmosphere seemed more relaxed in the next session. The husband recounted jovially how his wife had remembered much more than he would ever have expected, and that he had been able to take a breather at long last. Therapy could now usefully proceed.

We have tried to show throughout this chapter that the balance between remembering and forgetting is essential in therapy. Certainly, Selvini Palazzoli's hypothesis in her article, "Why a Long Interval Between Sessions?" (1980), can usefully be read in this way. A long interval allows clients to forget their relationship with the therapists and gives the relationship time to have an effect on them. Similarly, a long interval allows therapists to forget their relationship with their clients and enables them to observe new developments in future meetings with a fresh eye.

The Hayworth family we discussed in Chapter 5 can also be seen as a case of excessive remembering. If it is true that remembering depends to an extent on intense emotional contact, it is easy to understand that it was the therapist's defective memory during the session that made her continue to view the Hayworth family through the lens of the past, while the greater detachment of the team behind the mirror enabled it to forget the family of the past and see a family that was now projecting itself into the future.

However, there are cases where therapy comes to a standstill and further progress seems impossible. In some situations of prolonged impasse, the therapy system loses its ability to evolve. Time seems to stop and no more change is seen. In such cases, when repeated attempts to break the impasse have failed, we impose a longer interval between sessions, sometimes of several months, in order to promote forgetfulness in both clients and therapists and so open up possibilities for the future. In narrative terms, the interval encourages clients and therapists to deconstruct the story that emerged during therapy: therapy, too, becomes a story from which both therapists and clients must liberate themselves.

This deliberate attempt to forget therapy is, paradoxically, an excellent way of ensuring that it is clearly remembered. "True erasure of memory is oblivion, which happens involuntarily as a result of physical or psychic causes" (Bettetini, quoted in Giorello, 1990). It is precisely for this reason that, at the end of the prescribed interval, we do not resort to the usual *aide-mémoire* (clinical files, video recordings) or review the case together before the next session. As Georges Perec rightly says: "Remembering is an illness whose cure is forgetfulness" (quoted in Giorello, 1990).

7

FUTURE INTO PRESENT

IFFERENT TYPES OF THERAPY direct attention towards different areas of the temporal horizon. Short therapies (de Shazer especially), behavioral therapies (in particular those based on operational conditioning), and various uses of hypnosis are oriented towards the future. Systemic therapy, too, has ended up preferring orientation towards the future, in the sense that futures are constructed in the here and now of sessions themselves. Systemic therapy brings the future—or rather, many possible futures—into the present, and allows clients to choose the ones they prefer. The possibility of a future not determined by necessity, but open to sometimes unpredictable choices, gives clients hope; it helps them to break the deadlock and paralysis that is causing them so much suffering and to embark upon a new journey.

The temporal orientation of Western society is mainly responsible for the emphasis our culture places on the future. Although this does not imply a rejection of history (whether individual or social), we agree with Heinemann and Ludes (1978) that: "time [is] regarded as an abstract continuum whose future seems open and may be shaped by individuals and social interaction" (p. 162). Rapid and constant change in our social systems makes thinking based on the past less attractive to us. Post-industrial culture, with its formidable telecommunications structures, is constantly evolving: the objectives we set ourselves and the means we employ to achieve them can no longer be formulated in terms of what was possible in the past. It is what is possible now, or what we *expect* will be possible in the future, that counts.

As with the past, our conception of the future depends on a number of anthropological and social variables. Fatalistic cultures, for example, have limited or no expectations of the future: the future seems uncontrollable because it is conditioned by fate or the inscrutable will of God. The possibility that human beings can influence future events, thus, seems negligible. The temporal perspective depends on how historical, cultural, and social factors blend in any given system. There are situations where the future, of its very nature, breeds a sense of insecurity, where there are so many possibilities that an individual or a family cannot properly work them out, with an eventual "saturation of self" (Gergen, 1991) and the possible onset of paralyzing anxieties. In such cases, the person or the family tends to narrow the temporal horizon: the system denies certain future options, so it is less likely to be disturbed by an excess of expectations.

As Minkowski has pointed out (1933), and as our daily clinical work confirms, psychological and psychiatric disorders are often linked to what we might call "pathologies of the future." Both individual people suffering from serious psychiatric syndromes like schizophrenia and depression and also entire families suffering from psychiatric disturbance seem to develop an almost total inability to plan for the future.

FUTURE QUESTIONS AND HYPOTHETICAL QUESTIONS

Of the circular questions we looked at in Chapter 4, future questions and hypothetical questions are the most important in promoting new orientations and choices. The topic was first discussed in the article "Hypothesizing-Circularity-Neutrality" (Selvini Palazzoli et al., 1980a), and later in the book *Milan Systemic Family Therapy* (Boscolo et al., 1987), where the capacity of these questions to generate new organizations, meanings, and emotions in the future was stressed.

Penn (1985) invented the term *feed-forward* (the opposite of *feedback*) to describe the process triggered by future questions: the possible construction of new relationships and new mental maps.

> The consideration of these future maps places the family in a metaposition to their own dilemma, and the system increases its view of its own evolutionary potential. Pragmatically, future questions, in combination with positive connotation, promote the rehearsal of new solutions, suggest alternative actions, foster learning, discard ideas of predetermination, and address the system's specific change model. . . . At that moment I would say the family is in a process of feed-forward. (pp. 299–300)

Future questions — whether hypothetical or not — at first do not seem very different from each other, but in fact they belong to three quite distinct categories, each with its own objectives. Let us now see how hypothetical future questions relate to the theory of possible worlds (see Chapter 4).

Hypothetical questions, which introduce various "possible worlds" using modal logic, can also be asked about the past or the present. For example, hypothetical questions about the past enable us to construct a present, different from the one we know, in a possible world: "What would be happening now if the past were different from what it really is?" "If your son had never been born, what would your situation as a couple be like now?" "If you had decided to get divorced three years ago, what would your wife be doing now?" "If you had moved far away from your parents-in-law, what kind of relationship would you have with them now?" And so on. After a series of such questions, which may generate new possible worlds, the therapist can, if desired, move profitably from the conditional to the indicative mood to make these worlds "real." We shall give clinical examples of this process later on.

Future questions are totally open and totally unrestricted, apart from inevitable restrictions imposed by actual "reality." They allow clients to construct possible future worlds by exploring the temporal horizon of the family and any discrepancies there may be between the times of individual members. "What will your life be like in ten years' time?" "How long will the present situation remain unchanged?" "When will your daughter be ready to leave home?" "When will her parents accept that she is able to go?" And so on. Future questions thus have a dual function: they probe the family's ability to project itself into an unrestricted future and help it to see that the future can be reinvented.

By contrast, hypothetical questions about the future place a limit on the number of possible futures that can be imagined: they present clients with a possible world subject to constraints imposed by the therapy team itself. The therapist includes one or more possible futures in hypothetical questions and presents clients with a stimulating hypothesis. This enables him or her to challenge their premises quite openly: "If you decide to stop behaving like an anorexic, how do you think your parents will react?" "If you get divorced, what will your children do?" "If your father decides to show more concern for your mother than for her children, how will she behave?" In Tomm's list (1985), future questions are defined as descriptive questions, and hypothetical questions as reflexive questions.

"Pathologies of the future" are usually generated by a narrowing of the temporal horizon (absence of perspective; inability to envision the future; inability to project into the future) or a deterministic view of the future (inability to see possible worlds that are not an immediate projection of the existing world). Future questions work mainly on closures of the temporal horizon by extending and so challenging premises that assume that the present or past can never change. By contrast, hypothetical questions work mainly on deterministic views of the world: by challenging mechanistic premises, they make new worlds possible.

Emanuela: A Future in Chains

Let us now look at part of a case study. Future and hypothetical questions played a major role in broadening the perspectives of the Rocca family, with the result that one of its members was freed from her psychotic, almost autistic, isolation and from a stuck future. For our client, Emanuela, perspectives had been narrowing for some years, and a chronic psychosis was apparently establishing itself.

Emanuela Rocca's future had been closing in for years, and she was rapidly developing chronic psychotic symptoms. She was a 28-year-old woman, the eldest daughter of Gianni Rocca, a 54-year-old company director, and his first wife, Tracy, an Englishwoman who had resettled in London after divorcing her husband. Since the divorce ten years earlier, Emanuela had been living with her father and younger sister, Gabriella, while Filippo, her elder brother, had led an independent life and had found an excellent job with a finance company in a large city. The children had been educated in Italy and Britain. The mother had remarried a few years after her divorce, and kept in close touch with Filippo, her favorite child. Gianni had also remarried two years previously. His new wife, Bruna, was a primary school teacher who had not been married before. She was not yet living with him because she had to look after her mother, who was ill, in another town.

Emanuela had begun to show anxiety and depressive symptoms while at the university, and had gone to a psychologist for individual therapy. Therapy had been broken off a year later when the psychologist had moved. She had reacted violently to this "abandonment," and a few months later, on the day she was supposed to go and visit her mother in London, she had jumped from a bridge and broken both legs. The result of this experience was an outbreak of florid psychotic symptoms, and she was admitted to a therapeutic community. There was no improvement; on the contrary, she became increasingly introspective and gradually succumbed to a range of extremely serious mental and emotional problems. She had been given medication and had undergone rehabilitation therapy, but the therapist who had been in charge of her and who was present at the first meeting we had with the family said that his efforts to establish a relationship with her had largely failed and that she had ignored the group activities in the community.

In the first session, as in later ones, the father sat next to Gabriella, who was attractive and carefully dressed, while Emanuela, less noticeable than her sister, sat apart from them, curled up on a chair with a vacant expression on her face. The group was completed by Filippo, an elegant, polished young man, and the therapist. The first thing that surprised the therapist was that no mention was made of Bruna's absence. When this was pointed out, the father, quite unruffled, said that she was looking after her mother. Her name was never mentioned again during the session. Filippo seemed more absent than present, but mentioned on two occasions that he had little time for his family and was absorbed in his work and recent move to Rome. For her part, Emanuela showed a total unwillingness to cooperate with the consultant throughout the session, responding to his questions on most occasions with silent stares, eccentric behavior, and garbled attempts at speech.

Two major themes emerged during the session, one open, the other concealed. One was the powerlessness and frustration the father and Gabriella experienced when visiting Emanuela, who would often behave erratically and eccentrically with them, and sometimes even refused to see them. A search for possible reasons for this behavior produced no result. The second, concealed theme was a probable alliance between the father and Gabriella: some of the colleagues behind the mirror even fantasized that they were having an affair, but indirect questions aimed at confirming this possibility got nowhere. It was decided at the end of the session to ask only the father and the two daughters to come to the next session to investigate their relationship more thoroughly (Filippo seemed to have established an independent life of his own).

The second session revealed that the pact between the father and Gabriella dated a long way back, to before the divorce — Filippo had been the mother's favorite, Gabriella the father's. The couple behaved like parents trying to cope with a truant child. Exploration of Bruna's role in the family revealed that Gianni had probably married her not so much because he loved her but because he feared loneliness in the future (or, some members of the team speculated, because he needed camouflage). All his passion seemed directed towards Gabriella, who reciprocated in a less direct way. Gabriella spoke of Bruna as a "good, dependable woman" who was very attached to her mother. When asked about Bruna, Emanuela spoke of her as if she were a Martian.

The team was still doubtful as to whether Emanuela's problems were related to her relationship with her mother, consuming jealousy over her father's relationship with Gabriella, or jealousy towards her sister. Bruna was invited to subsequent sessions and openly appreciated having been invited. She did much to clarify our ideas during the third session. She seemed an uncomplicated, sensible woman who appeared almost amazed that she had married into a family she regarded as socially superior to her own. She seemed to be making every effort to be accepted by the daughters and enjoyed her friendly conversations with Gabriella, although she had made no impact on Emanuela, who rejected her totally. Bruna cleared up the doubt that had remained after the first session by openly admitting that she, too, had realized there was a "passion" between Gianni and his younger daughter.

Let us now look at a fragment of the session in which extremely important emotions were revealed.

THERAPIST: (*to Bruna*) You said you feel there is a strong passion between Gianni and Gabriella. Don't you feel excluded by it?

BRUNA: No, because I understand the bond between a parent and a daughter. I also feel very attached to my mother.

THERAPIST: Mightn't this make it more difficult for Gabriella to detach herself from her father later on?

BRUNA: I don't think so . . . hum . . . maybe . . .

FATHER: (*slightly embarrassed, insincerely*) But I hope my daughters will have their own lives, because my future is with Bruna.

THERAPIST: (*to the father*) Might it be that Emanuela has stopped developing because she's waiting for things to sort themselves out in the family? I mean, that Gabriella will become more outward looking and your situation (*pointing to Bruna and Gianni*) will sort itself out. Perhaps she's confused to see you married but separated. . . .

FATHER: Oh, I really wouldn't know, I don't know what goes on in her head.

THERAPIST: And you, Bruna?

BRUNA: Well, now that I think about it, I think Emanuela *would* be pleased to have her sister near her. I often see them arguing, but my impression is that deep down they like each other.

THERAPIST: (*to Emanuela*) Do you agree with that?

EMANUELA: (*looking away*) I'm not here. . . . I don't know.

THERAPIST: And you, Gabriella, do you agree?

GABRIELLA: I'd like to have my sister as a friend, but every time I try to get close to her she lashes out at me.

THERAPIST: In your view, Gabriella, is Emanuela stuck in the present because she can't accept that her father has chosen another woman, or because she feels excluded from the intense relationship that exists between you?

(*Gabriella blushes; the father squirms in his chair.*)

GABRIELLA: As my father said, I've given up trying to understand Emanuela as well. We'd be only too pleased if she decided to change the state she's in and forget all this strange behavior.

It should be noted that Emanuela seemed especially quiet and attentive during this dialogue. Within days of the session, she began to be more open with the staff and other guests in the community. In the following session, her improvement continued and—perhaps not surprisingly—the father went to live with Bruna, explaining that he was tired of traveling so much. Gabriella announced the date of her wedding.

At the start, Emanuela seemed excluded from the family because everyone seemed to have found a home except her: the father with Gabriella and then with Bruna, Filippo with his mother. All she had left was a therapist—whom she had lost—and the community. Another problem, brought forward by the father in the first session, was that financial troubles made it difficult for Emanuela to stay in the therapeutic community (which was very expensive). The relational hypothesis and the urge for Emanuela to leave the community became the basis for a series of questions in the fifth session that attempted to find out what Emanuela would do in the near future.

THERAPIST: (*to Gabriella*) I was wondering, if Emanuela suddenly decided to leave the therapeutic community and make a life for herself outside it, like all young women of her age, where do you think she would go? Emanuela has told me she doesn't know. What about you?

GABRIELLA: I don't know.

FATHER: I know. She'd come home to me. I'd be over the moon and she'd be really happy.

THERAPIST: OK, but let's imagine (it's a hypothesis, this) that she prefers to go to her sister, for example.

FATHER: Well, I don't think that'd be so easy because her sister has a boyfriend, they'll be getting married soon, she'll have her own life. . . .

Gianni is behaving like a good father, prepared to welcome his daughter with open arms, but he is also trying to prevent any powerful bond developing between the two sisters. Emanuela has already shown that she is anxious about her father and may be rejecting him, perhaps because she may fear he has incestuous intentions or fantasies about her, and because

Gabriella has recently relaxed her relationship with her father in order to find a boyfriend.

THERAPIST: But if Emanuela decided to leave the community when she's finished her course there, would she find all your doors open or not? Would she find them open or closed?

FATHER: Emanuela would have three options: live with her mother, live alone, or come and live with us.

THERAPIST: In your view, would she decide to come and live with one of you, or . . .

FATHER: No, not with her sister or brother, I don't think so.

THERAPIST: I mean temporarily, for a certain period, a week or two. . . .

The therapist is worried about the future and tries to discover if there will be anyone to look after Emanuela temporarily when she is forced to leave the community, so that she won't find herself living in a vacuum once again.

GABRIELLA: She could live with me. . . .

FATHER: You'll have your own life, with your husband. . . .

GABRIELLA: That doesn't matter!

There is an important redundancy in this conversation: the father seems unable to accept the loss of both daughters. He feels he is about to lose Gabriella, so he then tries to secure Emanuela.

THERAPIST: (*staring hard at Emanuela, as if trying to break through her apparent indifference*) Emanuela, we're talking about what would happen if you decided your course was over and you left.

EMANUELA: (*in an empty, unfeeling voice*) I mean, like, I was born in '62, so I'm now fairly old, and . . . I mean, I'd like to get married, sooner or later, only . . . that's all I'm worried about, for the moment.

THERAPIST: About getting married?

EMANUELA: Yes.

Her "schizophrenese" becomes even more incomprehensible when she is asked about leaving the community. The therapist focuses on "I'd like to get married."

THERAPIST: So your plan is to get married. To get married inside in the community? Or outside?

EMANUELA: But you can't get married in the community!

THERAPIST: So you'd get married outside the community. OK, but if you go outside the community, from what you say, you wouldn't live with them, you wouldn't go to your mother, you'd get married, you'd find a boyfriend. You'd make your own life.

EMANUELA: Yes, I think so. I mean, I hope so, because the community has been no use to me in that way.

THERAPIST: Pardon?

EMANUELA: Yes, I'd like to get married, what else can I do?

THERAPIST: You say the community's been no use to you?

EMANUELA: No . . .

THERAPIST: Have you already got some idea of what sort of man you'd like? Have you got your eye on someone?

EMANUELA: No, no one special.

THERAPIST: So what do you mean by "getting married"? Getting married to some man, is that what you mean?

EMANUELA: No, I don't know either.

THERAPIST: "If I leave the community I'd like to get married": that's what you said, isn't it?

EMANUELA: I don't know what to say about anything definite, really definite . . .

Once again, Emanuela gives indirect, evasive, incomprehensible answers to the questions. Ambivalence makes her fluctuate between contact with the therapist and withdrawal into her own world.

THERAPIST: Well, my question now is: if you decided to leave the community because your course is finished, which door would you knock on temporarily? Who would you like to stay with? Would you prefer to stay with your father and Bruna, or would you prefer to go to your mother in London?

EMANUELA: (agitated) Well, I don't think I can in my family, I don't know, really I don't know!

THERAPIST: If you had to make a choice, who would you choose?

EMANUELA: If I had to choose? What do you mean, if I had to choose? I mean, I don't have any plans!

THERAPIST: Well, I'd like to ask you one final question. When you say "I'll have to finish the course," when do you think you'll leave the community, if you do leave it? Could you tell me when?

EMANUELA: No.

Here the therapist's curiosity shifts to possible futures, and more specifically, to the delicate and possibly dangerous time when Emanuela will have to leave the community (perhaps obligatorily, owing to her father's lack of money). Her schizophrenese seems to contain two ideas: that everyone in the family gets married apart from her (her mother's second marriage in London, her sister's likely marriage, her brother who is "married" to his work and friends), and the worry that she will be deprived of the only refuge she has, the community. When pressed to be definite about leaving the community, her language becomes enigmatic. This is not surprising. As early as the seventies our experience with families with psychotic members led us to identify this as a fundamental theme. Unlike the anti-psychiatry champions of the time—Laing, Cooper, Basaglia—who saw schizophrenics as flag-bearers of freedom and change in the *status quo*, we realized that schizophrenics, more than anyone else, actually *defend* the *status quo*, or the family's homeostasis, as the term then was. A change in family relationships could deprive them of their only *raison d'être*, so psychosis seems the only possible solution to them.

THERAPIST: Well, for example, would it be weeks, a year, years, or never?

This future question has a dual function: it introduces the possibility of change in the future, and seeks to identify accurately the moment when it will occur. This imposes a constraint (and also introduces a possibility) that challenges the vagueness of Emanuela's thinking.

EMANUELA: I don't even know that. It could be ... that is, because my therapist came here and wasn't able to say, so I haven't abandoned that kind of stuff, I mean, it's not my job to say what I'll do, when I finish the course.

THERAPIST: But just guessing, when do you think you won't need it anymore?

EMANUELA: I haven't the faintest idea, to be honest.

THERAPIST: Is it possible that it might never end in your lifetime?

EMANUELA: No, I think I've done a lot of things. Doing family therapy really isn't any use to me, just as other therapy groups in the community are no use to me. That's why I stopped doing it in the community some time ago!

THERAPIST: So it's possible that, in a sense, you retreated into the community in the way people once used to retreat into convents? You know that some women used to retreat into convents forever;

they shut themselves up behind four walls and it was all over for them. Is that possible? Is it possible that, in the end, what you want is to shut yourself up in some community, in some hospital? . . .

As the dialogue progresses, a redundancy emerges between the therapist's questions about the post-community situation and Emanuela's replies, which are often confused but nonetheless fairly clear about her lack of alternatives outside the community. The therapist and client seem to be in opposing camps: the therapist has an implicit mandate from the referrer and the head of the family to solve the problem of her discharge from the community, and tries in various ways to open up perspectives for her. He seems to be fighting to open up three futures: that of the community, which will have to discharge her if it is not paid; that of the father, who doesn't earn enough to pay the community indefinitely; and that of Emanuela, who depends on the community because she sees no other way out. The conclusion seems to be that Emanuela has no choice, but this would probably condemn her to living in a void again. However, a rather less dramatic possibility seems to be taking shape. The fact that Bruna and the father on the one hand, and Gabriella and her fiancé, on the other, are moving closer together offers Emanuela a new future perspective in which family roles are clearly defined at last.

THERAPIST: Might it be that, in a way, you've withdrawn into a convent?
EMANUELA: I can't imagine it.
THERAPIST: You can't imagine it?
EMANUELA: No. It's possible . . . I don't know from what point of view
. . .

Then again, some may wonder whether introducing scenarios of this kind—a life confined to a hospital or community—might have a negative influence by persuading clients to adopt aims suggested by the therapist. We believe that in contexts where mutual understanding and a positive viewpoint have been established, the therapist's acceptance of all client choices promotes constructive development and reduces self-destructive tendencies.

The family did not come to the next session. The community therapist phoned the center a week later saying that the father had decided to break off therapy because Emanuela had changed so much in so short a time. She had begun to enjoy meeting the family, both in the community and at home, had thrown herself enthusiastically into the work of the community, and had become more open with others. Her language had almost returned to normal.

Six months later, she had a brief attack of delusional and hallucinatory symptoms, but managed to recover without relapsing into the autism of previous months.

Lucia: Renouncing a Kingdom

The effectiveness of circular questions, especially future ones, in revealing new and — we should add — less dangerous future scenarios is well illustrated by the case of Lucia, a seven-year-old child whose obvious intelligence was belied by extremely poor performance at school; also, her evident vivacity and constant attention-seeking at home contrasted with her avoidance of social contact at school.

She had been referred by her school to the local nursery and infants service (SIMEE) for the following reason:

> During her first year at school she had serious learning difficulties and could barely read or write. Her relationships were also extremely poor, lacking motivation, and always only marginally social. During her second year, she tried to participate in the life of the class but her insufficient skills, immature behavior, and infantile, standoffish attitude towards her classmates has restricted her. Her involvement in work and play has been marginal and passive as a result.

It was decided that she had to repeat her second year of primary school.

In addition to Lucia, the Marcheggiani family included the father Mario, a 45-year-old commercial agent, the mother Giulia, a 42-year-old housewife, and an 18-year-old sister, Anna, in her final year of accounting school. The SIMEE psychologist had decided to refer them to our center for therapy because Lucia's problems seemed closely related to the family situation. And in fact, it became clear in the first session that the Marcheggiani family was beset by a host of problems.

The father was a pessimist and depressive, always complaining about crises at work, which meant that he earned little and couldn't meet the family's expenses: in fact, half the family's income came from the wife's parents, who were physically and emotionally extremely close to all the family, especially their favorite, Lucia.

The mother had had a heart attack two years previously ("psychosomatic," according to her doctors) and had been hospitalized briefly. From then on she had had a "terror" of sudden death and always needed some member of the family close by her. Her virtual immobility had increased her weight enormously. It should be noted (although the family itself had not) that her heart attack had coincided with Lucia's starting primary school.

Anna seemed a taciturn, morose girl obsessed by problems at school. She had changed schools three times in recent years because of study problems. Having failed her exams the previous year, she now hoped that she could at last get her certificate and find a job immediately. She was often out of the house and spent much time at the *oratorio* (the center for youth held by the local church): she disliked looking after her mother and found the family atmosphere stifling because of her and her parents' daily efforts to teach Lucia to read and write, and her parents' repeated arguments.

In the first session, the moroseness of Anna and her parents would suddenly change whenever Lucia drew on her lively repertoire of non-verbal communication (she would get up, move about, walk around the room) and verbal joking, bravado, and sometimes rather cheeky comments ("Daddy's a wreck, and Mommy's a barrel. If she gets any fatter she'll break the chair").

The most evident redundancy was that her family's faces lit up whenever Lucia spoke, and switched off when she was silent. Lucia seemed to occupy center stage, from where she entertained the family (and the therapist). When the timing seemed right, the therapist began to challenge Lucia's assumptions.

> THERAPIST: (*to the father*) Lucia seems worried about you parents—
> she's always trying to cheer you up, amuse you. Who is she most
> worried about?
> FATHER: My wife.
> THERAPIST: It looks as if Lucia's got a full-time job . . .
> LUCIA: (*interrupting and pointing to her parents*) Yes, for both of them!
> THERAPIST: When you're at school, do you always think about home,
> how your mother is?
> LUCIA: (*laughing*) Yes, that's right. Mommy's too greedy.
> THERAPIST: She's so worried about you, she seems like a grandmother.
> (*noisy general laughter*)

The reader will have noticed the correspondence between Lucia's teachers' comments on her "infantile" behavior at school and her "grandmotherly" behavior in the session. We might hypothesize that this divergence will probably increase as time goes on because Lucia's behavior at home is immediately rewarded but frowned on at school, so that she will increasingly withdraw into her own world. Lucia seems to have grown up in a family that has allowed/asked her to adopt the roles of daughter, parent, and grandmother. The actual grandmother, because of the power the family has given her, seems to have made a major contribution to the "crowning" of Lucia in the Marcheggiani kingdom. Lucia's future already seems to have been decided for her: as a queen, she must command, not obey. Even to the therapist, with 30 years' experience behind him, she spoke as an equal, and sometimes even as a superior.

ANNA: It's true, it's true! She looks after us full-time, notices everything, what we do, what we eat, she checks everything.
THERAPIST: Like a grandmother.

Lucia now changes the subject, gets up and goes to her mother as soon as the latter seems about to speak. Lucia stops her and takes over the stage once more, making everyone laugh with her funny remarks. In one sense, Lucia seems to dislike being compared with her grandmother, but in another she seems to exaggerate her role, almost as a challenge, contradicting the therapist, shutting her mother up, making fun of everyone. The therapist now introduces the metaphor of the queen unable to rule simultaneously over the Marcheggiani kingdom and the kingdom of her school. Possible worlds are about to be introduced.

THERAPIST: I had the impression at first that you were the princess in this family, but now I think you're the queen.
LUCIA: (*seems visibly pleased*)
THERAPIST: Who commands most in this family?
LUCIA: (*thrusting her chest forward with an amusingly imperious expression on her face*) Me, of course. . . .
THERAPIST: And after you?
LUCIA: Grandmother, grandfather, and then my old wreck of a father, my barrel of a mother, and my Pinocchio of a sister.
(*much general laughter, naturally*)
THERAPIST: Who commands most, your grandfather or grandmother?
LUCIA: My grandmother.
THERAPIST: So there are two queens in this family, you and your grandmother.
LUCIA: I command more because I'm a bit more aggressive than she is.
THERAPIST: So, you go to your grandmother to learn how to give orders . . . interesting, very interesting. Well, Lucia, would you allow us to help your parents, because they came here for help, didn't they?

LUCIA: (*seems puzzled, thinks for a long time, then blurts out*) No!

THERAPIST: Do *you* want to do the job, then? Why don't you want us to do it? Haven't you already got a job at school?
(*Lucia seems to dislike this kind of question and gives an evasive, meaningless answer.*)

THERAPIST: Don't beat about the bush, Lucia. Answer me. Why do you do this job at home and not your job at school?

LUCIA: (*waves her arms about, obviously vexed*) But I do work at school. I can't read, but can write a little.

THERAPIST: Here you're a queen, at school you're not. Your teacher won't take orders like your mother. Your classmates won't obey you either, will they?
(*The parents and Anna agree; Lucia seems puzzled.*)

THERAPIST: It's difficult for you to leave this kingdom, isn't it?
(*The therapist goes out to talk to the team.*)

In this sequence, the therapist begins by approving of Lucia, promoting her from princess to queen, to her evident pleasure, and then links her to the other queen, the grandmother, who occupies the key position in the family. Lucia's self-regard is so great that she places herself above everyone, even her grandmother. Instead of challenging her on this, the therapist, like a loyal subject, asks her permission to help her parents, and hints that she might do more at school. Verbally, Lucia does not permit the therapist to concern himself with her parents, but sends nonverbal messages of puzzlement and indecision. The possibility of a different future for herself and her family is probably gaining ground in her mind.

The therapist's end-of-session comment was as follows.

THERAPIST: We find ourselves with a family that has various problems: (*to the father*) economic problems, pessimism about the future, (*to the mother*) anxiety and fear of death, (*to Anna*) school problems and fears about the future. Lucia seems to have taken the burden of this complex family situation on herself, and works full-time to entertain you, cheer you up. Her behavior shows her to be a delightful, intelligent and amusing child who often behaves like her grandmother, and her grandmother, together with her grandfather, has been looking after you for years. As we've said, she seems to have taken on a full-time job, so she has no time or energy left to think about school.
One of my colleagues expressed the worry that Lucia, by learning only how to command, will find her future relationships with others difficult or impossible. Finally, we were especially struck by Lucia's

negative response to our offer to help you, her parents. Before closing the meeting, and since we still haven't finished our investigation, we suggest that you don't change between now and the next meeting in a month's time, otherwise we might get confused. You especially, Lucia, should go on giving orders and acting as the queen in this family.

The team thought the family looked happy, apart from Lucia, who seemed sullen and even refused to shake hands with the therapist. The emotions shown by the various members of the family at the beginning of the session seemed to have been reversed. However, the team had the impression that Lucia, too, had engaged with the therapist but was hiding her positive feelings out of pride. If this impression is wrong, therapy will have got off on the wrong foot, the timing will have been wrong, and the early challenging of Lucia's assumptions will have been counterproductive.

The suggestion that no one should change before the next session was intended to challenge Lucia's illusion of being in control and put her in a dilemma: if she disobeys she will have to change her behavior, if she obeys she will have to accept the therapist's suggestion. This part of the intervention will not be to the liking of many colleagues who regard these concepts as obsolete, a legacy of the strategic period. We have no qualms about using types of intervention deriving from other theories of therapy. We adhere to the complexity paradigm, which says that the best way to see and act in the world is through a *network* of theories. In other words, we sometimes leave our own field to graze in others if, in certain circumstances, the grass there seems greener than ours. The important thing is to know *when* you are conforming to or departing from your preferred orthodoxy and to take full account of the differences between theory and practice in the model you use.

In the second session a month later, Lucia showed none of the excitable behavior—histrionic, amusing and amused, almost hypermanic—of the first session. She seemed quite calm and willingly offered information about the nuclear family's complex relations with the extended family. Here is an extract from our diary notes on the second session:

Lucia seems to be the nub of the relationships between the three generations, which produces a general confusion of roles. Lucia has spent much time with her maternal grandmother while the father was absent from work, and regards her as "more a mother than her mother." The grandmother treated the mother and Lucia in the same way, as if they were sisters. The grandfather was considered more fun than the father and was always meddling in the family's affairs. The nuclear family had no space of its own. Lucia, opposing the immobility of her father and sister, responded to the bored moroseness of her mother with creativity and liveliness. It is important that on three occasions during the session she got up to go and kiss and caress her parents when their conflicts were being discussed, as if to reassure them. At the end of the session, the therapist asked the sisters to stay at home, saying he would see only the parents in the next meeting.

Only the parents came to the third, fourth, and fifth sessions. They reported that Lucia was steadily improving at home and also, according to her teachers, at school. In the final session, the sixth, about a year after the first, the sisters were also asked to attend. What the therapist saw when he entered the therapy room was significant: the parents and Anna were sitting near each other, but Lucia was curled up on a chair some distance from them, studiously reading a book that she held so as to cover her face completely. It was as if she were saying, "I'm busy with school now, so you busy yourself with my family."

After the usual pleasantries, the therapist tried to involve Lucia in the conversation. Lowering her book and smiling, she pointed to her family and said, "I'll hand over to them, I have to read." In a humorous and rather stylish way, she indicated verbally and, most importantly, nonverbally during the session that she had withdrawn from the field, that her interests were now her school work and her friends. A note from the school brought along by the parents fully confirmed the change in her: being highly intelligent, she had easily made up lost ground and was now part of a large group of friends. Her sister Anna also seemed less morose, more relaxed, and optimistic about her future. Only the parents still seemed prepared to go on with therapy in order to resolve their conflicts.

Towards the end of the session, the therapist envisioned a different future for the couple which involved the wife especially.

THERAPIST: Mrs. Marcheggiani, have you ever thought of finding some sort of job outside the home?

MOTHER: Oh, yes . . . but my husband has never liked the idea. . . .

THERAPIST: But now your daughters are growing independent. I think that if you ever felt you wanted a job, any job, part-time or full-time, the situation might change in the future. . . .

MOTHER: (her face lighting up) It's true, it's true.

THERAPIST: I think that, first, a job would bring in some money, which would make your husband less anxious. It would also make you less anxious because your anxiety is strongly linked to your husband's. Second, you might lose weight, feel better physically, and that might reduce your anxiety still further. Third, and I think this is very important, the desire for a job outside the home would probably make all your fears, your phobias about being alone, disappear like magic. . . .

MOTHER: (with a sigh) I'm quite sure of it!

The therapist left the room for the ritual consultation with the team at the end of the session. On returning, he said that no psychological problems could be seen at present that justified the continuation of therapy. The family was visibly relieved and pleased, except for the father who, as he left, asked the therapist if he could call him in a few months' time. The therapist responded by telling him to let quite some time pass, after which the situation might have changed so much that there would never be any need for outside help again.

The overall impression was that the three females had—in reality or, for the moment, only imaginatively—forgotten their state of immobility, their impasse, and had embarked on a new journey into the future. The father's closing message seemed to suggest that he was worried about finding himself on his own in future. As we pointed out in Chapter 4, the team did not respond to the messages, first from the couple and then from the father, that they did not want to be abandoned. To have continued seeing the couple would have confirmed the "diagnosis" that they were a dependent, problem-ridden family; breaking off the relationship stressed that the family had its own resources from which the independent identities and lives for all its members could develop. We have sometimes found that breaking off the relationship can happen too soon. However, the risks involved are more than outweighed by the benefits that result from "depathologizing" clients. Should difficulties arise, the situation can easily be remedied by accepting clients back for further therapy.

Violent Couples: "You Provoke Me, I Hit You"

The problem of violence, especially in marriages and families, has become a controversial and complex issue among therapists. We shall limit ourselves here to the work of Gerry Lane and Tom Russell, two psychologists from Atlanta, Georgia, who have devised a therapy for violent couples (couples with a pattern of recurring violence) who have not responded to legal or other existing kinds of therapeutic intervention (Lane & Russell, 1986). Therapy is offered only to those couples whose violence has led neither to separation nor to the adoption of new modes of coexistence.[1]

---

[1]Such intervention is an attempt to solve problems of violence using words instead of social control. Violence should be neither underestimated nor treated like just another marital problem. It may call for drastic measures like the use of centers for battered wives, forced temporary separation or even prison in the last resort. As Russell and Lane stress, however, the problem remains that, although women are obviously the victims of violence, they often refuse to separate from their partners or even report them to the authorities.

Lane and Russell's contract with the court of Atlanta requires the court to respect the confidentiality of the sessions and not to interfere with therapy. The sessions with the couple, usually, are not more than three.

In the first session, great care is taken to establish a relationship of mutual trust with clients by gathering information about the life of the couple and its context. A set of circular hypothetical future questions is asked which speculate about eventual loss of control in aggressor and victim, possibly with serious, irreversible consequences:

> In our work we attempt to observe interactional patterns, elicit historical premises and causal attributions, which in our view maintain the recursive pattern of violence. We punctuate our concern about the violence and underscore the potential grave consequences without blaming in a causal fashion either partner. We do this through circular questioning and future questioning. We communicate to each partner their responsibility for their violent behavior and their responsibility for remaining in a violent relationship. For example, we might ask, "If this violence in your relationship continues, who will die first?" We might follow-up with such a question as, "If one of you kills the other and the other is in prison, how will your children be taken care of?" Still further, we might ask, "If one of you is dead and the other is in prison and your children grow up without you, who will they blame for not having parents?" We do not attempt to impose our maps or solutions onto the couple in regards to their dilemma. As stated previously, we adopted this stance after our observation of the ineffectiveness of such prior attempts to control the behavior of these couples caught in this repetitive pattern of violence. (Lane & Russell, 1986, p. 10)

As can easily be seen, Lane and Russell's future questions are what we call hypothetical future questions, i.e., questions which oblige clients to come to terms with a set of not always desirable options by explicitly placing constraints on the future: they take for granted that an escalation of violence will take place and that one of the partners will kill the other. To use Karl Tomm's terminology (1985), these questions explore differences of context in time, creating possible worlds in which relationships and actions develop in a context radically different from the present one.

We believe that these questions work not because they are a kind of terrorism, but because they conflict with the epistemology of violent people, which is similar to the epistemology of alcoholics conceived by Bateson (1972b). The epistemology of a violent person is based on a concept of control: he/she is convinced that (in the future) he/she will always be able to control his or her violent urges before he/she actually kills someone or is him/herself killed. By contrast, hypothetical questions predict loss of control in the aggressor (and the victim). When clients respond, as they usually do, by saying that *they* will be able to control themselves, they are given numerous examples of murder committed by ordinary people who believed they were able to control their violent impulses.

Interventions such as these direct the attention of violent people away from their partners, whom they see as the cause of their violence ("You provoke me, I hit you") to themselves ("I react to my own uncontrollable impulses"). In a sense, we could say that subjects who benefit from such intervention graduate from first-order to second-order cybernetics. Here, too, there are similarities with Bateson's alcoholics: the violent person sees the other person as the cause of his behavior, just as the alcoholic blames the bottle for his dependence on alcohol. However, this type of intervention works because the violent person "touches bottom" not in the present, as with alcoholics, but in a future brought into the present during therapy: if violence is carried to its logical limit, one member of the couple is in serious danger of being killed.

FROM AMBIFINALITY TO AMBITEMPORALITY

Cronen and Pearce (1985), developing the well-known concept of systems equifinality (von Bertalanffy, 1969), saw "ambifinality" as one of the distinguishing features of the Milan method. Because we now place so much stress on time in therapy, we have replaced "ambifinality" with another term, "ambitemporality." Before discussing why we did this, we would like to quote a longish section from Cronen and Pearce's article in which they describe the dynamic self-referential epistemology on which the Milan method is based:

> The Milan method is *not* just a collection of techniques which a therapist can *use*. It is a broad-based, sophisticated "epistemology," a way of thinking about and acting in social systems. . . . Milan therapists work at thinking of families systemically and dynamically. In this view, the structure of the family resides in the relationships among the members of the family, not in the attributes of each member. The structure is always a process of evolution. . . . But this evolution is not always in desirable directions. Sometimes the logic of a family results in pain, and through one means or another the family confronts a therapist. However, the "presenting problem" is often a poor description of the structure and action patterns of the family. Like most of us, families usually think in terms of individuals rather than systems, in terms of linear processes rather than reflexive revelations, and in terms of static "states" rather than dynamic "processes."
>
> In our judgement, the procedures which Milan-style therapists use can be seen as "expressing" a systemic, reflexive, dynamic epistemology which is in sharp contrast with that of most families. The therapy session itself, as well as the "intervention" and "prescriptions," is an invitation for the family

to participate in patterns of action which reflexively "reconstitute" this epistemology.

Cronen and Pearce then go on to describe the concept of "ambifinality":

Any discussion of "effects" or how things work in a system is difficult using a language whose bias is linear. In systemic epistemology, "causes" are not distinct from "effects" and the relevant variables cannot be "isolated" without killing the system. An ambifinal cause is one whose "effects" are "context dependent" or "contingent" on the state of the system in which it occurs.

The procedure which the Milan method uses to invite clients to participate in a systemic epistemology are ambifinal because they have different effects depending upon the characteristics of the system to which the invitation is given. Further, the various effects are sufficiently broad to pose a powerful impetus to change the existing logic of the system. (1985, pp. 70–71)

We said earlier that our interest in how human systems function in time led us to prefer "ambitemporality" to "ambifinality." A social system (e.g., the family) may be regarded as a collection of individuals each with their own time, or as a collection of individual stories (histories) which combine and interpenetrate to produce the story (history) of the larger system. As we have seen, the individuals in a family may have different times: one member may evolve out of step with the others, be arrested or regress in time while the others adapt, understand the situation or become contrary and intolerant, all of which obviously has an effect on the family atmosphere. Some or all members of the nuclear and extended family may become overinvolved with or hypercritical towards each other, thus producing the frustration and hostility typical of "high expressed emotion" (cf. Leff & Vaughn, 1985).

In such cases, the therapist tries to accept the various temporal perspectives of the family members impartially and to introduce new temporal correlations and coordinations. This may have an effect on the family's stalemate (temporal rigidity and atrophy) and make development possible.

The therapist seeks to introduce a temporal sequence that opens the present up to the future: absence of change is seen positively, but the possibility of change is also simultaneously entertained ("For the moment we understand that it's better for you to remain the way you are"). Thus, although the *status quo* is explicitly accepted, "for the moment" introduces the possibility of change. The use of phrases like "for the moment," "in this period," "up to now," "later" and "now is not the time" releases clients and therapists from the responsibility for change and restores it to time, to the future. To paraphrase Cronen and Pearce, the static logic of the system is powerfully stimulated towards change by introducing a new logic that opens it up to the future. This is a tautology, of course, but at least it is a therapeutic tautology. Whenever we hear "we are stuck in time," we respond with "your evolution is a matter of time." The tautology alters the thrust of the problem as originally formulated.[2]

Thus, ambitemporality means acknowledging and accepting the present while at the same time speculating about and accepting possible futures. The present is what it is, but the future can either reproduce or reject the present. Once again, the therapist challenges deterministic premises: "If our past always offers the same situation, which is also the present situation, our future can only be identical to the past." We respond to this nontemporality with an ambitemporality that assumes the possibility (although not the inevitability) of an unpredictable future.

Future or hypothetical circular questions can also effectively challenge certain diagnoses, prognoses or seemingly inevitable judgments based on an adjective-plus-verb *to be*, such as "he's weak," "he's delinquent," "he's schizophrenic," etc., which imply aspects of character that seem unlikely to change. Bateson (1972), for example, believed that prisons fail to reeducate and rehabilitate their inmates because they crystallize the very "delinquency" they are intended to eradicate. The difference between "a delinquent act" and "delinquency" is a difference in logical types: a delinquent act is a discreet event that may be repeated or not, but delinquency is a process that Bateson would put in the "learning II" category, in which are included what are commonly considered intrinsic aspects of a person's character. From the point of view of time, this process becomes timeless. "Delinquency" is, after all, the crystallization of a future: once a "delinquent," always a delinquent. As many have pointed out, this may also happen to schizophrenics: when they have no symptoms, they are not considered normal, they are merely defined as "schizophrenics in remission."

We have here a self-reflexive loop similar to the one we found in constructing the past. The future we create is determined by present necessities and premises, is shaped by the present, but an imagined future has a washback effect on the present which can create the conditions needed for its own realization. This is precisely how Watzlawick's (1984) self-fulfilling prophecies work.

We have referred to delinquency and schizophrenia here, but everything we have said applies to a whole range of other character traits. There

---

[2]This temporal reformulation introduces uncertainty and the possibility of change. Clearly, such interventions should be inserted into a context of complex interaction that is highly unpredictable: no one, whether client or therapist, can predict the outcome of such a statement, which is intended to be neither reassuring nor mandatory.

is a world of difference between saying "the child is bad" and "the child has (just now) done something bad." Circular questions, especially future and hypothetical ones, can challenge the timeless inevitability of these labels and help a new awareness of time and contingency to emerge.

As we have seen, the therapist accepts the various individual and collective times, presents and futures, encountered in the family. This enables the therapist to recalibrate family times and also to produce a new systemic synthesis: to take the diagnosis at face value (as if it were final); to treat the diagnosed person the same as all the others (as if the diagnosis were worthless); to introduce the expectation of change (as if the diagnosis might lose its validity in time). These are all stages in a therapy process based on ambitemporality, and they occur simultaneously.

Ambitemporality occurs even when the therapist suggests to clients that change should not happen and seems to halt time by "prescribing the symptom." For example, by saying, "It would be premature for you to change now," or "For the time being you could go on doing what you're doing now," another possible reality is placed alongside the reality of the client's symptom. A new future is revealed to the clients (and therapist).

Flight into the Future

The Maggi family—a 60-year-old mother widowed five years previously, and two daughters, 30-year-old Caterina, a chemistry graduate now working as a researcher in a large firm, and 24-year-old Teresa, an apprentice in a medical laboratory—came to our center at the suggestion of Caterina, who was worried about her sister's problems.

During the first session, Caterina, who had left the family five years before to settle in Milan, said that on her regular visits to the family she noticed that her sister was "steadily regressing," closing in on herself, losing interest in the outside world. This was worrying her mother, who often complained about it in her frequent telephone calls to the elder daughter.

Teresa, who did indeed seem subdued, morose, and neglectful of her appearance, said that she had no future, that her mother didn't understand her, that she felt vastly inferior to her sister and everyone else she knew. She blamed all this on her past, on the past life of her family, which had been rendered chaotic by the family apartment being located above the bar her parents managed. "We almost never ate together, because either my mother, or father, or everyone had to be in the bar." The father, who had never got on with his wife, had died of a heart attack five years previously. The relationship between the two sisters mirrored that of their parents: Caterina, who had been closer to her father, had never become attached to her sister and mother; Teresa had always "clung" to her mother (who subtly, though exasperatedly pointed out that Teresa followed her everywhere, like a shadow). It was reported that Teresa's "regression" had started shortly after Caterina's move to Milan.

One of the team's hypotheses in the first session was that Caterina had abandoned her family after the death of the father because of the gloomy atmosphere that had developed, and the mother had missed her. This had raised doubts in Teresa: her self-esteem was undermined and she had developed an obsessive need to be loved by her mother. Once again, a vicious circle had been created in which symptoms — the expression of a relational dilemma ("Am I loved or not?") — were achieving the opposite of what they were intended to achieve: reactions of pity, frustration, and exasperation.

When the therapist suggested another meeting, Caterina said she had just finished individual therapy that had lasted two years, and felt she had achieved her own equilibrium: in other words, she was handing over her mother and sister for "repairs" (in fact, she did not attend subsequent sessions). In seven sessions held over a period of a year, Teresa changed significantly, began to pay more attention to her clothing and appearance, joined a sports club, made a lot of friends, and even changed her whining tone of voice: she now spoke pleasantly and self-confidently.

All this changed the basis of her mother's worries about her: instead of worrying that her daughter was regressing, she was worried that she was *too* involved with the outside world. It was also reported that Caterina was now having problems: her boyfriend had left her three times and she was plunging into gloom. The team decided to invite Caterina along for a meeting, and she accepted.

The meeting proved very interesting. There was tension between Caterina and Teresa right from the start: they had argued violently during Caterina's visit the previous weekend, with Caterina accusing Teresa of neglecting the mother and being arrogant. Caterina had been especially offended by one of Teresa's remarks: that she had found a friend who was "like a sister" to her. The mother was plainly uneasy and said, with a sigh: "If these two could only get on, there'd be peace in the family."

The following hypotheses emerged during team discussion:

> 1. Teresa's growing independence, and so greater involvement in the outside world, had made the mother feel lonelier, so the mother had stepped up her attempts to involve Caterina in checking on her sister. This had put Caterina in the role of the husband-father who had died young. It should be noted that Teresa turned to Caterina three times during the session and said, "I want a sister, not a father!"

2. Teresa's rapid detachment from the family and development of a separate identity had led to a crisis in the family, especially in Teresa's relations with Caterina, who until then had been considered the responsible woman in the family, the woman who had been successful. The rivalry between the sisters had been reversed: the mother was beginning to see cracks in Caterina's formerly solid position ("Even at her age she still shows no sign of starting a family and having children").

3. Like other women who have been closer to their fathers than their mothers, or have entered an alliance with the father against the mother, Caterina, although enterprising and independent, also felt a strong unsatisfied need for affection and had difficulty in establishing a deep, ongoing relationship with another man.

These hypotheses formed the basis of an intervention that would mirror the themes of rivalry, separation, and exasperated conflict that seemed to be producing tension, and sometimes anguish, in the family. It was not easy task. As the team laboriously discussed the situation, suddenly a hypothesis emerged located in remote future time, a "flight into the future." It was soon accepted by the whole team.

THERAPIST: (to the mother) My colleagues behind the mirror, especially the women, think that you'll have to be patient before your dream of having two daughters who get on with each other can be realized. Even though they've always had their disagreements—and they're quite violent ones at present—they're irreversibly heading towards a sisterly relationship—a relationship of mutual acceptance—although of course they'll continue to disagree over some things. Let's let time do its work and meet again in three months' time.

Initial amazement was followed by relief and acceptance. We might comment on this intervention by saying that if the team had decided to intervene in past and present conflicts in the family, it would have remained within the time of the family system. This "flight into the future," i.e., a prediction of development in the future, made a less conflictual relationship possible between the mother and the two sisters.

The women's positive response to the intervention seemed to show that it mirrored their own hopes. Since this was the latest session, we are unable to report as yet on longer-term developments. However, we would say from experience that interventions like this can at times be extremely effective, even final. On other occasions, because the timing was wrong (see Chapter 5), they seem to be rejected totally. It should go without saying that, if this happens, the team drops everything and returns to the family's previous themes and times. A consultant or therapist always has to take full account of timing—he or she is dealing with complex living systems, not machines—but even so, it is difficult to time things perfectly. There is always an element of trial and error, as in exploring unknown terrain without maps. So timing is simply a means of orienting actions: its effectiveness is shown by the results it produces.

Let us look more closely for a moment at the relationship between a therapist's (or team's) "flight into the future" and timing in one of the most important stages in therapy and consultation: its termination. As we said in Chapter 4, we often terminate therapy or consultation when the therapist or team see highly significant change in clients: more fluent communication and information flow, greater ability to "see" different solutions to the same problem, an improvement in emotional atmosphere, and above all, a new ability to resolve conflicts. The problems and symptoms that were brought in for therapy may still partly be present, but the assumptions that would ensure their continuation are beginning to crumble. In short, when we see what we, in our jargon, call an "about-turn in the system," we tell our clients that our work is done.

After a brief moment of disorientation, clients usually approve of this decision, and often ask if they can come back later if some new crisis arises. Our follow-up shows that in most cases positive change continues after termination of therapy, while in a minority of cases contact is reestablished after a year or more. So the decision to terminate therapy or consultation may be seen as the outcome of a "flight into the future" on the part of the therapist and team, which in successful cases is also shared by clients.

SIMILIA SIMILIBUS CURANTUR: SPLITTING THE TEAM

Sometimes, especially when faced with powerfully symmetrical relationships or deeply rooted oppositions in the families or couples we see, we decide to use split intervention. The therapist returns to the therapy room with the message that the team has been unable to reach a unanimous decision. He or she then presents the views of the two "factions" within the team. One part of the team is usually in favor of maintaining the *status quo,* while the other favors change. In this way, the team reproduces the family's dominant relationship mode (split, therefore impasse) and introduces the possibility of change: *similia similibus curantur,* like cures like.

Time also plays an important part in such interventions. One-half of the team sees the present or past positively: "It's useful for you to stay the way you've always been," "We're worried—the best cure is for you to continue behaving as you are now." The other half sees the future positively: "It's useful that the change that has begun should continue." In this way, the two "factions" in the team identify (and make concrete) two different temporal realms by simultaneously ordering the family's experiences of time and creating interplay between its various temporal realms. The result is that the family's temporal horizon is radically modified. Let us now look at some case studies.

Maturity and Immaturity

It sometimes happens that individuals, families, or therapy systems get stuck in the present. To use Watzlawick's symmetry-complementarity model, we might say that systems get stuck in rigidly symmetrical or complementary modes which produce discomfort and suffering. Both modes lead to an impasse in therapy, as if time stops and the ability to change is lost. In the case study that follows, we shall examine an intervention devised by the therapy team to avoid entering into symmetrical interaction with the family, with the ultimate aim of initiating a process of change.

The Adorni family consisted of the father, a 50-year-old doctor, the 47-year-old mother, and two daughters. The elder daughter, age 25, had left the family home to marry a colleague, and had had a baby daughter. The younger daughter, Luisa, 16 when consultation took place, was suffering from a rather serious form of anorexia that had begun three years before, shortly after the birth of her niece.

The whole family came to the first two sessions, including the elder daughter, whom Luisa both admired and envied, especially since she had become a mother. One of the first hypotheses was that her anorexia was related to the intense relationship that had developed between Luisa's mother, her sister, and her niece. The father was a blunt, rather boorish man totally immersed in his work.

From the third session on, only the parents and Luisa, who was showing signs of gradual improvement, were invited to attend. Before, Luisa had completely withdrawn from social contact, but now she had grown close to a female friend with whom she was planning to share a small apartment. Her weight had increased moderately and her obsession with food had virtually disappeared, although menstruation had not yet resumed.

In view of these positive changes, the team decided to call only the parents in for the seventh session, because they felt therapy was now nearing its end. The parents' opposing ideas about Luisa provided the main theme of the session. The father said that his daughter's anorexia was a question of age: once she reached the age of 18, all her problems with food would vanish. The mother disagreed, saying that Luisa had not got over her difficulties yet and would certainly have had a relapse without therapy. What she feared most—apart from the death of her daughter— was that Luisa would shut herself up in the house again and resume her terrible battle with food. The husband responded impatiently, restating his views. The wife interrupted him, repeated her own views, and so on.[3]

In the team discussion, it was decided to accept "simultaneously" the opposing views of the husband and wife by placing them both on the same level and putting both "in the right." This was made possible by splitting the team.

> THERAPIST: We've had a long discussion in there, but we haven't come to any agreement. Some of us think the mother is right, that is, that the illness is serious and has to be dealt with in some way. Others of us think that the father is right, and that everything will sort itself out in time. After heated argument, we've decided to let time do its work. We've decided to interrupt therapy for a year, that is, until Luisa reaches her eighteenth birthday. If Luisa is then still experiencing the problems she has now, it means the mother is right and we'll begin therapy again.

The parents didn't show up the following year, but telephoned instead to say that Luisa was well, had lost most of her symptoms, had been living for some months with a friend in a small apartment, and was making good progress with her studies.

Two years after the last session, the father called one of the authors (who had been the therapist at the time) asking with some embarrassment if a meeting could be arranged for himself and his wife. When asked if Luisa had had a relapse, the answer was a decided "no": the couple was the problem now. An interview was granted. After a strange reluctance to say why they had requested the interview, the father finally blurted out, "Doctor, don't get annoyed, but we've come about the really big problem we've got with the dog!"

Shortly after moving into the apartment with her friend, Luisa had asked her parents to buy her a dog—a doberman no less—which they would have to look after for her because her apartment was too small: she

---

[3]Similar, though less emotionally charged, situations are often found in families with adolescent children, when the parents disagree radically over the age at which their children should be regarded as adult.

would visit them on weekends to play with the dog. Everything went well until the dog became huge and began behaving strangely with its owners: totally obedient with Dr. Adorni, playful with the daughter, but nearly dangerous with the mother, who was often leapt on, scratched, and bitten ("Show the doctor all the marks he's left on you").

The husband was worried about the harm that might come to his wife, believing that the dog might actually kill her. On two occasions he had decided to stun the dog with the butt of his pistol, but his wife had begged and warned him against doing so because it might bring on a serious relapse in Luisa. The father was unable to persuade Luisa to get rid of the dog: it was time, she said, that they learned how to look after the dog well, as she did on weekends. There was now such a stalemate between the father, the mother, the dog, and Luisa that the parents had come to the team for help. One hypothesis was that, on leaving home, Luisa had decided to leave a ferocious dog in her place which, "strangely," was now a threat to her mother's safety. Instead of rushing to get rid of the dog, Luisa was now using subtle threats to force her parents to keep it. This all seemed like Luisa's revenge on her mother. Another hypothesis was that the dog took up a lot of the mother's time, thereby preventing her from getting too attached to the elder daughter and her child. A third was that the dog had grown up under symmetrical pressure—and so had been exposed to opposing styles—from the two parents, and had become confused as a result. Certainly, the dog's behavior—unfortunately for the mother—was far from neutral.

At the end of the meeting, the therapist said that as soon as they got home the parents should call a meeting of the entire family, including the daughters and son-in-law, and say they had requested a meeting with the center's therapist (300 kilometers away) because they were worried the dog might go berserk. They should then all decide what was to be done. The ritual was successful, and the father cancelled the next meeting because they had all decided—Luisa included—that the dog should go to an animal training center.

The Adorni couple is a classic example of a symmetrical relationship ("I'm right!"/"I'm right!"), in which each member of the couple believes that accepting the other's point of view will make him or her the loser. A vicious circle is created by uniting two opposing causal chains with no "before-after" temporal sequencing. A situation rather like the 40-year Cold War stalemate between the USA and the USSR is created: neither side agrees to disarm first for fear of being attacked as a result. The Adornis' symmetrical relationship also included Luisa, whom they both unceasingly fought to gain control of.

By accepting both parents' maps, the team's split intervention in the seventh session established a complementary relationship between the team and the couple, thus avoiding a symmetrical relationship that would probably have escalated in the way the couple's own symmetrical relationship had done. Everyone taking part in therapy adopted a complementary stance towards time: the final decision concerning whether Luisa's symptoms had really disappeared for good had been left to the passing of time. In a sense, time had been made the final arbiter.

Bateson provides an interesting discussion of symmetrical relationships in his article, "The Cybernetics of 'Self'" (1972b), from which we quoted earlier. He compares the alcoholic's symmetrical relationship to drink with man's relationship to nature. Both commit the epistemological error of assuming they can control what they see, the bottle or nature as the case may be. In the intense and prolonged relationship that develops between a therapy team and clients, the team's complementary relationship with both the couple and time may serve to correct what Bateson calls "epistemological error."

At this point we have to ask whether it was the split intervention that made therapy successful or some other factor. An unqualified "yes" would be simplistic and reductive, and place too much faith in the healing effectiveness of *ad hoc* intervention. The split occurred in a complex relationship that had developed over time: if the same intervention had been made in the first session, it would probably have had no effect whatsoever. As we have said, it is impossible to establish once and for all what produces change. All we can do is suggest explanations.

Agreement and Disagreement

The Valentini family consisted of a couple of middle-aged parents — the father a professional, the mother an office worker — with a 20-year-old son, Ettore, and an 18-year-old daughter, Cinzia. Ettore, described as a "mommy's boy" since early childhood, had always demanded attention from his parents, while Cinzia, a more independent child, had seemed able to live her own life without depending overmuch on her family.

A year before the start of therapy, Ettore had suffered a schizophreniform crisis with delusions and hallucinations. His florid symptoms had promptly disappeared after brief hospitalization and therapy, and seemed to have left no permanent aftereffects, although there were still residual negative symptoms like apathy, inertia, and loss of interest in the outside world. He spent his life indoors, had lost the few friends he had had, and had withdrawn from high school. He spoke little, and when he did it was mainly to argue with his mother. His worried parents had been keeping a close eye on him, but to little effect.

Excellent results were obtained after five family therapy sessions (we shall not go into all the detail here). Ettore's progress was quite evident from the fact that he had started going out of doors again and seeing his old school friends; he was even keen on going back to school the following year.

At the start of the sixth session, the father began by saying that Ettore was now well on the way to recovery and seemed to be steadily regaining his independence. Ettore, for his part, adopted the role of "outsider" in the session, as if to state once and for all that he no longer had anything to do with his family. Immediately after, however, his father raised a new topic which, frankly, seemed to astound him. He and his wife, who had always said they had got on well with each other, had started arguing. The wife accused her husband of expecting to be waited on, of being selfish, while he replied that she no longer took any interest in the family. In short, the whole session developed into a sparring match between the husband and wife, with an occasional contribution from Cinzia, while Ettore remained serenely silent.

During the team discussion, the rather simplistic hypothesis emerged that Ettore had finally decided to break away from his mother by changing and viewing events in his family from the outside. With Cinzia already excluded from the family game for some time, the parents had found themselves free to think about each other now that they no longer had to think about their children, and both—but especially the mother—felt alone.[4] Possibly the mother had been feeling alone for a long time before and had attached herself to Ettore because the husband did not fulfill her needs. The change in Ettore was accompanied by a change in the mother, who felt the need to think more of herself, a need that the husband could not accept.

The team felt they had to draw attention to both the change in the son and the uneasiness of the parents by keeping open the prospect of further change. They decided on the following intervention.

THERAPIST: We have noticed that positive change has begun both in Ettore, who has started thinking about his own future, and in his parents, who have started airing their conflicts and strains openly in the family. In our experience, this happens in all families. The children become independent and their parents are at last able to bring

---

[4]It often happens that the disappearance of symptoms when a psychotic child leaves the family produces not relief in the parents, as might be expected, but a crisis of loss, which usually disappears soon afterwards.

their normal, healthy marital conflicts out into the open after remaining silent for the general good of the family.[5] In short, we see from these changes in the whole family that a process of positive change has been initiated. However, the members of the team disagree over what the future holds. Some of us think that the process of change is now irreversible and that therapy should be terminated. The others think there is some doubt as to whether it is irreversible. So we've decided to meet in six months' time to see if the change is irreversible or not.

The intervention produced interesting reactions in the various members of the family. Nodding his head with real relief, Ettore said, "So far as I'm concerned, therapy should be terminated." The mother, staring anxiously at the therapist, ventured: "But we're stuck in this situation. We need help! Can't you give us some sort of advice now?" The father and daughter made no comment on the intervention.

Two points should be made about this case study. From the family's point of view, i.e., from the point of view of the observed system, it is interesting that their time frames changed once therapy had started. Ettore clearly opted for change, for a time that flows forward into the future. The mother and father remained stuck in the static time of their conflict, although they tried to redefine their position. Finally, the daughter seemed to alternate between the two positions (change, no-change).

The observing system's (i.e., the therapeutic team's) assessment of the situation was even more interesting. The team accepted both Ettore's change and the conflict that had broken out between the parents as positive developments, each with its own temporal perspective oriented towards the future. By splitting into two groups—one believing that the change was irreversible, the other that it was reversible—the team had been able to adopt the opposing positions of the son and mother. In this way, the intervention amplified indeterminacy by introducing ambitemporality: change vs. immobility, time fixed in the present vs. time flowing into the future. The intervention thus had a dual effect: the future was presented in a positive light; and indeterminacy was introduced, not placing any constraints on the future. The family could now evolve in any direction.

Such indeterminacy restores to clients the authority that had previously

---

[5]Positive connotation avoids passing negative judgement on the couple's disagreement: indeed, the couple can now exist as a couple at last. Before, they were simply their child's nurses.

been delegated to the therapeutic team alone. Clients expect the therapist to supply knowledge, certainty, solutions and guarantees, to arbitrate the meaning and extent of change: the therapist responds with indeterminacy, uncertainty, a sense of possibility. Clients are now free to attribute their own meanings to their ideas and actions. We might say that splitting the team delegates change to time, or rather, to the future.

A Tea-Party Family

A split intervention is sometimes given at the end of the first meeting in cases where the clients' need for therapy has not been stated very clearly, where the motivation of the various members of the family is uneven (some want therapy, others not), or where there is no apparent uneasiness or suffering in the family itself. Let us look now at a case of the third type, what we like to call "tea-party families"—families that come to therapy for the kind of relaxing, noncommittal conversation they would get if they had been invited round for a cup of tea and a chat.

The three members of the Beria family were unusually carefree and high-spirited when they came to the first meeting; at the least, their mood seemed out of keeping with a serious therapy context, as if they just come for a relaxing chat with friends and acquaintances. The parents, who owned a tie-manufacturing business in Northern Italy, were both extremely obese. Mrs. Beria, as if to emphasize the fact that she was an entrepreneur, came with a laptop computer in her bag. Their 18-year-old daughter, Carlotta, was the designated patient. Obese like her parents, she had had a splenectomy at the age of 14, and a serious accident at 15 when a car had run her down and broken her tibia and fibula. Since she suffered from blood deficiency, it had been impossible to operate and her leg had remained in plaster for more than a year.

Three years later she still walked with great difficulty, although no permanent orthopedic damage had been found. She had virtually no friends, and most of her interaction had been with health workers, nurses, and physiotherapists. She refused to leave the house (she weighed 200 lbs.), and although she did some housework, she remained totally closed in on herself.

Her parents complained that she was too dependent on the mother, but Carlotta complained in turn that her parents—her mother especially—spent too much time out of the house. However, this conflict was contradicted by nonverbal behavior that revealed unconditional acceptance of the *status quo*. As regards their individual times, the team had the impression that the girl was immobilized in time, while her parents oscillated between the "future" of their company and a static present dominated by a daughter who was becoming fatter and fatter. Carlotta, for her part, not only seemed incapable of change but also tended to regress into an increasingly parent-dependent childhood past.

One hypothesis was that the parents oscillated between their company and their daughter because both were needed to avoid creating a void in their marriage. This also explained the contradictory nature of their demands: "Change us (superficially) but don't change us (emotionally)." The team decided to end the first session with an intervention that would reflect the family's dilemma: either separate or stay together, change or remain immobile.

> THERAPIST: After the first meeting with a family, we're usually able to say if there's a problem that needs therapy. We usually agree on this, but in your case things are different. A part of the team thinks that Carlotta has already made her life choice, to be a support to her parents in their old age. They think this choice has been accepted by her parents. So, since you all agree, there's no need for therapy.
>
> But the other part of the team thinks that therapy *is* needed. They think that beneath a superficial absence of worry, Carlotta is in fact genuinely ill at ease about her existential situation. She wants to be independent, to project herself outside her family, like any girl of her age. And, naturally, her parents share her desire. As you see, the team finds itself at an impasse. We've decided to see you again after the summer holidays for a second meeting. In the meantime, we'd like to ask you to tell us your reaction to what we've said, to tell us what you think will help us to get out of the impasse we find ourselves in now, and enable us to decide whether we should go on meeting.

The family reacted to the intervention as if everything that had been said was totally obvious. Towards the end of the intervention, the Berias nodded their heads vigorously, in nonverbal confirmation of the therapist's verbal message. When they had left, the team briefly discussed what had happened and reached two provisional conclusions. Most importantly, the family seemed to have accepted both the possible worlds described by the team (evolving time, static time). Secondly, from what the therapists themselves had seen, therapy had already begun. From the moment when they had accepted the two possible worlds, the clients had implicitly begun a therapy relationship with the team.

The family's attitude had changed by the second session—the noncommittal tea-party atmosphere of the previous month had been replaced by the more appropriate image of a family that felt uneasy about its problems and was looking for help. All this was verbalized, especially by the father. Rivalry between the father and daughter also emerged: they fought to gain the love of the wife/mother, who in turn seemed in difficulty about how to respond to these two types of love. Now that there was engagement, it was possible to go ahead profitably with the meetings.

8

TIME AND RITUALS

R<small>ITUALS ARE STEEPED IN TIME,</small>
so discussion of time itself cannot avoid dealing with them. In this chapter
we shall first look at some aspects of ritual in general, and then at rituals
in the family. We shall explore the relationships among time, ritual, and
myth in culture, the family, and the individual. This done, we shall be
able to look at rituals in therapy and the temporal aspects of their use,
which we shall illustrate with brief clinical cases.

THE MEANING OF
RITUALS AND TIME

According to Mircea Eliade, the reality of primitive Man is properly located outside time, in sacred ritual acts which reactivate unchanging ar-
chetypes and reactualize them by rendering them concrete. His book,
The Myth of the Eternal Return (1954), provides impressive and abundant
evidence in support of this idea. Man is only fully himself in the rituals
which mark and structure his truly significant actions: linear time, the
time of becoming, is empty and meaningless. As a result, Man most truly
"is" not when he abandons himself to subjective time, but when he reen-
acts archetypal actions that were (are) performed once and for all by divine
figures *in illo tempore*, outside time.[1]

---

[1]This is why popular memory is archetypal, not historical. In popular legends
based on historical figures, "real" and biographical events acquire exemplary, archetypal elements that in the end become their most important features. For the
people who repeat them, however, exemplary stories are truer than real stories.

In primitive societies, linear time, the time of becoming, must be regularly halted in its course to be regenerated through ritual[2]: "all rituals imitate a divine archetype: their continual reactualization occurs in a single, identical mythical moment located outside time" (Eliade, 1954). Total involvement in rituals enables their participants to experience sacred reality. This has produced the rites that structure the lives of men in all primitive societies, the "rites of passage" described by Van Gennep (1961) that transport the individual into the "neutral time" in which he or she progresses from one stage in his/her life to another. Rituals also punctuate and structure the various times of everyday existence. A human who participates in a ritual not only *is*, but is also *in his or her proper place*, and so in his or her proper time: when he has undergone his rite of passage, a young man is recognized as an adult by the society to which he belongs; a young woman, after marriage, is recognized as a spouse, and so on.

For the moment, we propose to accept Van der Hart's definition of ritual:

> Rituals are prescribed symbolic acts that must be performed in a certain way and in a certain order, and may or may not be accompanied by verbal formulas.
>
> Besides the formal aspects, an experiential aspect of rituals can be distinguished. The ritual is performed with much involvement. If that is not the case, then we are talking about empty rituals.
>
> Certain ritual are repeatedly performed throughout the lives of those concerned; others, on the contrary, are performed only once (but can be performed again by other people). (1983, pp. 5–6)

As will be clear from this definition, the rituals that interest us here are those which, at the very least, have social sanctioning. Individual rituals play a different role since they are concerned with personal habit or even psychopathology (obsessive ritualism). A ritual is an *act* that gives symbolic meaning intelligible form: the sequencing and ordering of the acts are at least as important as the meanings they convey. Using the terminology of semiotics, we could say that in ritual the signifier has the same importance and dignity as the significatum (the meaning conveyed by the signifier) and that both are essential to defining the sign-act that constitutes the rite. The use of verbal formulas is only a secondary characteristic, and never in itself constitutes a rite.

The second part of Van der Hart's definition seems to contradict the popular Western idea of ritual as formal behavior devoid of any real per-

---

[2]We shall be using "rite" and "ritual" as synonyms throughout.

sonal involvement in the ideas and values that come into play (Merton, 1984). One example might be religious services "performed in a purely ritualistic way . . . externally, without involvement" (Van der Hart, 1983, p. 6). Authentic rituals are the ones found in traditional cultures, those performed in families, or those we all experience during the course of our lives: sets of socially prescribed gestures which nonetheless involve real emotional commitment.

The third part of Van der Hart's definition introduces time into the concept of ritual. There are two kinds of ritual. The first includes those rituals that are experienced only once (or only during the course of important events, such as serious illness) and that introduce a *discontinuity* in time, a shift from one clearly defined time to another. Van Gennep (1961) called them "rites of passage" (*rites de passage*), citing typical examples like the passage from adolescence to adulthood we noted earlier. "Healing rituals" (Van der Hart, 1983) are similar to rites of passage: since they are performed when unexpected problems arise, they are less general and more closely linked to individual people and contexts.

By contrast, the other kind of ritual involves repetition. Since these rituals are repeated at regular intervals, they introduce *continuity* and regularity into the passing of time. They include "rites of intensification"— collective group activities that reinforce the cohesion of the group as it copes with external events — and "teletic rituals" (Firth, 1972) — acts which mark the entry or exit (even temporarily) of an individual into or from a group. Since our major concern here is with rituals in time, we shall refer to rituals of the first type as "rituals of discontinuity" and rituals of the second type as "rituals of continuity."[3]

Finally, like other forms of symbolic and sign expression, rituals are flexible. No matter how exact their formal structuring, rituals include flexible "open" sections that can be modified according to circumstances or environment.

Rituals have important temporal connotations. Both Mircea Eliade (1954) and Norbert Elias (1989) base their accounts of how our experience of time has developed on the experience of ritual (sacred time). Elias even places the origin of the measurement of time in ritual, citing the example of small African tribal societies in the last century in which one of the priest's main tasks was to observe the rising of the sun every day. When the sun rose from behind a certain cliff, it meant that it was a favorable

---

[3]"Rites of inversion," which according to Van der Hart (1983, p. 9) may belong to either of the two larger categories of one-time or repeated rituals, involve exchanges of roles within a group and are a case apart.

time for sowing. Then, and only then, was the priest able to utter the words of the propitiatory rite that allowed the tribe to commence sowing.

Van Gennep (1961) outlined the structure of rites of passage extremely well. His outline, that can be applied with a minimum of variation to any kind of rite, clarifies the role of time in rituals. At the very start (zero time), the subject of the ritual is living in ordinary, everyday time. A *rite of separation* is then performed in which the person's ties with the group— the past—are drastically cut (preliminal phase). He or she then enters the "margin" period (*marge*) in which time is annihilated: one is outside time, in Eliade's sacred dimension (liminal phase). The best known example of this marginal state is the 40 days Christ spent in the desert. When this phase ends, a *rite of aggregation* reinstates the person in the group (post-liminal phase), but he/she is now a different person because he/she has access to a future that was once closed to him or her, and is forbidden to turn back into the past. In rites of continuity, a similar shift outside the flow of ordinary time reconfirms the unique reality of a person's individual existence, which the ordinariness of secular life tends to deny.

In terms of time, then, the prime function of ritual is the creation of a "suspended" time. *Time is annihilated during ritual*: participants are placed outside the flow of everyday time; when this happens, it is possible to reorganize their time in radical ways, although the form of this reorganization varies according to ritual.

In a rite of passage, two other conditions are created in addition to the suspension of time: the past is dissolved, and possible futures are opened up. As in therapeutic dialogue, the ritual breaks a chain of events and the past's stranglehold on the future is lifted, thereby making it possible to move from the past into the future. Perhaps the most apt metaphor for what happens in such rituals is the arrow of time: the rite of passage marks (creates) an irreversible transition.

By contrast, a rite of continuity structures and regularizes time by being repeated at regular intervals. By identifying a regularly repeated sequence in time, such rites give impetus to collective life. It is no accident that they are linked historically to regularly repeated events, such as the mass, the New Year, or the cycle of the seasons, and that the wheel of time is the metaphor that best describes them: a rite of continuity marks (creates) a regular series of repetitions that point to a present moment lying outside the flow of time (Eliade, 1954).

RITUALS IN THE FAMILY

According to Gluckman (1962), rituals are essential to multifunctional groups, i.e., groups in which the same people simultaneously perform different roles (support, socialization, production and distribution of goods) in a defined space. The effect of ritual here is to prevent role differences among members of the group from developing to the point where the self-destruction of the group becomes a real possibility (each role implies all the others, so disorder cannot easily be tolerated).

The kind of order we achieve in our society through the spatial compartmentalization of activity (home, workplace, school, meeting places) is achieved in tribal societies through the regularity of ritual. In other words, where there is no spatial compartmentalization, it is necessary to have temporal compartmentalization: ritual synchronizes members of the group and regulates their interactions in time. In Western society, the most important multifunctional group is still the family, so it is not surprising that most of our rituals occur in the family.

Western industrial society is now regarded as ritualized to only a small degree, and what rituals have remained seem impoverished and instill little emotional involvement when enacted: to many they have become empty rituals. Gluckman (1962) claims that this is the result of spatial compartmentalization in society: if various spheres of activity are clearly separated, the coordination obtained through ritual seems superfluous.

However, it is also true that this compartmentalization is more apparent than real, at least in some situations. The family is still a multifunctional group in which close contact among members has been maintained. Even in societies as clearly compartmentalized in space as ours, impoverishment of ritual creates confusion of times. As we have seen in earlier chapters, it is very difficult to know when a young person may be regarded as adult, or when a period of mourning is over. We have only a few residual rites of passage (baptism, marriages, funerals) and they do not always indicate correspondingly radical changes in the mental maps of those involved: two people may well form a new family without the sanctioning of marriage, or may marry without really breaking away from their respective families of origin.

However, the family environment is always ritualized to a certain extent. These rituals are usually small-scale rites of continuity serving to consolidate family cohesion and perpetuate what Reiss (1981) calls the family paradigm, rather than full-scale rites of discontinuity. Bossard and Boll (1976) also regarded rituals as part of daily life in families, although still prescribed and symbolic to some extent. Thus, the evening meal, with the whole family present, is a rite of intensification; Sunday dinner is generally more elaborate and ritualistic, while the even more complicated Christmas dinner may assume the characteristics of a full-scale annual rite.

Firth (1972) has noted that families also enact "teletic rites" as well as rites of intensification. The way two married partners say goodbye to each other when they separate in the morning and greet each other in the evening when they are reunited is very important in defining their relationship and their respective roles in the home: their tone of voice, the distances they maintain, the kiss or lack of it and also the way they kiss are all ways of defining a relationship through daily repetition. When carried to its logical conclusion, Firth's theory would turn any habitually repeated action into a ritual, so that rites would lose much of their emotional power. For this reason, we prefer to define as "family rituals" only those acts which, by placing themselves outside the family's ordinary time, enable all its members to perceive a point of discontinuity that lends rhythm and regularity to family life.

Family rituals perpetuate the belief and meaning system of the family and confirm its roots in past generations. Determined by the social life of the family, they are transmitted from one family nucleus to another, creating continuity with the past, regulating the structuring of time,[4] and placing constraints on future development.

The kinds of ritual usually enacted in a society mainly depend, according to Douglas (1973), on group "structure" and "pressure." Group structure means here the whole society's shared system of classification, the social order which is "social" precisely because it is accepted and practiced by everyone in the society. By contrast, group pressure is the set of usually active restrictions that members of the group impose on the behavior of others. In the former case, we have an internalized variable; in the latter, externally imposed censure and censorship.

When group structure and pressure are both powerfully present in a society, we have "established authority" in which interaction is highly ritualized and rites of passage and intensification are commonly found. If weak structure is combined with powerful pressure, the society tends to be "enmeshed" (Minuchin, 1974), with strongly demarcated boundaries but confusion within. The contradictions that often develop in these societies create the need for individualized rituals like rites of healing and purification. Finally, a society in which both structure and pressure are weak is disengaged: rituals are rarely used, and conflicts are usually controlled by withdrawal. This is what happens in Pygmy tribes, where interindividual constraints are extremely weak and the complex rituals of neighboring tribes are considered ridiculous.

---

[4]Children are particularly sensitive to ritual sequences. If they are used to being put to bed by the mother while their father reads a bedtime story, even a slight change in sequence will produce a negative reaction.

Family groups, like societies, vary according to the importance they attach to ritual. Van der Hart (1983) distinguishes "positional" families—in which the group counts more than the individual, hierarchical positions are well established, and rituals are widely practiced and crucially important—from "person-oriented" families—in which the individual counts more than the group, hierarchies are less clearly defined, and ritualized behavior is rare. In what Minuchin (1974) calls "enmeshed" families, external boundaries are strong and group cohesion is high, but hierarchies are poorly defined and ineffective. Rituals tend to be confused and few and far between. As we shall see, these distinctions are of some importance to therapists. Imber-Black and her colleagues (1988) suggest, for example, that the degree of spontaneous ritual in a family should be carefully assessed during the course of therapy, so that the therapist knows to what extent the family is able to accept ritual, up to what point it will collaborate in it, and what degree of ritual complexity is accessible to it.

THERAPY TIME AS RITUAL TIME

Therapy time is certainly a separate time, one which those involved in it (therapists as well as patients) experience very much as a sort of sacred time.[5] It is interesting that a number of psychotherapies are in many ways similar to Van Gennep's rites of passage. In psychoanalysis, for example, the model for many other types of psychotherapy, there are many devices that radically separate therapy time from ordinary time. Changing Van Gennep's categories only slightly, we could say that analysis begins with a consultation (preliminary phase), which is followed by therapy as such (liminal phase), and ends with a conclusion in which the parting of the therapist and patient has to be formulated (postliminal phase). When this is done, the patient has been "reaggregated" to the ordinary world.

If this analogy seems rather forced, the similarity between rites of passage and systemic family therapy sessions is quite evident. Sessions begin with a pre-session team meeting while the family waits in the therapy room (preliminary phase); the session proper then follows, with team discussion (liminal phase); and finally, there is the conclusion of the session, when the date of the next meeting is arranged and a reformulation, intervention, prescription, or ritual may be given that will "accompany" the family back into its world (postliminal phase). Note that this last phase may take the form of a simple conclusion, like the *ite, missa est* that concludes a mass.

---

[5]"Sacred" is used here in Mircea Eliade's sense, as outlined in *The Myth of Eternal Return.*

We do not mean by all this that psychotherapies were ever intentionally designed to resemble rites of passage, but it is interesting that their basic structure has unknowingly been repeated. And in fact, the function of psychotherapy in our society is similar to the basic function of rites of passage in primitive societies—to sanction the passage of an individual or group from one state to another (in our particular case, from "illness" to "sanity"). It is no surprise, then, that all therapies have the form of rites to a greater or lesser degree.

In some areas of modern society, psychotherapy is now seen as a sort of necessary "accompaniment" to life, a never-ending analysis that keeps a client engaged with one or more therapists for years. This "deritualization" of therapy can, understandably, confuse therapy with life itself because therapy is deprived of one of its essential elements, that it should be a *parenthesis*—something bracketed apart from ordinary daily life.

In a conversation with John Turner, an English anthropologist whom one of the authors (Luigi Boscolo) met in California in 1989, a different view emerged. Turner brought forward an interesting aspect of the issue "life versus therapy":

> I think you classify therapy and life as existing in two separate categories. Why? It is the first time in human history people are paying for friendship. ... The commercialization of relationships is growing; as more people want to improve their psyche and their soma, they will seek people to help them do that; and, as people have higher and higher standards for what they want in a relationship (relationships are now like commodities that can be traded in for better one, or worked on to upgrade like computer hardware), they will want more and more to find commercial surrogate relationships that have in them the good qualities they find so difficult to produce in traditional friendship and love. ...
>
> So your notion of life and therapy being two discrete categories of existence no longer fits with the modern phenomenon of therapist as a bona fide member of people's kinship systems. This I think is a social and cultural phenomenon that goes hand in hand with the phenomenon of people marrying at a later age, and the steep increase in single households. We are becoming a society of social atoms, with more disconnectedness than at any time in history. So, it makes sense to have a commercial connectedness, which is therapy. ...
>
> Luigi, if your mission is to convey that therapy and life are different, I think you will be like the English king who tried to turn back the tide. I think it is a noble enterprise, but you will find your feet wet a lot of the time. ... I think your plea for awareness about the separateness of life and therapy will be submerged by the tide about the commercialization of improving relationships and the commercialization of kinship. I am glad to hear you making the plea for awareness because it will affect those you contact, but I am concerned that you don't know what forces you are up against. You talk about culture, so perhaps you know all this.

The tragedy (for me) is that not only have things got to the point where it is now the norm in urban, college-educated America for people to induct a therapist into their life and their kinship system, but it will become more and more common. And since the rest of America follows California, and the rest of the Western world follows America, the commercialization of surrogate friends and relatives will increasingly be a global custom. (personal communication, 1989)

MYTHS, STORIES, AND RITES

The Milan group used a therapy ritual for the first time in the early seventies, with the "Casanti family," as described in Chapter 9 of *Paradox and Counterparadox* (Selvini Palazzoli et al., 1978). This was a therapy done with a family which had an anorexic daughter. After a few sessions, she seemed to have recovered, at least so far as her food intake and weight were concerned. Several months later, however, the family contacted the center again to say that the daughter had made a serious attempt to commit suicide. Therapy was resumed. The team members agreed that they were dealing with a potent family myth that bound the three generations together: all members of the family owed unquestioning obedience to the grandfather, the "boss" of the family. The apparent healing that had led to the termination of therapy had in reality been a defense of this myth, which now seemed to be under some threat. It could be said there had been a "flight into health."

The team decided that what was needed was an intervention that would create solidarity and cohesion in the nuclear family, and encourage the formation of clearer boundaries between it and the larger extended family while avoiding direct conflict between the two. This was achieved by prescribing a ritual, performed after dinner, in which the nuclear family met for an hour behind closed doors and each member spoke in turn for 15 minutes about his or her relationship with the extended family. The family was forbidden to discuss or comment on what was said once the ritual was over. This ritual thus became a counter-myth, although this was never explicitly stated by the therapists:

> We can therefore conclude that our prescription of a ritual is meant not only to avoid verbal comment on the norms that at that moment perpetuate the family play, but to introduce into the system a ritualized prescription of a play whose new norms silently take the place of old ones. (Selvini Palazzoli et al., 1978, p. 97)

Thus, therapeutic rituals emerged as *alternatives* to family myths, which is highly suggestive if we bear in mind the close relationship between rite and myth.

In *1984*, George Orwell invented a world in which history is constantly being rewritten by watchful civil servants in the specially created Ministry of Truth, so that history always conforms to and justifies the government's present policies. Myths — all myths — are very similar to the kind of history Orwell's Ministry of Truth disseminates: they are always being rewritten, but on the assumption that they always remain the same. Myths do not record development in time. Homer did not know he was producing yet another syncretization of our ancestral journey home when he wrote of Ulysses' journey home. For each and every Greek rhapsodist, his own version of the myth was the only unchanging one, the myth as it had always been. Similarly, the last person to sing of the Knights of the Round Table did not weigh the implications of the fact that various versions of this story — always similar but always different — had been produced over the centuries.

According to Ferreira (1963), who first elaborated the concept, a family myth is an expression of beliefs shared by and implicitly accepted by all members of the family, although they may not state this in so many words. Ferreira saw myth as a static construction, in keeping with the concept of "family homeostasis" that dominated thinking at the time: myths never changed.

Thirty years later, with the narrative paradigm now at its height, Alan Parry (1991) writes:

> A myth, in this view, represents a story that embodies or encodes a person's, or even a people's, unquestioned beliefs about the way things are. . . . As encoding a person's fundamental beliefs and assumptions about given circumstances, a myth influences the selecting process concerning which events are highlighted as the stories the person includes as summing up herself and her life. This, then, is the "hermeneutical circle" . . . according to which our beliefs determine our understanding and our understanding determines our beliefs. (p. 52)

This means that myth is part of a circular, evolutionary process. As Bagarozzi and Anderson (1989), among others, observe, personal or family myths, like social and cultural myths, are highly flexible. They can be modified, but without the people who actually experience them realizing it. Thus, a family myth might be a variation on a socially accepted myth (so many of the family myths we observe in Italy are variations on the *buona mamma* theme found throughout Italian culture), and a personal myth might in turn be an individual's adaptation of a family myth.

In primitive societies, myths are located, as Eliade would say, *in illo tempore*, in a time outside the profane time of becoming, which never changes because sacred and profane are totally separate. In our society, personal and family myths are not immutable in this way. Sometimes we are not even aware of them, so they may change without our realizing it. A myth of perfection incarnate in one member of a family may change to a myth of decadence if the family in question proves consistently unable to live up to expectations. But it is perfectly possible that no one in the family is aware of this change. Psychotherapy can influence the so-called epistemological premises, or underlying unconscious assumptions, that myths represent in narrative or metaphorical form. Within the wider system, in culture, there is a whole body of people — poets, artists, sociologists, philosophers and writers — who portray these myths and their evolution in time.

Let us look now at the work of David Reiss (1981), who has carried out interesting research into the nature of family culture. He sees family myths as cognitive constructs shared by the whole family, comparable to the concept of family paradigm that is central to his work (see Chapter 3). In our view, myth differs from Reiss' family paradigm in at least two ways: first, and most importantly, myth is a metaphorical expression of the family's cognitive constructs[6] (synchronic vision); secondly, it is a narrative or "story" in the way White and Epston (1990) use the term, and so develops in time (diachronic vision). The unusual thing about myth is that it has the structure of a story — a beginning, a middle, and an end — but of a story that has already happened in some other time different from ordinary time. Myths unravel in time, but are located outside time.

As Jerome Bruner says (1986), any narrative has two facets. Frank Kermode (1967) follows the Russian Formalists in defining them as *fabula* and *sjuzet* (plot). The *fabula* is the basic nontemporal theme of any story, the *sjuzet* the sequence of events that enables it to develop. These two facets can also be seen in the stories (including myths) that individuals or families tell about themselves, in which a timeless thematic root metaphorically expressing the meaning and value systems of the individual or family is actualized in time by narrative.[7]

If myth is a metaphor of a dominant meaning system, and so located

---

[6]According to Lévi-Strauss (1962), myth is always metaphorical. It may be regarded, then, as a metaphor of certain cognitive constructs that have special emotional significance.

[7]We have defined "myths" as special kinds of stories — apparently fixed and unalterable, with a high emotional charge — that produced the mythologies of the Ancient World. However, all the stories we tell about ourselves, including history, have some mythical element. In many ways, "myth" and "story" overlap and express different facets of the same basic concept — a meaning system communicated through narrative modes, styles and diachronic sequencing.

outside time, ritual offers the possibility of acting on myth by reintroduc-
ing the flow of time. Lévi-Strauss (1974) claimed that myth and ritual
are two different ways of expressing the same meaning system: in his
terminology, myth and ritual express the same structures. Therapeutic
ritual may be seen as a metaphorical act that releases a system's potential
for development. The Casanti family had carried a myth over two generations, but the myth had not developed in step with the surrounding environment and had become a prison for the new generations, with the
appearance of symptoms. We would say now that the Casanti family,
faithful to its myth, was beginning to lose its ability to coordinate its
own times and social times. Once the myth, and its influence, had been
identified, an *ad hoc* ritual was invented that released the family's potential
for development.

In the past, individual and collective lives were highly ritualized. Various phases in the human life cycle were marked by precise rituals, which
in Western countries differed only in content and always had the same
formal function. Most of these rituals have withered or even died away
completely in modern society. Only local rites survive in regions, cities,
towns, and even further down the social scale, individual families. Some
would say that modern society's lack of well-being, its "symptoms," are due
to a lack of ideologies, values, and religious belief, and most importantly,
to the loss of traditional rituals.

We would now like to describe an example of a spontaneous ritual of
exchange—they are very common in primitive societies—which occurred
during the course of a therapy and gave the team concrete evidence of
change in a significant relationship. This was an episode in the therapy of
the Hayworth family, which we discussed in greater detail in Chapter 5.
During the second session it soon became clear that one of the main
obstacles hindering resolution of conflicts and enmeshment between
mother and son was the mutual indifference and hostility of the son and
daughter. The family believed that the son, Sandy, had inherited from his
father the recklessness and charm he bestowed so liberally on women but
had so far proved unable to turn to any practical advantage in work. This
seriously worried his mother and sister, who saw no prospect of a secure
job or independent future for him. By contrast, the sister, Vera, seemed a
"normal" woman, a hard worker, rational and rather rigid, who would always lead an orderly, boring life and never kick over the traces.

The therapeutic team decided to end the second session by expressing
the hope that the two children might exchange character traits—Vera
would give Sandy some of her seriousness and stability, and Sandy would
give her some of his creativity and charm. Immediately after the end of
the session, before leaving the room, Sandy and Vera stopped in front of

the large mirror and, almost without realizing it, exchanged jackets to see what they looked like, observing each other intently as they did so. Both were clearly satisfied when they came to the next session. Sandy spoke thoughtfully about his work and future, while Vera was all jokes and smiles. They also seemed to understand and appreciate each other much more, while the mother seemed gloomy rather than relieved that her son had begun to live more responsibly.

With no prompting, the two children had performed a ritual exchange of clothing, a type of ritual Van Gennep (1961) classifies as a rite of passage, and more specifically, as a rite of fellowship and marriage. Not only this: their ritual act really did count metaphorically as the redefinition of the relationship envisioned in the therapy prescription, a relationship in which both children should exist on the same level and give each other something of themselves. It might be objected that this was not a ritual but simply a gesture, but we think their gesture acquired ritual significance because it occurred in a separate space (and time) in the presence of witnesses. There is a similarity between the therapists (witnesses) and the therapy context, and a priest and a marriage ceremony, in which the bride and groom exchange rings.

RITES OF PASSAGE, RITES OF CONTINUITY

Before illustrating our therapeutic rituals with clinical cases, we would like first to list the basic assumptions of our approach.

1. A ritual obliges an individual or family to behave in ways specified by the ritual itself; these are different from the behaviors adopted in the past that have led to suffering and the emergence of symptoms. In trying to perform their ritual, the clients sometimes find a "third solution," which may resemble neither their previous solutions nor the ideas of the therapist. As well as new meanings and emotions, rituals also introduce new behaviors. This passage from thinking to doing seems to be one of the reasons for the success of rituals with chronic psychoses, where family groups seem immune to words, hypotheses, or interpretations.

2. One fundamental aspect of ritual is that it puts all members of the family on the same level when they actually perform it. This may simply mean meeting for an hour a week to exchange thoughts and emotions about a given theme specified by the therapist, or going together to the cemetery to think about the death of a relative,

or at a given time every week reporting among themselves information received from people outside the family so to avoid the risk of creating secrets, and so on.

Bringing all members of the family together in this way enables them to develop a new vision of themselves and others, and introduces a circular vision linking ideas, emotions, and people in ways that substitute linear, moralistic ways of thinking. However, the most typical feature of ritual is that it urges people to find a point of contact, of agreement, that can generate new shared ideas. This is reminiscent of rituals like the mass or Holy Communion, which bring the faithful together, or certain secular rituals like political, corporate, or sports meetings.[8]

3. Ritual thus promotes the harmonization of individual and collective times. Any therapeutic ritual involves demarcation and ordering of time because it creates rhythm and sequence. When the flow of time is blocked, as in paradoxical situations, ritual can sometimes reinstate the sequences that have been obliterated.

4. Generally speaking, the aim of ritual is not to provide a literal vehicle for content, although in certain cases (in psychosis, for example) a simple ritual may serve to transmit content. Rituals are formulated in order to act on *processes*, to trigger change: in other words, we think the form of a ritual is more important than its content.[9] Many of the rituals we prescribe are even cryptic, in the sense that their content is obscure to clients. In this way, the risk of purely didactic interaction is avoided, and our rituals become examples of what is called "hypocoding" in semiotics (Eco, 1976): clients are faced with symbolic acts whose code they do not completely understand, so they are encouraged to create new codes and new meaning systems for themselves.

5. Another aspect of ritual—equally important because it provides an emotional experience all members of the family can share at the same level—is that clients are forbidden to speak of anything that happens during the ritual in the intervals between rituals. The aim

---

[8]In *Naven* (1958), Bateson observes that rituals like the Naven become more important the fewer "legal" sanctions there are, as with the Iatmul who had no laws in the European sense of the word. So rituals are important in social areas where interaction is freely negotiated, such as the family, but less so in tightly controlled areas, like the workplace (although even here things are not quite so simple as they may at first appear).
[9]As Imber-Black and her colleagues (1988) apparently believe. They describe rituals at length, and ways of developing them in interaction with families.

here is to create a clear break between daily and ritual experience, which obliges clients to behave differently in each case and enables them to live as if they were two different families. Without this prohibition, families would, of course, talk about their ritual experience during their ordinary lives, and this would destroy the differences introduced by the ritual, rendering it "ordinary" and ineffective.

Before going on to our clinical cases, we would like to distinguish in therapy the two kinds of ritual we mentioned at the beginning of this chapter: rites of continuity (time's cycle) and rites of passage or discontinuity (linear time, time's arrow).

Rites of passage mark a single point of discontinuity around which an irreversible change occurs. For example, a family with adolescent children who are not yet considered independent and responsible is given a one-day-a-week ritual, to be repeated until the next session, in which the children have to behave in an independent, responsible way and the parents have to create the conditions for this to be possible. By contrast, rites of continuity mark a cyclical movement that governs the system's future development. Here parents might be asked to spend alternate days being the "parent on duty" (Selvini Palazzoli, Boscolo, Cecchin, & Prata, 1978a).

Burying the Past

A rite of passage can be used when action is needed on a past problem that continues to influence the present. In such circumstances, the ritual can unblock the flow of time. The case we cite here was described by Imber-Black (personal communication). A family of three people — mother, father and son — had gone for therapy because of a problem with the son. The "official" problem was quickly solved, but then another much more serious problem emerged. The parents were prone to interminable bouts of often violent arguing that were making family life a hell. When the therapist asked what caused the fights, the reply was that they argued over an event in the distant past which they could not reveal to anyone under any circumstances, not even to the therapist.

The therapist thus found herself with the task of helping them to solve a problem she knew nothing about! She invented an ingenious ritual. She took an ordinary cardboard box and asked each of the parents to write a narrative on a piece of paper about the secret event that was making them argue all the time. When they had done this, she told them to fold the sheet of paper in four and put it in the box. This done, she asked an odd-job man at the clinic to find some shovels and picks (it was winter at the time), and made the couple dig a hole beneath an oak tree and bury the box. We might say that the therapy had brought the past into the present and buried it. This done, the therapist said to them: "From now on, whenever you start fighting you must stop and come right here, where the box is buried, to talk things over."

The husband and wife arrived for the next session in good spirits. With some embarrassment, they reported that when they had started arguing for the first time after the previous session, they had got in the car and come to the oak tree where, instead of arguing, they had burst out laughing. From then on, all their arguments had been stillborn. The ritual had proved effective, and therapy was terminated. We might say that the ritual had succeeded in physically embodying the popular idea that the past is past and should be buried. The idea that the past cannot be changed because it is past was introduced, and the couple was made to bury the past symbolically, thus creating a new context—arguing under an oak tree and over a buried cardboard box—totally at variance with the context of their frequent fights.

Odd and Even Nights

The success of the early-seventies rituals described in *Paradox and Counterparadox* (Selvini Palazzoli et al., 1978) and a number of articles (Selvini Palazzoli et al., 1974, 1978a), encouraged us to devise new rituals. For example, the article, "A Ritualized Prescription in Family Therapy: Odd and Even Days" (Selvini Palazzoli et al., 1978a) describes a continuity rite we have since used extensively. We originally devised it for use in those common cases of families in which parents interfere with each other's parental functions and so confuse their children. The idea was to create a temporal sequence that allowed each parent to behave as he or she wished with the children without the other interfering.

The parents were told that on even days (Tuesday, Thursday and Saturday) one of the two would be the "parent on duty," while the other would take over on odd days (Monday, Wednesday and Friday). The children were instructed to check that this happened, and to point out and make a note of any insubordination or forgetfulness in their parents. As in all rituals, there had to be a period when life could go on as usual, so the family was asked to "behave spontaneously" on Sundays.

The "odd and even days" ritual was and still is extremely useful in ordering and sequencing daily relations between parent couples and children. A similar "odd and even nights" ritual proved useful in cases where the nocturnal life of a family was associated with pathologies, sometimes very serious ones. In our experience, some families—especially those with a psychotic or pre-psychotic member—often have unusual or even bizarre nocturnal lives. Adolescent sons or daughters sometimes still sleep in their parents' bed between their parents, or sleep with just one of the parents while the other withdraws to another room.

Our example here was a family consisting of three people—mother, father and son. The father was a young company director from a family with old money. When they got married, his wife had persuaded him to build their family home so that the door of the children's room would be opposite the door of the parents' bedroom. In this way, she would always be able to "keep an eye on the children." Only one child was born—Giacomo—who was nine when therapy began.

Giacomo had been suffering from serious bouts of night terror for about a year, accompanied by nightmares and genuine feelings of panic. A nocturnal panic disorder (*"pavor nocturnus"*) had been diagnosed and individual psychotherapy undertaken, but to no avail. In the meantime, Giacomo's life had been seriously affected: his school work was deteriorating and he often fell asleep at school during lessons.

Given the nature of the symptom, the therapist dwelt at length on the family's nocturnal life during the first session. Giacomo was the center of his parents' lives, always under observation, always watched over and made a fuss of. Over the past year, the whole family had gradually begun to suffer from insomnia. As soon as they heard some sound of distress from Giacomo's room, the parents would rush in and often themselves spend a sleepless night there.

Usually, bathrooms and bedrooms have no keys in such families. Before prescribing the nocturnal ritual, the therapist told the parents they would have to put the keys back in the bathroom and bedroom locks. Giacomo was free to leave his bedroom door locked or unlocked, but the parents had to lock their bedroom door from ten at night to eight in the morning every day. On odd nights the father would be the "parent on duty"; on even nights the mother. Behavior was to be spontaneous on Sundays. The parent on duty could intervene as he or she wished in anything that might happen to Giacomo during the night. Whenever it was decided to comfort Giacomo in his room, the other parent had to be locked in the parents' bedroom. Obviously, Giacomo was forbidden to enter his parents' bedroom at night.

The aim of the prescription to put the keys back was to make it possible to choose between collective and private time, a choice which, from everything the family had said so far, seemed impossible at the moment. The odd and even nights ritual, with the prescription that the parent on duty had to lock the parents' bedroom door, was intended to help the couple to create their own time and space separate from their son.

Of course, the therapist developed a number of hypotheses about the origins and nature of the family's life (especially its nocturnal life). The parents' love for and attachment to the child seemed far stronger than their love for each other: supporting this hypothesis was the fact that Giacomo would be sole heir to a large fortune amassed over generations, meaning that he lived at the center of a complex web of affections and interests. Alternatively, by concerning themselves with Giacomo during the night, the parents avoided having sex. Or, reversing the situation, it was Giacomo, with his nocturnal fears, who prevented the parents from having sex, and so from being a couple, by keeping them out of the traditional place for couples, the bedroom. The further idea emerged that the three members of the family had been unable to form a hierarchy. As Giacomo had grown, there had been a dilution of roles so that *all three* could plausibly be regarded as children (especially by the extended family). Also, the parents' constant concern for their son was preventing them from being together, and so from producing other children.

In the second session the family reported a dramatic change. The parents said they had obeyed our instructions to the letter, even though doing so had caused a lot of suffering, especially on the mother's part. In one month Giacomo had had only two minor nocturnal panic attacks, both during nights when his father was on duty. Giacomo seemed relieved and implicitly thanked the therapist for having freed him from his parents by allowing him to reestablish contact with the day-time world. Therapy continued for a further three sessions with the parents only, to discuss their own problems as a couple. During that period Giacomo had no further attacks. He loved going to school and worked extremely well there.

This ritual radically changed the nocturnal life of the family member by introducing a clear distinction between the parents' roles and the son's role, thereby allowing all three to start evolving again as a family. Apart from the hypotheses mentioned earlier, the ritual itself was based on relational patterns described by the family that were affecting day-night rhythms and sometimes having a serious effect on the school and social life of the son.

This was a simple, monosymptomatic case. But psychosis cases, often with much more important, more highly animated night lives than day lives, are more complex and more difficult to cope with. Knowledge of this nocturnal life is very important for the therapist because it can point to significant role confusion and enmeshment that may be less apparent during the day. So whenever we see families with a psychotic member, we investigate their night lives very closely because they do not usually talk about them spontaneously. Any kind of nocturnal interference between parents and children tends to arrest development, leaving children stranded in life at the infantile stage. If the children also become attached to one parent rather than the other, the situation is rendered potentially disastrous. These problems, and the ambiguities they involve, are nurtured in the secret, hidden time of the night: daylight (and the scrutiny of others) renders relationships more distinct and much tidier.[10]

Simultaneous Times, Separate Times

The Pericoli family consisted of the parents — both office workers in their forties — and their daughter Cristina, a highly intelligent and extroverted 10-year-old. Two years previously, Cristina had developed obsessive symptoms that in time had affected the social life of the whole family. For about a year, the parents had been permitted to leave the house only to go to work, on pain of serious agitation crises and threats of suicide on the part of their daughter if they disobeyed. In addition to being obsessively worried about the passing of time, and also personal hygiene (which called for rigorously ritualistic ablutions and washing), she was also obsessed by the night. A complex evening ritual involving the whole family had developed more than a year earlier. If it was not performed correctly down to the last detail, Cristina became prey to incurable insomnia.

When it was bedtime, the parents had to take Cristina to their bedroom and spread out on the bed an immaculate sheet with no trace of a crease or wrinkle. The daughter's continual protests about creases could prolong this ceremony to 20 minutes or more. Then the father had to go and sleep in Cristina's room while the mother slept in a bed next to the parents' double bed. Cristina would first get into bed with her mother. When she began to feel sleepy, she would jump into the double bed and remain there until morning.

This account of her rituals was important to the team in formulating its hypotheses, but direct observation of the family during sessions proved even more important. Cristina sat between her parents with her legs apart, as if on a throne. She was dressed like a little girl and held a tiny doll in

---

[10]One particularly instructive example, for us, was a family with a 17-year-old daughter suffering from a serious anorexic disorder accompanied by obsessive-compulsive behaviors of a highly ritualistic kind. Until two years previously, the daughter had slept in her parents' bed wrapped around her father's body, holding on tight to a lock of his hair, while the mother slept in another room. During puberty, the daughter had begun to fear that fat corpuscles from her father's body would penetrate her body, so she went back to sleeping in her own bed. Her symptoms rapidly worsened: she broke off all contact with the outside world, again because she feared fat corpuscles would penetrate her own body, and cut down drastically on food. Feeling dirty, she developed ritual cleansing behaviors.

her hand, but this infantile appearance would often suddenly give way to (verbal and nonverbal) behaviors more appropriate to adults or even old people. Behaviors appropriate to small children, parents, and grandmother were observable in equal measure. For their part, the parents seemed to fear her judgment greatly and secretly tried to ingratiate themselves with her, while often disagreeing with each other, even to the point of open argument.

Although the parents complained they had lost their freedom because of Cristina's problems, they also gave the impression of having dedicated their lives to winning the love of the daughter. Time after time, episodes were described in which all attempts to establish a dual relationship between two members of the family were frustrated by the third member, as if the formation of a couple — any couple — was a source of anxiety to the third, and so unacceptable. It seemed that each of the three kept the other two under scrutiny, so that no one could ever have (or was allowed to have) private time.

In the second session, the team devised a ritual to separate the three members of the family, allowing each to develop a time distinct from the times of the others in a context that would coordinate their respective times and promote change and evolution. The ritual involved separating the family into a couple and a single person on each of the first three days of the week. Monday was "Mommy and Daddy's day" when the parents were to concentrate on each other and ignore their daughter, while Tuesday was "Daddy and Cristina's day" and Wednesday was "Mommy and Cristina's day." On the other days of the week the family was to behave spontaneously. Significantly, Cristina heaved a great sigh of relief when the ritual had been explained to her: "So I'll be free on Thursdays!"

In the third session, Cristina was noticeably calmer, while her parents seemed more tense and argumentative. The ritual had been obeyed only partially. The mother had given way to the temptation to interfere with the father-daughter relationship on Tuesdays (one of the team hypothesized, perhaps not very convincingly, that the mother was afraid of incest between the father and daughter). At the end of the session the family was told to continue with the ritual. The following month the parents came without Cristina, who had gone to visit a school friend in her maternal grandmother's village to see "a great TV program." The team received the clear impression that Cristina had started to reclaim her own private time and had used the excuse of the TV program to send her parents for therapy. The therapists understood her message and saw the couple for a further four sessions, in which constant improvements in Cristina were reported (she, incidentally, had taken to sleeping normally, with no need for rituals, ever since the first evening she had spent at her grandmother's house). In the meantime, the parents gradually seemed to be regaining the status of a couple.

This has been the description of another success; however, should we conclude that this *ad hoc* ritual was the ideal one for this family? Would an odd-and-even-day ritual have been just as effective? Would therapy without a ritual have been enough? Once again, there is no definitive answer. It is impossible to predict the effect a ritual will have with any accuracy. On the other hand, rituals need not actually be performed to be effective: they have influence on the imagination of clients, independent of actual performance. In our view, the effectiveness and outcome of a ritual depend on the meaning its recipients give it within the broader relational context (which also includes the therapist). Equally, therapy itself may be regarded as a ritual. Speaking of shamanistic healing, Lévi-Strauss (1974) says that to be effective it has to be accepted on trust by the patient, society, and therapists themselves. One simple criterion for deciding whether to use a ritual or not may be to evaluate the overall meaning it will acquire in the therapeutic system as a whole.

Mourning

Our next family was brought to our center by a trainee having supervision. It consisted of a father and mother, both 50, a daughter aged 30, and a son aged 26. A younger son, Moreno, had died two years earlier. The problem was Giovanna, the daughter, who, after an undisturbed adolescence, had started to develop increasingly chaotic behavior. She had taken to heroin and was becoming increasingly self-destructive, while her family wavered between condemnation and exaggerated protectiveness.

The session revealed that the family's present interaction had developed after the death of the younger son in a car accident. After a long period of mourning, Giovanna had resumed her normal social life, but the mother had immediately criticized her strongly for being so insensitive: how could she go out and enjoy herself when her brother had only just died? Giovanna replied that people have to think of life, not just of death, but this only convinced the mother still further of her insensitivity. So a classic vicious circle was created, in which the other members of the family supported the mother against the daughter, who then began to develop transgressive and self-destructive behaviors. The therapist who had asked for the consultation had been unable to remedy this deteriorating situation which in his view was heading in a potentially extremely dangerous direction with little prospect of change.

In the opinion of the consultant, the family seemed to be unable to mourn for Moreno because it had polarized into two opposing camps —

life and death—represented by Giovanna on one side and the rest of the
family on the other. It was as if times for mourning and times for ordinary
activities could never be sequenced properly in the daily life of the family.
The family was living neither in the present (life), as Giovanna wished,
nor in the past (mourning), as the mother wished.

The consultant felt that a ritual was needed to break the vicious circle
and to introduce temporal sequencing into the family. One day a week—
Tuesday—would be Moreno's day, when all the members of the family
were encouraged to remember him, recall episodes in his life, display
photos of him around the house and perhaps go together to the cemetery.
On the other days of the week, they were strictly forbidden to speak of
him. Naturally, they could think their own thoughts, but if someone spoke
of him the others would have to intervene to ensure that the prescription
was obeyed.

Three months later, the therapist reported that the consultation (but,
in his view, the ritual most of all) had produced an unbelievable change.
Giovanna had stopped taking heroin almost immediately and had started
looking for work again, and the whole family atmosphere had completely
changed. Further checks a year later confirmed that this change had been
lasting.

In this case, a number of factors may have contributed to success of
the ritual. First, the consultant had stressed the centrality of Moreno's
death and the importance of proper ritual mourning; this, when accepted
by the whole family, had helped to create a climate of agreement. Moreover, by prescribing, in sequence, a day devoted to death and six days
devoted to life, the ritual had implicitly conveyed the message that both
Giovanna and the other members of the family were right. Real life, present time—to which six days a week were devoted—was brought into contrast with the imaginative life of the family, the past—to which one day a
week was devoted. All the members of the family were obliged to shift
from "real" time to mourning time and back again, and reorient themselves
in a temporal sequence in which the past was now less important than the
present and, we would add, the future. The family was thus able to *experience* sequentially the distinction between past and present.

A similar ritual could also be used with mixed-parent families, now
increasingly common in Italy, in which there are often conflicts with satellite families: if, for example, a son accepts his stepfather or stepmother, he
may feel, or be made to feel, disloyal to his natural parents, and vice
versa. Here, too, where it seems impossible to create temporal sequences
between past and present, between mixed-parent family and original families, ritual can be very beneficial.

The Pintus family—a father, 17-year-old son and stepmother—had come for consultation because the son, placed in the custody of his father for a year by the court, had begun to develop behavioral disorders. He had committed a serious sexual crime at the age of 12 (shortly after his parents had separated) and had lived for several years in a juvenile rehabilitation home. The court had then put him in the custody of the father. After a promising start in his father's new family, the son had started to develop behavioral disorders again.

A situation in some ways very common in mixed-parent families was apparent right from the start: no one was allowed to speak about emotions and feelings relating either to the present mixed-parent family or to the two previous ones. More specifically, the boy was implicitly forbidden to speak about his mother. He found himself in a paradoxical situation, then: "If I think about the present, I'm bad because I shouldn't completely forget the family I've left. If I think about the past, I'm bad because I'm ignoring my present family." The problem had been created by this ambiguous simultaneity of past and present.

A ritual was prescribed. One day a week, the three members of the family had to meet and speak about the boy's past, his mother, the mother's family, and the previous relationship between his father and mother, so that the stepmother could also participate in a story to which, in effect, they all belonged. They were also advised to telephone the mother and speak to her. On the other days of the week, however, it was forbidden to speak about the past: anyone who did so had to be brought into line by the others. Here, too, the ritual proved successful because it enabled family members to speak and think sequentially about both the present mixed-parent family and the two satellite families without any of the families being regarded as a taboo subject.

9

THREE CLINICAL CASES

IN PREVIOUS CHAPTERS WE HAVE given a general outline of our approach to time in therapy. We should now like first to present two complete case studies in which the role of time is analyzed in detail at every stage in the therapeutic process. Both therapies were conducted by Luigi Boscolo, assisted by a team of trainees. We shall then report on a consultation, again conducted by Luigi Boscolo, on a schizophrenia case at a psychiatric hospital in Switzerland.

DAVID: BREAKING A
VICIOUS CIRCLE

The family came from a small town in Northern Italy. Both parents were about 30 years of age. The father, a plumber, and the mother, a housewife, had an only child, David, who at the time of therapy was in his third year at primary school. David suffered from Down's syndrome, but in terms of intelligence was well above average for his condition. As a result, he found himself the focus of well-meaning, amused attention, especially from adults; it was as if he permanently lived his life at the center of a stage.

David had been assigned a special support teacher at school to oversee not so much his academic progress as his behavior. At first sight, he was a lively, likeable child, although both at school and at home he was restless, impetuous, and undisciplined, forever on the move. He would resolutely reject any form of external control, continuing his ceaseless movement and constantly shifting his attention, as if trying to force adults to take an interest in him. At home, his mother had to keep him under constant observation because he would touch everything and dismantle anything he could lay his hands on: lampshades, telephones, radios. He would regularly break two or three pairs of eyeglasses a month, and rejected any form of prohibition. In short, he would never do what he was told.

And yet, everyone liked him because he was fun. He would sometimes talk about himself in the third person, and spoke in a nasal voice, occasionally mispronouncing his words, with the result that he was regarded as something of a comic character. He had already undergone individual therapy, but with no success. However, his mother had kept on asking his therapist for help, and he, feeling totally helpless, had eventually advised her to try family therapy. All in all, David seemed to have a knack for making those around him feel helpless. At school he had become a sort of amiable jester, performing his routines under the watchful eye of his support teacher. At home, his mother was totally bound to him, unable to take her eyes off him for an instant. In the evening, his father would return from work to take over from the mother.

In the first session the parents' helplessness, discouragement and resignation were written clearly on their faces, while David made obvious at once, with mocking laughter and sudden movements, that he would obey no rules, and indeed, would disrupt the conversation and draw attention to himself whenever he wished. His behavior reminded the therapist of children suffering from attention deficit disorder. After a few minutes, during which David had obstinately refused to sit down, the therapist began to see whether he could establish a collaborative relationship with him: "Look, this is my place. You can sit down now." David's only response was to start running round the room, and also to slap his father on the head. His father resignedly accepted this. David then showed signs of leaving the room.

At this point, he was stopped: "Listen, if you leave this room it means you're stupid; if you stay, it means you're clever. Make up your mind which." David hesitated, remained in the doorway for a few seconds, then resolutely came back into the room. Immediately after, however, he found another way of disrupting the conversation by starting to finger the magazines on the table and then throwing them noisily onto the floor in an irritating way.

Seeing that this attempt had failed, the therapist decided to confront him by emphasizing that all this was happening in his territory: "David, you're in my place here and you have to obey the rules. If you don't put those magazines back on my table in five minutes, I'll throw you out!" David did not bat an eyelid, as if he hadn't even been listening. A few seconds before the five minutes were up, the therapist, watch in hand, asked him to tidy up the magazines. David's response was to challenge him with a sarcastic smile. The therapist stood up calmly, and when David refused to leave the room, lifted him by the collar of his jacket and gently put him down in the corridor outside. He then returned to the therapy room, where the parents were sitting motionless with amazement. The mother said she was afraid David might damage the offices. The therapist replied that the secretary would most probably realize he was doing it and stop him. By putting David out of the room, the therapist had communicated nonverbally his resistance to David's tendency to define unilaterally the rules of the relationship; moreover, he let the parents know that he was prepared to run some risk to make his resistance clear.

After about a quarter of an hour, the therapist in fact began to feel uneasy about what the destructive child might do to the equipment that was lying around. He went out and was surprised to find David sitting motionless on a chair in the waiting room like a wounded animal, apparently rather shocked at the brusque manner in which he had been removed from the room. Now it was time to change tack and make up. As is well known, nonverbal behavior is more effective with children than verbal behavior, so the therapist suddenly got down on his hands and knees on the carpet and asked David, in a persuasive voice, "Where should I go now?" David seemed impressed and asked him to crawl to the end of the corridor. The therapist, still on all fours, did what he asked. Having carried out David's request two times more, he then got up and said, "Now it's your turn!" And David obeyed.

By means of this game, the therapist had succeeded in breaking the stalemate of their symmetrical stance; he had loosened up their interaction by adopting a new stance totally complementary to the child's, thus enabling him to adopt a complementary stance, too. Having himself given orders to the therapist, David was immediately prepared to be obedient. A sequence had been established in which both participants gave orders and carried them out in turn. Once the therapist had agreed to be a child in the presence of another child, David felt able to accept his own social role as a child, if only playfully for the moment.

The session then went ahead with less difficulty, and it was easier to examine the system of interactions that developed around David. It became clear that, although he was continually receiving orders, accompanied by threats of punishment, he regularly ignored the orders and the threatened punishment was never carried out: inevitably, the inconsistency of this response to his disobedience was only perpetuating it. In other words, the behavior of David and those around him had achieved its own kind of equilibrium. One of the therapist's aims was to avoid interfering with this equilibrium, instead creating conditions in which new behaviors could be established.

Looking ahead for a moment, it is interesting that the couple showed no significant relational problems, either as husband and wife or with their extended family, over the entire course of therapy: their problems did not seem to have been produced by any identifiable family or couple "psychopathology." The basic problem seemed to be the "handicap" or "illness" label that was conditioning how they responded to David's behavior and that was inducing in them a forced—and frustrated—tolerance of his excesses. As a result, the context David lived in was preventing him from developing his full potential.

Another important reason for the persistence of David's hyperactivity was that he was liked, and so continually attracted attention to himself. He was used to living on a stage all the time, with an audience he always had to keep amused. During the session, for example, the parents would sometimes burst into amused laughter as they watched David, only to return immediately afterwards to their usual expressions of frustration and impotence.

Returning now to the session, David, although he had already had his ups and downs in his relationship with the therapist, had clearly shown that he was prepared to change his behavior, and his parents seemed impressed by this, even if they still looked somewhat doubtful.

Two options emerged from the team discussion: either to go on seeing the whole family or to call in just the parents. The second was chosen, in the hope that the parents would be able to regain their lost "competence" as parents now that they had been given the chance to relish the prospect of it actually happening.

It was decided to communicate the final intervention only to the parents while David drew on a blackboard in an adjacent room.

THERAPIST: We'd like to give you a very important task to carry out at home. It's a hard one, and it'll be difficult to see it through. We expect that David will rebel against this task in any way he can, and you'll be tempted to give up. If this happens, you'll end up obeying David, not us. We're not giving you this task as a duty. On the contrary, it's extremely important that you decide together at home whether you want to do it or not. If you feel doubtful about it, don't do it.

With the parents' agreement, the therapist proceeded to prescribe an odd-and-even-day task (Selvini Palazzoli et al., 1978a).

THERAPIST: On the even days of the week—Tuesday, Thursday and Saturday—you (*the father*) will be the parent "on duty." When you're at work on those days, and David asks your wife something, she must say: "Sort it out with your father when he comes home." No more than that. On the odd days—Monday, Wednesday and Friday—you (*the mother*) will be on duty. On Sundays, behave just as you wish.

The main aim in prescribing this ritual was to make the parents *do* something specific that would help them to break out of their word-bound helplessness. This was certainly a case where actions would speak louder than words. The odd-and-even-day ritual is usually prescribed to conflict-bound parents who disrupt each other's relations with their children. In this case, however, the main aim was to place David in a new situation in which his parents would alternately abdicate their usual willingness to be available to him at all times. In addition, their responsibility towards David would now be more or less equally shared. This was advantageous, since the team believed that this was a "symbiotic" mother-son relationship in which the mother never managed to take her eyes off her son for an instant. Finally, the ritual would introduce time into the relations between parents, in the form of a temporal sequence the family did not yet seem to have developed for itself.

In the second session, the parents reported an improvement in the general situation, although a high price had been paid. From day one, David had systematically tried to impose his previous behavior on his parents, but they had scrupulously carried out their task and had thwarted all his attempts to disrupt it. It is interesting that David addressed most of his requests to his father when the latter was "off duty." Both parents reported with amazement that, after repeated attempts to engage his father's attention, David had called him "Daddy" for the first time, after a lifetime of calling him only by his name. As time passed, David adapted to the new situation and began to be quieter and more manageable.

In the third session with the parents, the main theme was the mother's enslavement to her son—the fact that she had to keep an eye on him all day long to prevent him from causing trouble. Of course, there were no keys in the house, so no door could ever be kept locked, with the result that neither parents nor David could ever enjoy their personal time and space.

The final intervention was based on this theme.

THERAPIST: I've been talking things over with my colleagues, and I'd like to ask you to do something if you can manage it, but it must be you who decide whether you want to or not. So we'd like to ask you to think it over for a couple of days, and then go ahead with our program if you both agree you can do it.

As in the intervention at the close of the first session, the therapist's tone was deliberately unassertive. In families where obedience and control are a problem and orders are never carried out, it is counterproductive to adopt a stance that in any way appears authoritarian. The therapist avoided symmetry with the parents just as he had with David himself. Asking them to discuss beforehand whether the task was feasible or not reinforced their decision and prevented disagreement.

THERAPIST: Well, when you go home, and if you agree, call David and say: "Look, David, you're eight years old now, and like all children of your age you know that when your parents go to the bathroom you shouldn't follow them. From now on, we're going to lock the door when we go to the bathroom. Since for the moment you show no signs of being able to keep your hands to yourself, we're also going to lock the kitchen and bedroom doors. You'll stay in the dining room where there's nothing you can break. And remember, we won't unlock the doors for any reason." Do you think it's possible to do this? If you think you can, do it straightaway, maybe when you're alone at home.

FATHER: What if we're both at home?

THERAPIST: Then it's pointless locking the doors. When you're both at home, it would be better if you (*the mother*) went out for a breath of fresh air now and again, leaving you (*the father*) alone at home for an hour or two. While she's out, you should go to the bathroom at least once. When you go to the bathroom, take your watch and decide to stay inside for at least ten minutes, if you can manage it. (*The father looks rather apprehensively at the mother.*) It's a risk. Do you feel like trying it?

FATHER: The dining room can be left unlocked. There are the chairs, but the worst he can do is knock them over. . . .

THERAPIST: You must remove all medicines, which are the biggest source of danger to children. We have to remove these dangers in order to avoid an even bigger one. David is eight, so he still hasn't had the experience of being separated from adults for even a moment. He always feels safe and secure because he's *always* being observed, and he does all these things to show off in front of the people who observe him. Even when he was here, he tried to make himself observed all the time. He's never had, and he never can have the experience of not being observed. So it'll be new to him, but it's an experience all children must have. If you feel you're strong enough to give it a try . . .

FATHER: Yes, yes, it can be done.

MOTHER: Yes, it can be done, it'll be difficult at first . . .

The parents gradually shift from apprehension at hearing the therapist's proposal to agreeing to give it a try. Any kind of lecturing or imposition would probably have produced the inevitable "we can't do it," so the therapist leaves it up to the parents to decide one way or another, now or later. By doing this, he avoids holding them to an immediate decision and makes it possible for them to develop their own competence in their own time. The therapist respects the times and rhythms of his clients, adjusting his time to theirs.

> THERAPIST: Anyway, we leave it up to you. Then, if you agree to do it, explain things to David. Don't repeat yourselves. If he keeps on asking for an explanation, say: "We've already told you why." Don't accept arguments. And continue with the task we gave you the other time.

The prescription is an especially complex one. It is mainly based on the themes of agreement between the parents, David's growing out of early childhood, and the introduction of temporal sequences in a family that has lost all sense of development, a family in which time is both chaotic and at a standstill. The prescription has four parts:

> 1. Although leaving them freedom of choice, the therapist asks the couple to agree in advance on the task they will have to perform.
>
> 2. Their first action works as a ritual. The couple will have to make its announcement to David together, "once and for all," using a preestablished formula. It may be regarded as a "rite of passage" marking David's promotion from an age when he must always be observed to one when there must be moments when he is alone. For this reason, the formula contains many references to "what normally happens at a certain age."
>
> 3. The wording of the prescription contains references to time such as "for now," "up to now," "for the time being," which serve to introduce the idea of change into a system where time has come to a standstill.
>
> 4. Finally, the sequencing of the actions asked of the parents transforms the words of the ritual into *facts*, thereby marking David's new maturity (he is no longer a small child, and can no longer be totally irresponsible).

In the next session, the parents reported that the situation had improved beyond their wildest expectations. As the mother apprehensively began to lock the door every time she went to the bathroom, none of the behavior they had feared actually happened. David proved quite able to tolerate her absence and showed no desire to wheedle his way into the bathroom. A fortnight later, she even risked going out to do some shopping at a nearby market. Upon returning, not without some trepidation, she found her son had remained happily in the dining room. She had now rediscovered what it meant to be free and started going out more often. In the meantime, David's behavior at school was improving constantly. In the fifth session, the family seemed to have been relieved of a huge burden.

The therapist himself immediately noticed David's new attitude. He sat obediently next to the therapist, as happy as pie, and never once disrupted the conversation. His behavior was the exact opposite of what it had been in the first session, as if he had moved from a rigidly symmetrical stance to a rigidly complementary one. In order to test this new relationship style, the therapist asked him to be disobedient at least once during the rest of the session, and then continued talking to his parents. Halfway through, David politely asked: "Excuse me, could I go to the room with the blackboard so I can draw for a while?" The therapist gave his consent.

The session — and the therapy — ended with a comment from the therapist stressing that the change they had seen would be a lasting one, and that there was no point in going on with the therapy.

The relieved and smiling parents went with the therapist to fetch David from the adjacent room, and were dismayed to find that, instead of drawing on the blackboard, he had used the eraser steeped in blue ink to scribble (indelibly) all over the white wall. Visibly embarrassed, the father looked at the therapist and said he was sorry about what had happened. Suddenly, the therapist remembered that he himself had caused the disaster: he had ordered David to be disobedient, and David had promptly obeyed him!

ANTONELLA: THE SWEATER GIRL

The Viola family, from a Lombardy town in Northern Italy, was referred to our center by a psychiatrist who had been treating their daughter Antonella for three years. The family consisted of the father, a 54-year-old artisan, the mother, a 48-year-old housewife, and their three children. The eldest, Giovanni, was a 25-year-old engineering student; Antonella, 23, was studying philosophy; and the youngest, Gustavo, 20, was studying commerce and economics.

Antonella had started to have problems three years earlier, beginning with painful gastric symptoms like burning, nausea, heaviness and swelling of the stomach. In parallel with this, she had decided that she was over-weight, and so had started the war on food typical of an anorexic syn-drome.

Antonella's stomach disorders cleared up after hospital treatment fol-lowed by outpatient care. Thereupon, however, her obsession with food and being overweight caused her to develop a series of phobias, which included fear of catching a whole range of different diseases, fear that her food was bad, fear of losing control, and a constant fear that something terrible was going to happen. However, what tormented her the most was that a change in external temperature might cause the saprophytic bacte-ria in her mucous membranes to turn virulent, with the danger that they would invade her body and destroy it. For this reason, she kept her body temperature under control with pullovers and sweaters—cotton in sum-mer, wool in winter—which she wore literally in layers, one on top of the other, removing or putting them on at the slightest variation in tempera-ture. Her fear had gradually increased to a point where, two years ago, she had left the university and stopped seeing her friends in order to remain at home: the temperature there was more constant and predictable, and so easier to control.

First Session

Antonella's strange, grotesque appearance was immediately noticeable at the first meeting. Her thin body was swathed in large sweaters, which made her look like an American football player. As if these were not enough, she also had other heavy sweaters draped over her right arm. Her mother sat in the middle of the room flanked by her two sons. The father sat on the outside next to the youngest son Gustavo, with Antonella next to her elder brother Giovanni on the other side.

On being asked why the family had been referred to the center, the mother said that Antonella was suffering from "nervous anorexia and psy-chosis." It was obvious that this statement produced no emotional reaction in those present, as often happens in chronic cases.

The start of the session was devoted to describing Antonella's fears and eccentricities. She acknowledged that her fears were indeed strange, but added that "she couldn't do anything about it." When asked if she also suffered from "the fear of being well," she agreed that she did. Whenever she began to feel a bit better, she said, she would also feel afraid that she would soon have to pay for her undeserved well-being.

The family story that emerged during the first session contained serious conflict with the father's original family, which had strongly affected relations in the family nucleus. The Violas lived in one of three flats in a building that once belonged to the father's parents. The children described their paternal grandmother and aunt as extremely meddlesome people who had had free access to the family's home for years, coming and going as they pleased without even knocking and always trying to poke their noses into their affairs. In time, this had led to increasing disagreement between the mother (supported by her sons) and her husband's family. The father's attempts at mediation had been unsuccessful. In consequence, the parents had never got on, and Antonella, who had suffered a great deal as a result, had exhausted herself in vain attempts to bring them closer together.

One of the main accusations the mother and sons had against the father was that he was "weak, lacking in initiative." The father had always been strongly attached to his family: he had inherited his artisan's trade from them and had "taken over" the family workshop from his sister, but had now been working for some years as an employee in a craft firm. So although he had failed to live up to the expectations of his youth, he still remained the family's only source of income.

During the course of the session, it became clear that the family was divided into three subsystems: the mother and sons (who would often indirectly criticize and make fun of their father while their mother tacitly encouraged them to do so); the father, a sad, rather taciturn man; and Antonella, now completely isolated, who came to life only when speaking about her problems, otherwise seeming bored and distracted.

At a certain point, the therapist realized that the father seemed to have abdicated his role as a father, and asked the family which of them had taken his place. Both the mother and sons pointed to Giovanni, the "clever one" all the others turned to, as the father substitute. In fact, Giovanni showed more concern for his sister than the others did, announcing that he would help her in the future with his own money and would be prepared to have her living with him should he ever get married. Gustavo was seen as the "handsome one," his mother's pet, while Antonella said she looked like her father and was the "ugly one" in the family, one of life's losers. She said she would never marry and have children, and dreamed of going into a hospital for the rest of her life. These statements produced no great concern in the rest of the family, which showed more interest in its feuds with the paternal family and its criticisms of the father, who, it turned out, had been treated in the past for depression in a psychiatric ward. When the therapist pointed out to the father that the whole family seemed to despise him, and asked whether he had ever thought of "putting an end to it all," he answered, "Yes, of course, I often think of suicide. I might even do it, but only when all my children have got their degrees. Only when I've done my duty as a father."

During the course of the session, it came to light that Antonella had been undergoing individual psychotherapy for a year and a half, and that her therapist had not been informed that she had been referred for family therapy. To conclude the session, the therapist fixed an appointment for the following month, on the condition that Antonella's therapist agree that the sessions should proceed.

Second Session

A week before the date fixed for the second session, the mother telephoned the therapist to say, in aggrieved tones, that Antonella's individual therapist had not agreed to allow individual therapy to take place at the same time as family therapy, adding that, so far as she herself was concerned, the first meeting had been extremely positive and she hoped it would be possible to continue the meetings in future. The team hypothesized from this that family therapy had been sought only by those members of the family who had been disappointed with individual therapy.

Surprisingly, the mother telephoned again three months later to say that Antonella had dismissed her therapist because of "lack of results" and asked for another session, which was fixed for mid June.

When the family arrived, the only apparent difference was that Antonella had changed from wool sweaters to cotton ones. At the start of the session, the therapist returned to Antonella's fear of changes in temperature, using a metaphor that linked the various members of the family and cast serious doubt on the medical diagnosis of her illness.

ANTONELLA: Whenever I go out, I automatically have to think whether I'm going to be hot or cold, whether I should put on or take off a sweater, whether I'll be able to keep my temperature constant. . . .

THERAPIST: It's like a kind of research, isn't it? You're perhaps a little like a university researcher who's studying the effect of temperature on body cells, a very systematic kind of research. When you're at home, do you do your research alone, or as part of a team? Do you ever ask for help?

ANTONELLA: Yes, no, well usually yes. I ask: "What do you think, would it be better for me to put this sweater on, or to leave it in the car?"

THERAPIST: So you mean you ask them what the temperature is, is that it?

MOTHER: Yes, yes, she asks . . .

THERAPIST: I see. But in your family, who is your most faithful assistant in the research you do?

ANTONELLA: The who one I feel is closest to problems of temperature is Gustavo.

THERAPIST: Closest in the sense that he's better at guessing what it is?

ANTONELLA: Yes, maybe. He advises me quite often. In fact, he's been going around with me lately. . . .

THERAPIST: And is Gustavo interested in this research into temperature?

ANTONELLA: No, he says it's stupid.

MOTHER: (*laughs*)

ANTONELLA: He says it's pointless.

THERAPIST: But he does what you say.

ANTONELLA: No, usually he doesn't. Usually he gets fed up with it.

THERAPIST: But something interesting might come of this research. A constant might be found, yes, let's say a constant . . .

ANTONELLA: An average.

THERAPIST: A temperature that's standard in relation to a given constant; a relationship, let's say, between environment, clothing, the number of sweaters you need, their thickness . . . there might be a constant there . . .

MOTHER: Hmm, but there's no end to it because every day is a new day.

THERAPIST: Giovanni is studying engineering. Perhaps he could take charge of the research.

MOTHER: Every day is a new . . .

ANTONELLA: It's as if every day is newborn, as if the previous day has been totally useless!

THERAPIST: Is Giovanni interested in this research?

ANTONELLA: He's the one who gives me the most advice. I do it to get out of the house, because if I could always stay at home, I would.

THERAPIST: Excuse me, I'd just like to ask my colleagues behind the mirror if one of them has had any experience of this kind of research. (*goes out*)

Analysis of this segment of conversation reveals the following points:

1. The therapist is using metaphorical discourse to introduce other possible worlds: most importantly, a world in which Antonella is

redeemed from being branded as sick or deviant. The "research" metaphor not only restores her *status* as a university student but also implies collaboration with other members of the family. In answer to the question "When you're at home, do you do your research alone, or as part of a team?" Antonella says, "Yes, no, well usually yes." It seems here that the metaphor is beginning to be accepted by the family, which encourages the therapist to continue with it. Another possible "reality," i.e., a different interpretation of events, begins to emerge.

2. Some questions in this metaphorical framework are linked to the therapist's hypothesis about relationships within the family. Thus Giovanni, the son who seems to have taken the place of the father, is named "chief" researcher.

3. At a certain point, the therapist suggests that the research might produce a "constant," a new metaphor reflecting the immobility of Antonella's life, her desire to achieve an unchanging, constant state. The research for a constant temperature may be seen as an attempt to halt the onset of the future.[1]

4. The mother responds to the metaphor of the constant with a striking statement: "There's no end to it because every day is a new day." Antonella echoes her with a fine analogy: "It's as if every day is newborn, as if the previous day has been totally useless!"—a statement that describes the arrest of time in very simple, yet almost poetic, terms. We have here a circular time that rotates on itself, that never becomes part of life, never becomes irreversible like time's arrow.

5. It may also be that Antonella is in effect describing her situation as a case of zero learning. To say "every day is newborn" is to deny that experience can have any influence on the future. As Bateson (1972) would say, there is no learning and so new contexts cannot be constructed. If every day means starting again from scratch, there can be no development, life can never become story or history.

6. This exchange is a good example of the differences between our earlier systemic approach and the one we use now based on constructivist principles. In the past, we saw the therapist with his or her metaphors and hypotheses as an active agent, and clients as passive. Now we prefer to see hypotheses and metaphors as elements which

---

[1]From the psychoanalytic point of view, this could be seen as regression to an intrauterine state.

emerge from therapist-client and client-therapist interaction. Accordingly, we now also prefer to speak of co-creation and co-evolution.

7. It should be noted that the analysis so far has been an *a posteriori* one in which the authors, as "observers," have been observing the therapist who "observes" the family, i.e., the interactions and assumptions of the actors in the dialogue are seen through the lens of the authors' present theoretical and practical "biases."[2]

8. All this takes place in a clearly defined network that includes, in addition to those already mentioned, any future readers and reviewers of this book, as well as its editors and publishers. The complexity paradigm (Bocchi & Ceruti, 1985) seems to be the appropriate frame for all these points of observation.

THERAPIST: (*reentering the room*) According to my colleagues, your search for a constant temperature is a metaphor. I mean it stands for something else, for some other deeper search you're involved in but haven't had any results from yet. Do you know of any situation where temperature is constant?

ANTONELLA: (*reflecting*) Well, I don't know . . .

THERAPIST: The womb could be a place where temperature is always constant. You are absorbed in a search for a kind of security you will never find outside it. Your search for a constant might also be a metaphor for your research into how others see you. I mean: "How does my father see me, how do my mother and brothers see me?" My colleagues think that your brothers don't have your doubts about temperature and so they don't put on sweaters as you do because deep down they have a clear idea about what their position is in the family. And not just now, either—they've always had it. You, on the other hand, always seem to have been deeply uncertain about your position.

On returning to the therapy room after consulting with his colleagues, the therapist introduces two new metaphors, Antonella's refusal to come to terms with life and her rivalry with her brothers (which is developed a little later on). The family seems impressed by these metaphors, implying that Antonella is stranded in time, while her brothers have been able to

---

[2]During the session, the therapist makes choices based on client feedback and the circularity of relationships. At the time, he was unaware of all these implications, which only became clear later, in a new context.

evolve because they have always been sure of their relationships with other members of the family.[3]

> THERAPIST: Is the idea clear? You're like someone holding a daisy who says: "He loves me, he loves me not; my mother loves me, my mother loves me not." This kind of dilemma, well, you're a philosopher, so you know about it, don't you? The answers you get to these questions don't remove your existential doubts, they only perpetuate them. Usually, when you get answers to questions like these, they clear up doubts about temperature. One of my colleagues said I should ask if this idea makes any sense to you.
>
> ANTONELLA: (*with a puzzled expression*) Yes, perhaps, because I feel nothing, I feel I am nothing.
>
> THERAPIST: And you, Mrs. Viola, does what my colleague says make sense to you?
>
> MOTHER: (*in a clear, confident voice*) Yes, absolutely, it certainly makes sense to me.
>
> FATHER: Yes, I agree.
>
> THERAPIST: Let's assume it makes sense, then. How do you explain why Antonella feels this dilemma, but not her brothers?
>
> GUSTAVO, GIOVANNI: (*laugh nervously*)

During the course of the session, the therapist first introduces a theme which emphasizes the *possibility* of change. The research metaphor suggests a beginning and an end, as well as a positive result, the discovery of a "temperature constant," so it may be possible to release Antonella from her static existence. Immediately after, however, the therapist refers to the arrest of time Antonella mentioned at the start of the sequence. The daisy metaphor suggests a potentially infinite oscillation between "I am wanted" and "I am not wanted." If the research metaphor points to time's arrow, the daisy metaphor points to time's cycle, to perpetual fluctuation. Finally, the therapist relates this fluctuation to the family system. Antonella may never finish her research because no one in the family seems to be giving her an answer.

---

[3]The family's agreement with the therapist's hypothesis might lead the therapist to believe that he is getting at the "truth," that he is on the verge of understanding the psychological disorder he has been asked to treat. In our experience, the therapist should take care not to delude himself here, and should think simply in terms of a new story, conditioned (though not determined) by the constraints of the past.

Gustavo and Giovanni's nervous laughter seems an attempt to distance themselves from the dialogue. They may have been deeply impressed by what they heard, so their laughter may conceal guilt about their success in manipulating their parents at the expense of their sister, who seems totally isolated and confused. At this point, the family seems on the verge of change. The parents agree about the meaning of the metaphor: Antonella cannot finish her research because no one in the family is giving her the answers she needs. The brothers' embarrassed laughter, compared with the seriousness and sympathy of the parents, throws new light on relationships in the family and shows that it might be possible to reorganize the family system, to co-create a new story.

ANTONELLA: I could never accept myself as I was. I was disgusted with myself physically, and also because I was never any good at school, because I had to work so hard . . .

THERAPIST: This idea that you found yourself disgusting, where do you think it came from?

ANTONELLA: Well, the idea of being fat . . . I weighed 65 lbs. more than I do now when I began to feel ill.

THERAPIST: But did this idea of being disgusting come from other people too?

ANTONELLA: Well, sometimes . . .

THERAPIST: For example, do you think you disgust me now?

ANTONELLA: No, not now.

THERAPIST: Does it sometimes happen that you think I find you disgusting?

ANTONELLA: I don't know . . .

MOTHER: But she isn't fat. She isn't fat, so she can't be disgusting anymore.

ANTONELLA: I'm not fat anymore, I can't be disgusting anymore.

THERAPIST: Is it your mother who's disgusting, then? (*laughs*)

ANTONELLA: No, no.

THERAPIST: (*who is overweight*) Am I disgusting, too?

MOTHER: No, no. But for her, Antonella, it's like that. For me, no. Perhaps I don't disgust her.

The questions here try to relate a personal characteristic (fatness) to ideas that have gradually developed within the family and to others in the "here and now": the fatness of the mother and also of the therapist himself.

There is an implicit message that ideas about a given personal characteristic can be different, and may change. Moreover, the tendency of the mother to read Antonella's thoughts and answer for her should also be noted in this brief exchange. Later on, in the third session, we shall compare the mother's disgusted reaction to Antonella's new fatness with the reactions of the rest of the family.

> THERAPIST: Your father said at a certain point that, in the past, your brothers used to go their own ways while you were always at home and knew what was going on there.
>
> ANTONELLA: Yes, yes.
>
> THERAPIST: Did you suffer because of this?
>
> ANTONELLA: Yes.
>
> THERAPIST: What made you suffer most, then?
>
> ANTONELLA: Well, the arguing.
>
> THERAPIST: Between whom?
>
> ANTONELLA: Mother and father, because of father's family. There were times when they went at it day and night, without stopping . . . we were tired of it . . . all of us.
>
> THERAPIST: Whose suffering caused you most suffering? Your father's suffering, your mother's suffering?
>
> ANTONELLA: My mother's.
>
> THERAPIST: Your mother's. And your father's?
>
> ANTONELLA: Well, I saw that he was weak. . . . I thought it was strange that he had to react in that way. It wasn't like him to react like that.
>
> THERAPIST: Were you there during all your parents' arguments?
>
> ANTONELLA: Yes, yes, all of them. I remember them, it's as if they were happening now.
>
> THERAPIST: But your brothers went their own ways, didn't they?
>
> ANTONELLA: My brothers, well, yes, they weren't around so often. I remember they went off more often. I remember nights when we were all up. Once, I was trying to sleep because I had a Latin test the next day . . . and they were downstairs shouting . . .

Analysis of this segment brings to mind Selvini Palazzoli and colleagues' theory (1989) of psychotic games in the family, which sees psychosis as the final outcome of a six-stage game in which the son or daughter who eventually becomes psychotic is the child involved in the parents' "couple stalemate." Adopting this model, we would now have to look for denial of the parent-daughter alliance, parental "cheating," "dirty games," and other things that would make Antonella's behavior the logical outcome of the family game. We feel, however, that the idea that a single family typology can explain both the origin and development of a psychosis is too reductive, and that other systems have to be taken into consideration.

Later, the therapist continues to probe the relations between the nuclear family and the extended family. The most important element seems to be the father's position. Giovanni, who often serves as the family's spokesman, reports that his father has had to "swallow a lot of bitter pills" given to him by his family of origin, his wife, and his children, adding that this "served him right, because he asked for it." The phrase "bitter pills," like "research" and "constant," is what we have elsewhere (Boscolo et al., 1991) called a key word.[4]

> THERAPIST: (*to the father*) Who might have the sugar to sweeten all the bitter pills you've had to swallow, and are still swallowing?
>
> FATHER: My wife.
>
> THERAPIST: But you've accepted that she'll never give you this sugar anymore; you've got used to black coffee now?
>
> FATHER: I'm sure that, in the present situation . . . because I must say, it also has to be said that all these things that are coming out now are coming from Antonella; really it's because of her that all this is coming out, because you try to bear up, but at a certain point you can't go on anymore. They (*to his sons*) go off, but we parents can't just get up and go. So that's that, and of course, what must out will out.

The father avoids answering the question by shifting the conversation to the subject of Antonella. He does this repeatedly throughout the session, which may indicate, with all the abuse that is being heaped on him, that he is trying to regain the blameless position of a father who is worried about his ailing daughter. However, the inconsistency of many of his answers (such as the last one) could be seen as an example of deviance communication (Singer & Wynne, 1965).

> THERAPIST: (*to the mother*) Do you receive sugar from anyone at home?
>
> MOTHER: (*looking at her two sons*) Yes, yes, from my children, naturally.

---

[4]The article cited also envisions a linguistic analysis of this part of the session.

THERAPIST: They give your life meaning, let's say. But your husband, as Giovanni also said, now seems trapped in a dead-end situation, swallowing all those bitter pills, just waiting for them to come, for things to happen to him.

MOTHER: Yes, he's resigned, he's resigned to it.

THERAPIST: He's resigned to taking it, then. But I think there's also some resignation in Antonella about her life, too, her future. What struck many of my colleagues is that, in the past, she got the idea into her head that she was disgusting.

MOTHER: When she's fat, she is, yes.

THERAPIST: No one knows where this idea came from. But when one idea begins to develop, others start appearing. If you're disgusting, you aren't acceptable on the outside. You start asking, "Who could ever want me? Would any man ever want me?"[5]

MOTHER: Yes, yes, it's a habit.

THERAPIST: She might think: "Even if he wants me, he'll leave me when he realizes I'm disgusting." Or else: "How disgusting if I have a child; I'm disgusting, so God knows how disgusting the child would be!"

MOTHER: Yes, that's right, because if I weren't fat she would not be fat.

While the brothers tend to criticize their father and look kindly on their sister, the mother tends subtly to undermine her daughter's self-image. This is probably one of the main causes of Antonella's insecurity and self-hatred. The father could give his daughter support or even enter into an alliance with her, as the mother has done with her sons, but he doesn't because he is totally wrapped up in his fatalistic resignation.

THERAPIST: So at this point it's better to have done with it, decide you aren't suitable, give yourself a label. I mean (*to the mother*) I think your daughter has been labeling herself since an early age . . .

FATHER: But you see, she's never accepted herself physically. Because, I don't know, her problems started when she began to develop. "I have to use these things, I always have to do these things, why should I do them, those things are . . . "

THERAPIST: That reminds of something my colleagues said. They think

---

[5]The therapist's attempt to draw out an "ecology of ideas" should be noted here since it is characteristic of systemic approaches.

this temperature is a metaphor of a search for something. This something might be: "Am I a boy or a girl? Do I want to be female or male?" Deep down she may have thought she would have liked to be a boy because she may have noticed that the boys receive more love in this family. It may be that Antonella, born after Giovanni and before Gustavo, noticed that they made her mother happy, and said to herself: "If I were a boy too. . . . " Her mother said it a short while ago: "They give me sugar."

MOTHER: (*embarrassed*) But not just the two of them, all three of them!

The mother's sharply critical reply, which openly contradicts her previous statements, is common in seriously disturbed families and obviously helps to fuel dilemmas in relationships: "Am I wanted or not? Do they want me to be a boy or a girl?"

THERAPIST: (*to Antonella*) Perhaps you began to think: "I'm disgusting as a female; if I'd been born male things would have been better." And it's even worse to be female and fat, isn't it?

ANTONELLA: (*with a disgusted expression*) Oh, mother!

THERAPIST: To be tossed down the toilet and flushed away.

FATHER: No, because now, well, now she ought to get her hormonal state back to normal . . . she should accept herself as a person . . .

MOTHER: As a woman.

THERAPIST: (*to Antonella*) You feel no desire, I suppose.

ANTONELLA: No.

THERAPIST: You feel no sexual desire?

ANTONELLA: No.

THERAPIST: Are you relieved about that?

ANTONELLA: Pardon?

THERAPIST: Would you like to feel desire or not? I suppose not. Wouldn't you like to have erotic thoughts or ideas? Don't you ever have erotic thoughts?

ANTONELLA: No.

THERAPIST: Does that make you happy?

ANTONELLA: I don't know, I don't know.

In this central part of the session, a series of hypotheses emerge that enrich the past and present and introduce future possibilities. In other words, the therapist is encouraging the production of alternative stories about the past and present that may offer glimpses of possible future worlds. Later on, the therapist will shift the temporal horizon towards the future.

THERAPIST: I'd like to ask you another question before going to talk to my colleagues. The question I'd like to ask is this: when your brothers get married and start families of their own, which family would you like to live with, if you really do decide to stay with the family? With Giovanni, with your parents, or with Gustavo? Which is the one you would choose?

ANTONELLA: Perhaps with them.

THERAPIST: Who do you mean?

ANTONELLA: My brothers. Then, I don't know . . .

THERAPIST: Which brother? Which family?

ANTONELLA: It makes no difference.

THERAPIST: It makes no difference. Do you sometimes think about these things? Do you sometimes like the idea of becoming one of those spinster aunts, like in the old days, who never got married . . .

ANTONELLA: Yes, I do.

THERAPIST: Who looked after their nephews and nieces . . . do you think about it sometimes?

ANTONELLA: No. I don't think so far ahead. I mean, only now is real to me.

Once again, Antonella reveals the narrowness of her temporal horizon:

1. She seems to be trying to return to early childhood and reject adulthood (oral regression, in Freudian terms).

2. For her, "only now is real," but this "now" totally envelops her, so her story can never develop.

Clearly, her assumptions are fueled by the feedback she receives, which continually returns her to her starting point in a series of never-ending circles. The therapist now openly challenges the assumption that time is static. He initiates a series of questions about the future by offering new hypotheses no longer about what *has* been, but about what *could* happen. Answering such questions opens up Antonella's (and her family's) temporal horizon to the future.

THERAPIST: So you think: "Perhaps I'll live with them." Who would you prefer to live with, if you could choose?

ANTONELLA: I don't know. I don't know.

THERAPIST: If they had the choice, which of the three families would choose you, do you think?

ANTONELLA: (*to her brothers*) Not them, I think, because I'm unbearable.

THERAPIST: Your parents, then?

ANTONELLA: Yes, my parents, they would choose me.

THERAPIST: They'd be clamoring to have you, would they?

ANTONELLA: Oh, no. No.

THERAPIST: So they wouldn't be clamoring to have you.

FATHER: Yes, come on.

ANTONELLA: No, certainly not.

MOTHER: Well, not all that much, no.

ANTONELLA: No. I'd be a burden more than anything else.

GUSTAVO: Well, if you were in your present situation, it'd be . . .

ANTONELLA: Yes, well I don't see myself being any different from the way I am now.

MOTHER, GIOVANNI: (*laugh*)

ANTONELLA: I can't imagine myself in another situation, except the one I'm in now.

THERAPIST: You could do another kind of research: ask your brothers and parents how they would like you to be for them to accept you.

ANTONELLA: Well, that's just it. Perhaps the way I was before. Maybe just the way I was a year ago.

GIOVANNI: No.

ANTONELLA: The way I was four years ago.

THERAPIST: Look, let's imagine for a moment that your brothers start their own families in a few years' time, and you continue to have the idea of yourself you have now . . . because you might change this idea, you might start thinking at a certain point that you're a young woman like any other, a woman who can have a family if she wants to, or not have one if she doesn't want to. Have an outside life, a career—I don't know, live the way ordinary people do. You might think you're an ordinary person like everyone else, like us here. We're ordinary people, aren't we?

The therapist's future questions introduce possibilities for the whole family, a future scenario in which the brothers have gone away to start families of their own, leaving the parents and Antonella in a sort of no-man's land. As this future scenario develops, Antonella sees no way out, no possibility of independence in the future. She sees only stasis and dependence. Her statement "I can't imagine myself in another situation, except the one I'm in now" shows how seriously limited her temporal horizon is. Two readings seem possible — either her anguish and despair are narrowing her temporal horizons or her restricted temporal horizon is causing her symptoms. However, we believe this apparent dichotomy is inherent in language itself: it would be more "systemic" to speak here of a self-reflexive loop.

The therapist's final intervention introduces all the possible options Antonella has: remain as she is, change, get married, not get married, make a career for herself, lead an "ordinary" life, etc. The therapist does this to broaden Antonella's range of options, and also to avoid losing his neutrality by forcing her into a prescribed solution.

THERAPIST: Let's imagine you stay with the same idea . . .

ANTONELLA: That I'm not normal.

THERAPIST: That you're not an ordinary mortal, but someone disgusting, fit for the trash can. Let's imagine your brothers get married and you go to live with one of them. How do you see your parents, in a few years' time, on their own . . .

ANTONELLA: What would those two be like?

THERAPIST: Without children.

ANTONELLA: Without children? Oh, it'd be one big fight.

FATHER, MOTHER, GIOVANNI: (*smile*)

THERAPIST: One big fight?

ANTONELLA: Yes.

FATHER: You'd like . . .

THERAPIST: Mightn't your mother start giving your father a little sugar, I don't know . . .

ANTONELLA: Maybe.

THERAPIST: This might happen without the children around, mightn't it?

ANTONELLA: Perhaps, it might happen . . .

THERAPIST: Probably your father doesn't really need sugar. Just the gesture of receiving it.

ANTONELLA: I don't know.

GUSTAVO: All father needs is to suffer.

The future the therapist envisions here is that the separation of the children from parents will lead the parents to stop their feuding and reach a new understanding. Antonella seems to accept the prospect, but not Gustavo. The dialogue gives them the chance to "discover" that everyone's behavior is linked to context rather than to immutable personal characteristics.

At the end of the session, the therapist goes out to consult with the team. When he returns, he offers this conclusion.

THERAPIST: My colleagues and I have talked things over, and for the moment we've come to this conclusion. We aren't worried about you, Mr. Viola, because you've been used all your life to swallowing bitter pills. We aren't all that worried about Antonella either, because she knows very well it's up to her to choose in the future whether to go on with the idea that she's worthless, or to have a new idea, that she's valuable, just like everyone else. That's her decision, so we aren't worried. No, it's her mother we're worried about.

According to my colleagues, and I agree with them, the mother in this family has been used to having sugar, and by getting used to something, you come to depend on it. So, in the near future, when her sons get married, and there are other wives demanding sugar, the mother's supply may suddenly be reduced. We feel that you (*to the mother*) have never experienced what your husband has in the past. You haven't been immunized yet. Is what I am saying clear?

MOTHER: Yes.

THERAPIST: You haven't got used to this yet, and we feel you'll be in a vulnerable position in the future. It might be that, with all this sugar you're taking—I'm speaking metaphorically here—you're coming down with a kind of relational diabetes!

MOTHER: (*agreeing*) Dangerous.

THERAPIST: That's why we feel that *you* are in a vulnerable position, much more than your husband. It might be as well for the family to think this over for a while. At present, we see that Antonella is trying in some way to get her mother used to swallowing one or two bitter pills. No matter how hard you try, Mrs. Viola, you can't persuade Antonella to change, so in this sense you're swallowing bitter pills, at least for the moment.[6] These bitter pills are good for you, they'll

---

[6]In Selvini Palazzoli and Viaro's model (1988), Antonella's behavior here may be described as that of a *Type B* anorexic. In such cases, the daughter who becomes anorexic is the father's favorite. She "admires her father and considers him far superior to her mother. She can see no excuse for the way her mother rants at

make you stronger, immunize you like your husband. Immunity in
life can also come from adversity. We think it might be a good idea if
your sons helped you by starting to give you less sugar and getting
you used to living with less sugar.

GIOVANNI: (*agitated, in an excited voice*) I don't think it's like that. I see
him (*pointing to his father*) as closed, incapable of making friendships,
but (*turning to his mother*) she hasn't got any problems.

THERAPIST: Mr. Viola, what I can tell you now is that Giovanni is
giving your wife another lump of sugar.

MOTHER: (*agrees vigorously*)

THERAPIST: Do you see now? Mrs. Viola, do you see as well?

MOTHER: Yes, I see, I see. Giovanni sees too, but . . .

THERAPIST: These lumps of sugar are what we see at the moment.
What your son says is neither right nor wrong. It just confirms that
he immediately wanted to give you a lump of sugar and his father
a bitter pill. Our idea is that, during the time before the next session, your sons should help you, too, by trying to give you a bit less
sugar.

Everyone gets up: the mother and father show their agreement with the
therapist; Giovanni seems less angry though rather embarrassed; Gustavo
seems uninterested; Antonella seems relieved.

A number of points should be made about this intervention.

1. The family came to therapy with a diagnosis: Antonella is suffering from anorexia and psychosis. The therapist restated the problem
in terms of existential rather than clinical suffering.

2. Concern shifted from Antonella, who is now seen to have a range
of possible future choices if she wishes, to the mother, who runs the
risk of contracting "relational diabetes."

3. The "relational diabetes" metaphor was suggested to the therapy
team by Giovanni, who said that his father had always "swallowed

___

him" (p. 132). When the anorexic symptom appears ("stage 4"), "dieting is seen
from the start as a challenge to the mother. . . . The decision to diet is often
sparked by some specific behavior on the part of the mother that is especially
disturbing to the father or the daughter. No matter how the lowered intake of
food begins, it rapidly develops into silent protest and rejection of the mother"
(p. 133).

bitter pills," adding sarcastically that this "served him right." The metaphor also served to make the family reflect on the possible dangers of the mother-Giovanni alliance against the father.

4. Antonella's behavior has also acquired positive connotations because of the positive effects her "bitter" pills may have on her mother.

5. Finally, after Giovanni's latest attempt to establish himself as the leader of the group by criticizing the intervention, the therapist turned to the father, thereby disassociating himself from the elder son's attempts to enter an alliance with the mother against him.

If we look briefly at this second session as a whole, the importance of time is immediately apparent. The conversation began with analysis of Antonella's present situation—her existential stalemate—created by relationships within the family, and the shakiness of relationships outside the family. As well as serving to link various meanings within the family, extensive use of metaphor in this session made it easier to connect the family's range of individual and family times. After some hesitation, the rest of the family eventually came to share Antonella's "research" metaphor, and Antonella, as an acknowledged "researcher," came to be accepted in the family's here and now.

Later on, Antonella's story was woven into the total family situation, including its relations with the parents' original families. Hypothetical questions about the past made it possible to imagine alternative worlds by easing the stranglehold of the past on the present, and so widening the temporal horizon. At first, Antonella seemed trapped in endless flux, in static circular time, but as the session progressed the possibility of making time flow once again began to emerge. It was as if a river that had silted up into swamp had started to flow again.

Third Session

The third session was held after a long summer break. Antonella seemed happy and was noticeably heavier. Whereas before she tended to avoid food, she now ate continuously. In reply to the therapist's first question about how the summer had gone, the mother said: "For her (*Antonella*), not very well."

By contrast, Giovanni began by saying how much better his sister was, pointing to a *joie de vivre* that had previously been totally lacking. During the summer, Antonella had not only started going out again, but had even gone to the seaside and had started seeing her friends again. Her temperature phobia had disappeared, so she no longer wore her sweaters. Her former good spirits and sense of humor had returned. The only problem was her overeating. It should be noted that while the whole family agreed on the improvement, her mother seemed rather puzzled and drew attention to Antonella's serious weight problem. She seemed disgusted when she looked at her daughter!

The final intervention was based on the hypothesis that Antonella would find her way out of her present situation if she could redefine her relationship with her mother and feel accepted by her. It was decided to prescribe a ritual.

> THERAPIST: We feel that there is a strong bond between Antonella and her mother and vice versa, even though they have been disappointed with each other over recent years. We would like to ask you, Antonella, and you, Mrs. Viola, to devote one day a week, Wednesday, to trying to understand each other. On that day, the other members of the family should avoid becoming involved with you, and you should keep how you have spent the day a secret.

Obviously, this ritual is intended to encourage a new relationship between the mother and daughter. The temporal sequence that separates the mother-daughter couple from the rest of the family, facilitated by the therapist's prescription of secrecy, seems well adapted to this purpose.

Fourth, Fifth, Sixth Sessions

Antonella steadily improved. Stimulated by her return to university study, she went on a crash diet and lost most of the excess weight she had put on, but not her good spirits and sense of humor. The return to university after two years was a great achievement for her and further increased her self-esteem. It is significant that Antonella sat between her two brothers during the last two sessions, and that they no longer treated her like a poor little sick girl. Indeed, they often consulted with one another, and on more than one occasion told their parents that it was "time to pack in the quarreling" and work out how to live together in future.

Outcome

In January 1991—just over two years after the completion of therapy— the therapist phoned the family to see what the outcome of therapy had been. The mother answered and reported that the change had continued.

Interestingly, Antonella had decided the year before to resume her weekly visits to her therapist to "talk about her personal problems."[7]

The family atmosphere had improved markedly, with the children gradually involving themselves more in study and the outside world, and the parents getting on with each other much better. When asked what she thought about family therapy, the mother reported that all the members of the family, with the sole exception of Antonella, had openly acknowledged that family therapy was extremely useful. Antonella could not make up her mind whether therapy or other events had opened up new perspectives in her life.

ALDO: "TIME HAS STOPPED!"

We would now like to report a consultation held in 1989 at the request of a young psychiatrist who was looking after a young man named Aldo as an outpatient. Aldo, 26, had been diagnosed schizophrenic five years previously. Symptoms had first appeared during a journey to Tibet: a systematized delusion in which the Dalai Lama governed his life and the lives of the people with whom he came into contact. He had been in a psychiatric hospital for some time, but had relapsed on being discharged and so had had to return. He had been living with his family for some months, causing such havoc that his father and brother had said they wanted him to leave, or go back to hospital.

Those present at the consultation were Aldo, his parents and the psychiatrist in charge. Aldo's brother Giulio, 20 years old, an apprentice weaver, could not attend because he was doing military service.

We should say first that the systemic consultant often departs from normal procedure when he/she initially meets a family with a psychotic member. Much more time is devoted to dialogue between the consultant and the psychotic patient than with other members of the family. The main reason for this is that families usually talk more with the psychiatrist than with the psychotic himself/herself, who is deemed incapable of "normal" reasoning and so also of "meaningful" dialogue. With their frequent antagonism, negative attitudes and strange behavior, psychotics often seem

---

[7]As happens in some cases of families with adolescent or young adult patients, individual therapy is initiated or resumed upon completion of family therapy. The reason for this may be that family therapy, by solving family problems, encourages the process whereby members of the family separate and define their own identities. Some of them receive a further stimulus towards independence by undergoing individual therapy.

to justify this belief, so that dialogue tends to narrow down and polarize around the "sane" family members and the psychiatric expert. If this is allowed to happen, a consultant in effect accepts the "diagnosis" that the patient is incapable of understanding or volition, and so of reasoned thought, with the result that the patient tends to be excluded.

By contrast, we try to establish dialogue with the psychotic. He/she is no longer regarded as "different" or "mad," and this tells him or her and others that he/she can speak normally when he/she wants to. Whenever the patient says something incomprehensible, the consultant or therapist challenges: "I asked you a question, but I didn't understand your answer. You probably have your own reasons for answering in a way I can't understand. I'll keep on asking questions, but it'll be up to you to decide if and when you want your answers to be understood."

This is the first step towards establishing a link with the psychotic patient. It will succeed if the consultant or therapist accepts the "reality" and logic of the psychotic, as is done with the "reality" and logic of "sane" people, implicitly confirming the legitimacy of both and so retaining a neutral position. With his or her world and logic accepted in this way, the psychotic can in turn begin to accept the world and logic of the consultant, who thus becomes a bridge between the world of "madness" and the world of "normality."

In response to the consultant's first question, "What's the situation like now?" Aldo spoke of the past, his journey to Tibet five years earlier, how the spirits of the Dalai Lama had brought him enlightenment—"an idea, a system of ideas"—that would give him a true vision of the world and human relationships. Aldo's attempt to "reform" his family, especially the mother, whom he described as aggressive and authoritarian, was significant. The consultant immediately showed curiosity about and interest in the extraordinary story Aldo was telling, and subtly entered into his way of reasoning. Aldo gradually showed that he accepted the consultant as an important expert and offered him the key to enter his world. For him, the consultant had become "one who understands," someone who knew what was happening to him and understood his ideas. Now the consultant could also begin to compare Aldo's vision of the world with his own, paying special attention to tiny emotional signals indicating the limits Aldo would not allow him to go beyond. It is commonly found that an initial "good" engagement at this point gives the consultant "credit" that he can spend during the course of the session. When all the credit seems to have been spent, he must proceed very cautiously.

Well on in the session, when a good level of contact had been established with Aldo, the consultant decided to confront him with a nondelusional reality.

THERAPIST: Why is it, Aldo, that these spirits of the Dalai Lama—so powerful, more powerful than all the people around you, as you've said—have led you to live like a madman, to be taken to a psychiatric hospital? My colleague here is a psychiatrist, isn't he? You aren't just visiting here, you're here to be cured, you're on medication: why is it that this idea has led you to live like . . .

ALDO: Like a madman!

THERAPIST: Yes, exactly.

ALDO: Now I'll ask you a question: are we living in the present, the future or the past?

THERAPIST: What do you think?

ALDO: I think there's no such thing as time. That's the problem.

THERAPIST: Well, you must have good reasons . . .

ALDO: And I can never understand if I'm in a past, a present, or a future. So I go mad. Because I don't want to live here for eternity. This is another problem.

When faced with the effect of his delusional ideas in his daily life, Aldo takes refuge in a time that doesn't exist, in turn asking the consultant to explain which time he, Aldo, is living in. His Sibylline phrase, "I go mad. Because I don't want to live here for eternity," seems to suggest that flight into madness is a defense against the horror of his personal situation, which he tragically experiences as time that has stopped, time immutable, eternity. This interpretation points to the temporal prison Aldo seems to be living in: it is eternal because there is neither past, present, nor future. If Aldo were to lose his present equilibrium and succumb to acute schizophrenia, his life would probably become total chaos, an existence in fragmented time in which past, present, and future intersect in strange ways and perceptions of duration and rhythm change enormously.

The consultant continues the analysis—his attempts to understand the vision (and its effects) of a man overwhelmed by psychosis.

THERAPIST: Now I'd like to ask you a question, too. Let's imagine that this idea that has possessed you and is forcing you to live in this way . . . let's imagine that this idea went away, and you became free. What would you do? What would your life be like?

ALDO: It would be a life . . . it would certainly be much happier.

At the start, Aldo had an imposing air of superiority and seemed content to "be possessed" by the spirit of the Dalai Lama, but here, for the first time, he seems doubtful, as if he has glimpsed a happier world. His tone is sober, almost depressed. The questions have released him from an eternal present, in which nothing changes, into the flow of time, in which he begins to glimpse obscure future scenarios.

> THERAPIST: It certainly would be a happier life, as you say. And what would you do if this happened? For example, would you find a job, and what job would you like?
>
> ALDO: The problem is I'm not stupid. I'd like to be stupid.
>
> THERAPIST: No, sorry, would you answer my question?
>
> ALDO: What question was that?
>
> THERAPIST: Let's imagine that this idea went away, just as it came.
>
> ALDO: I'd be stupid.

This is reminiscent of Haley's description—in his classic article "The Family of the Schizophrenic: A Model System" (1959)—of the way schizophrenics ignore notions like emitter, receiver, message, and context, concepts that make communication possible. Haley would say that Aldo is trying to avoid defining his relationships with others.

Some of Aldo's responses to the choices he is offered reveal confusion and a great deal of ambivalence. It is significant that Aldo used the word "stupid" immediately after what seemed to be a new insight: "It would be a life . . . it would certainly be much happier." The "stupidity" seems intended not so much as a way of avoiding the idea of work as a defense against introspection, from acknowledging what his real situation is. As soon as Aldo glimpses the possibility of another life—which he probably fears he cannot cope with—he retreats into regression or, as he himself says, into stupidity. We begin to understand here how communing with the spirit of the Dalai Lama serves to camouflage a feared weakness or impotence: in psychodynamic terms, it serves to camouflage a narcissistic wound.

We might hypothesize that in his pre-psychotic life Aldo had experienced a situation of loss, insecurity, and anxiety about the future. His father and brother, a harmonious couple, had been resentful and hostile towards him and rejected all his attempts to be accepted. Furthermore, his relationship with his mother had been disastrous. He continually disobeyed and offended her, and she became the target of his delusions. Aldo's situation seemed one of isolation and alienation.

> THERAPIST: Just a moment. It seems that by obeying this idea you're behaving stupidly, in a certain sense. This idea makes you do every-

thing it wants. You aren't free. You seem to be living like someone who's stupid . . .

ALDO: No, like a madman. You have to distinguish the words very carefully. Because stupid is very different from mad.

THERAPIST: But this idea came to you. Not to your brother or mother. It came to you. So we might ask why this idea came to you and not, for example, to your brother. Have you ever asked this question to yourself?

ALDO: Because I've entered the spiritual world, but my brother hasn't, even though he's got all the advantages in the world.

Obviously, this statement points to great rivalry between the brothers, so great, in fact, that if the brother is respected "in this world," Aldo is respected in the spiritual—and so superior—world of the Dalai Lama. It seems likely that the mother had covertly begun to favor the brother rather than Aldo before his symptoms appeared.

Note how the consultant raises the stakes in the final set of exchanges. Most importantly, he brings Aldo back to the world of the "sane" with a hypothetical question: "If you'd never had this (delusional) idea, how would you be living now?" Aldo seems to accept the hypothesis by comparing the two worlds—the world of stupidity and the world of madness, both timeless—then he hesitates. He seems unable to enter the world of reality, the world of development and change.

The consultant presses him still further with another challenge: it's precisely because he has this idea that Aldo seems stupid. Moreover, the consultant stresses stupidity rather than madness because stupidity is less serious but also more challenging. Thus, he continues to enter and leave Aldo's (psychotic) world—in and out, out and in, in rapid succession— seeking to relate to Aldo, compare himself with him, accept his world and his logic, offer him the chance to enter the commonsense world of ordinary logic. Aldo can thus enter a discourse that makes him acknowledge the existence of several different realities, several different worlds. He can experience the Other as a person similar to himself.

THERAPIST: Now I'd like to ask you again: if you didn't have this idea, which makes you live stupidly, or like a madman, as you say, in the sense that you can't shake free of it, you're totally enslaved by it . . . if you could shake free of this idea, what do you think you'd be doing now?

ALDO: I'd be working.

THERAPIST: Which job would you be doing?

ALDO: Ah! I'd still be an industrial designer.

THERAPIST: You'd be an industrial designer. Would you have a girl-friend? . . . Would you be married?

ALDO: Yes.

THERAPIST: When would you have got married?

ALDO: When I was 22.

THERAPIST: What's your marriage like?

ALDO: I'm married to a really bright woman, with two nice children.

THERAPIST: Brighter than your mother?

ALDO: Calmer, she doesn't shout.

THERAPIST: Is she like your mother, this woman?

ALDO: No.

THERAPIST: Very different from your mother?

ALDO: Yes, yes. The opposite.

THERAPIST: You mean, a calm woman. But your mother isn't very calm?

ALDO: No.

THERAPIST: She isn't very calm, in the sense that she wants to impose herself on you, be obeyed?

ALDO: Yes, certainly.

THERAPIST: You sometimes find yourself facing a dilemma: should you obey the idea, the Dalai Lama, that is, or your mother? Because your mother, too, has said that she's trying to make you obey her. Do you sometimes find yourself in a dilemma where your mother wants to be stronger than your idea? Have you ever asked yourself this question?

ALDO: My mother is never stronger . . .

THERAPIST: But she tries to be?

ALDO: My mother tries to be stronger than my ideas, than my idea, but my idea is stronger than my mother.

At this point, when Aldo seems to accept the possibility of returning to the world of common sense, hypothetical questions create a different real-ity in the here and now which no one—certainly not Aldo, and not even his parents and the psychiatrist—thinks can ever happen, unless in some remote future. Aldo and the consultant now jointly construct a scenario in which Aldo works, gets married, and has children: he's a person who can get on in life. The shift from the conditional to the indicative mood makes the scenario seem more real. In our experience, especially with pre-chronic cases, truly dramatic discontinuous change can occur in which psychotic symptoms disappear completely. In cases where change is slower, the shift into "normality" often involves a depressive phase. There is indeed an element of depression in some of the exchanges in this session: it is important for a consultant, in these circumstances, to have a positive view of the world.

Aldo's response shows he has entered this possible world: his tone of voice changes (it is now less languid and affected), he seems ready to cross the bridge to the real world. The consultant is also, as it were, on the bridge, waiting for Aldo to come to him.

It may seem at times that the consultant's language is exerting pressure on the client (the references to appearing "stupid" or "mad," for example), but this should be seen in the context of the relationship as a whole. It is well known that in the context of a "negative" relationship—two conflicting partners, for example—the phrase "I love you" has nothing like its face value. Equally, "I hate you," in the context of a positive, loving relationship, should be read very differently.[8]

In the final exchanges—we are about halfway through the session here—the consultant links the mother to Aldo's imaginary wife. The family's interaction can now be explored in greater detail, and the parents can be involved in the conversation. The father and mother had listened to Aldo and the consultant's verbal fencing extremely carefully, amazed at seeing their son and the consultant engaged in a lengthy and often meaningful dialogue. This often comes as a revelation to close relatives of psychotics. Usually, conversations between psychotics, family members, and outsiders either remain stillborn or creak forward in a repetitive, sterile way because shared meanings cannot be established.

THERAPIST: Does your father try to be stronger than your ideas as well?

ALDO: My father never speaks.

THERAPIST: Ah, he never speaks. . . . When you say you'd marry a woman different from your mother, a calmer woman that is, someone who doesn't tell you what to do, who doesn't give orders . . .

---

[8]In the mid seventies, the original Milan team (Selvini Palazzoli, Boscolo, Cecchin, and Prata) sent a letter to Gregory Bateson, asking his opinion on some of the final interventions the team had invented and transmitted to the families by the therapist. Some time later, Bateson sent a short letter in which he made a positive comment but refrained from expressing his opinion on the effects they may have had on clients, since: "I don't know the tone you used in conveying your messages."

ALDO: Let's say there's nothing wrong with receiving orders from people who deserve to give orders.

THERAPIST: I see, so your mother . . .

ALDO: The Tibetan Lamas and I . . .

THERAPIST: I see, but leave the Lamas out of it for the moment. You say you'd like a wife who's completely different from your mother.

ALDO: It's odd, isn't it? Lots of people want their wives to be like their mothers. That's what I don't understand.

THERAPIST: But you want to change. We'll see why later, it seems important. Anyway, you're saying: "My mother is someone who tends to give orders, and my brother and my father obey." If they don't, your mother raises her voice and makes herself obeyed. But not with you, she can't do it, because you, Aldo, have somebody else to obey: the system. I imagine your mother tries. . . . Can I ask your father?

ALDO: Yes.

THERAPIST: Does your wife try to make herself obeyed? Does she succeed?

FATHER: Partly. Perhaps by imposing herself, well no, not imposing herself, by blackmail. She says, "Look, if you don't do this . . ." and then he does it, but he sees it as blackmail.

THERAPIST: And then?

FATHER: Then everything returns to normal, the story repeats itself. He always does things because he's forced to.

THERAPIST: So the sparks fly between them sometimes, do they?

FATHER: Yes, sometimes, that's why I advised him to live on his own, to avoid all this fuzz. I'm sorry about it, mainly because I haven't got all that much money. It'll be hard, but if he can manage it, all the better for him . . . and for us.

THERAPIST: (to the wife) Can I ask you something? What does your husband do when there are these rows with Aldo, when the sparks fly?

MOTHER: Well, he's against it, he says he can't go on this way . . . he says he doesn't want to hear any more arguing . . .

ALDO: He doesn't want to hear any more shouting . . .

MOTHER: Yes, shouting, because I keep calm for a while, I try not to shout, but when I see that things aren't OK I just give up . . . and start shouting.

THERAPIST: So you raise your voice?

MOTHER: Yes, because sometimes I really want to shout, you know?

THERAPIST: And he (*pointing to Aldo*) raises his voice, too?

ALDO: No!

THERAPIST: (*to the father*) When your wife raises her voice . . .

FATHER: He's calm.

THERAPIST: Ah, he's calm. He's learned the Indian way.

MOTHER: He doesn't listen. Things go in one ear and out the other.

FATHER: So then she starts getting agitated.

THERAPIST: So what does your husband do then? Does he try to stop you?

MOTHER: He tries to stop me because he says it's pointless. And . . .

THERAPIST: (*to Aldo*) Does your father manage to stop your mother?

MOTHER: I try sometimes, to stop myself, but shouting is one of my faults.

THERAPIST: (*to Aldo*) Do you sometimes do this to help out your father? For example, when you see your father's upset, suffering, because your mother's shouting too much . . .

ALDO: Yes.

THERAPIST: Oh, so you help out your father sometimes when you see him suffering. But couldn't you also help him by obeying your mother?

ALDO: Help out in what way?

THERAPIST: For example, if you obey her your mother will be quiet, and if she does that, your father will feel better, won't he?

Using a series of triadic circular questions based on the theme of agreement between the various members of the family, the consultant ascertains that there is a high level of disobedience, of disagreement in the family. At another point in the session, the father says he is afraid his younger son, Giulio, will act on his intention to leave the family. Apparently, Giulio had been threatening his parents for some time with the ultimatum, "It's either Aldo or me," because family life had become impossible. This injunction could also be interpreted as "Either you obey me or you obey Aldo." As we shall soon see, it is interesting that the father, in alliance with Giulio, would like to be rid of Aldo, but that, as was to be expected, the mother disagrees. As for Aldo, on the one hand he wanted to stay at home, on the other hand to leave. When questioned, the psychiatrist was unsure whether to support father's, mother's, or Aldo's wishes;

his clinical judgment appeared shaky (as often happens to psychiatrists faced with families like this), and he hoped the consultant would find a solution. This is the classic situation in which the "hot potato"—i.e., the decision of what to do with the patient—is thrown from one person to another. We shall see how the consultant deals with all this at the end of the session.

THERAPIST: (*to the mother*) Your husband said it'd be better if Aldo went to live on his own somewhere. Do you agree?

MOTHER: Well, no, I don't agree that it'd be better for him to leave home. What he says isn't true, that I don't love him. I'd always prefer to have my son at home. But he does things that are wrong, he refuses to work, he just wants to go on holiday. I've never heard him say he *likes* something, that he'd like to do this or that . . .

THERAPIST: Do you agree with your husband that it's better Aldo leaves home?

MOTHER: (*she seems anxious, worried*) I don't know, I'm sorry . . . I'd like him to stay at home. . . . It's not as if I want to send him away, but I'd like him to obey me, at least in the little things I ask . . .

THERAPIST: But you've already tried. Your husband says "you've tried so much, but. . . . " Why don't you agree with your husband?

MOTHER: I don't understand. Sometimes I try to say nothing so as not to make him angry, but . . .

THERAPIST: But when your husband says to you "You've tried so much, why go on deceiving yourself?" why don't you obey him?

MOTHER: That'd mean letting him do what he wants, not say anything about it anymore. I know he'd just stay at home and do whatever he likes!

THERAPIST: (*to Aldo*) Do you understand your father's position? For the sake of peace in the family, it'd be better if you left home.

ALDO: I've already left home.

MOTHER: Yes, two days ago!

THERAPIST: Ah, two days ago. But in the near future, do you agree with your father's idea that you should leave home, or do you feel better at home?

MOTHER: (*She seems alarmed at the idea that the decision to send Aldo away is about to be taken.*) No, he . . .

THERAPIST: Just a moment!

ALDO: How do you know?

THERAPIST: Would you prefer to stay at home with them or leave?

ALDO: Let's say I'd prefer to stay at home, but since I can't stand the family atmosphere there, I'd be happy enough to leave.

THERAPIST: So what advice would you give your father? Would you advise him to keep you on at home?

ALDO: No.

THERAPIST: Look, have you got a job at the moment?

ALDO: No, I worked for ten years as a gardener.

THERAPIST: But you don't anymore?

ALDO: I stopped two months ago.

THERAPIST: Why did you stop?

ALDO: Because I'm becoming serious.

THERAPIST: What do you mean?

ALDO: I can't explain, I can't tell you . . .

THERAPIST: Was it your system of ideas that ordered you to stop?

ALDO: It was me who decided to stop. I don't like it that time doesn't move.

Let us try to explain the strange, incomprehensible answers Aldo gave in these exchanges. When asked why he had stopped working as a gardener, he answered, "Because I'm becoming serious," and refused to explain. Presumably, this isn't the kind of job he would have liked to be doing, so "I'm becoming serious" may mean that he has to look for something very different. The refusal to explain may indicate reluctance to talk about his frustrated ambitions. When he says that he decided to stop because he didn't like it that time doesn't move, this may be a metaphor of the boredom he feels for a job he finds meaningless. Boredom and a feeling of emptiness take over and slow or paralyze his life. In such phase, time may slow to a standstill, with a perception of timelessness, while in an acute phase it becomes fragmented.

THERAPIST: That time doesn't move. You feel that time doesn't flow?

ALDO: No, it doesn't flow.

THERAPIST: I see. I find that entirely logical. It doesn't flow because the system is stationary. In your life the systems are stationary, immobile. Let's take the example of a child. As he grows, time flows. When he becomes an adolescent, he enters the period when it's usual to leave the family system and enter an external system, which might be a new family, a profession, a company, the army . . . do you follow

me? So time flows. But for you, I understand you, time has stopped
because you're still in this system (*indicating his parents*). Totally. I
think the system of ideas you've brought over from Tibet is forcing
you to remain here in this system, with this family that is . . .

Note how Aldo increasingly speaks "schizophrenese" in the next fragment. The consultant tries to introduce a possible story using a logic
Aldo himself hints at. This story, which tries to bring Aldo back from the
mountains of Tibet to the Po plain, makes Aldo's schizophrenese indirect
and evasive. It is interesting to see how clearly fragmented time is. The
consultant's attempt to build his own and Aldo's ideas into a framework—
a story—with meaning and internal consistency, which could encourage
the reestablishing of temporal sequence, contrasts with Aldo's experience
of fragmented time.

ALDO: Time stopped when I came back from India.
THERAPIST: Exactly. It stopped when you started obeying unquestion-
   ingly these ideas you've developed, this system of ideas you've got in
   your head. In this sense, you obey your ideas but not your parents . . .
ALDO: But all my conflict with opposites . . .
THERAPIST: Yes, I understand. Deep down you're really, let's say, the
   sort of person who likes to get on with his father and mother, who
   likes to receive affection and suffers because he can't have these
   things. I imagine you sometimes think of death, and your ideas tell
   you "Why don't you have done with it, why not kill yourself?" I think
   that might even be . . .
ALDO: . . . a solution.

When later he read this part of the transcript, Boscolo, the consultant
in this case, was very surprised to note the shift from positive ideas—
getting on with people, receiving affection—to the sudden appearance of
death and suicide. The hypothesis is that he identified very strongly with
Aldo's dramatic existential situation at that point: a total dead-end in life.
Many might feel this is dangerous because it could detonate Aldo's emotions and really drive him to suicide. In our experience, however, speaking
of suicide, as we have indicated elsewhere, has if anything the effect of an
exorcism: the client, and possibly also the other members of the family,
feel understood and so less desperate.

THERAPIST: Exactly. A solution because time has stopped, it stopped
   when you came back from Tibet. By nature you're probably an obedi-

ent person, someone who could be affectionate, etc., etc., like your brother. I imagine your brother, too, would like to tell your mother she's a drag, but he stops himself . . . do you see? He's more malleable, more adaptable, something like that. In some way you're now possessed by the idea, the mission, that you've got to sort them out (*the parents*). When you said "opposites," he (*indicates the father*) wants to make you talk more because your mother doesn't like it when he doesn't speak, when he's silent, and she would like to shut you up. This means that your father talks more and mother talks less.

So for years time has stopped, you've avoided the chance to find a job, to make friends, even find a wife, have children . . . time has stopped. I understand: time has stopped because you continue to live in this system here (*points to parents*). Or (*to the psychiatrist*) in this system here where they look after you, feed you, etc., etc.

ALDO: No, it isn't like that at all.

THERAPIST: You say it isn't like this at all, but time has stopped. Even if they left home, or if you went away, nothing would change. Even if you go a thousand miles away, you still can't stop thinking about how to change them both. It's become a sort of mission that's taken possession of you, that prevents you from pursuing the biological imperative of young people and adolescents when they leave the family system and move into external systems. Your family is what it is, your parents are what they are, will be what they will be. If you look outside, direct your attention outside the family, as I said before, time will start flowing again and you'll leave all this stagnation behind. Now you're in a state of total stagnation, you're totally immobile. Is what I'm saying clear?

ALDO: Yes.

THERAPIST: Anyway, I'd like to stop a moment here. Can you come back in 20 minutes?

The consultant uses the themes and metaphors that emerge during the conversation, giving priority, as we saw earlier, to dialogue with the client by both accepting and challenging his vision of reality. In the frame of therapy and consultation, this hopefully may have a constructive, creative effect, while in other frames the effect may be different, even confusing or destructive, depending on the relational context.

The circular structure of the discourse, constantly returning to previous themes to establish connections (including temporal ones), may allow a different, liberating story to emerge. The final intervention took up the themes that had emerged during the session, especially those raised by future or hypothetical questions. The basic reason why the psychiatrist and family had asked for consultation—to sort Aldo out, whether at home, away from home or in the hospital—is placed in the background to give priority to the idea that Aldo's time has stopped, with the consequent loss of coordination with the times of the other family members and his peers.

In the final intervention, the consultant brings the future into the present by hypothesizing about possible worlds. He envisions a linear, deterministic world that perpetuates the present situation alongside other possible worlds in which time starts flowing again and life evolves.

THERAPIST: I've talked things over with my colleagues, and we agree that some years ago you, Aldo, took on the full-time job of changing your family, especially your parents. Because time has stopped for you. You have adopted a new "mind"—or a new "mind" has adopted you, the "mind" of the Dalai Lama—in an attempt to change your parents, to make them different, to make your father speak, who usually doesn't say much, and make your mother be quiet, who usually talks too much. In this sense, time has stopped for you because, as was said before, time flows in adolescence and adulthood when you leave the family system and move into other systems, like new interests, new work, new friends, marriage, children, etc., etc. But you stopped five years ago. You decided to stop in time to reform your family, change it.

At present you're working in two systems—the family system and the psychiatrist's system. I'm speaking now as a representative of the psychiatrist's system, that is, psychiatrists, psychologists, nurses, psychotherapists, etc., whose job is to look after people with problems until they can resume their own lives again. My colleagues and I have thought about your possible futures. It may be that this task you've undertaken, reforming your family, will take you all your life; or it may happen that you'll get tired of trying, or think there's no longer any reason to go on trying. If that happens, you'll start thinking of yourself, of your life, rather than them. You'll start getting ideas about finding a job, friends, etc., etc. But you'll only be able to do this when deep down you no longer have a reason to be so concerned about them. If you asked me, "Doctor, what do you think about them?" I'd answer that they'll basically be as they have been. They can't be different from what they are. Your father will tend to be silent, your mother talkative.

ALDO: Why don't they change?

THERAPIST: It's an illusion. It seems you're driven by the illusion that you can change them. Have I answered your question?

ALDO: Yes, more or less.

In the language he uses, it is as if the consultant has frozen the family and its time so that Aldo has the choice of either remaining immobile in time or developing. He links Aldo's life to his brother's life, suggesting that Giulio may have had the same problems but ended up opting for development and change.

THERAPIST: More than likely, your brother once had the idea of changing his parents, but then gave up and accepted them as they are. So to conclude, we see that your life has been seized up for several years, that your interest in changing this family, this system, takes all your energy, all your time. For the time being, we think you'll go on like this.

In many ways, the consultant reflects the client's wish to bring about change. Just as the client is trying hard to change his parents, so the consultant, in suggesting various scenarios ranging from the *status quo* to evolution, is trying to change his client. But there are fundamental differences. First, the consultant avoids creating temporal symmetry with the client by implicitly suggesting that their relationship will not continue *ad infinitum*, that he will leave the scene at a certain point. Second, he thinks not in terms of "either ... or", but "and ... and." He offers more than one option.

THERAPIST: (*to the family and psychiatrist*) The main reason why you brought me in, to know where Aldo would be best off living at the moment—at home, away from home, or in hospital—is of only secondary importance to me, although it is important. Aldo knows very well how to behave if he wants to be accepted at home or if he wants to go into the hospital, he knows very well what behavior best suits either solution. Just as he knows very well how to behave if he wants to live away from home. What I said a short while ago is the most important thing. Don't expect that Aldo will suddenly give up his idea of reforming his family. I expect he'll go on in the same way for some time yet. Should he give up the idea in future, he'll also give up the family system and the psychiatric system and he won't even need his system of ideas anymore. He'll find another system.

Follow-up

Two years later, the consultant met the psychiatrist who had been looking after Aldo and found out what had happened since the consultation. Aldo had been living in a sheltered home, was still on medication and visited his psychiatrist less frequently, was working occasionally and living a fairly independent life.

10

THE TWO MESSIAHS

WE CHOSE THE CASE WE DESCRIBE here because of its unusual clinical development, the narrative structure of the stories it presents, and the important subjective time changes in the member of the family who had been diagnosed as schizophrenic. After a brief overview of the case, both authors will analyze and comment directly on most of the final session.

The Ponzi family, which lived in Milan, was referred to our center in June 1987 by a psychologist who insisted that this was an especially serious case, a "special case." For the past five years, the family had been in constant touch with either the psychiatric ward of the hospital or the psychosocial community center where the referring psychologist worked. The parents, immigrated from Southern Italy, were unassuming and rather old, the father an employee of a food firm, the mother a switchboard operator in a large company. Both were on the verge of retirement. The mother had a slight limp caused by a congenital hip dislocation. Before the onset of psychosis in 1982, the 30-year-old son had worked as a surveyor in an important Milanese manufacturing company.

Symptoms had suddenly appeared when he discovered that his immediate superior at work earned twice his salary but did only half the work he did. His protest had been so strong—and ill-advised—that he had been fired on the spot. At first, Fabrizio reacted by withdrawing into a stubborn two-week silence during which his parents had begged the company directors to have him reinstated. In the end, he was given the chance to work for the same firm again, but in a different city 200 kilometers from his home.

Fabrizio refused the offer, and began to develop paranoid symptoms, with the result that he soon had to be hospitalized in a psychiatric ward. This was the start of a career as a chronic psychotic, during which he was forcibly hospitalized six times because of his violent behavior. He often physically and verbally abused his parents, was always asking them for money, and would buy cars, which he then either wrecked or resold. In the periods between crises he would look for and easily find work, but his jobs lasted only a few days because he invariably ended up arguing with everyone at work and getting himself fired. He behaved intolerably at home, like a dictator. He would often shout at and hit his parents, so that his parents or neighbors sometimes had to call the police and have him forcibly taken to the hospital.

His most usual way of describing his parents was "cripple" for his mother and "*terrone*" for his father because of his southern accent (*terrone* is an insulting term used by northern Italians to sneer at southern Italians). He refused to collaborate with psychiatric staff and quickly rejected the therapy programs suggested to him. His parents continuously sought help from public service agencies, hoping to have him hospitalized for a longer period, but Law 180 in Italy allows for only brief periods of hospitalization, so Fabrizio had become a sort of tennis ball, bouncing back and forth between his home and the hospitals that admitted him. His referral to a private center like ours was—according to the referrer—yet another attempt to remedy this festering chronic situation.

Only the parents came to the first session because Fabrizio had refused therapy. They described their tribulations with their son, and also with public service agencies, which they now detested because the family had so often been abandoned and disappointed. The father especially stated that he was totally mistrustful of psychology and psychotherapy and felt his son would never change, while the mother seemed more hopeful that things might change, stating that "hope is the last to die." The father conveyed his hostility not only towards hospitals and clinics, but also towards his son. By contrast, the mother suffered for her son and worried about his future.

An interesting story about the mother's family emerged even in the first session. She had been orphaned at the age of 15 with her brother Aldo, seven years her younger, and looking after him had become her mission in life. She had brought him with her as her dowry when she married, had imposed him on her husband, and had made him stay on at school until he got his certificate. Aldo stayed with them until he had completed his military service, whereupon his brother-in-law had made him leave, saying "he's taken advantage of our hospitality for too long."

Fabrizio was six at the time and seemed to get on well with his uncle, who had been "like a brother" to him. Relations with Aldo, which the mother had never broken off, resumed when Fabrizio fell ill and the parents had asked him for help. Fabrizio did not seem to have appreciated Aldo's help, which only seemed to have worsened the situation. Two years later, relations between the Ponzi family and Aldo's family were broken off again.

In our notes on the first session we wrote that, before Fabrizio's illness, the mother had probably been in love with her "two sons" and had devoted herself to them totally, in effect excluding her husband. As a result, Fabrizio probably grew up confused about his role in the family. Attempts to engage him in therapy in the early sessions proved useless. The parents came willingly to sessions, even though this entailed great financial sacrifice for them. However, the only result after eight sessions was that the father and mother had grown closer and had begun to live more as a couple.

By the eighth session, then, with the son still refusing to attend, it seemed as if nothing more could be done. The therapist stated this clearly to the parents, and suggested they get in touch with the social services agencies again, if only "to avoid throwing money away."

One day in September 1990, more than two years after the final meeting with the Ponzis, the center's secretary handed the therapist a clinical file and announced that "the Ponzi case is in the therapy room." As he began to discuss the file with his training group, the therapist suddenly remembered the case and began to fear that something irreparable had happened. He rushed to the curtain covering the one-way mirror and, to his amazement, saw three people: the parents and, sitting between them, the son.

The therapist entered the therapy room extremely curious to know what had happened since he had last seen the parents. The parents welcomed him with big smiles and surprised him by saying how grateful they were to him: he had helped them a lot, had given them hope; the mother said that during the final session she had begun to see her husband differently and to feel closer to him. Laughing, she said, "For me, he's been promoted from Division Two to Division One," adding that her son had decided to come to the center after seeing the change in his parents.

Fabrizio, still basically morose although smiling weakly, confirmed that he had come because since his parents were happier and closer to each other he felt more alone. Now he hoped to benefit as they had from contact with the therapist. The session served mainly to explore the family's past life. The importance of uncle Aldo, as well as the dramatic events they had all experienced after the initial outbreak of Fabrizio's psychosis, clearly emerged during the session. It is interesting that Fabrizio's memories seemed disconnected, as if he found it difficult to link the various events of his story in a coherent way.

What follows is a verbatim report of most of the second session, along with our comments on it.

THERAPIST: What have you got to say to us today?

MOTHER: Well, er, let's say there's . . . there's been some improvement. Yes, I'd say he's pretty calm at the moment.

FABRIZIO: The situation has flattened out a bit.

THERAPIST: Flattened out?

FABRIZIO: Yes, flattened out, that's right.

THERAPIST: Can you tell me what "flattened out" means?

FABRIZIO: Well, no ups or downs, stalemate.

THERAPIST: And you're used to having powerful feelings in your life, aren't you?

FABRIZIO: Yes.

BOSCOLO: It's interesting to look at the central role of language in the opening section of the session and relate it to recent developments in narrative and hermeneutics research. The mother began by smiling and saying that there had been some improvement. By contrast, Fabrizio smiled faintly in agreement but gave a different account, saying that the situation had "flattened out." We have two different descriptions of the same experience. The therapist introduces a third description: for there to be improvement, the powerful emotions of the past (when Fabrizio was seriously ill) have to be brought to the surface. As we pointed out in our article on key words (Boscolo et al., 1991)—that is, "bridging" words that span a range of meanings—a whole description may conflict with the two bridged descriptions, as is the case here. This conflict may change how things are seen, may generate new meanings, new alternative stories.

BERTRANDO: Not only that. I remember how in the previous session Fabrizio came out with a lot of disconnected story elements that had no chronological sequence. I'm curious to see whether in this session they will came together to form a coherent story. Before, Fabrizio seemed to have only ideas that floated around a vacuum.

THERAPIST: Do you see the past as flat, or the future as flat?

FABRIZIO: The future.

THERAPIST: Do you also see your past as flat, or not?

FABRIZIO: Well, maybe I'm also beginning to see the past as flat, I mean, yes, I'm beginning to see the past as flat as well.

BOSCOLO: *Note how the therapist introduces first the present and future, and then the third component of the temporal horizon, the past, to see if there are any discrepancies. Fabrizio is beginning to see the past as flat too, which shows that his temporal horizon is closing in. At this stage, I think we can see that deterministic links are being forged between past, present, and future, confirming that a flat, unsuccessful past can only produce an unsuccessful present and future. It'll be interesting to see later on how the therapist tries to loosen these links. One way would be to start introducing differences, perhaps using hypothetical questions about the past, present and future.*

BERTRANDO: *We could try to find out why, now, in this moment, he has started seeing the past as flat, by asking him what would happen in his life if his negative ideas changed so that he could see his past and present differently, and so on.*

BOSCOLO: *Yes, that seems a good idea. The link between past, present, and future reminds me here of Jim, the Australian, whose mother had remarried when he was four, after the death of his father (see Chapter 5). During the consultation, Jim told a whole story about the past which his mother didn't share at all. He said he'd become schizophrenic from the age of five without anyone realizing it, but his mother said he'd been a normal child until the year before, when he'd become unbalanced. Only from then on did he seem different to her, before no. After the onset of symptoms, he seems to have emerged from his confused state with a clear vision of his past which was different from everyone else's, including his parents' and teachers'. It was as if he'd had a flash of psychotic insight that had given him a new vision, which had dispelled his anxiety, like St. Paul's vision on the road to Damascus. He found new meaning in the idea that he had been treated unfairly in the past, and projected the cause of his suffering onto others, especially his mother. By doing this, he reconstructed a past to give meaning to his present. More than likely, he found he couldn't cope when the time came for him to leave home—he was 22—and face the challenge of life outside. He became anxious and afraid, went psychotic, and constructed a new story to justify his "illness," the hospital, the psychiatrists, and his arrested independence. His present became linked to a past story that explained why he felt alone, impotent, mad. Mental illness experienced as physical illness and external events like his father's death and his mother's remarriage, which, according to Jim, seems to have brought on his illness, relieved him of all responsibility for his present and future.*

BERTRANDO: *Yes, I remember he foresaw a depressing future, a solitary life with his pottery. But here, Fabrizio says he sees the present and future, and now also the past, as flat. In a sense, he's telling us we're right to say there's a self-reflexive loop linking the present to the past and future. Basically, he's saying that since his present is now so flat, so unsuccessful, it can only produce the same effect in his past and future. It's he who's telling us that there's a loop that joins the three components of the temporal horizon.*

FABRIZIO: I'm trying to reconstruct my past.

THERAPIST: You're being your own historian. You know that anyone who tries to describe his experiences is really a historian? History includes his past . . .

FABRIZIO: I like the past better than the present or future.

THERAPIST: Your past. But when you say "I see it as flat," what do you mean?

FABRIZIO: There are days . . .

THERAPIST: I think that when you were talking about your parents the other time, you also saw their life as flat, you saw them as flat people. What do you mean when you say now that your past is flat? That you had desires and ambitions that you've failed to realize? Tell me.

FABRIZIO: I didn't see the future as very . . . I didn't see a very rosy future, I mean . . . I can't explain.

MOTHER: What?

FABRIZIO: Ah, yes, I had ambitions and I can't realize them.

THERAPIST: Do you feel agitated?

FABRIZIO: Intolerant more than agitated. Intolerant.

THERAPIST: Intolerant of what?

FABRIZIO: Most things. I feel intolerant.

THERAPIST: Do you find you have difficulty in connecting your thoughts? Can you read a newspaper?

FABRIZIO: I can read the main items.

THERAPIST: But you find it difficult to read a whole article?

FABRIZIO: Yes.

THERAPIST: How long has it been like this?

FABRIZIO: Nearly always. It's always been a defect of concentration in me.

THERAPIST: You seem livelier than the last time.

FABRIZIO: I don't know. Maybe.

MOTHER: Perhaps because he had the Haldol injection yesterday and he's feeling the effects of it. He's always a bit groggy for two or three days afterwards. He has an injection every fortnight, and he takes a Valium every morning . . .

THERAPIST: Are you still feeling a bit groggy?

FABRIZIO: Yes.

THERAPIST: (*to the father*) How do you see the situation?

FATHER: Well, it seems fairly calm to me. After we came here, he said, "You've put pressure on me, I'm always . . ."

MOTHER: . . . the center of attention.

FATHER: The center of attention. Yes, because he felt a bit under pressure the first time we came here.

THERAPIST: Could you tell me, Fabrizio, how you felt during the talk we had a month ago?

FABRIZIO: I felt empty inside.

THERAPIST: But was it good or bad for you, this feeling empty inside?

FABRIZIO: Maybe now, after thinking about things between the first and second meeting, I'm not really sure if it's a good thing to feel so empty. Some things should be forgotten.

FATHER: Yes, that's where he thinks the fault lies. Going to therapy can be bad for you. That's how he sees it, because he says, "By digging too much you uncover the hatred between us." That's what he thinks. That's my impression.

MOTHER: That's what he told Dr. Bianchi, his psychiatrist. He said he felt afraid about digging all this up, going back in the past.

THERAPIST: Yes, that's what he's saying now.

BOSCOLO: *At a certain point, Fabrizio says: " . . . I'm not really sure if it's a good thing to feel so empty. Some things should be forgotten." He seems to agree with the warnings given to young therapists dealing with psychotics in individual psychodynamic therapy. These warnings say you should avoid probing the unconscious, avoid interpreting it, because the client's defenses are so weak. They should be reinforced, the client's attention should constantly be directed to themes relating to the ego and "reality." It's as if Fabrizio is saying here: "I need to forget, not to remember!" In family therapy, I think these fears about digging down deep are mitigated by the reality framework created in the dialogue between the therapist and the various members of the family. This framework allows the therapist to dig down deep to look for lost connections, disturb hidden secrets, uncover positive experiences buried under later negative experiences that seem to have invalidated them. All this enables a new past to be constructed, an alternative story that can illuminate the present and the future.*

BERTRANDO: *I'm struck by the father when he says that Fabrizio is afraid to dig up the hatred between them. The father probably thinks that, in digging it up, Fabrizio might fly off the handle and spoil everything. I think Fabrizio is afraid because digging down inside him might lead him to discover that he doesn't exist, the horror of nothingness, that there's a void inside him. As Binswanger (1967) would say, he's afraid of discovering that he has no project for his life, as if he doesn't exist, as if he "isn't in the world." This is one of the commonest fears of psychotics: the fear of nothingness.*

THERAPIST: Digging can bring up negative things, but when I dig I'm also looking for positive things in you, now and in the past. Do you understand what I'm telling you? You're afraid of finding negative things, but I'm saying that I'm more optimistic than you, in the sense that I expect to find positive things not just about you, but also about your family. From what was said the other time, I think that in the past you thought of rejecting your family, of repudiating your parents for some reason. In this sense, the digging I did the last time aimed at exploring your feelings in the past, the negative—and, I'd add, positive—feelings a son can't help having about the people who made him. Deep down, you can't have helped having *some* positive feelings about the two people who made you, even if you've ended up experiencing your relationship with them in a negative way.

FABRIZIO: Maybe it's a question of points of view.

THERAPIST: Perhaps. The last time you spoke of your disappointment in your parents over the years. In this sense, you're saying it's better not to speak about it, it's better not to dig. But I think that digging might give you the chance to discover, make contact with the positive feeling you can't help having had, perhaps when a small child, about the people who made you.

BOSCOLO: *Here I'm benignly challenging Fabrizio's assumptions. I'm saying that, for me, the purpose in digging is not just to look for negative things, but also to find positive ideas and experiences that he must have had in his life. Here, the trust the therapist inspires is very valuable because the client can connect with him, and thus may open up to the possibility of "seeing" his life in a new way. I begin by stating as convincingly as possible that there must have been positive experiences in Fabrizio's past. I'm drawing on my own experience here, as well as on some of the literature, especially Harold Searles' essays on the treatment of schizophrenia (1966). In one of his essays, Searles says that schizophrenics tend to make the analyst believe that their mothers are monsters, distillates of negative feelings and ideas. He says that a therapist who believes this is compromised for good. The analyst should look resolutely for positive feelings in the mother and mother-child relationship that have been repressed. That's what I'm doing here with the Ponzi family. I'm gradually preparing the scene for a reconstruction of the past that will include the whole family system and allow not only conflicts but also periods of affection and solidarity to emerge. These periods are often repressed for fear of rejection or censure by the alter ego.*

BERTRANDO: *By saying to him, "You must at some stage have had positive feelings about the people who made you," you're reconfirming his most powerful, most positive roots. It's well-known that a person can't leave his family unless he's had some clear confirmation. His abuse of his parents over the years—hitting them, calling them things like "squalid," or even "terrone" and "cripple"—shows that he's rejecting his roots. In a sense, this reveals the narcissism of the psychotic who, by projecting all his negative feelings onto his parents, in effect shoots himself in the foot because they are the people who made him. You'll remember that in the previous session you asked him point blank, "Fabrizio, how do you explain the fact that two such squalid, insignificant parents have produced such an intelligent son?" The question seemed to stun him—so much so that he laughed with embarrassment and said, "Christ, yes, that's an intelligent question!" It should be added that, by constructing a more positive past, you can influence the present by making his existence as acceptable as that of any other person, freeing him from the need to build castles in the air.*

BOSCOLO: *From what we're saying, it's possible to understand how often psychotics have to go through a depressive phase in their shift from psychosis to "normality." I remember a patient diagnosed as a chronic schizophrenic who said to me, "I'm afraid of becoming normal, because normality is boredom."*

FABRIZIO: I don't remember anymore.

MOTHER: That's right, doctor, he's forgotten all the positive things. How many times have I tried to remind him of the things that were a reason for happiness . . .

FABRIZIO: Yes, but I forget them because there haven't been any others since then. There's always some connection with other people in your memories, people who come between things, who've established relationships, etc. This . . . this makes me intolerant.

BOSCOLO: Fabrizio is talking here about outsiders entering into dyadic relationships; this unleashes powerful feelings of rivalry, envy, jealousy, and hatred, as Freud (1901) points out in his discussion of the Oedipus complex. So do Melanie Klein (1928), Haley (1959) in his analysis of the perverse triangle, and others. Only when the Oedipus complex or perverse triangle has been unraveled can positive feelings of gratitude, love, acceptance of the outsider, emerge. Pasolini's film Teorema *gives a striking example of a third person breaking into a relationship. If I remember correctly, it begins with a traveler, a handsome young man of uncertain sexuality, coming to a village where a middle-class family lives. Gradually they all fall in love with him, including the servants. They all try to have him to themselves. He condescendingly goes to bed with all of them, maintaining his Olympian calm while deadly hatreds break out among his hosts, so that—again if I remember correctly—someone sets fire to the villa. In this atmosphere of death and destruction, some members of the family die, and others go mad. With the same Olympian calm, the traveler slowly leaves the villa and heads towards another one he can see in the distance. The film ends there.*

THERAPIST: Let's talk a bit about what your mother was saying earlier, that you're sleeping about eight hours a day at the moment.

FABRIZIO: Yes.

THERAPIST: Can you sleep at night?

FABRIZIO: Yes, pretty well, not always.

THERAPIST: Do you dream at night? Do you wake up because of dreams, nightmares?

FABRIZIO: Dreams.

THERAPIST: Are they usually good or bad?

FABRIZIO: They're good, usually.

THERAPIST: They're good, usually.

FABRIZIO: Yes ... then I wake up and see reality, which is bad.

THERAPIST: Have you had any particular dream lately?

FABRIZIO: No. It depends on the day, how I spend it. If it's a day when I've met someone nice, I dream afterwards at night about everything that might have happened, but if they were negative ...

THERAPIST: So can you tell me about a positive dream? What is a positive dream for you?

FABRIZIO: A beautiful woman.

THERAPIST: A beautiful woman, and then? A night with a beautiful woman, or a life with a beautiful woman?

FABRIZIO: A life.

THERAPIST: A life. Is that positive?

FABRIZIO: Yes, it's positive, if you can have it.

BOSCOLO: *Since the family was a bit worried about digging into the past, the therapist, careful about timing, leaves the subject to simmer for a while and turns everyone's attention to dreams. In our work, we rarely ask clients to tell us about their dreams, although we do if the situation demands it. The contents of their dreams are immediately linked to present reality.*

MOTHER: There's something else I must say ...

FABRIZIO: I'd like to do an English course to improve my language ...

BERTRANDO: *The mother immediately says something to draw attention away from the beautiful woman, and throws out an injunction to talk about something else, probably work. She may be jealous of other women who might take her son away from her. Symbiotic parent-son/daughter relationships are common in psychosis; the patients, in these cases, are utterly sensitive to the parents' injunctions.*

BOSCOLO: *The mother is saying, "Talk about something else." This is also a message to the therapist to talk about something else, maybe about work. For the moment the therapist obeys her, because he also wants to prevent a symmetrical relationship from developing.*

FABRIZIO: I'd like to learn English well because it would open up new prospects for me.

THERAPIST: Work prospects?

FABRIZIO: Yes.

THERAPIST: Those positive dreams about beautiful women you were talking about earlier, do you also have them about work?

FABRIZIO: Ah yes, I wake up so many times thinking I'm starting a new job in an ideal environment, I mean, where people don't bother you, in a nutshell. I dream that this is really happening. Then I find out it isn't . . .

THERAPIST: Maybe one really important dream might be to meet a beautiful woman and be the director of a company . . .

FABRIZIO: No, not that.

THERAPIST: A great artist?

FABRIZIO: A great artist, yes; I imagined that some time ago when I was avoiding my friends and I had no one anymore and I was completely alone. I stayed at home painting, hoping to make a go of it with painting. Then I realized I wasn't up to it.

THERAPIST: When you talk about work prospects, what do you mean? What would you find rewarding?

FABRIZIO: Now I don't even feel very . . . very . . . I mean, I'd prefer a job like, I don't know, in an architecture studio, since I'm a surveyor, that had some connection with what I studied, but I feel more . . . I'm not very lucid at the moment, so maybe I'd prefer a manual job. Even if I'm wasting myself, at least I'd be kept busy in some way.

THERAPIST: If I remember correctly, you've had a lot of different jobs in the past, haven't you?

FABRIZIO: Yes, I've had several.

THERAPIST: You haven't had any trouble finding a job.

MOTHER: No, he hasn't.

FABRIZIO: I never have.

THERAPIST: But it's been difficult to hold onto your jobs.

FABRIZIO: Hold onto them, yes.

THERAPIST: What do you think the main reasons were for this, that you could never hold onto a job?

FABRIZIO: Well, because I'm too fussy, I mean, one part of me gets attached to everyone, I respond to everything, but another part of me always wants pure justice, I'm always looking for perfect relationships, I'm always looking for perfection, and in relationships with other people, especially today, it just doesn't exist, because people turn things to their own advantage. . . .

THERAPIST: You're choosy, then.

FABRIZIO: Yes, I find it difficult to have relationships with other people because they always try to be smart or, worse still, they're small-minded or hypocritical.

THERAPIST: So then what happens?

FABRIZIO: I feel bitter and keep myself to myself. That's probably why I'm alone, because I can't find anyone I feel I can be open with.

THERAPIST: So you have a strong sense of justice?

FABRIZIO: Yes, a strong sense of justice.

THERAPIST: Have you always had this strong sense of justice?

FABRIZIO: Ever since I did military service.

BOSCOLO: Fabrizio's obsession with justice and his intolerance of ambiguity remind us of those theories that attribute the genesis of psychotic symptoms to relational situations based on disconfirmation and contextual ambiguity; I could quote double-bind theory here, or psychotic family games theory. Fabrizio, who is so concerned with justice and perfection, reminds me of Ciompi's (1983) theory, based on a biological predisposition to stressors, which emphasizes, in the genesis of schizophrenia, the difficulty in discriminating and ordering ambiguous information coming from inside and outside. This means that—to an extent—parents aren't responsible for psychosis, unlike in other theories. Psychiatry has interpreted "schizophrenic illness" in various ways. Traditional psychiatry sees it as the outcome of genetic, biochemical, or anatomical changes in the central nervous system; psychodynamic psychiatry sees it largely as the outcome of mental conflicts; social psychiatry attributes it to relationships, and anti-psychiatry to total institutions.

BERTRANDO: We might say that any hypothesis is partial, deals with only one aspect of the problem. No single hypothesis can account for all aspects of a psychosis. At the beginning, the hypothesis about time seemed adequate, but now Ciompi's hypothesis about ambiguity seems more appropriate. Later on, other hypotheses may emerge.

BOSCOLO: That's right, and I'd add Searles' hypothesis we mentioned earlier, but later on maybe some aspect of Selvini Palazzoli et al.'s (1989) hypothesis about psychotic games might fit better. The important thing is that ideas and hypotheses emerge naturally from discussion, so that they don't become true hypotheses and trap us into one-track thinking. It's always the client who provides the meanings that count. The client might notice a certain similarity between the therapist's way of thinking and his/her own. The therapist might say things the client has always thought, but has never succeeded in organizing into a description, into a definite linguistic form. Or the therapist might say things the client is already beginning to guess or think vaguely, that are already in the air. It's as if, with the client's help, the therapist makes discoveries about the client which then become the client's own discoveries.

BERTRANDO: *Just a moment! Your efforts to explain circularity in therapy dialogue seem to be coming unstuck. Listening to you, I get the impression that you place the therapist on a different level from the client, that you're tending towards the idea that the therapist "knows" what's good for the client. In other words, your neutrality is being threatened. I can already hear the comments of colleagues who believe in therapy conversation, narrative, hermeneutics . . .*

BOSCOLO: *It's difficult to give you an answer. . . . I can say that your impression—or the one I've given you—is partly a result of the tyranny of language (as we all know, it's difficult to avoid linear sequence in language), and partly the outcome of my biases and the hypotheses I've adopted. I think that a mass of circular questions, like a mass of carefully chosen hypotheses, prevents the client from knowing what the therapist thinks, and that's good for clients because in the end they have to make their own choices. In this sense, neutrality has to be seen diachronically, because you can't be neutral if you see it synchronically. Remember, too, that the therapist or consultant has a special kind of knowledge in a therapy or consultation context, precisely because of one's expertise: hypotheses deriving from personal experience and various theories of human behavior, including, of course, the important theory of common sense, are part of the job. I must repeat yet again that hypotheses should always simply be instruments; they should never become truths. Each client will get what he or she can or wants to get from these hypotheses and other aspects of the therapy relationship.*

THERAPIST: It was military service that brought this on, then?

FABRIZIO: I saw military service as a bit like a punishment.

MOTHER: Because they sent him to Messina, and that's a long way from home.

THERAPIST: Too far from home? Did you miss your family when you went to Messina?

FABRIZIO: No, because they gave me everything I needed.

THERAPIST: So you didn't miss your family?

FABRIZIO: No, no, I had friends because, by chance, we were all from the north and there were other people from Milan in my dormitory, so I made friends and adapted pretty well.

MOTHER: Although if he didn't phone, I would call the camp.

THERAPIST: You're saying that you two missed him very much.

MOTHER: Yes, we did.

THERAPIST: Did they miss you very much?

FABRIZIO: (*showing curiosity*) Did you miss me a lot?

MOTHER: I should say so! We always came down straightaway when we could, don't you remember?

FABRIZIO: If I don't, I realized it anyway. I was only 18 then, you know . . .

THERAPIST: You were telling me that you had this strong sense of justice. Does it make your life a bit complicated? Can it complicate your life?

FABRIZIO: Yes, it can.

THERAPIST: One can decide to stay at home to avoid unjust situations, but inevitably, whether you like it or not, if you go into the outside world there are always unjust situations, even if you try to avoid them. I was wondering if in your past life, before you did military service, you sometimes had the feeling that a situation was unjust.

FABRIZIO: There was another person who I thought was stealing my privileges as an only child: I felt a bit cheated by this person.

THERAPIST: Who was it?

FABRIZIO: My mother's brother. He lived at home with us, years ago, and I felt he had succeeded . . . succeeded in getting from my parents what I hadn't been able to. He stole the best of their youth from me.

BOSCOLO: *It's interesting what happened when he began to talk about this uncle: he looked to the right and left, as if he were checking his parents' reactions. The father seemed a bit agitated: his body language showed the subject was important to him. Perhaps some secret was being touched on.*

BERTRANDO: *There is a logical connection, anyway. The problem of justice led to the problem of the uncle, because you asked: "Did something happen before you did military service?" and he answered: "There's a person . . . "*

BOSCOLO: *Yes, a connection was created between his military service in Messina and his uncle.*

BERTRANDO: *That's what I meant when I said he doesn't have a story (a plot) but only, as Bruner says, a theme (a fabula): that is, a theme prevails on a narration. He's got a timeless theme—"justice/injustice"—that he conjugates in a timeless way. What prevails in him is the idea that an injustice has been done to him.*

BOSCOLO: *But only vaguely, I think. He doesn't seem much aware of it.*

BERTRANDO: *Yes, no diachronic connection comes out of it, an injustice was once done to him and this is immediately connected to all the injustice there is in the world. He's referring to a timeless "justice/injustice" theme: every event is seen by him through the lens of this theme. This reminds me of what Prigogine (see Prigogine & Stengers, 1984) says about the dichotomy between (natural) "law" and (contingent) "event." If you reason in terms of laws, you place yourself outside time; if you reason in terms of events you place yourself inside time, introducing unpredictability and irreversibility.*

BOSCOLO: *One could say that Fabrizio decontextualizes or, better, goes out of context. The same thing happens when one sees reality through the lens of a strong myth, a religious belief, or a delusion.*

BERTRANDO: *That's right. When he thought he was treated unjustly by his company, the "justice/injustice" theme was reactivated without being placed in context. Like transference in analysis.*

BOSCOLO: *It's interesting that he doesn't relate the injustice he feels to his rejection of his parents.*

BERTRANDO: *The connection between the issue of military service and this remote act of injustice came out through your questioning.*

BOSCOLO: *This may be an example of "split time" in the schizophrenic's experience. It's as if experiences are unconnected.*

BERTRANDO: *Yes, we could say that Fabrizio's experiences have been scattered in time, as if they're quite separate from one another, discontinuous. He seems unable to create a diachronic description of his life.*

BOSCOLO: *But Jim (see Chapter 5) seems to have constructed a new story after his psychotic break, a story that goes from the death of his father to the present day in a coherent temporal and causal sequence.*

BERTRANDO: *I can say that Jim projected into his past his present distorted view of himself and his own world. It is as though he had a "psychotic insight" which gave a new meaning to his past and intro-*

duced deterministic constraints ("I'm a schizophrenic") on his present and future. Schizophrenics may have different ways of distorting time. Jim the Australian has one. Aldo the Swiss (see Chapter 9), another. He had to stop his own life and wait for his parents' dilemma to sort itself out before he could move on. Temporal connections appear to be relaxed or strengthened in different stages of the psychotic process. The maximum breakdown occurs in the acute phase; then temporal links seem to rebuild themselves in the intervals between psychotic episodes.

BOSCOLO: A month ago, in a consultation, I saw a case of two parents and their 10-year-old boy, who had a long story of elective mutism. He spoke only with his mother, rarely with his father; at school he spoke only with his teacher, never with anyone else. In the first session he just looked at me and never spoke. The story that emerged was that the parents were still tied to the families of origin. Towards the end of the session, I began to say that the boy didn't speak because he was signaling that his parents weren't married yet, that they were finding it difficult to marry. He didn't speak to his grandparents because he was waiting for his parents to marry. Then I added that he would remain silent until the parents had decided to start a "real" marriage, not just a legal one. Shortly after I'd said this, to his parents' amazement, he started talking to me a little. I saw his therapist in a supervision group today, and he told me, all excited, that when the boy left the consultation he couldn't stop talking: he amazed everyone by talking to all of them. It's significant that, in a meeting with the parents, the therapist noticed that they used the phrase "since we were married" three times, as if the consultant's idea had in some way become their reality. Now there's a family: the parents are married and the child speaks.

BERTRANDO: This could be seen as a rite of passage: they got married during the session, or rather, when they realized during the session that they weren't married yet. The session functioned like a rite: a new family was born, where "speaking" again could make sense.

BOSCOLO: That's interesting. They entered a new time dimension, by accepting my metaphor (because the idea that they weren't married was only a metaphor), which became a reality for them both, so in a sense their time frame shifted. It's as if they had gone back to the day when they were and weren't married.

BERTRANDO: One could see a relationship between ritual and narrative. The ritual produced a discontinuity in time, but time regains its continuity in a new story.

THERAPIST: Who did he get most from? Perhaps from your mother because he was your mother's brother?

FABRIZIO: Yes.

THERAPIST: Do you remember suffering some of this injustice? Were you aware of injustice?

FABRIZIO: Yes, I suffered a bit.

THERAPIST: As you remember it, did he, you know, manage to attract your mother's attention, or was it your mother who . . .

FABRIZIO: No, no, I remember that . . .

THERAPIST: Was she in love with him?

FABRIZIO: I remember the selfishness, the selfishness of this person, this uncle, who succeeded, with his selfishness, getting everything. I was small . . .

BOSCOLO: *It's interesting how he says, "This uncle managed to get everything with his selfishness." After becoming psychotic, Fabrizio was so violent with his parents that he succeeded in using up all their savings. Psychotically, he's probably trying to get what he didn't have but his uncle did: there's a kind of vengeance here that's quite common, for example, in adolescents who think they haven't gotten what they deserve from their parents or society.*

FABRIZIO: I mean, I both understood and didn't.

THERAPIST: But you suffered then?

FABRIZIO: Yes.

THERAPIST: Have you ever thought that you suffered then because this uncle had taken your place?

FABRIZIO: Yes.

THERAPIST: He was an uncle, but he was also a son.

FABRIZIO: Yes, he was also a son.

THERAPIST: To both your parents, or was he most attached to your mother?

FABRIZIO: To both.

THERAPIST: Did you wonder, "Does my mother love me or my uncle more?" Did you wonder about that?

FABRIZIO: No, I never had that problem.

THERAPIST: Or, "Who does my mother think is better, more intelligent, me or my uncle?"

FABRIZIO: (*pauses*) No, I felt equal in that sense.

THERAPIST: So what made you feel that your uncle had usurped your position in the family?

FABRIZIO: Yes, he was an outsider. I could feel it, he had nothing to do with the family I had been born into.

THERAPIST: Perhaps you had this idea. Not only did the presence of this outsider who had taken your place as a son weigh on you; maybe you also thought, for example, that this uncle had taken your father's place, that your father too was a bit in your situation.

FABRIZIO: Yes.

THERAPIST: Do you remember thinking that?

FABRIZIO: Yes, yes, because he was more intelligent, more active, he was . . . he knew how to talk to people, he was . . . he lived in a world of rather rich people, I mean, there was almost nothing he didn't have, he had more financial possibilities . . .

FATHER: That happened later when he left home, but when he was with us I had to give him money, a bit here, a bit there. The possibilities came later.

BOSCOLO: *My impression is that Fabrizio always wondered: "Does my mother love me more or this uncle?" and the mother never gave him a clear answer. If he'd had the chance to have his father on his side, to get on well with him, he'd probably have avoided his painful experiences. I think the father is less open, more ambiguous than the mother. At least the mother is clear; she liked them both. The father was jealous both of the son and of his brother-in-law, who monopolized his wife's affections. He was jealous of his son for the same reason. I've never felt the father has any empathy for Fabrizio. So the latter found himself in a situation where he felt he counted for nothing.*

BERTRANDO: *We could also hypothesize that all three males were competing for the same woman, whose responses may have been confusing. Fabrizio seems to have been in the worst position, probably because there was a triangle that existed before he was born, because his mother's brother had been incredibly important to her since before her marriage. Metaphorically, the mother was already "married" to her brother before marrying her present husband.*

BOSCOLO: *And the father always tried to take the place of this brother-in-law. This reminds me once more of the theory of psychotic games in families (Selvini Palazzoli et al., 1989). At first one could see an alliance between the mother and son, which later became question-*

*able, in the sense that no one knew where the mother stood in
relation to the father and the uncle, so that the context was created
for the development of psychotic behavior. The abuse toward parents, the money he extracted with violence from them, his breaking
off relations with Aldo—all can be seen as Fabrizio's vengeance for
the wrongs he suffered. His psychotic rejection of his parents over
so many years seems a response to a situation in which he could
never understand what was what.*

BERTRANDO: *This reminds me of the double-bind theory that was so
important to our approach in the past.*

MOTHER: That's because he was small, because my brother left when
he was six. That's what amazes me, how certain things have been
blown up out of all proportion, because that's what his feeling . . .

THERAPIST: Fabrizio, when you were six, where did your uncle go?

MOTHER: He went to live on his own.

THERAPIST: Yes, but in Milan, near you?

MOTHER: In Milan.

THERAPIST: So you continued seeing him?

MOTHER: Yes, sometimes.

THERAPIST: How old was he when he left?

MOTHER: He was 24 or . . .

FATHER: Yes, 24.

MOTHER: He'd done his military service.

THERAPIST: He'd already done military service?

MOTHER: Yes.

BERTRANDO: *The mother says Aldo left when Fabrizio was six; that's a
delicate age, as we well know. It was the same with Jim: everything
began when he was six. From the psychoanalytic point of view, we
could say that everything has been laid down by that age.*

BOSCOLO: *But that's not true at all. Similar events later on can be very
important. When a member of a family leaves home for good, to
start a career or get married, he or she may sometimes become more
important than before. We sometimes love those who leave us the
most, not the ones who stay behind: many novels and films deal with
this theme. It runs through all Antonioni's films. It's like people who
die: they become nicer, more praiseworthy, than they were in life.
When he left home, Aldo seems to have been more present in his
sister's thoughts and affections, and this may have increased Fabriz-*

io's insecurity considerably. If Aldo really had burnt his bridges and gone out of their life, Fabrizio would at last have been able to experience being the favorite child. From what happens later on, we know this story is still going on, that the uncle is even more powerful than before, precisely because he isn't in the home. This is a common dynamic in psychotic families.

THERAPIST: So he went away. Where did he do his military service?

MOTHER: In Como.

THERAPIST: In Como, so (*to Fabrizio*) nearer home than you. Perhaps you felt there was a bit of injustice there. How come you ended up in Messina, while your uncle came to Como, virtually on the doorstep?

FABRIZIO: Yes, now I've followed the argument. I see it, but I didn't know he'd done it in Como.

FATHER: Don't you remember?

MOTHER: We took you to see him.

FATHER: We even went to visit him.

MOTHER: You see . . . he has tremendous blanks, but I remember things when I was a child . . .

BOSCOLO: This is an interesting example of the selectiveness of memory. He doesn't remember because it's too painful to remember. Forgetting has proved stronger than remembering here because it was a painful experience.

THERAPIST: You said you were a bit worried about "digging." I'll do it slowly. My impression is that you've been crushed by negative things so much that you've lost sight of the positive things in your past. I'll try to dig gently to find out what they are. (*to the parents*) Did you send Aldo to school?

MOTHER: Yes, I made great sacrifices for my brother because we were orphaned when I was 15 and he was eight, and the family was very united, the way families used to be, and I hung on to what little I got from my parents, so . . .

THERAPIST: Did you have only the one brother?

MOTHER: Yes, raising him became my mission in life. I paid for it, physically and financially . . .

THERAPIST: In a sense, your son and your husband had to make a bit of a sacrifice, too, because they also had to accept the person you felt you had a duty towards.

MOTHER: Yes.

THERAPIST: Were they a bit neglected?

MOTHER: It's true, no, they weren't neglected, in all conscience I can say they weren't because my son especially was always the first.

BERTRANDO: *It's interesting that the mother first says yes, but then retracts. She seems to have real problems admitting that she too has done something wrong, just like her husband.*

BOSCOLO: *I notice the mother keeps putting her hand over her heart when she speaks of her mission, while Fabrizio, who seems more perplexed here, touches his chin and seems a bit absentminded, less alive, as if he doesn't want to hear when his mother talks about her brother and her "mission."*

BERTRANDO: *Yes, he seems to withdraw, he doesn't follow the conversation. Sometimes he even puts his hands over his eyes, so as to almost not see.*

MOTHER: (*pointing to her husband*) He was neglected a bit.

THERAPIST: He was neglected?

MOTHER: Yes, it's true.

THERAPIST: He stayed in Division Two?

MOTHER: Yes, he stayed in Division Two. I've changed my mind about him over the years, I've come to appreciate him more. My husband's very impulsive but I'm very sensible: that's why I feel hurt sometimes.

THERAPIST: It's to be hoped, I think, that your son will also be promoted from Division Two to Division One, don't you agree?

MOTHER: Yes.

THERAPIST: When Aldo left home, did you go to visit him or did he come to see you?

MOTHER: He left home a bit suddenly because my husband . . . at a certain point . . . since he was at university . . . as my son quite rightly said, Aldo is a selfish person and he took advantage of the situation a bit. I have to admit that. So my husband got fed up with it and quite rightly said to me: "We've got a family, we've got a son and this Aldo's 24: it's time he stood on his own two feet." He left home, found a job, and got married.

FABRIZIO: (*as if to justify his own failure to himself*) Times were different then.

MOTHER: Yes, they were different times.

BOSCOLO: *The mother's embarrassment in saying how Aldo left is interesting. She seems to have trouble hiding that she feels a little guilty because she wasn't the one who sent him away. It's also important that Fabrizio returns from his isolation at precisely this point.*

BERTRANDO: *He times it just right, coming in to justify himself, because he always feels his uncle is better than him.*

THERAPIST: (*to Fabrizio*) He was very attached to your mother, he wanted her financial and emotional resources, but it seems your father put his foot down.

FATHER: Perhaps he doesn't remember that . . .

FABRIZIO: No, I remember.

MOTHER: You remember?

FABRIZIO: Yes, I don't know if this is connected in some way to what we were saying before, but I'll say it anyway. My mother had this mission to look after her brother, then she got married and had a child, me. I was born as the savior, like a Messiah, I felt the center of attention.

THERAPIST: I wonder, though, if you thought there might be two Messiahs at home: you and your uncle.

BOSCOLO: *We're getting to the heart of things here. Psychosis dazes you; you can't distinguish between two or more alternatives. Fabrizio said he came as a Messiah after his mother had had the mission of looking after her brother. Either he was made to believe he was the Messiah, or he deceived himself into believing it. Either he was deceived, or he deceived himself. With his questions, the therapist begins to question whether Fabrizio was the true Messiah, or rather, begins to suggest that there's no such thing as a Messiah.*

BERTRANDO: *It's in unclear situations like this, situations that produce such ambiguity, that the mind gets muddled, because if the family had simply rejected him and said, "You don't matter in the slightest," the situation would have been clear—"You don't count, it's your uncle who's most important to us." Similar situations make people become antisocial, set fire to their parents' home, and all the rest of it. He was told, "You're the most important of all," but this verbal message was invalidated nonverbally, and in fact, by all the money* and affection the mother lavished on the uncle. Fabrizio may have begun to have problems about being discriminated against when he was sent to Messina for his military service, while his uncle went to Como, a stone's throw from home.

BOSCOLO: See how in these story fragments he says, "But I was the Messiah." He ought already to be saying, "Now I understand I wasn't the Messiah," or showing emotions appropriate to having realized this.

BERTRANDO: That's the point: as we said before, his time experiences are scattered and disconnected. He returns to those story fragments as if the past had collapsed into the present.

BOSCOLO: But we're talking here, in the present, about his story, the reconstruction of his story up to this moment. I think that if he could accept the reconstruction, he'd start thinking differently. For example: "I thought I was the Messiah, but now I realize that my uncle was probably the Messiah; I deceived myself or was deceived into believing that I was the Messiah." Or, "Messiahs don't exist and have never existed, the idea that my mother was Mary and my father Joseph came from me." And so on, depending on which hypothesis you choose to adopt. That would make him change his description. He doesn't seem to be ready yet. The mother has just revealed that she had a mission to look after her orphaned brother, that her sacrifices were rewarded by bringing him up successfully, by being able to send him to university so he could find a good job. You'd expect Fabrizio, after saying he didn't have the pleasure of being the only son (although in reality he was), to slap his forehead and say, "Eureka! I understand!" Probably a few more sessions will be needed, but you can already see that the past inside him is being challenged.

BERTRANDO: From the way you speak about him, it looks as if the sine qua non for change is Fabrizio's insight, as a psychoanalyst would say. But from a systemic point of view, the explanation ought also to include the other members of the family, the psychiatrists . . .

BOSCOLO: Of course. As the therapist and the family investigate important relationships and emotions in Fabrizio's past, as well as the influence the past may be having on his present, the whole therapy system — including the team — may be led into a new story. This usually happens without any special insight, particularly in clients — without the sort of "eureka!" I've just mentioned. But there may be other factors that hinder the reconstruction of a different past and the possibility of a new future: intensity and duration of psychotic *experience, difficulty in facing the challenge of the outside world after years lost because of "mental illness," the rubber wall surrounding the family that refuses to let a member go, and so on.*

FABRIZIO: Yes (*laughs*), that's it, two Messiahs in the home . . .

THERAPIST: Your mother said her son came first. In fact, she seems to have had two missions, looking after Aldo and looking after her son.

MOTHER: That's right.

THERAPIST: So in a sense you had two children.

FABRIZIO: Yes, in effect she did.

THERAPIST: Your mother had two missions, but what about your father? Didn't he feel excluded, or exclude himself? With two missions, your mother must have been rather busy as a mother, don't you think?

FABRIZIO: No, to finish what we were saying earlier, about my birth and all that, well, afterwards I wasn't treated like a man, like a male, in the way I'd have liked. At a certain point it should have been possible for me to leave home, make my own life, but this hasn't happened, I haven't realized myself, I haven't started my own family. He (*i.e., the uncle*) has managed to do it, somehow.

THERAPIST: But I wonder: have you gone on comparing yourself to him all these years? Did you think . . . what's your uncle's name?

FABRIZIO: Aldo.

THERAPIST: Did you sometimes think: "What's Aldo doing now? What success is he having with women? A lot? A little?"

FABRIZIO: Yes.

THERAPIST: Or, "How much money has Aldo got?"

FABRIZIO: It's not as if I made problems about money . . .

THERAPIST: But in your view, how was . . .

BERTRANDO: *I notice that Fabrizio slid over your comment about his father being excluded. I don't know how much this was due to his deliberately ignoring it or to his obsession with Aldo. One could say that, by not hearing the comment about his father, Fabrizio confirms the pattern of ignoring the father in the family. A hierarchy seems to have been established in the family, with the mother at the top, then Aldo and Fabrizio, and the father last. Wouldn't it have been better for the therapist to have drawn attention to the father's exclusion, so as to reinstate him (if he was ever in it) in his rightful position, the role he should occupy, rather than to go on talking about the relationship between the mother, Aldo, and Fabrizio? There's the risk of confirming the family hierarchy.*

BOSCOLO: *Yes, I'm afraid you're right. The therapist seems satisfied with his own metaphor, the metaphor of the two Messiahs. Fabrizio's laugh seems to show that something struck home, and this anchored, almost hypnotized the therapist, even though Fabrizio resumed his earlier rigidity and control immediately afterwards. This can be the case of a dangerous falling in love of a therapist with his metaphor.*

BERTRANDO: *Fabrizio has gone up and down a stepladder. He seems to have a very strange way of putting things in sequence. For example, he says, "I wasn't treated like a man, like a male, so I never managed to leave home." In fact, the opposite sequence seems more appropriate, "I was treated like a child, and I basked in it, so as time passed I did nothing to help myself start behaving like a man." Or, "I was never given the chance to leave home in a certain way, like a man." He mixes up things; he has serious problems with sequencing.*

BOSCOLO: *It's interesting that, when he laughed at the idea of the two Messiahs, if he hadn't been a psychotic he would probably have begun to put all his past together and realize that he'd been either a fool or just ingenuous to have built castles in the air the way he did. Significant change would have been triggered, and this would have brought therapy rapidly to an end. In most cases, this happens after five or six sessions, but not with psychosis or chronic schizophrenia, where the situation is much more complex.*

BERTRANDO: *As Singer and Wynne (1965) have said, families like this seem to be surrounded with a rubber wall that absorbs all shocks. For example, when the therapist speaks about the two Messiahs, Fabrizio laughs, seems to arrive at some insight, which momentarily fools the therapist, but then he resumes the puzzled, rather confused expression he had earlier.*

BOSCOLO: *Reframing interventions, including the invariant prescriptions used by Selvini Palazzoli and her collaborators, never produced conclusive results in our center. My impression is that complex cases like these need complex responses. The presence of the team is very important in preventing the therapist from being absorbed by the rubber wall. In some cases, psychotherapy itself—family or individual—isn't enough and has to be supplemented with group or rehabilitation therapy.*

THERAPIST: So your uncle got on in life . . .

FABRIZIO: Well, not so much now, he's got a few problems at the moment . . .

MOTHER: He's got big problems, economic problems, problems with his wife, problems with his 15-year-old son who's getting into all kinds of mischief . . .

BOSCOLO: *I think they were both entranced by her, son and brother. Aldo must be confused, too: "Is she my mother, my sister, or my wife?" That's why his marriage has never really worked out, and why he's now on the verge of separation. And the sister keeps on calling him! There's a transgenerational pattern repeating itself here: now Aldo's son may find himself in the same situation Fabrizio was in the past, in which the parents are split and there's an alliance between one parent and a child.*

BERTRANDO: *They're all paying for it, Fabrizio, Aldo, the father—as an excluded husband, as a Division Two male—and the mother, who's had to put up with a husband she couldn't stand for years, with Aldo who was always making problems for her, and above all with Fabrizio, who's been tyrannizing her for years and sometimes even hits her. You might ask how behavior that produces so much suffering and frustration can go on repeating itself. One explanation could be that they've all become victims and players in an unstoppable game in which each is able to sustain the illusion he or she is winning secondary advantage over the others.*

BOSCOLO: *I'm puzzled by the father, though. He seems cunning to me, someone who plays a dirty game, as Selvini would say. The mother no, she's the saint, she has a mission and just gets on with it, never tiring, never getting down from her pedestal. You could see things in the opposite way, the mother as the unlucky one, as the victim of circumstances and people who've put her on a pedestal she doesn't want to be on. Her two "children" help to maintain the idea of how good and capable a person she is, of what a saint she is. Naturally, the husband plays a part in the mission, too.*

BERTRANDO: *Yes, that's true, but the husband was less happy. He's beginning to feel content only now that Aldo is having problems. The two Messiahs with problems have made him seem more important.*

BOSCOLO: *I think he was fairly content before, as well, secretly content that one day his wife would recognize how patient and giving he's been. Members of couples often project reparation for wrongs done to them into the future, like married couples in therapy, where each partner expects his or her goodness and rightness to be recognized in the future.*

FABRIZIO: I was irritated, I mean, we don't speak to each other, only my mother speaks to him.

THERAPIST: How long haven't you been speaking to each other?

FABRIZIO: Er, more than three years.

THERAPIST: So neither you nor your father speak to Aldo?

FATHER: In the past, if he phoned and heard my voice he would ring off straightaway. If he hears my voice now, he'll talk to me as well.

THERAPIST: (*to the father*) Did you not speak because you were angry with him, or did he think you were angry with him?

FATHER: We were a bit short with each other because in a certain period . . .

FABRIZIO: (*showing sudden interest and turning to his father*) No, answer the question properly. Did you think he was angry with you, or were you angry with him. . . ?

FATHER: Because I was angry with him.

FABRIZIO: Ah, you were angry with him?

FATHER: Because there came a point when I was fed up and I told him: "If you poke your nose into my affairs again and you do me more harm than good, you'd better just clear off, forget about us, leave us in peace!"

THERAPIST: What problems has Aldo got at the moment?

MOTHER: Financial problems, and his wife. It seems his wife is having her menopause, so she's bit off her head, too. They've also got a young son, he's 15, 16 years old, who's very intelligent and did well at school until last year, but then he went off his head too and he's smashing the house up now. My brother doesn't know how to react. He phoned just the other day, and . . .

FABRIZIO: For example, there can now be rivalry with the son as well, because he's managed to have a son and I haven't.

FATHER: He's 15; you're 30.

BOSCOLO: *It's odd. The mother's saying that all Aldo's family is in turmoil: they're in financial trouble, the wife's going off her head, the son's smashing up the home . . . and Fabrizio is still fixated on the past. He says, "He's managed to have a son, I haven't," ignoring everything the mother's saying, which seems very important. He almost seems to have some disturbance in his thinking . . .*

BERTRANDO: *He can't read the context properly.*

BOSCOLO: *You could say he always thinks about himself, that he's stuck in time and can't enter life, although he sees it going on all around him.*

THERAPIST: Fabrizio, I think there are two knots in your life. Once they've been untied, you really will begin to understand who you are, because up to now I've had the impression you aren't sure who you are, or rather, you don't know who you are.

FABRIZIO: Me?

THERAPIST: Yes, You haven't found your identity, you're searching for it, but you still haven't found it.

FABRIZIO: Not yet, it's true.

THERAPIST: To paraphrase Pirandello, you're like a character looking for an author. You know who Pirandello is?

FABRIZIO: Yes, a bit.

THERAPIST: They found their identity in the end, but you're still looking, so . . .

FABRIZIO: For my exact identity.

THERAPIST: We're here to try to see if this identity can finally come out so you can understand what you want to be, what you want to do, because I think you've been pretty confused in recent years.

BOSCOLO: *The therapist is saying here, "You're looking for an identity, and neither you nor we know what it is." Doing this is like saying to him we have to go and look for something that didn't exist before.*

BERTRANDO: *This opens up a future. What is being said is, "You haven't found an identity yet," which is different from saying, "You haven't got an identity." That means he's searching and there's a chance he may find it. That's the important thing, I think. He hasn't found it up to now, but he may find it in the future.*

THERAPIST: You haven't spoken to Aldo for three years?

FATHER: No, me yes, now.

THERAPIST: How come you're speaking to him now?

MOTHER: (*defending her husband*) He came to us because he was desperate . . .

FATHER: He turned to us lots of times, often just to get things off his chest, because he's in real trouble now. He was important once, maybe, but now the wheel of fortune has turned.

THERAPIST: (to Fabrizio) But you haven't spoken to him for three years? Why not?

FABRIZIO: Because that person has always made me feel uneasy.

THERAPIST: Uneasy, in what sense uneasy? Do you see yourself in a mirror when you look at him?

MOTHER: And to think they even look like each other, too.

THERAPIST: Why uneasy?

FABRIZIO: Uneasy because . . . because I remember that he treated me badly when I was a child. When they left me with him . . . I remember that I once banged my head, he dropped me . . .

BOSCOLO: *He's even unlucky enough to look like him! You know the theory of the double? Everyone has a double. It's interesting, rather odd, the therapist's phrase, "Do you see yourself in a mirror when you look at him?" as if they were identical twins.*

BERTRANDO: *Yes, and whenever he has some doubt, she always makes it worse, unknowingly increases it, with her charming voice. I think this makes him even more confused. From the order he says things in, he could almost be holding a daisy and saying: "Are we brothers or are we uncle and nephew? Or are we father and son?"*

BOSCOLO: *Yes, he must have wondered, or rather, hasn't wondered: "Which family do I belong to, who is my father?" because more attention has been paid to Aldo than to his biological father. I remember a consultation I did in Germany a couple of years ago. It was a family of four people, two parents about 30 with two small children. A few months previously the father had developed the fantasy that his children were his father's children, that his younger sister was the daughter of his eldest brother. He'd had to be hospitalized because of the state he was in, and he'd just been discharged. During the consultation, he totally ignored his children because he said they weren't his. He looked enigmatic, distracted. Careful investigation of the ties with his original family showed that his delirium was closely linked to his intense relationship with his mother, who had always set him against his father, and a secret envy of his older brother, who had always been more successful than him. Towards the end of the session, he seemed visibly shaken when I said that out of deep loyalty to his mother, so as not to betray her, he was fighting against his love for his wife and children. It's interesting that in this case, consultation—and only one session at that—was enough to solve the problem.*

BERTRANDO: *Mightn't it be that when the mother notices the resemblance between Fabrizio and Aldo, and so excludes the father, Fabrizio fantasizes that his uncle is his father: "If I'm like my uncle and not like him, my father, and my father doesn't count, then maybe I'm the result of incest between brother and sister." A psychoanalyst would have the time of his life here!*

FABRIZIO: I mean, I remember these things from my childhood, that I was left with him now and again and he treated me as if I was a burden to him.

THERAPIST: Did you have the impression that he was more cunning, not more intelligent, more cunning than you, for example in involving your parents?

FABRIZIO: Yes, in a neurological examination I once had, they told me I'm more incapable than disabled.

THERAPIST: Ingenuous?[1]

FABRIZIO: Ingenuous, yes, but they considered me incapable, that's what they said.

BOSCOLO: *The therapist is ready here with another key word, ingenuous instead of incapable, introducing a more positive frame.*

FABRIZIO: I can't manipulate situations, I can't . . .

THERAPIST: It would be pretty hard to find people in the outside world who think the way you do, who have such a strong sense of justice. Most people elbow their way through life, try to find a place in the sun at the expense of others.

FABRIZIO: Who maybe deserve more . . .

THERAPIST: Pardon?

FABRIZIO: Who maybe deserve more.

THERAPIST: Yes, certainly, who maybe deserve more. In this sense, the outside world works fine. But compared with Aldo, you felt . . . less cunning, more ingenuous? Even though you're maybe more intelligent?

FABRIZIO: Yes, more ingenuous. Since I had a high opinion of myself,

---

[1] In Italian, "ingenuo" means "naive."

and in certain moments this high opinion of myself came out, I felt cheated because although I felt more intelligent than him, I could never express this intelligence.

THERAPIST: Is this a source of great anguish?

FABRIZIO: Yes.

THERAPIST: For example, do you see your father as ingenuous or as cunning, more as an ingenuous person or more as a cunning person?

FABRIZIO: Cunning.

THERAPIST: Cunning. And your mother?

FABRIZIO: I don't think she's cunning any more, I feel she's fuller, more realized.

BOSCOLO: *Well, he confirmed the hypothesis about the father being cunning. The phrase about the mother is interesting, because the experience that makes you see your mother in this way instills basic trust in you if her love is unconditional. If the opposite is true, it's a disaster.*

BERTRANDO: *The correlation between the mother's fullness and Aldo's emptiness is interesting.*

THERAPIST: In your view, from your memories, how did your father cope with the fact that your mother spent so much time looking after this brother and you? Did he feel excluded?

FABRIZIO: No, because he isn't incapable, he always managed to find something for himself, he managed OK, he wasn't a victim.

THERAPIST: Yes, but what if he managed because there were no alternatives . . .

FABRIZIO: No, because he's cunning by nature.

BOSCOLO: *He said: "My father managed OK because he's cunning by nature," so here a cunning person would be defined, in terms of what we said about schizophrenia and ambiguity, as someone who accepts ambiguity, and an ingenuous person would be someone who can't accept ambiguity.*

BERTRANDO: *Yes, in fact a cunning person not only accepts ambiguity, but can also create it in others. A cunning person plays with ambiguity.*

THERAPIST: (*to Fabrizio*) I remember that, in the second meeting with your parents more than a year ago, I said I saw your family as the Holy Family: your mother as Mary, you as Jesus . . .

FABRIZIO: Christ.

THERAPIST: Yes, Christ, the Messiah, and your father as Joseph.

FABRIZIO: Yes, yes (*laughs*), I can't help laughing. It's a great metaphor, but it's also close to the truth.

THERAPIST: Your father had to be like Joseph because there was this mission, because the real Joseph's role had already been fixed, there'd been orders from above. The prophets had already said that this Jesus would come, born of a virgin mother, a Jesus who would be very attached to her, while Joseph was rather left out of it all, excluded, and maintained the family by making tables and chairs. That other time your parents said: "In some way we feel closer now." He's been promoted, he isn't Joseph anymore. Your mother and father say they feel more like a couple. You yourself confirmed it. Don't you remember saying: "I think my mother and father are closer than they used to be"?

FABRIZIO: Ah, yes, now I remember.

THERAPIST: Your father's been promoted now.

FABRIZIO: Yes, there's been a change in them, but my personality has remained stable, I mean I'm fixed, I feel fixed now . . .

BOSCOLO: *This is interesting: the idea that they've changed, that they've entered a developmental perspective in which time flows, while Fabrizio's time is immobile. This temporal notion of stalemate, where nothing moves, has already come out in Fabrizio's idea of flatness. It seems he decided to come to therapy after seeing the change in his parents' relationship, their development, which made him acutely and painfully aware of his own immobility in time. I'm reminded of Aldo (see Chapter 9) who, under the delusional influence of the spirit of the Dalai Lama, saw time as immobile, like an eternity in which past, present, and future are indistinguishable. In religious thought, temporality, eternity, is projected onto a divine figure, but if we feel we're falling into it in our ordinary mortal lives, we feel anguish. This reminds me of Kierkegaard. Life is all one with the passing and the flow of time. I think Fabrizio wants therapy to make his time start flowing again so he can coordinate himself with other people's times and the times of the world around him. In other words, he's asking to return to life.*

THERAPIST: But your family's situation seems more complicated to me. There wasn't just one Jesus, but two, two Messiahs, a family with two Messiahs (*Fabrizio laughs*). In the real Holy Family there was only one. Fabrizio, I think you've had to deal with another Jesus, I think it's been hard trying to find out who the real one and who the false one is. "Am I the real Jesus, or is the other one?"

FABRIZIO: Yes, I've had that doubt.

THERAPIST: And you've had it pretty badly, too.

FATHER: You've invented things you shouldn't have, useless things.

BOSCOLO: *Father seems to have little introspection into Fabrizio's dilemmas.*

BERTRANDO: *In fact, the patient seems to have more insight than his parents.*

BOSCOLO: *Exactly. The parents seem less willing to make connections between past events in the family and the present symptomatic situation. Although they're in a family therapy context, they tend either not to "see" or else to deny possible connections between their behavior and their son's problems, which they regard just as a sign of nervous illness. These denials that other members of the family may have contributed to a psychosis may happen because it's difficult, unacceptable, to feel you're responsible for such serious symptoms. One tends to accept medical diagnoses of physical illness more easily, rather than diagnoses based on human relationships. Families are usually very happy to accept diagnoses that point to individual, physical origins for psychosis because they obtain a clear, simple explanation of a very complex situation and are relieved from direct responsibility for the symptoms.*

BERTRANDO: *Another explanation could be that, since the couple have had seven sessions before, they may believe that the work on them had already been done, that the problem now was only of their son.*

BOSCOLO: *That's a very plausible hypothesis. In the first session the tone was: "Now we've brought our son, we hope you'll have the same success with him you had with us."*

BERTRANDO: *Exactly, they already think they're OK. One could say they already have a therapeutic past but he doesn't. One thing that struck me very much was how the family, especially Fabrizio, responded to the metaphor of the Holy Family. You used it with the parents in the second of the seven sessions you did with them. It may have contributed greatly to the change in their relationship as a couple, with the promotion of the husband from Division Two to Division One and the easing of pressure on Fabrizio, who, feeling himself alone, has come to the center to see if we can sort him out too. I was especially struck by Fabrizio's reaction when you talked about the Holy Family, the Messiah, Jesus Christ and so on. His basically expressionless face changed, lit up, showing that the metaphor had hit the mark. Sometimes metaphors can have a huge impact, for example when certain key words are used in therapy (see Boscolo et al., 1991). If accepted as a representation of their reality (Fabrizio said: "That's right, that's exactly the way it is"), they can produce discontinuous change and, as in this case, create an untenable, absurd situation, a family with two Messiahs.*

(The therapist goes out and returns after a long discussion with the team.)

THERAPIST: I've talked to my colleagues to get the situation into perspective, and they also think that in your family, in the past, Fabrizio has, through no one's fault, been placed in an ambiguous situation. I said you were like the Holy Family, a very close family, but a family that found it had not one Jesus but two, two Messiahs. So it had the problem of having to decide who the real one was, and so on.

FABRIZIO: *(agreeing)* What role I have, what role I don't have . . .

THERAPIST: Yes, who is the more important Messiah, who is the less important one. My colleagues also found this situation very important, in the sense that it explains why you, Fabrizio, have found it difficult to develop a clear identity in time. We all seek our own identities, seek to know who we are and are not, what we want and don't want, so you've always been rather confused. We're here, then, to see if these doubts can be cleared up so you too can find your identity. That's why we're here. Is that clear or not?

FABRIZIO: Yes.

THERAPIST: We've also talked a lot about the relationship you all share with an important character in your family called Aldo. We've looked at this relationship over time, in the distant past and over the last three years. You haven't spoken to him recently, Fabrizio, but you, Mrs. Ponzi, have always maintained contact with your brother. You *(to the father)* began speaking to him again three years ago. By the way, I didn't understand when, in answer to my question: but when he heard your voice, did your brother-in-law ring off because he thought you were angry with him or because your brother-in-law . . . no . . . sorry, brother-in-law . . . I'm getting confused . . .

MOTHER: Yes, brother-in-law!

THERAPIST: *(laughing, a little embarrassed)* It's a bit difficult to get your bearings in this family! As I was speaking I suddenly wondered: is he or isn't he a brother-in-law? When I said it I suddenly thought he was the brother. . . . I think that's quite significant, don't you?

MOTHER: I should say so!

THERAPIST: I'm confused. Don't say I'm going schizophrenic. Anyway, did you put down the phone because you were angry . . .

BOSCOLO: *I think it's significant that I really was confused at that moment. My confusion may have reflected Fabrizio's confusion over his relationship with his family. The phrase "I'm confused. Don't say I'm going schizophrenic," was intended as an indirect attack on labeling.*

BERTRANDO: *You mean, schizophrenic becomes synonymous with confused.*

BOSCOLO: *Confused, but not ill.*

FATHER: Because I'd treated him badly, I'd told him: "Don't bother to phone."

THERAPIST: Anyway, we've analyzed the situation now, including in the light of these recent serious problems of Aldo's, with his wife, his son, and so on. He's always been very close to you, for better or worse, and you've always been very close to him. We think it's very important now to give you a task which, of course, you must first think about, and then scrupulously perform if you agree to it.

The task is as follows: we think it's very important now that communication with Aldo and his family should be shared by all three of you. We're asking you to choose a day of the week — Tuesday, for example — and devote it to speaking about Aldo, his family, and the relationship you share with them. Every Tuesday until our next session, you should hold a meeting of an hour or two, after lunch or after dinner, in which you exchange all the information about Aldo and his family you have acquired during the previous week. This information should be discussed in the family meeting, where you'll decide things together, or work out together the responses you think are best in the circumstances.

MOTHER: Together.

THERAPIST: Together. One of you will be appointed to make the response you have decided on together. Is that clear?

FABRIZIO: Anyone can be appointed?

THERAPIST: You must all decide who is to be appointed. You can discuss it in the meeting and decide whose turn it is by majority vote.

What you should do is important, but what you *shouldn't* do is just as important. What you shouldn't do is this: on all the other days of the week, you are forbidden to talk about Aldo and his family. Naturally, you can think about them, but you're forbidden to speak. If one of you breaks the rule, the others must make that person keep the rule. Thoughts about Aldo and the family should be voiced only in the Tuesday meetings. Even you, who are husband and wife and so on more intimate terms, must not speak of Aldo. Is that clear? You must speak of Aldo only on Tuesdays in the family meetings. The family meeting will decide what to do: it might decide to break off relations and tell Aldo to solve his own problems, or it may decide to lend a hand, but it must be a collective decision.

FATHER: Unanimous.

THERAPIST: Unanimous, yes, by common assent.

FABRIZIO: If he happens to phone . . .

THERAPIST: When he phones, whoever answers should report the content of the call on Tuesday in the family meeting. If someone asks: "What did he say?" the answer should be, "I'll tell you on Tuesday." Is this clear?

FABRIZIO: I understand what we should do, but I still haven't quite grasped what we shouldn't do.

BOSCOLO: *I think it's important that Fabrizio finds the task extremely interesting. He seems more alert, asks for explanations and confirmations. It's probably the first time he's ever had the chance to manage and control communication between the two families, the thing that caused him uncertainty and anguish in the past. When giving the ritual, it's important to be precise about when and how it should be performed to avoid any risk of it being nullified. Among other things, its purpose is to establish a clear boundary between the two families. A ritual like this can have a profound effect on the organization of family life, and sometimes produce sudden, lasting change. I wouldn't be surprised if Fabrizio succeeds in breaking his stalemate after this session and starts becoming more independent.*

THERAPIST: What you shouldn't do is speak to each other about Aldo and his family during the week. To summarize: there must be no communication with Aldo that isn't reported in the family meeting. This is fundamental. No communication between you three about Aldo and his family should remain secret. It must be reported in the meeting. What comes out during the actual meetings should not be discussed in the intervals between meetings. You can talk about Aldo and his family only on Tuesdays. That's final. Even if one of you is dying to speak, keep quiet, otherwise you disobey the prescription. Is that clear?

MOTHER: What if nothing has happened, if Aldo hasn't phoned . . .

THERAPIST: You can use the two hours on Tuesday to talk about events concerning Aldo and his family in the past, present, or future. You can discuss how you feel about those events, or imagine the story of your two families had been different and decide what might have happened.

BOSCOLO: *Telling them to spend the two hours on Tuesday talking about Aldo and his family, even if nothing new has happened, means acknowledging and accepting "what the system brings"—that Aldo and his family are central to their lives. The ritual changes the rules of the relationship between the two families: Fabrizio's family can talk about Aldo's only one day a week. This establishes a clear temporal sequence defining when it's all right to talk about Aldo, and when it isn't. Before, Fabrizio could never be certain he really existed; now he can begin to exist six days a week.*

REFERENCES

Allwood, J., Anderson, L. G., & Dahl, O. (1977). *Logic for Linguistics*. Cambridge: Cambridge University Press.

Andersen, T. (1987). The reflecting team: Dialogue and meta-dialogue in clinical work. *Family Process, 26*(4), 415–428.

Anderson, H., & Goolishian, H. (1988). Human systems as linguistic systems: Preliminary and evolving ideas about the implications for clinical theory. *Family Process, 27*, 371–393.

Anderson, H., Goolishian, H., & Winderman, L. (1986). Problem determined systems: Towards transformation in family therapy. *Journal of Strategic and Systemic Therapy, 5*, 1–14.

Assmann, A. (1993, April 3–7). *Cultural and individual construction of time*. Paper presented at the International Congress, "The End of Grand Designs and the Flowering of Systemic Practice," Heidelberg.

St. Augustine (1991). *Confessions* (H. Chadwick, Trans.). London: Oxford University Press.

Ausloos, G. (1986). The march of time: Rigid or chaotic transactions, two different ways of living time. *Family Process, 25*, 549–557.

Bagarozzi, D. A., & Anderson, S. A. (1989). *Personal, marital and family myths*. New York: Norton.

Balbo, L. (1991). *Tempi di vita. Studi e proposte per cambiarli*. Milan: Feltrinelli.

Bandler, R., & Grinder, J. (1975). *The structure of magic*. Palo Alto: Science and Behavior Books.

Bateson, G. (1958). *Naven* (2nd ed.). Stanford, CA: Stanford University Press.

Bateson, G. (1972). *Steps to an ecology of mind*. New York: Ballantine.

Bateson, G. (1972a). Cybernetic explanation. In *Steps to an ecology of mind* (pp. 399–410). New York: Ballantine.

Bateson, G. (1972b). The cybernetics of "self": A theory of alcoholism. In *Steps to an ecology of mind* (pp. 309–337). New York: Ballantine.

Bateson, G. (1972c). The logical categories of learning and communication. In *Steps to an ecology of mind* (pp. 279–308). New York: Ballantine.

309

Bateson, G. (1972d). From Versailles to cybernetics. In *Steps to an ecology of mind* (pp. 469–477). New York: Ballantine.

Bateson, G. (1978). The birth of a matrix or double bind and epistemology. In M. M. Berger (Ed.), *Beyond the double bind* (pp. 38–64). New York: Brunner/Mazel.

Bateson, G. (1978a). Bateson's workshop. In M. M. Berger (Ed.), *Beyond the double bind* (pp. 197–229). New York: Brunner/Mazel.

Bateson, G. (1979). *Mind and nature: A necessary unity.* New York: Dutton.

Bateson, G., Jackson, D. D., Haley, J., & Weakland, J. H. (1956). Toward a theory of schizophrenia. *Behavioral Science, 1:* 251–264.

Bateson, M. C. (1984). *With a daughter's eye. A memoir of Margaret Mead and Gregory Bateson.* New York: Morrow.

Berger, P., & Luckmann, T. (1966). *The social construction of reality.* New York: Doubleday.

Bergson, H. (1889). *Essai sur les données immédiates de la conscience* (Essay on the immediate data of consciousness).

Binswanger, L. (1967). *Being-in-the-world: Selected papers of Ludwig Binswanger* (J. Needleman, Ed.). New York and London: Harper Torchbooks.

Bocchi, G., & Ceruti, M. (Eds.) (1985). *La sfida della complessità.* Milan: Feltrinelli.

Boorstin, D. (1983). *The discoverers.* New York: Random House.

Borges, J. L. (1962). *Funes.* In J. L. Borges, *Ficciones* (Anthony Kerrigan, Ed.). New York: Grove Press.

Borges, J. L. (1964a). *New refutation of time.* In J. L. Borges, *Other inquisitions: 1937–1952* (Ruth L. C. Simms, Trans.) (pp. 171–188). Austin: University of Texas Press.

Borges, J. L. (1964b). Pascal's sphere. In J. L. Borges, *Other inquisitions: 1937–1952* (Ruth L. C. Simms, Trans.) (pp. 6–9). Austin: University of Texas Press.

Borwick, B. (1990). *Circular "questioning" in organizations: Discovering the patterns that connect.* Unpublished manuscript.

Boscolo, L., Bertrando, P., Fiocco, P. M., Palvarini, R. M., & Pereira, J. (1991). Linguaggio e cambiamento. L'uso di parole chiave in terapia. *Terapia Familiare, 37:* 41–53.

Boscolo, L., Cecchin, G., Hoffman, L., & Penn, P. (1987). *Milan systemic family therapy. Conversations in theory and practice.* New York: Basic Books.

Bossard, J. H., & Boll, E. S. (1976). *Ritual in family living.* Westport, CT: Greenwood. (Reprint of the 1950 edition)

Bowen, M. (1978). *Family therapy in clinical practice.* New York: Jason Aronson.

Bowlby, J. (1982). *Attachment, volume I: Attachment and loss.* New York: Basic Books.

Bruner, J. (1986). *Actual minds, possible worlds.* Cambridge, MA: Harvard University Press.

Campbell, D., & Draper, R. (Eds.) (1985). *Application of systemic family therapy: The Milan approach.* London: Grune & Stratton.

Capra, F. (1991). *The tao of physics* (3rd ed.). Boston: Shambhala.

Cecchin, G. (1987). Hypothesizing-circularity-neutrality revisited: An invitation to curiosity. *Family Process, 26:* 405–413.

Ceruti, M. (1985). La hybris dell'onniscienza e la sfida della complessità. In G. Bocchi & M. Ceruti (Eds.), *La sfida della complessità* (pp. 25–48). Milan: Feltrinelli.

Chapple, E. D. (1970). *Culture and biological man.* New York: Holt, Rinehart and Winston.

Ciompi, L. (1983). How to improve the treatment of schizophrenics: A multicausal illness concept and its therapeutic consequences. In H. Stierlin, L. C. Wynne, M. Wirsching (Eds.), *Psychosocial intervention in schizophrenia* (pp. 53–63). Berlin: Springer Verlag.

Cohen, J. (1967). *The time in health and disease.* Springfield, IL: Thomas.

Coser, L. A., & Coser, R. L. (1963). Time perspective and social structure. In A. W. Gouldner & M. P. Gouldner (Eds.), *Modern sociology* (pp. 638–650). New York: Harcourt, Brace and World.

Cronen, V. E., Johnson, K., & Lannamann, J. (1982). Paradoxes, double binds and reflexive loops: An alternative theoretical perspective. *Family Process, 21:* 91–112.

Cronen, V. E., & Pearce, W. B. (1985). Towards an explanation of how the "Milan method" works: An invitation to systemic epistemology and evolution of family systems. In D. Campbell & R. Draper (Eds.), *Application of systemic family therapy: The Milan approach.* London: Grune & Stratton.

Curi, U. (Ed.) (1987). *Dimensioni del Tempo.* Milan: Franco Angeli.

Curi, U. (1987a). *Introduzione.* In U. Curi (Ed.), *Dimensioni del Tempo* (pp. 11–18). Milan: Franco Angeli.

Dalla Chiara Scabia, L. (1979). *Logica.* Milan: Mondadori.

Davis, J. (1988). Mazel tov: The bar mitzvah as multigenerational ritual of change and continuity. In E. Imber-Black, J. Roberts, & R. Whiting (Eds.), *Rituals in families and family therapy* (pp. 177–208). New York: Norton.

de Saussure, F. (1966). *Course in general linguistics* (W. Baskin, Trans.). New York: McGraw-Hill. (Original work published in 1922)

de Shazer S. (1988). *Clues. Investigating solutions in brief therapy.* New York: Norton.

Deissler, K. G. (1986). *Recursive creation of information. Circular questioning as information production, part I.* Unpublished manuscript.

Dell, P. (1981). Some irreverent thoughts on paradox. *Family Process, 20:* 37–42.

Dossey, L. (1982). *Space, time and medicine.* Boston: Shambhala.

Douglas, M. (1973). *Natural symbols.* London: Barrie & Jenkins.

Eco, U. (1976). *A theory of semiotics.* Bloomington: Indiana University Press.

Einstein, A. (1961). *Relativity: The special and general theory* (W. Robert, Trans.). New York: Crown. (Original work published in 1905)

Einstein, A. (1983). *Sidelights on relativity.* New York: Dover Press. (Original work published in 1916)

Eliade, M. (1954) *The myth of eternal return* (W. R. Trask, Trans.). Princeton: Princeton University Press.

Elias, N. (1989). *On time.* Oxford: Basil Blackwell.

Elkana, Y. (1984). Relativismo e filosofia della scienza dal baconianesimo vittoriano al giorno d'oggi. In M. Piattelli Palmarini (Ed.), *Livelli di realtà* (pp. 205–233). Milan: Feltrinelli.

Erickson, M. (1954). Pseudo-orientation in time as a hypnotic procedure. *Journal of Clinical and Experimental Hypnosis, 2:* 261–283.

Erikson E. (1968). *Identity: Youth and crisis.* New York: Norton.

Ferreira, A. J. (1963). Family myths and homeostasis. *Archives of General Psychiatry, 9:* 457–463.

Firth, R. (1972). Verbal and bodily rituals of greeting and parting. In J. S. La Fontaine (Ed.), *The interpretation of ritual; Essays in honour of A. J. Richards.* London: Tavistock.

Fleuridas, C., Nelson, T. S., & Rosenthal, D. M. (1986). The evolution of circular questioning: Training family therapists. *Journal of Marital and Family Therapy*, *12(2)*: 113–121.

Fraisse, P. (1976). *The psychology of time* (J. Leith, Trans.). Westport, CT: Greenwood.

Fraisse, P. (1974). *Psychologie du rythme*. Paris: Presses Universitaires de France.

Fraser, J. T. (Ed.) (1981). *The voices of time*. Amherst: University of Massachusetts Press. (Original work published in 1966)

Fraser, J. T. (1981a). *Toward an integrated understanding of time. Introduction to the second edition*. In J. T. Fraser (Ed.), *The voices of time*. Amherst: University of Massachusetts Press.

Fraser, J. T. (1989). *Time and mind*. New York: International Universities Press.

Fraser, J. T., & Lawrence, N. (Eds.) (1975). *The study of time, vol. 2*. Berlin: Springer Verlag.

Freud, S. (1901). Fragment of an analysis of a case of hysteria. In J. Strachey (Ed. and Trans.) *The standard edition of the complete psychological works of Sigmund Freud* (vol. VII, pp. 3–122). New York: Norton.

Freud, S. (1916–1917). Introductory lectures on psycho-analysis, part III. In J. Strachey (Ed. and Trans.) *The standard edition of the complete psychological works of Sigmund Freud* (vol. XVI). New York: Norton.

Gardner, H. (1985). *The mind's new science. A history of cognitive revolution*. New York: Basic Books.

Garfinkel, H. (1967). *Studies in ethnomethodology*. Englewood Cliffs, NJ: Prentice Hall.

Gergen, K. (1991). *The saturated self*. New York: Basic Books.

Giorello, G. (1990, November 11). Ma Platone preferiva il Lete. *Corriere della sera*.

Giovannelli, G., & Mucciarelli, G. (1979). *Lo studio psicologico del tempo*. Florence: Cappelli.

Gluckman, M. (1962). Les rites de passage. In M. Gluckman (Ed.), *Essays of the ritual of social relations*. Manchester: Manchester University Press.

Goodman, N. (1978). *Ways of worldmaking*. Indianapolis: Hackett Publishing.

Halberg, F. (1979). Les rythmes biologiques et leurs mécanismes: base du développement de la chronopsychologie et de la chronoéthologie. In *Du temps biologique au temps psychologique*. Paris: Presses Universitaires de France.

Haley, J. (1959). The family of the schizophrenic: A model system. *Journal of Nervous and Mental Disease, 129*: 357–364.

Haley J. (1990). *Strategies of psychotherapy* (2nd ed.). Rockville, MD: Triangle Press. (Original work published in 1963)

Hampshire, S. (1982). *Thought and action*. London: Chatto & Windus.

Hawking, S. W. (1988). *A brief history of time. From the big bang to black holes*. New York: Bantam Books.

Heidegger, M. (1962). *Being and time*. San Francisco: Harper. (Originally published in 1927)

Heinemann, K., & Ludes, P. (1978). *Zeitbewustein und kontrolle der Zeit*. In K. Mammerick & M. Klein (Eds.), *Materialien zur Soziologie der Alltags*. Sonderheft 20/1978 der Kolner Zeitschrift für Soziologie und Sozialpsychologie, Opladen.

Heisenberg, W. (1962). *Physics and philosophy*. New York: Harper and Row.

Hoffman, L. (1971). Deviation-amplifying processes in natural groups. In J. Haley (Ed.), *Changing families. A family therapy reader*. New York: Grune & Stratton.

Hoffman, L. (1981). *Foundations of family therapy*. New York: Basic Books.

Hoffman, L. (1988). A constructivist position for family therapy. In *Radical Constructivism, Autopoiesis and Psychotherapy*, a special issue of the *Irish Journal of Psychology, 9(1)*: 110–129.

Hofstadter, D. R. (1979). *Gödel, Escher and Bach: An eternal golden braid*. New York: Basic Books.

Husserl, E. (1966). *Zur Phanomenologie der Inneren Zeitbewuntseins, 1893–1917*. The Hague: M. Nijoff.

Imber-Black, E., Roberts, J., & Whiting, R. (1988). *Rituals in families and family therapy*. New York: Norton.

Jaques, E. (1982). *The form of time*. New York: Crane, Russak & Co.

Jauch, J. M. (1973). *Are quanta real? A Galilean dialogue*. Bloomington: Indiana University Press.

Jaynes, J. (1976). *The origins of consciousness in the breakdown of the bicameral mind*. Boston: Houghton Mifflin.

Jervis, G. (1989). *La psicoanalisi come esercizio critico*. Milan: Garzanti.

Kant, I. (1969). *Critique of pure reason* (1781). (Norman K. Smith, Ed.). New York: St. Martin's.

Kermode, F. (1967). *The sense of an ending*. Oxford: Oxford University Press.

Kerr, M. E., & Bowen, M. (1988). *Family evaluation*. New York: Norton.

Klein, M. (1928). Fruehstadien des Oedipuskonfliktes. *Int. Z. Psychoanal., 14*: 65.

Kuhn, T. (1962). *The structure of scientific revolutions*. Chicago: University of Chicago Press.

Lander, H. (1987). *L'enterprise polycellulaire*. Paris: Editions ESF.

Lane, G., & Russell, T. (1986). *Eliciting change in couples violence. A second order systemic approach*. Paper presented to the 9th Family Therapy Network Symposium, Washington, DC.

Leff, J. P., & Vaughn, C. E. (1985). *Expressed emotion in families*. New York: Guilford.

Leibniz, G. W. (1973). *Discourse on metaphysics* (2nd ed.) (G. R. Montgomery, Trans.). Peru, IL: Open Court.

Levi, P. (1986). *Survival in Auschwitz*. New York: Macmillan. (Originally published in 1947)

Lévi-Strauss, C. (1974). *Structural anthropology, Vol. 1*. New York: Basic Books.

Lévi-Strauss, C. (1962). *Totemism*. Boston: Beacon Press.

Luce, G. G. (1971). *Biological rhythms in human and animal physiology*. New York: Dover Publications.

Luria, A. R. (1987). *The man with a shattered world*. Cambridge, MA: Harvard University Press.

Luria, A. R. (1987a). *The mind of a menmonist*. Cambridge, MA: Harvard University Press.

Marsh, J. (1952). *The fullness of time*. London: Nisbet & Co.

Maruyama, M. (1968). The second cybernetics: Deviation-amplifying mutual causal processes. In W. Buckley (Ed.), *Modern systems research for the behavioral scientist* (p. 491). Chicago: Aldine.

Maturana, H., & Varela, F. (1980). *Autopoiesis and cognition*. Boston: D. Reidel.

Maturana, H., & Varela, F. (1987). *The tree of knowledge: The biological roots of understanding*. Boston: New Science Library.

McTaggart, J. M. E. (1927). *The nature of existence*. Cambridge: Cambridge University Press.

Merleau-Ponty, M. (1945). *Phénoménologie de la perception*. Paris: Gallimard.

Merton, R. K. (1957). *Social theory and social structure*. New York: Free Press.

Merton, R. J. (1984). Socially expected duration: A case study of concept formation in sociology. In W. W. Powell & R. Robins (Eds.), *Conflict and consensus: A festschift for Lewis A. Coser* (pp. 262–283). New York: Free Press.

Michon, J. A. (1979). Le traitement de l'information temporelle. In *Du temps biologique au temps psychologique*. Paris: Presses Universitaires de France.

Miller, G. A. (1956). The magic number seven, plus or minus two: Some limits on our capacity for processing information. *Psychological Review, 63*: 81–97.

Minkowski, E. (1933). *Le temps vécu*. Paris.

Minsky, M. (1985). *The society of mind*. New York: Simon & Schuster.

Minuchin, S. (1974). *Families and family therapy*. Cambridge, MA: Harvard University Press.

Morgan, G. (1986). *Images of organization*. Beverly Hills, CA: Sage.

Morin, E. (1985). Le vie della complessità. In G. Bocchi & M. Ceruti (Eds.), *La sfida della complessità* (pp. 49–60). Milan: Feltrinelli.

Newton, I. (1966). *Sir Isaac Newton's mathematical principles of natural philosophy of his system of the world*, 2 vols. (translated by Andrew Motte in 1729, revised and edited by Florian Cajori). Berkeley: University of California Press.

Orme, J. E. (1969). *Time, experience and behavior*. London: Iliffe Books.

Ornstein, R. E. (1969). *On the experience of time*. Hammondsworth, England: Penguin.

Ornstein, R. E. (1975). *The psychology of consciousness*. New York: Viking Penguin.

Orwell, G. (1983). *1984*. New York: NAL Dutton.

Parry, A. (1991). A universe of stories. *Family Process, 30*: 37–54.

Pearce, W. B. (1989). *Communication and the human condition*. Carbondale: Southern Illinois University Press.

Penfield, W., & Rasmussen, T. (1950). *The cerebral cortex of man*. New York: Macmillan.

Penn, P. (1982). Circular questioning. *Family Process, 21*: 267–280.

Penn, P. (1985). Feed-forward. Future questions, future maps. *Family Process, 24*: 299–310.

Piaget, J. (1970). *The child's conception of time*. New York: Basic Books. (Originally published in 1946)

Piaget, J. (1937). *La construction du reel chez l'enfant*. Neuchatel: Delachaux et Niestlé.

Poincare, H. (1913). *Dernières Pensées*, Chapter 2.

Popper, K. (1982). *Unended quest* (rev. ed.). Peru, IL: Open Court.

Prigogine, I., & Stengers, I. (1979). *La nouvelle alliance. Metamorphose de la science*. Paris: Gallimard.

Prigogine, I., & Stengers, I. (1984). *Order out of chaos*. New York: Bantam Books.

Quispel, G. (1957). Time and history in patristic christianity. In J. Campbell (Ed.), *Man and time*. Princeton: Princeton University Press.

Reale, P. (1982). *La psicologia del tempo*. Torino: Boringhieri.

Reinberg, A. (1979). Le temps, une dimension biologicale et medicale. In *L'homme malade a du temps*. Paris: Pernond et Stock.

Reiss, D. (1981). *The family construction of reality*. Cambridge, MA: Harvard University Press.

Ricoeur, P. (1988). *Time and narrative, vol. 3*. (K. Blamey & D. Pellaner, Trans.). Chicago: University of Chicago Press.

Rumelhart, D. E. (1975). Notes on a schema for stories. In D. G. Bobrow & A. M. Collins (Eds.), *Representation and understanding*. New York: Academic Press.

Russell, B. (1984). *History of western philosophy and its connection with political and social circumstances from the earliest times to the present day.* New York: Simon & Schuster. (Original work published in 1948)

Sabbadini, A. (1979). *Il tempo in psicanalisi.* Milan: Feltrinelli.

Schafer, R. (1983). *The analytic attitude.* New York: Basic Books.

Schein, E. H. (1987). *Process consultation, Vol. II. Lessons for managers and consultants.* Reading, MA: Addison-Wesley.

Searles, H. F. (1966). *Collected papers on schizophrenia and related subjects.* New York: International Universities Press.

Selvini Palazzoli, M. (1980). Why a long interval between sessions?. In M. Andolfi & I. Zwerling (Eds.), *Dimensions of family therapy.* New York: Guilford.

Selvini Palazzoli, M., Boscolo, L., Cecchin, G., & Prata, G. (1974). The treatment of children through brief therapy of their parents. *Family Process, 13(4):* 429–442.

Selvini Palazzoli, M., Boscolo, L., Cecchin, G., & Prata, G. (1978). *Paradox and counterparadox.* New York: Aronson.

Selvini Palazzoli, M., Boscolo, L., Cecchin, G., & Prata, G. (1978a). A ritualized prescription in family therapy: Odd days and even days. *Journal of Family Counseling, 4(3):* 3–9.

Selvini Palazzoli, M., Boscolo, L., Cecchin, G., & Prata, G. (1980). The problem of the referring person. *Journal of Marital and Family Therapy, 6:* 3–9.

Selvini Palazzoli, M., Boscolo, L., Cecchin, G., & Prata, G. (1980a). Hypothesizing-circularity-neutrality, *Family Process, 19:* 73–85.

Selvini Palazzoli, M., Cirillo, S., Selvini, M., & Sorrentino, A. M. (1989). *Family Games.* New York: Norton.

Selvini Palazzoli, M., & Viaro, M. (1988). The anorectic process in the family. A six-stage model as a guide for the individual therapy. *Family Process, 27(2):* 129–148.

Singer, M. T., & Wynne, L. C. (1965). Thought disorder and family relations: IV. Results and implications. *Archives of General Psychiatry, 12:* 201–212.

Sluzki, C. (1992). Transformation: A blueprint for narrative changes in therapy. *Family Process, 31:* 217–230.

Smith, M. W. (1952). Different cultural concept of the past, present and future. *Psychiatry, 13:* 395–400.

Sonnemann, V. (1987). Il tempo è una forma di ascolto. Sulla natura e le conseguenze di un disconoscimento kantiano dell'orecchio. In U. Curi (Ed.), *Dimensioni del Tempo.* Milan: Franco Angeli.

Spencer Brown, G. (1972). *Laws of form.* New York: Bantam Books.

Steiner, G. (1978). *Heidegger.* London: Fontana Press.

Stroud, J. M. (1956). The fine structure of psychological time. In H. Quastler (Ed.), *Information theory and psychology.* New York: Free Press.

Tanizaki, J. (1985). *Naomi* (Anthony Chambers, Trans.). New York: Knopf.

Telfener, U. (1987). Heinz von Foerster: Costruttivismo e psicoterapia. In H. von Foerster, *Sistemi che osservano* (pp. 27–38). Rome: Astrolabio.

Thom, R. (1989). *Structural stability and morphogenesis* (D. H. Fowler, Trans.). Reading, MA: Addison-Wesley.

Thompson, E. P. (1967). Time, work, discipline and industrial capitalism. *Past and Present, 38:* 56–97.

Tomm, K. (1985). Circular interviewing. A multifaceted clinical tool. In D. Campbell & R. Draper (Eds.), *Application of systemic family therapy: The Milan approach.* London: Grune & Stratton.

Tomm, K. (1984). One perspective on the Milan systemic approach: II. Description of session format, interviewing style and interventions. *Journal of Marital and Family Therapy, 10:* 253–271.

Tomm, K. (1987). Interventive interviewing: I. Strategizing as a fourth guideline for the therapist. *Family Process, 26:* 3–13.

Tomm, K. (1987a). Interventive interviewing: II. Reflexive questioning as a means to enable self-healing. *Family Process, 26:* 167–183.

Tomm, K. (1988). Interventive interviewing: III. Intending to ask circular, strategic or reflexive questions? *Family Process, 27:* 1–15.

Toraldo Di Francia, G. (1990). *Un universo troppo semplice.* Milan: Feltrinelli.

Van der Hart, O. (1983). *Rituals and psychotherapy. Transition and continuity.* New York: Irvington.

Van Gennep, A. (1961). *Rites of passage* (M. B. V. Zedon & G. L. Caffee, Trans.). Chicago: University of Chicago Press. (Original work published in 1909)

Varela, F. J. (1975). A calculus for self-reference. *International Journal of General Systems, 2:* 5–24.

Vicario, G. (1973). *Tempo psicologico ed eventi.* Florence: Giunti Barbera.

von Bertalanffy, L. (1969). *General system theory. Foundation, development, applications.* New York: Braziller.

von Foerster, H. (1981). *Observing systems.* Seaside, CA: Intersystems Publications.

von Foerster, H. (1985). Cibernetica ed epistemologia: storia e prospettive. In G. Bocchi & M. Ceruti (Eds.), *La sfida della complessità* (pp. 112–140). Milan: Feltrinelli.

von Glasersfeld, E. (1987). *The construction of knowledge.* Seaside, CA: Intersystems Publications.

Watzlawick, P. (Ed.) (1984). *The invented reality.* New York: Norton.

Watzlawick, P., Beavin Bavelas, J., & Jackson, D. D. (1967). *Pragmatics of human communication.* New York: Norton.

Watzlawick, P., Weakland, J. H., & Fisch, R. (1974). *Change: The principles of problem formation and problem resolution.* New York: Norton.

White, H. (1981). The value of narrativity in the representation of reality. In W. J. T. Mitchell (Ed.), *On narrative.* Chicago: University of Chicago Press.

White, M., & Epston, D. (1990). *Narrative means to therapeutic ends.* New York: Norton.

White, M. (1984). Pseudo-encopresis: from avalanche to victory, from vicious to virtuous cycles. *Family Systems Medicine, 2:* 2.

Whitrow, G. I. (1980). *The nature and philosophy of time* (2nd ed.). New York: Oxford University Press.

Whorf, B. L. (1956). *Language, thought and reality* (J. B. Carroll, Ed.). Cambridge, MA: MIT Press.

Wiener, N. (1961). *Cybernetics, or control and communication in the animal and the machine* (2nd ed.). Cambridge, MA: The Technology Press of MIT. (Original work published in 1948)

Wynne, L. C., McDaniel, S. H., & Weber, T. T. (1986). *Systems consultation. A new perspective for family therapy.* New York: Guilford.

Wynne, L. C., & Wynne, A. R. (1986). The quest for intimacy. *Journal of Marital and Family Therapy, 12(4):* 383–394.

Zerubavel, E. (1981). *Hidden rhythms. Schedules and calendars in social life.* Chicago: University of Chicago Press.

INDEX